# Imagining Nuclear War in the British Army, 1945–1989

# Imagining Nuclear War in the British Army, 1945–1989

SIMON J. MOODY

OXFORD
UNIVERSITY PRESS

# OXFORD
## UNIVERSITY PRESS

Great Clarendon Street, Oxford, OX2 6DP,
United Kingdom

Oxford University Press is a department of the University of Oxford.
It furthers the University's objective of excellence in research, scholarship,
and education by publishing worldwide. Oxford is a registered trade mark of
Oxford University Press in the UK and in certain other countries

Published in the United States of America by Oxford University Press
198 Madison Avenue, New York, NY 10016, United States of America

British Library Cataloguing in Publication Data
Data available

Library of Congress Control Number: 2019946752

ISBN 978-0-19-884699-4

DOI: 10.1093/oso/9780198846994.001.0001

# Preface

The idea for this book came in 2008 when, as an undergraduate at the University of Salford, my erstwhile personal tutor, the indomitable Professor Eric Grove, insisted I borrow an 'interesting little book' of his. The book in question was Andrew Bacevich's *The Pentomic Era*, which described how the US Army attempted to overcome the organizational challenges posed by the arrival of tactical nuclear weapons in the 1950s. It both fascinated and appalled me in equal measure. Did armies really plan to fight with nuclear weapons on the battlefield? How would that even be possible? What purpose would it serve? Intrigued to discover how my own countrymen in the British Army tackled the same problems, I set out to the library in search of further literature, only to find it did not exist. Considering the stakes involved with any type of nuclear planning, this struck me as a curious omission in the historiography of the British Army, and a narrative which deserved to be told. At the time of writing, the British Army is withdrawing the last of its forces from Germany, bringing to an end a seventy-five-year deployment during which time it stood watch over the Iron Curtain ready to engage Warsaw Pact forces in nuclear land combat should the Cold War suddenly go 'hot'. This book does not seek to cast value judgements on the morality of nuclear weapons—that is for the reader to contemplate—but it is an empirical study which shines some light on the experiences of a professional military organization which was forced, through government policy, to plan for a war which most persons regarded as beyond the imagination.

I have been privileged in both my professional and personal lives to be surrounded by a number of supportive and encouraging individuals. I would like to thank in particular Dr Angel O'Donnell and Professor Ashley Jackson for taking the time to provide helpful feedback on sections of this manuscript at various points in its development. I am also grateful to the two anonymous reviewers whose constructive criticisms were indispensable to the finished product. I alone am responsible for any errors of fact or interpretation. Special thanks go to Mr Jackson Perry, who conducted some excellent work as my research assistant in the summer of 2015, and who has been incredibly patient in waiting for the project to come to fruition. I would also like to thank the Trustees of the Liddell Hart Centre for Military Archives and the Zentrum für Militärgeschichte und Sozialwissenschaften der Bundeswehr for granting me permission to reproduce material for which they hold the copyright.

This book was written over a two-and-a-half-year period, spanning three homes in two different cities, London and Oxford. None of this would have been possible without the love and support of my wife, Amy. This book is dedicated to her, and to our wonderful son, Robin, as a small token of my appreciation.

Simon J. Moody

*Oxford*
*February 2019*

# Contents

# List of Maps

# List of Abbreviations

| | |
|---|---|
| ADM | atomic demolition munition |
| AFCENT | Allied Forces Central Europe |
| AORG | Army Operational Research Group |
| AORE | Army Operational Research Establishment |
| APC | armoured personnel carrier |
| ARMEX | Arms Executive |
| BAOR | British Army of the Rhine |
| C-in-C | Commander-in-Chief |
| CAS | Chief of the Air Staff |
| CDC | Civil Defence Corps |
| CDS | Chief of the Defence Staff |
| CENTAG | Central Army Group |
| CGS | Chief of the General Staff |
| CIGS | Chief of the Imperial General Staff |
| CNS | Chief of the Naval Staff |
| DBD | Directorate of Battle Doctrine |
| DCD | Director of Combat Development |
| DGAT | Director-General Army Training |
| DGMT | Director-General of Military Training |
| DOAE | Defence Operational Analysis Establishment |
| DPS | Defence Planning Staff |
| DS | Directing Staff |
| DSACEUR | Deputy Supreme Allied Commander Europe |
| FRG | Federal Republic of Germany |
| GLCM | ground-launched cruise missile |
| GOC | General Officer Commanding |
| ICBM | inter-continental ballistic missile |
| INF | intermediate-range nuclear forces |
| IRBM | intermediate-range ballistic missile |
| JIC | Joint Intelligence Committee |
| JPS | Joint Planning Staff |
| LRTNF | long-range theatre nuclear forces |
| NAG | New Approach Group |
| NATO | North Atlantic Treaty Organization |
| NORTHAG | Northern Army Group |
| NPG | Nuclear Planning Group |
| OMG | operational manoeuvre group |
| PPGs | Provisional Political Guidelines |
| RUSI | Royal United Services Institute |

| | |
|---|---|
| SACEUR | Supreme Allied Commander Europe |
| SACLANT | Supreme Allied Commander Atlantic |
| SHAPE | Supreme Headquarters Allied Powers Europe |
| SLBM | submarine-launched ballistic missile |
| TDC | Tactical Doctrine Cell |
| TEWT | tactical exercise without troops |

# Introduction

Throughout the Cold War, military and political elites in Britain consistently described the prospect of using nuclear weapons in land warfare as pure fantasy— an impossible military operation which would take place during an unreal stage of war. The destruction that would be unleashed on the battlefield by the widespread use of so-called 'tactical' nuclear weapons suggested this would be a battle that not only could not be won, but that could not even be fought as an operation of war. The outbreak of general war between NATO and the Warsaw Pact was widely believed to precipitate a process of escalation which could result in the destruction of the Northern hemisphere, along with all the fighting forces within it. The effects of an all-out nuclear exchange would be such that the outcome of any conventional fighting in Europe would be insignificant by comparison, with the actions of NATO's shield forces rendered irrelevant. Such apocalyptic visions of future war prompted the Chief of the Defence Staff (CDS), Lord Mountbatten, to ask his NATO colleagues in 1965: 'what then would be the object in the few survivors rushing around shooting up everybody in sight, well knowing that their actions could achieve absolutely no rational military or political aim?'.[1]

The action Mountbatten described as being devoid of any military or political utility was in fact the primary mission assigned to the British Army within national and alliance strategy from the 1950s until the end of the Cold War: deterring Soviet aggression in Europe by demonstrating the will and capability to fight with nuclear weapons in defence of NATO territory. This mission was unlike any other assigned to the Army before or since, and presented a number of practical and conceptual difficulties. The traditional concepts that had hitherto guided strategic and operational planning for conventional warfare appeared to no longer be relevant in the nuclear age,[2] even calling into question the continued relevance of ground forces of the type that had performed important combat functions during the wars of the first half of the twentieth century.[3] As an

---

[1] The National Archives, Kew [TNA], DEFE 4/186, COS 1918/21/6/65, SHAPEX 65—Valedictory Address by Chief of the Defence Staff, 21 June 1965.

[2] For an overview of the problems facing conventional forces in the nuclear age, see Otto Heilbrunn, *Conventional Warfare in the Nuclear Age* (London: George Allen & Unwin Ltd, 1965) and Michael Carver, 'Conventional Warfare in the Nuclear Age' in Peter Paret (ed.), *Makers of Modern Strategy: From Machiavelli to the Nuclear Age* (Oxford: Clarendon Press, 1986).

[3] In a contemporary article typical of those that challenged the utility of conventional forces in the nuclear age, the author claimed that 'ground forces are an anachronism arising from an effort to adapt armies to conditions they cannot cope with ... in [thermonuclear] war, there is small place for armies

*Imagining Nuclear War in the British Army, 1945–1989*. Simon J. Moody, Oxford University Press (2020).
© Simon J. Moody.
DOI: 10.1093/oso/9780198846994.001.0001

erstwhile Supreme Allied Commander Atlantic (SACLANT) planner testified, 'the concept of fighting a nuclear war was "inherently incoherent" but the services had to strive nonetheless to develop contingency plans for this "surreal mission"'.[4]

The British Army therefore emerged from the high-intensity conventional fighting of the Second World War into a rapidly and significantly changing military environment overshadowed by the mushroom cloud of the atomic bomb. Although the service was continually engaged in various counter-insurgency and expeditionary operations throughout the Cold War, it was the Army's nuclear mission in Germany that was the most enduring of these commitments and where the strategic stakes were highest.[5] Like most armies, the *raison d'être* of the service stemmed from its identity as the organization that fought decisive battles and won wars. After all, it was the victory of the Desert Rats in the second battle of El Alamein which saw church bells ring in Britain for the first time since the start of the war, and it was the men of the British 2nd Army who had marched from Normandy to the Rhine, delivering the death knell to German resistance in the West. The same organization, whose very essence was predicated on its ability to 'close with and kill the Queen's enemies', now existed in a strategic milieu whereby the extreme limit of that mantra was the assured destruction not only of enemies of the Crown, but also of organized civilization as it was once known.

In spite of the importance of the Army's preparations for fighting a nuclear land war in Europe, it remains a curious gap in the historiography. Historians of the post-war British Army have traditionally focused their attention on explaining how the service was able to develop a supposedly first-rate counter-insurgency doctrine after 1945,[6] and few attempts have been made to explore how the Army

---

and navies'. Thomas R. Phillips, 'The Atomic Revolution in Warfare', *Bulletin of the Atomic Scientists*, Vol. 10, No. 8 (October 1954), pp. 316–17.

---

[4] Cited in Beatrice Heuser, *The Evolution of Strategy: Thinking War from Antiquity to the Present* (Cambridge: Cambridge University Press, 2010), p. 269.

[5] For example, the British Army fought against insurgents in Palestine (1945–8), Malaya (1948–57), the Canal Zone (1951–4), Kenya (1952–6), Cyprus (1955–9), Aden (1963–7), and Northern Ireland (1969–2007), and committed sizable ground forces to the Korean War (1950–3) and the Falklands War (1982). Indeed, between 1949 and 1970, the United Kingdom initiated thirty-four military interventions in more than twenty countries. See John van Wingen and Herbert K. Tillema, 'British Military Intervention after World War II: Militance in a Second-Rank Power', *Journal of Peace Research*, Vol. 17, No. 4 (1980), pp. 291–303.

[6] Huw Bennet, *Fighting the Mau Mau: The British Army and Counter-Insurgency in the Kenya Emergency* (Cambridge: Cambridge University Press, 2012); David French, *The British Way in Counter-Insurgency, 1945–1967* (Oxford: Oxford University Press, 2011); John A. Nagl, *Learning to Eat Soup with a Knife: Counterinsurgency Lessons from Malaya and Vietnam* (Chicago, IL: University of Chicago Press, 2005); Thomas R. Mockaitis, *British Counter Insurgency in the Post-Imperial Era* (London: Macmillan, 1995); Mockaitis, *British Counterinsurgency, 1919–60* (London: Macmillan, 1990); Michael Dewar, *Brush Fire Wars: Minor Campaigns of the British Army since 1945* (London: Robert Hale, 1984).

overcame the conceptual and practical challenges of preparing for nuclear land combat.[7] The orthodox narrative of the post-war British Army is one of a conservative institution tied to out-of-date concepts and a stagnant military doctrine resulting from an institutional reluctance to change.[8] Some historians argue that it was the legacy of the erstwhile Chief of the Imperial General Staff (CIGS), Field Marshal Bernard L. Montgomery, which cast a long debasing shadow over subsequent generations of officers,[9] and that it would not be until the reforms of Field Marshal Sir Nigel Bagnall in the 1980s that the Army finally broke free from its doctrinal straitjacket.[10] This is far from the case. New research on the post-war military thought of Montgomery demonstrates that he was in fact cognisant of the changing character of conflict, and was the first post-war CIGS to instigate a thorough review of the Army's written doctrine in light of the nuclear revolution.[11] This book develops further this revisionist interpretation of the post-war British Army. By placing the conceptual component of the Army's fighting power as the referent object of analysis, it shines new light on the Army's contribution to NATO's strategic deterrent on the front line of the Cold War in Germany.

The British Army found itself as a potential agent of nuclear warfare as a consequence of a critical juncture in British strategic culture that saw fundamental

[7] David French's *Army, Empire, and Cold War: The British Army and Military Policy, 1945–1971* (Oxford: Oxford University Press, 2012) did much to fill the gap in this literature, although only two chapters were devoted to the British Army of the Rhine's planning for nuclear war. The contribution made by the Canadian Army to NATO's Northern Army Group has been the subject of recent enquiry in Andrew B. Godefroy, *In Peace Prepared: Innovation and Adaptation in Canada's Cold War Army* (Vancouver: University of British Columbia Press, 2014) and Isabel Campbell, *Unlikely Diplomats: The Canadian Brigade in Germany, 1951–64* (Vancouver: University of British Columbia Press, 2013).
[8] See, for example, Allan Mallinson, *The Making of the British Army* (London: Bantam Press, 2009), pp. 384, 407; Paul Cornish, 'Learning New Lessons: The British Army and the Strategic Debate, 1945–50' in Hew Strachan (ed.), *Big Wars and Small Wars: The British Army and the Lessons of War in the 20th Century* (Oxford: Oxford University Press, 2006), pp. 54–5; Correlli Barnett, *Britain and Her Army, 1509–1970: A Military, Political, and Social Survey* (London: Penguin, 2000), pp. 485–90; Paul Cornish, *British Military Planning for the Defence of Germany, 1945–50* (London: Macmillan, 1996); Hugh Beach, 'British Forces in Germany, 1945–85' in Martin Edmonds (ed.), *The Defence Equation: British Military Systems Policy, Planning and Performance* (London: Brassey's, 1986), pp. 157–73; Alun Gwynne Jones, 'Training and Doctrine in the British Army since 1945' in Michael Howard (ed.), *The Theory and Practice of War* (London and Bloomington, IN: Indiana University Press, 1975), pp. 313–23; Gregory Blaxland, *The Regiments Depart: A History of the British Army, 1945–1970* (London: William Kimber, 1971), p. 341.
[9] For example, John Kiszely, 'The British Army and Approaches to Warfare since 1945' in Brian Holden Reid (ed.), *Military Power: Land Warfare in Theory and Practice* (London: Routledge, 1997), pp. 183–7.
[10] Alexander Alderson, 'Influence, the Indirect Approach and Manoeuvre', *The RUSI Journal*, Vol. 157, No. 1 (2012), p. 38; Alexander Alderson, 'The Army Brain: A Historical Perspective on Doctrine, Development and the Challenges of Future Conflict', *The RUSI Journal*, Vol. 155, No. 3 (2010), pp. 11–12; Colin McInnes, 'The British Army's New Way in Warfare: A Doctrinal Misstep?', *Defence and Security Analysis*, Vol. 23, No. 2 (2007), p. 129.
[11] Simon J. Moody, 'Was There a "Monty Method" after the Second World War? Field Marshal Bernard L. Montgomery and the Changing Character of Land Warfare, 1945–1958', *War in History*, Vol. 23, No. 2 (2016), pp. 210–29.

changes to its foreign and defence policies. As an island nation separated from Continental Europe by its channel moat, Britain had always enjoyed something on an 'illusion of choice' when orchestrating its grand strategy before 1945: to enter into European affairs or use its sea power to develop links elsewhere. Yet, as a status quo power, Britain had always possessed a vested interest in balancing power in Europe to prevent one single state from dominating the Continent, and at times this had necessitated the commitment of an expeditionary force to Europe, as was the case in 1914 and 1939. Although Mons and Dunkirk both became moral lessons on the inherent dangers of such military expeditions, the deteriorating relationship between the Soviet Union and the Western Powers during the late 1940s finally convinced British policy-makers of the need for greater political and military cooperation with their continental neighbours as a bulwark against the Communist threat.[12] This led to the signing of the Brussels Pact with France and the Benelux countries in 1948, which contained a mutual defence clause pledging military assistance to any party subject to armed attack in Europe.[13] From a British perspective, the military rationale for this new-found appetite for continental commitments was clear, as the Chiefs of Staff identified in 1947:

> The days when we could afford to remain on the defensive, while gathering our great strength for the knock-out blow, ended with the advent of the cross channel pilotless missile and with the dropping of the first atom bomb.[14]

Thus, it would simply not be possible at the start of another major war for Britain to donate token ground forces for continental defence and remain on the defensive while her war production industries lurched into motion, as she had done in two world wars. Rather, in this new strategic environment, Britain would have to fight the opening stages of a future war with forces-in-being; that is, those units that were already deployed and prepared for war at the onset of hostilities. National security was now synonymous with collective security, and Britain could no longer afford to stay isolated in her island fortress.

The Brussels Pact paved the way for the signing of the North Atlantic Treaty a year later. NATO was, for all intents and purposes, a *de facto* nuclear alliance designed to 'keep the Russians out, the Americans in, and the Germans down', according to its first Secretary General Lord Hastings Ismay. The United Kingdom was now part of what would become an increasingly entangled alliance, transforming overnight British defence policy, and ending Britain's splendid isolation

---

[12] Alan Macmillan, 'Strategic Culture and National Ways in Warfare: The British Case', *The RUSI Journal*, Vol. 140, No. 5 (1995), p. 35.

[13] For further information see John Baylis, 'Britain, the Brussels Pact and the Continental Commitment', *International Affairs*, Vol. 60, No. 4 (1984), pp. 615–29.

[14] TNA, CAB 21/1800, DO(47)44, Future Defence Policy, 22 May 1947.

from the Continent. Since its inception, NATO became the major channel for British defence efforts and was intended, by implication at least, as a permanent alliance.[15] Through its 'special relationship', Britain also became the transatlantic hub linking the United States to European security. The three pillars of British post-war defence policy were now NATO, the special relationship, and nuclear deterrence.

It was deterrence with nuclear weapons that became the primary means through which the UK sought to contain Soviet influence in Europe. The British attachment to nuclear deterrence as the best, and only, means of ensuring national security in the uncertain post-war world has been described by John Baylis and Kristan Stoddart as being born of a 'deterrence habit of mind', which itself was a reflection of British strategic culture.[16] The ideational influences which shaped this nuclear monomania in Whitehall were the perceived unique vulnerability of the UK to attack with nuclear weapons; the identification of the Soviet Union as a threat to the status quo; a faith in the commonality of interests between East and West to avoid nuclear war; the hope that nuclear weapons might abolish war in all its forms; and a symbolic attachment to nuclear power as a manifestation of Britain's autonomy and independence.[17] This deterrence habit of mind manifested in Britain's preference for a 'pure-deterrence' strategy for NATO, which amounted to a pledge of faith that the consequences of nuclear war would be so repugnant that the Kremlin would be sufficiently deterred from embarking on war in Europe to further its policy aims.

The outward expression of Britain's commitment to European defence was the British Army of the Rhine (BAOR). BAOR began life as a post-war administrative headquarters in Northern Germany responsible for supporting the civilian authority in the British zone of occupation, but it soon became the most powerful field force in the British Army, designed from the ground up to be able to fight on a nuclear battlefield. Along with its sister formations in Northern Army Group (NORTHAG), BAOR was an integral component of NATO's conventional/nuclear 'shield' of ground forces tasked with defending a 140-mile front from south of the river Elbe to the city of Kassel.[18] Manpower in BAOR stood at a high of 75,000 in 1953, but troop reductions saw it shrink to 60,000 men in 1970, before peaking again at 66,000 in 1985.[19] The reality was that BAOR was often

[15] Beatrice Heuser, *Nuclear Mentalities? Strategies and Beliefs in Britain, France and the FRG* (Basingstoke: Macmillan, 1998), p. 36.
[16] John Baylis and Kristan Stoddart, *The British Nuclear Experience: The Role of Beliefs, Culture, and Identity* (Oxford: Oxford University Press, 2015), pp. 16–41.
[17] Heuser, *Nuclear Mentalities*, pp. 3–52.
[18] Robert Evans, 'The British Army of the Rhine and Defense Plans for Germany, 1945–1955' in Jan Hoffenaar and Dieter Krüger (eds.), *Blueprints for Battle: Planning for War in Central Europe, 1948–1968* (Lexington, KY: University Press of Kentucky, 2012), pp. 204–11.
[19] John S. Duffield, *Power Rules: The Evolution of NATO's Conventional Force Posture* (Stanford, CA: Stanford University Press, 1995), p. 234.

undermanned as the Army struggled to resource its many overseas security commitments against a backdrop of shrinking defence budgets.[20] The organization of 1(BR) Corps, BAOR's principal fighting formation, was subjected to a number of changes throughout the Cold War as a result of fluctuating military, political, or economic circumstances. In the 1950s, 1(BR) Corps consisted of three armoured divisions and one infantry division (Map 1), which were reduced in the 1960s to three combined-arms divisions. In 1976 a major reorganization took place in which the brigade level of command was eliminated and command over units was then exercised by four divisional headquarters. This decision was reversed in 1982 in favour of a deployment of three stronger armoured divisions.[21]

Throughout the Cold War, both power blocs developed and operated a plethora of nuclear weapons, each with specific roles and functions designed to be employed at different levels of conflict. 'Nuclear weapon' is an umbrella term used to describe atomic bombs, which derive their explosive power from a nuclear fission reaction, and the much more powerful thermonuclear or hydrogen bomb (H-bomb), which produces much of its energy from a nuclear fusion reaction. Nuclear weapon yields are measured in kilotons (kt), a unit of explosive power equivalent to a thousand tons of TNT, and megatons (mt), equivalent to a million tons of TNT. Nuclear warheads could be transported to their intended target by a variety of delivery vehicles including missiles, aircraft, and artillery. At one end of the spectrum were the most powerful 'strategic' nuclear weapons. Such weapon systems were deemed 'strategic' in the sense that they possessed the necessary range to hit any target on earth, and could be profitably used against opposing strategic nuclear forces ('counter-force' targets) and people and property ('counter-value' targets). Strategic nuclear weapons and systems included the 20kt Blue Danube gravity bomb carried by British Valiant and Vulcan strategic bombers, the Polaris A-2 submarine-launched ballistic missile (SLBM), which carried an 800kt warhead, and the Titan II inter-continental ballistic missile (ICBM), which could detonate a mighty 9mt thermonuclear device over its target. Complementing strategic nuclear weapons were intermediate-range nuclear forces (INF), which were intended for use against military and civilian targets within a theatre of operations. These weapons were of a shorter range than their inter-continental cousins, and could hit targets between 2,780km and 5,560km. Weapon systems in this category included the American Thor and Pershing II intermediate-range ballistic missiles (IRBM), with yields of 1.44mt and 250kt, respectively, and the Soviet SS-20 IRBM, which carried a 150kt warhead.[22]

[20] French, *Army, Empire, and Cold War*, pp. 217–23.
[21] David Miller, *The Cold War: A Military History* (London: John Murray, 1998), pp. 234–5.
[22] Miller, *The Cold War*, pp. 406–17.

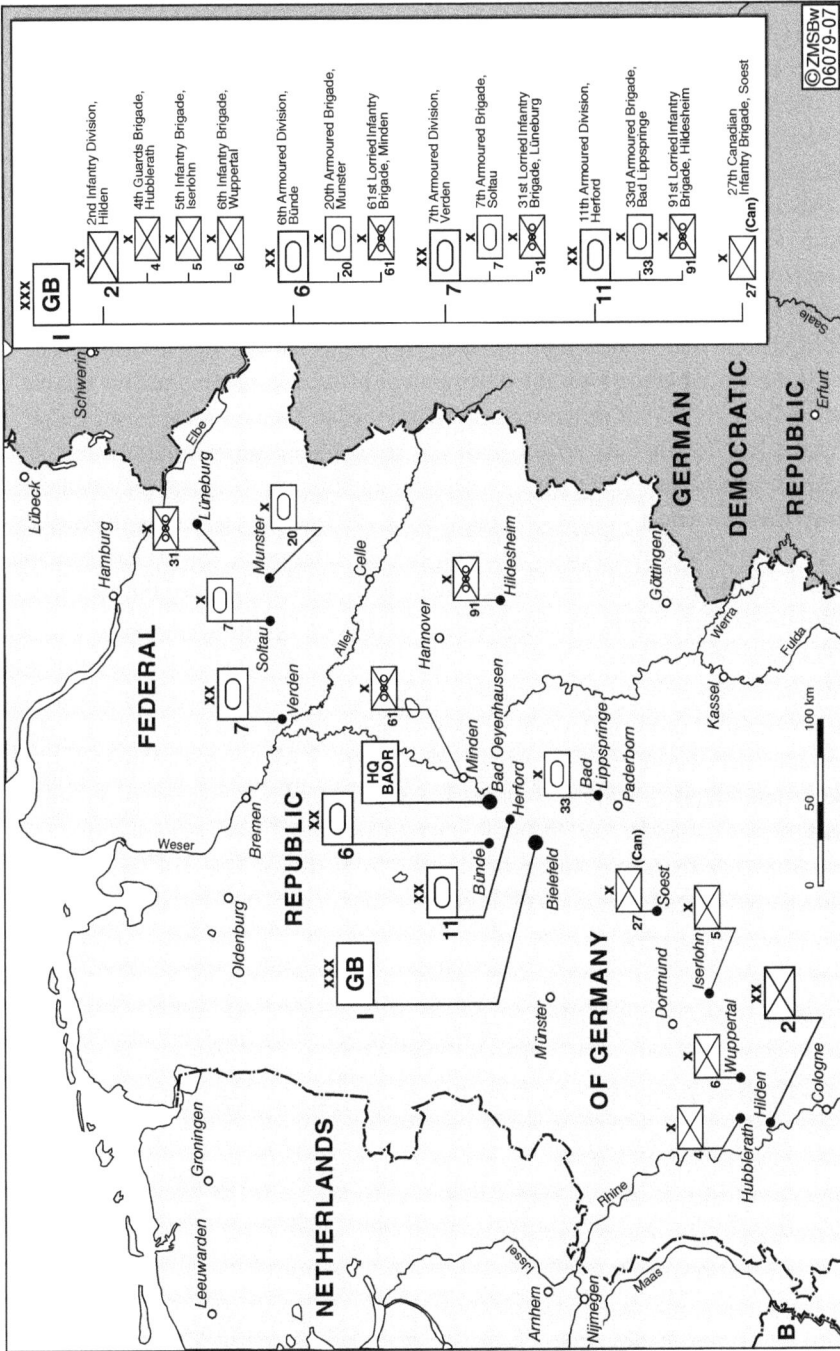

Map 1. (06079-07). Location of BAOR's divisions in the 1950s.

At the opposite end of the spectrum to strategic nuclear weapons were so-called 'tactical' or 'battlefield' nuclear weapons, which were designed to be employed by military forces in the field in support of conventional combat operations. These weapons emerged not from a statement of operational requirement by armies or air forces, but as an offshoot of the Manhattan project, when American scientists realized that it had become technically possible to develop small nuclear warheads which could fit into short-range missiles and artillery shells.[23] A stereotypical tactical nuclear weapon was generally regarded as having a nominal yield of 20kt, which was around the same size as the atomic bomb which obliterated the Japanese city of Hiroshima. The United States began to deploy tactical nuclear weapons to Europe in the early 1950s in the form of the 280mm cannon, and later with Corporal and Honest John missiles, with which BAOR was furnished. The British Army did embark on the development of its own tactical nuclear missile system, Blue Water, but the project was abandoned in 1962 for fiscal reasons, after which it had to purchase off-the-shelf the second-generation American missile Sergeant, which possessed a 60kt warhead for 'tactical' use. Sergeant provided the Army with a tactical nuclear capability until 1972, when the jointly developed Anglo-American Lance missile entered NATO armouries. The Lance system carried a warhead of variable yield between 1 and 100kt and formed the backbone of the British Army's nuclear capabilities until the end of the Cold War.[24]

Few weapon systems in history have generated the level of curiosity, confusion, and controversy as have tactical nuclear weapons. Part of the problem stems from the ambiguity of the term 'tactical' nuclear weapon, which appears something of a misnomer considering the destructive power of the weapons. It is for these reasons that scholars and practitioners have struggled to reach a consensus on what constitutes a 'strategic' or 'tactical' nuclear weapon.[25] For example, the US Department of Defense distinguishes tactical from strategic nuclear weapons by their intended use or mission,[26] while other commentators prefer to define nuclear

[23] Ibid., p. 349. The first scientific study to consider the tactical use of nuclear weapons was Project Vista, which took place between 1951 and 1952 at the California Institute of Technology. See David C. Elliot, 'Project Vista and Nuclear Weapons in Europe', *International Security*, Vol. 11, No. 1 (1986), pp. 163–83.

[24] For a review of early British short-range nuclear weapon procurement policies see Kaoru Kikuyama, 'Britain and the Procurement of Short-Range Nuclear Weapons', *Journal of Strategic Studies*, Vol. 16, No. 4 (1993), pp. 539–60.

[25] Lawrence Freedman believes it is nonsensical to talk of 'strategic' and 'tactical' nuclear weapons since it is as difficult to imagine a non-tactical weapon as it is a non-strategic war. Lawrence Freedman, *The Evolution of Nuclear Strategy*, 3rd ed. (London: Palgrave Macmillan, 2003), pp. 117–18.

[26] See Joint Chiefs of Staff, *Dictionary of Military and Associated Terms* (Washington, DC: Department of Defense, 2008), pp. 523, 541. William Van Cleave highlights weaknesses and ambiguities with this mode of classification. He demonstrates that certain 'strategic' weapon systems such as ICBMs and B52 bombers may, theoretically, be employed at the tactical level of war, whilst atomic artillery and atomic demolition munitions could conceivably be used for strategic effect. William Van Cleave and S. T. Cohen, *Tactical Nuclear Weapons: An Examination of the Issues* (New York, NY: Macdonald and Jane's, 1978), pp. 13–14.

weapons by their observable capabilities; mainly their means of delivery vehicle or yield of warhead.[27] Attempts to draw distinctions between nuclear weapons became a source of great friction within the NATO alliance, not least between its European and North American members. As the West German Chancellor Helmut Schmidt explained in a 1987 television interview for the US Public Broadcasting Service:

> [The Americans] had the peculiar habit of calling strategic only such weapons which could hit their own soil and their own cities and I said to them well the first one...so-called battlefield nuclear which hits people on German soil for the German nation is a strategic event. They had great difficulty to understand this. They were academics, you know. They had never...and couldn't image the impact and the psychological impact of a nuclear weapon exploding among soldiers or among the civilian population.[28]

It was not only the nomenclature of tactical nuclear weapons that caused conceptual difficulties for the Alliance. As will be shown, there was also considerable confusion about their intended use and functions. The original conception of tactical nuclear weapons as defensive armaments which could be used by NATO to counterbalance Soviet manpower superiority was not a result of careful analysis but rather, according to the British government's Chief Scientific Adviser Solly Zuckerman, 'a reasonable hope in the days when the West manifestly had a bigger nuclear arsenal than the USSR'.[29] It soon became clear by the 1960s, when nuclear equipoise had been achieved on the Central Front, that the use of any nuclear weapon in land combat might lead to misunderstandings between the belligerents, miscalculation, and the prospect of uncontrolled escalation to the use of strategic nuclear weapons, with all of the death and destruction that would entail.[30]

Such considerations raised a number of difficult questions in NATO about the use of tactical nuclear weapons, the most important of which were identified by Beatrice Heuser and Kristan Stoddart as: if a conventional defence was failing, would the Alliance be prepared to fight a geographically limited nuclear war in Europe rather than capitulate to the Soviets? Did the credibility of NATO's deterrent posture require a 'seamless robe' of nuclear weapons reaching from

---

[27] Even classifying nuclear weapons on the size of their yield can be misleading. As Nigel Calder observes, even 'modest' battlefield nuclear weapons which are designed to be used against tanks and airfields can be employed equally as well against cities—the traditional target for strategic nuclear weapons. Calder cited in Dietrich Schroeer, *Science, Technology and the Nuclear Arms Race* (New York, NY: John Wiley & Sons, 1984), pp. 293–4.

[28] Interview with Helmut Schmidt, 'War and Peace in the Nuclear Age', 1987.

[29] Solly Zuckerman, *Nuclear Illusion and Reality* (London: Collins, 1982), p. 60.

[30] The seminal works on the theory of nuclear escalation are Herman Kahn, *On Escalation: Metaphors and Scenarios* (Washington, DC: Hudson Institute, 1965) and Bernard Brodie, *Escalation and the Nuclear Option* (Princeton, NJ: Princeton University Press, 1966).

the battlefield to deep strikes into Soviet territory? Could tactical nuclear weapons be used in a demonstrative role to disabuse the Soviets of their aggression without escalating to all-out nuclear war? Was it desirable to have American tactical nuclear weapons based in Europe with the consequent lack of participation in decision-making? Was it more credible to have European tactical nuclear weapons based in Europe, independent of an American veto?[31] There were also more basic, but no less challenging, questions about the military application of tactical nuclear weapons on the battlefield: can an army function on a nuclear battlefield? Do tactical nuclear weapons favour the defender or the attacker? Does tactical nuclear war require more or fewer men?[32] As will be shown, the British Army largely ignored such questions and implied that there were no unusual problems with fighting a tactical nuclear war. The result was that many of the questions remained unanswered, leading one Pentagon official to conclude in 1975 that 'nobody knows how to fight a tactical nuclear war. Twenty years of effort by many military experts have failed to produce a believable doctrine for tactical nuclear warfare'.[33]

The unbelievable nature of nuclear war, 'tactical' or otherwise, has been described by Matthew Grant and Benjamin Ziemann as representing a 'war against the imagination'.[34] Nuclear war was imaginary in the sense that, in lieu of any practical experience, it could only ever exist within individual skulls. As the great nuclear oracle, Herman Kahn, noted, 'thermonuclear wars are not only unpleasant events, they are, fortunately, unexperienced events'.[35] The atomic bombings of the Japanese cities of Hiroshima and Nagasaki in 1945 provided a shocking, yet ultimately limited, insight into the destructive power of nuclear weapons. Indeed, it was the non-use of nuclear weapons that became one of the most important phenomena of the nuclear age, giving birth to a normative prohibition on nuclear weapon use in the international system which endures to this day.[36] Thus, although 'the bomb' would cast a long shadow over the Cold War confrontation, the consequences of nuclear war, especially in the context of a mutual exchange of H-bombs, remained something of a mystery. While observers have at times struggled to conceptualize the effects of such a nuclear conflagration

---

[31] For further discussion of these questions see Beatrice Heuser and Kristan Stoddart, 'Difficult Europeans: NATO and Tactical/Non-Strategic Nuclear Weapons in the Cold War, *Diplomacy & Statecraft*, Vol. 28, No. 3 (2017), pp. 455–6.

[32] Philip W. Dyer, 'Will Tactical Nuclear Weapons Ever Be Used?', *Political Science Quarterly*, Vol. 88, No. 2 (June 1973), p. 220.

[33] Alain C. Enthoven, 'U.S. Forces in Europe: How Many? Doing What?', *Foreign Affairs*, Vol. 53, No. 3 (1975), p. 525.

[34] Matthew Grant and Benjamin Ziemann, 'The Cold War as an Imaginary War' in Matthew Grant and Benjamin Ziemann (eds.), *Understanding the Imaginary War: Culture, Thought and Nuclear Conflict, 1945–90* (Manchester: Manchester University Press, 2016), p. 2.

[35] Herman Kahn, *Thinking about the Unthinkable* (London: Weidenfeld and Nicolson, 1962), p. 143.

[36] For a thorough analysis on how the nuclear 'taboo' evolved see Nina Tannenwald, 'The Nuclear Taboo: The United States and the Normative Basis of Nuclear Non-Use', *International Organization*, Vol. 53, No. 3 (1999), pp. 433–68.

as 'beyond the imagination',[37] imagination ultimately remained one of the principal means of thinking about an unknown and unknowable future.

This is not to say that the possibility of nuclear war did not shape the lived experience of the Cold War. For many individuals, 'imagining the devastation of nuclear weapons was at the root of how they experienced British nuclear culture', and nuclear anxiety became a pervasive and persistent feature of national life after 1945.[38] While the individual experience of ordinary people who were forced to live under a nuclear sword of Damocles is an important narrative strand in British nuclear culture, such visions of nuclear war were largely detached from strategic logic. As Kahn cautioned:

> It is generally easy for laymen to believe that a city-busting attack would be the most likely beginning to a thermonuclear war. Visualizing themselves as the defenders, they naturally think of the attacker as vindictive or malevolent, and interested primarily in hurting them. But it is irrational for an attacker to ignore his own priority of interests in order to hurt the defender. The attacker is usually not nearly so interested in hurting the defender as he is in the dual objects of achieving his military objective and escaping destruction himself.[39]

It was perhaps the air of unreality about an inter-continental nuclear war fought with thermonuclear weapons which encouraged the construction of nightmarish scenarios to fill the imaginative void. In continental Europe, however, the recent historical experience made war all too imaginable.[40] The prospect of a geographically limited 'tactical' nuclear war breaking out in Germany was much more convincing than the type of push-button spasm war often envisaged in popular culture. Thus, while for the majority of persons, the possibility of nuclear war tended to be 'a private image rather than a shared reality', the same could not be said for the British Army.[41] Out of all the actors involved in the workings of the British nuclear state, it was the Army that had to confront the atom on its starkest terms; nuclear war had become a distinct reality, an occupational hazard. The spectre of nuclear warfare would not simply vanish overnight, and the Army could not stop trying to think about the problem because it was difficult to think about. At the front line of any conventional or nuclear war in Europe, the Army had to

---

[37] Matthew Grant, *After the Bomb: Civil Defence and Nuclear War in Britain, 1945–1968* (Basingstoke: Palgrave Macmillan, 2010), p. 3.

[38] See, Jonathan Hogg, *British Nuclear Culture: Official and Unofficial Narratives in the Long 20th Century* (London: Bloomsbury, 2016), p. 173.

[39] Kahn, *Thinking about the Unthinkable*, p. 61.

[40] Vojtech Mastny, 'Imagining War in Europe: Soviet Strategic Planning' in Vojtech Mastny et al. (eds.), *War Plans and Alliances in the Cold War: Threat Perceptions in the East and West* (London: Routledge, 2006), p. 15.

[41] Joseph De Rivera, 'Facing Nuclear Weapons', *American Behavioural Scientist*, Vol. 27, No. 6 (1984), p. 742.

engage in an active process of imagination which framed the abstract notion of nuclear warfare within the grounded reality of objective and pragmatic military planning. Thus, there was a reality to the imaginary war for professional soldiers not experienced in the same manner by private citizens. That is not to say that soldiers serving in BAOR would not have had their own, private images of nuclear war. Soldiers were, after all, husbands, fathers, and brothers who would no doubt have constructed their own narratives of nuclear war and their personal role within it. Furthermore, during the 1950s, it was ordinary young men who had been conscripted into the Army to fulfil their National Service duties who would have taken the brunt of a Soviet atomic blitzkrieg in a Third World War. Only through the production of an oral history of BAOR, which is another missing piece in the historiography of the post-war British Army, informed by suitable studies on military psychology and masculine culture, will it be possible to ascertain how men truly *felt* about the possibility of being an agent of nuclear warfare.

What both the civilian population and the Army did have in common was that both groups initially located their reference points for thinking about nuclear war in the shared experience of the Second World War. For civilians on the home front, it was the collective experience of the blitz which provided a ready reference point for imagining what nuclear war might look like. Matthew Grant has demonstrated how the prevailing cultural power of the Second World War made it difficult to separate conventional from nuclear war in popular discourse. Having lived under the shadow of the bomber, it did not take a giant cognitive leap for Britons living in the atomic age to imagine how nuclear armed bombers and missiles could wreak destruction on their cities, at least before the arrival of the H-bomb appeared to obliterate these ties to the lived experience.[42] The Army similarly drew its intellectual reference points for thinking about a future tactical nuclear war from the great land campaigns of both the First and Second World Wars. Throughout the Cold War, the Army presented tactical nuclear war as being akin to conventional war, but with much bigger explosions. Infantry and armour would manoeuvre over the battlefield as they had in Normandy and North Africa, and the enemy would be defeated through hard and bitter fighting. Mary Kaldor has argued that the 'military-technological' style of Cold War military planning was reminiscent of the Second World War. It conceptualized nuclear weapons as tools for strategic bombardment or as more powerful forms of artillery, and involved conventional forces employing mass-produced vehicles designed for armoured operations.[43] Andrew B. Godefroy has shown how the

---

[42] Matthew Grant, 'The Imaginative Landscape of Nuclear War in Britain, 1945–65' in Matthew Grant and Benjamin Ziemann (eds.), *Understanding the Imaginary War: Culture, Thought and Nuclear Conflict, 1945–90* (Manchester: Manchester University Press, 2016), pp. 98–104.

[43] Mary Kaldor, *The Imaginary War: Understanding the East–West Conflict* (Oxford: Basil Blackwell, 1990), p. 214.

Canadian Army structured its thinking in a similar fashion, suggesting that it might have been planning for the war it wanted to fight rather than the one it might actually fight.[44]

That the Army took as its intellectual reference points the recent historical experience was not surprising. History provides a shared experience useful both in stimulating the imagination and in facilitating communication by the use of reference and analogy.[45] As David K. Hecht has argued, it would be a logical fallacy to claim that nuclear weapons were so revolutionary as to represent an ahistorical force, since 'how can anything new be analyzed except using pre-existing notions? Pre-existing ideas represent external factors that, inevitably, must be a part of how an innovation must be understood'.[46] There is a risk, however, that the professional culture of an officer corps distorts how those external factors are understood and transmitted through the rest of the organization. Elizabeth Kier has shown how the 'basic assumptions, values, norms, beliefs, and formal knowledge' of military organizations 'shapes its members' perceptions and affects what they notice and how they interpret it', and that this cultural interface 'screens out some parts of "reality" while magnifying others'.[47] Such distortions of reality were certainly true for the British Army, which sought to conflate as far as possible nuclear and conventional warfare. By focusing its members' attention on those features that were recognizable, it was hoped that nuclear warfare could be understood by a community of professional soldiers who, if deterrence broke down, would be called upon to fight on a battlefield of unprecedented violence and chaos.

There were clear limitations, therefore, in how far the Army was willing, and able, to imagine the consequences of nuclear war to the extent that its thinking often suffered from a 'cognitive dissonance'. In the field of psychology, cognitive dissonance describes a state of mental discomfort when persons are exposed to contradictory information that is inconsistent to their prior beliefs, ideals, or values. To reduce this discomfort, the sufferers will often add new parts to the cognition causing the psychological dissonance, or actively avoid contradictory information likely to exacerbate it.[48] I use the term loosely here to describe how the Army conceptualized nuclear warfare within the familiar paradigm of conventional warfare, whilst avoiding information which cast doubt on its ability to

[44] Andrew B. Godefroy, *In Peace Prepared: Innovation and Adaptation in Canada's Cold War Army* (Vancouver: University of British Columbia Press, 2014), pp. 140–1.

[45] Kahn, *Thinking about the Unthinkable*, p. 172.

[46] David K. Hecht, 'Imagining the Bomb: Robert Oppenheimer, Nuclear Weapons, and the Assimilation of Technological Innovation' in David H. Cropley (ed.), *The Dark Side of Creativity* (Cambridge: Cambridge University Press, 2010), p. 79.

[47] Elizabeth Kier, *Imagining War: French and British Military Doctrine Between the Wars* (Princeton, NJ: Princeton University Press, 1997), p. 28.

[48] Leon Festinger, 'Cognitive Dissonance', *Scientific American*, Vol. 207 (1962), pp. 93–106. Coincidentally, the original article was interrupted with an advertisement for 'The World's First Fully Mobile Nuclear Power Plant'.

operate effectively on the nuclear battlefield. The active avoidance of difficult or unwanted ideations about nuclear warfare was not unique to the Army, however. Peter Schwenger has argued that even if persons can overcome the reluctance to think about nuclear warfare, this does not necessarily mean that they are able because of a mental 'numbing'. He goes on to say:

> ...nuclear war is unthinkable in one sense because none of the images that characterize [sic] our previous experiences is adequate to this one. What images we can come up with are so painful, so unacceptable, that they, or the emotions associated with them, are blocked...[49]

This numbing phenomenon had been well documented by psychiatrists during the Cold War who concluded that while many persons had considered the possibility that a nuclear war could occur and were frightened by it, a considerable amount were still in denial about its consequences.[50] Anecdotal evidence also reveals a tendency on the part of those who came into contact with the bomb in a professional setting to block out unwanted thoughts about nuclear war. For example, Matthew Grant tells how in the aftermath of the Cuban missile crisis, Prime Minister Harold MacMillan confessed to President John F. Kennedy that 'when one lives on Vesuvius, one takes little account of the risk of eruptions'.[51] In the same vein, a BBC radio producer felt suddenly compelled to broadcast a feature on the H-bomb since 'like many people, I have simply avoided thinking about these bombs and their implications during the last ten years'.[52] It may be, as Eva Horn has suggested, that nuclear weapons represented a 'Promethean gap', indicating the 'discrepancy between the human ability to produce technology and the inability to imagine the repercussions and consequences of these technologies'.[53]

The British Army could not have failed to be affected by this type of mental numbing. Indeed, one of the core functions of any military organization is to reduce anxiety in its members, which is partly achieved through the process of 'bull(shit)'. Norman F. Dixon has described in vivid detail how 'bull' became one of the most irrational yet significant aspects of military culture which involves 'ritualistic observance of the dominance–submission relationships of the military hierarchy, extreme orderliness and a preoccupation with outward appearance'.[54] Manifestations of 'bull' include parades, drills, the polishing of cap badges, and

---

[49] Peter Schwenger, 'Writing the Unthinkable', *Critical Enquiry*, Vol. 13, No. 1 (1986), p. 35.
[50] De Rivera, 'Facing Nuclear Weapons', pp. 739–40.
[51] Grant, *After the Bomb*, p. 9.      [52] Ibid., p. 78.
[53] Eva Horn, 'The Apocalyptic Fiction: Shaping the Future in the Cold War' in Matthew Grant and Benjamin Ziemann (eds.), *Understanding the Imaginary War: Culture, Thought and Nuclear Conflict, 1945–90* (Manchester: Manchester University Press, 2016), p. 34.
[54] Norman Dixon, *On the Psychology of Military Incompetence* (London: Pimlico, 1994), pp. 176–7.

saluting. Such activities perform an important function for military organizations in that they ensure a level of orderliness, cleanliness, discipline, personal pride, obedience, and morale, which enhance solidarity and group cohesiveness, thereby contributing to overall combat effectiveness. The most important function of this imposed uniformity is its ability to reduce anxiety and fear, which helps soldiers overcome some of the psychological challenges of preparing for combat. The value of such conditioning would undoubtedly be at a premium in nuclear war. The downside, however, is that 'bull' is inherently anti-intellectual and designed to perform the role of distractor and time-filler. This too has its benefits for military organizations in that a mind concentrated on boring and repetitive tasks has little room for intrusive thoughts.[55] Such anxiety-reduction methods can certainly perform a useful function for combat soldiers, but do not necessarily engender a frame of mind that is comfortable with uncertainty or possessed of great creativity and imagination. The effects of 'bull', which was alive and well in the post-war British Army,[56] might have contributed to an inability, at an organizational level, to think about nuclear warfare in emotional or human terms. Indeed, Jessica Douthwaite has argued that the routinization of civil defence training in Britain during the 1950s 'dulled the imagination through the hypothetical, abstracted concepts written into rehearsals material'.[57] If this was true of a pseudo-military organization such as the Civil Defence Corps, it would have been felt much more acutely in a professional military force.

Language, and the vocabulary of discourse about nuclear weapons in particular, could also have played a role in shielding the Army from some of the realities of nuclear warfare. Like most fields of professional study, a large array of metaphors and terms of art surrounded nuclear strategy. Such language has been a source of concern for some observers outside of the defence establishment, who have worried that the 'techno-strategic' language employed by defence intellectuals removed them from the human realties behind the weapons they discussed. Having witnessed the professional discourse of nuclear analysts during a summer workshop on nuclear weapons in 1984, Carol Cohn observed that the discussions were 'carefully and intricately reasoned' and devoid of any sense of 'horror, urgency, or moral outrage'. The elaborate use of abstraction and euphemisms was such that 'they never forced the speaker or enabled the listener to touch the realities of nuclear holocaust that lay behind the words'.[58] The use of acronyms and technical jargon allowed the speaker to feel mastery over technology which was powerful 'beyond human comprehension'. For Cohn, the process of learning

---

[55] Ibid., pp. 182–3.

[56] For an example of 'bull' in action see French, *Army, Empire, and Cold War*, pp. 78–9.

[57] Jessica Douthwaite, '…"what in the hell's this?" Rehearsing Nuclear War in Britain's Civil Defence Corps', *Contemporary British History*, advance online publication (2018), p. 5.

[58] Carol Cohn, 'Sex and Death in the Rational World of Defense Intellectuals', *Signs*, Vol. 12, No. 4 (1987), p. 690.

to speak the language was itself a part of what removed the experts from the reality of nuclear war.[59] She concluded that:

> Listening to the discourse of nuclear experts reveals a series of culturally grounded and culturally acceptable mechanisms that serve this purpose and that make it possible to 'think about the unthinkable', to work in institutions that foster the proliferation of nuclear weapons, to plan mass incinerations of millions of human beings for a living. Language that is abstract, sanitized, full of euphemisms; language that is sexy and fun to use; paradigms whose referent is weapons; imagery that domesticates and deflates the forces of mass destruction; imagery that reverses sentient and non-sentient matter, that conflates birth and death, destruction and creation—all of these are part of what makes it possible to be radically removed from the reality of what one is talking about and from the realities one is creating through the discourse.[60]

Of course, those men who did, perhaps unfairly, 'plan mass incinerations of millions of human beings for a living' held very different views about the value and function of the language denigrated by Cohn. Herman Kahn, the archetypal defence intellectual, believed that a factual, dispassionate, and even colourful mode of expression was preferable for those who sought to analyse and critique nuclear strategy. After all, 'why would one expect a realistic discussion of thermonuclear war not to be disturbing?'.[61] Likewise, Sir Michael Quinlan, who spent a long career in the Civil Service working on many aspects of British nuclear weapons policy, defended the use of such euphemisms and metaphors as the only vehicle for communicating the various abstract concepts which, in lieu of any practical experience, were the only frames of reference for understanding nuclear war. The accurate use and comprehension of this language was therefore of special importance in the nuclear field in order to facilitate thought and dialogue.[62] The often dry language employed in the official documents on which much of the research for this book is based confirms that professional discourse about the employment of nuclear weapons was detached and unemotional. Cohn is correct in that such language facilitated thinking about the unthinkable; that was its purpose so that the fighting forces could develop rational military plans in support of defence policy. Abstractions such as 'trip-wire', 'escalation', and 'threshold', for example, provided convenient and readily understood metaphors for what are complex processes and interactions, thus aiding the imagination.

---

[59] Ibid., p. 704.    [60] Ibid., p. 715.
[61] Kahn, *Thinking about the Unthinkable*, p. 24.
[62] Michael Quinlan, *Thinking about Nuclear Weapons: Principles, Problems, Prospects* (Oxford: Oxford University Press, 2009), pp. 15–16.

The use of imagination to foresee the conditions of future war was not a new cognitive process unique to those who lived under the shadow of the bomb, but has always been a routine institutional activity for peacetime military organizations.[63] At a basic level, imagining the most likely conditions of future war increases the likelihood that the military force will be better prepared to adapt successfully to the new environment. The ultimate decider of whether major innovation occurs in peacetime military organizations is a complex web of technological, organizational, and cultural factors,[64] but corporate imagination performs a crucial function for a very simple reason, as Williamson Murray explains:

> Unlike other organizations, military forces in peacetime must innovate and prepare for a war 1) that will occur at some indeterminate point in the future, 2) against an opponent who may not yet be identified, 3) in political conditions which one cannot accurately predict, and 4) in an arena of brutality and violence which one cannot replicate.[65]

The nature of the Cold War removed some of these political uncertainties for Western defence planners, and the British Army had a clear and identifiable opponent in the Soviet 3rd Shock Army, which was located just across the intra-German border. It was the final point, however, that proved much more difficult since the Army was forced to think about an arena of such brutality and violence that it has often been regarded as unthinkable. Synthetic representations of nuclear warfare, in the form of war-games and military exercises, provided one means through which the Army could replicate the conditions of the nuclear battlefield, but they often raised uncomfortable questions which were drowned out by the organization's cognitive dissonance. Those military organizations that are unable to imagine the knowns and unknowns of the future operating environment, or else draw a faulty picture of that imagined future, can be extremely costly when the next war comes about.[66] One of the dangers in relying on imagination as a guide for future planning is that it is impossible to determine whether assumptions are correct before they are tested in the crucible of war. As Michael Howard observed about the soldier:

---

[63] 'Peacetime' here means that the military force is not actively engaged in war-fighting, as opposed to 'peaceful' relations between states.

[64] For an overview of the different schools of thought on military innovation see Adam Grissom, 'The Future of Military Innovation Studies', *Journal of Strategic Studies*, Vol. 29, No. 5 (2006), pp. 905–34.

[65] Williamson Murray, 'Innovation: Past and Future' in Williamson Murray and Allan R. Millett (eds.), *Military Innovation in the Interwar Period* (Cambridge: Cambridge University Press, 1996), p. 301.

[66] The classic example here are the assumptions made by the French Army in the inter-war period. See Elizabeth Kier, 'Culture and Military Doctrine: France Between the Wars', *International Security*, Vol. 19, No. 4 (1995), pp. 65–93.

... his profession is almost unique in that he may only have to exercise it once in a lifetime, if indeed that often. It is as if a surgeon had to practice throughout his life on dummies for one real operation; or a barrister only appeared once or twice in court towards the close of his career; or a professional swimmer had to spend his life practicing on dry land for an Olympic championship on which the fortunes of his entire nation depended.[67]

The stakes involved in military innovation are therefore high, and in the nuclear age, the costs of getting it wrong for the British Army would have been disastrous. However, in spite of the conceptual and practical difficulties posed by tactical nuclear weapons, the Army had little choice but to try and adapt to the new paradigm of nuclear-age land warfare. Although the British Army has been stereotyped as a 'quintessentially gentlemanly institution ... suspicious of change and reluctant to adopt new ways of doing things',[68] the service has nonetheless consistently proved itself capable of adapting, in times of peace and war, to the changing character of conflict.[69] In spite of the limitations in the Army's thinking about nuclear warfare, it was similarly successful in adapting to a military environment where only nuclear weapons appeared to matter. Indeed, between 1945 and 1989, the Army progressed through each of the three phases of military innovation identified by Thomas G. Mahnken as being signals that military organizations are undergoing a process of change: speculation, experimentation, and implementation.[70]

During the speculation phase in the late 1940s and 1950s, the Army sought novel ways to solve the operational problems posed by the introduction of tactical nuclear weapons. The period witnessed a proliferation of books, journal articles, speeches, and studies advocating new theories of war, and professional service journals were inundated with speculative ideas about nuclear weapons and the future operating environment. Speculation soon gave way to experimentation in the 1960s as the Army began to test innovative concepts in new field training exercises and war-games. The study of military history also saw something of a renaissance in the British Army as the lessons-learned process was mobilized to

---

[67] Michael Howard, 'The Use and Abuse of Military History', *The RUSI Journal*, Vol. 107, No. 625 (1962), p. 6.

[68] David French, *Military Identities: The Regimental System, The British Army, & the British People c. 1870–2000* (Oxford: Oxford University Press, 2005), p. 3.

[69] See, for example, Aimée Fox, *Learning to Fight: Military Innovation and Change in the British Army, 1914–1918* (Cambridge: Cambridge University Press, 2017); Brian N. Hall, *Communications and British Operations on the Western Front, 1914–1918* (Cambridge: Cambridge University Press, 2017); Robert T. Foley, Stuart Griffin, and Helen McCartney, 'Transformation in Contact: Learning the Lessons of Modern War', *International Affairs*, Vol. 87, No. 2 (2011), pp. 253–70; John Stone, 'The British Army and the Tank' in Theo Farrell and Terry Terriff (eds.), *The Sources of Military Change: Culture, Politics, Technology* (London: Lynne Rienner, 2002), pp. 187–204.

[70] Thomas G. Mahnken, 'Uncovering Foreign Military Innovation', *Journal of Strategic Studies*, Vol. 22, No. 4 (1999), pp. 30–4.

help unravel some of the mysteries of nuclear warfare. By the end of the Cold War, the British Army had developed, and was routinely utilizing, a wide array of different learning tools to test the effectiveness of new approaches to war-fighting. Successful experimentation resulted in the implementation of new doctrine, organizations, and forces structures. The most tangible changes occurred in written doctrine and Staff College curriculum. Indeed, the Army's doctrine evolved considerably over the decades to reflect its new nuclear mission in Germany, beginning with Montgomery's post-war review in 1948 and ending with the adoption of the Bagnall-inspired *British Military Doctrine* in 1989.

The study takes an interpretive approach to understanding how the British Army imagined nuclear warfare through the analysis of a large body of literature produced and used by the Army. Primary sources include internal communications, training manuals, doctrine pamphlets, Staff College curriculum, reports from operational research establishments, and articles in professional service journals. Official documents from other departments of state, and international organizations such as NATO, reveal insights into the policy decisions which shaped the Army's external world. Oral histories and personal testimonies provide atmosphere to the individual experiences of the men who served in BAOR. The book is weighted more heavily on the experiences of the Army in the 1950s and 1960s for two reasons. First, there are gaps in the archival record created by the many sensitive and secretive discussions about nuclear weapons and nuclear strategy that went unrecorded. This is compounded by the fact that there is no 'BAOR archive', or that it is yet to be found. The consensus appears to be that these documents have been destroyed, which was common practice for the Army in Germany when operational plans were rescinded. The result is that primary source material relating to the activities of the British Army, especially in the nuclear field, begins to trail off by the late 1970s in the British National Archive system. Second, the golden age of thinking about the nuclear battlefield in the British Army was during the first two decades of the Cold War. This was the formative period when the service began to adapt its thinking to the new challenges brought about by the arrival of tactical nuclear weapons. Images of nuclear war forged in these early years would have an enduring legacy, and shaped all further concepts about the future operating environment. As will be shown, by the late 1970s, notions of fighting a tactical nuclear war had fallen completely out of vogue, nuclear instruction had all but ceased at the Staff College, and the Army's doctrine was taking on a much more conventional theme.

The book is organized thematically into six chapters, each of which considers one of the core areas of intellectual activity across the British defence establishment: political-strategic planning, military-strategic planning, future operating concepts, professional military education, operational research, and doctrine development. From the corridors of Whitehall to Staff College classrooms, these interconnected themes present a portrait of the British Army's thinking about tactical nuclear weapons.

Chapter 1 examines how British policy-makers viewed the arrival of tactical nuclear weapons, employing as a vehicle the 1950s debate on the relative merits of the opposing strategic theories of 'massive retaliation' and 'graduated deterrence'. It shows how the British government rejected any suggestion to draw distinctions in peacetime between strategic and tactical nuclear weapons because of a strong belief that such an announcement would undermine the overall deterrent effect of nuclear weapons. Gripped by a 'deterrence habit of mind', civilian leaders viewed tactical nuclear weapons not as meaningful military tools, but as weapons of escalation whose use would trigger a strategic nuclear exchange between the superpowers. The rejection of any kind of graduated deterrence through the use of tactical nuclear weapons set a precedent in how British policy-makers conceived the utility of tactical nuclear weapons, which would have important consequences in the following debates about NATO strategy.

Chapter 2 analyses how the British deterrence habit of mind manifested in a preference for a pure-deterrence strategy for NATO. The forums of NATO were a market for strategic ideas, and competing visions of nuclear warfare reflected the often incompatible strategic preferences of its member states. Bargaining and compromise resulted in significant changes to defensive concepts throughout the Cold War and saw the emergence of two distinct strategies, massive retaliation and flexible response, which provided the conceptual framework for the Army's own thinking about nuclear war. The chapter draws out the most important assumptions made about the character of nuclear warfare, the political and military utility of tactical nuclear weapons, and the perceived role of ground forces within NATO's deterrent posture. It shows how the British reluctance to accept that military organizations could perform a useful function during or after a strategic nuclear exchange set an ominous tone for the Army's own theorizing about future war.

Chapter 3 considers some of the first attempts by the Army to imagine nuclear warfare. It provides a survey of the types of articles that appeared in the seven most popular service journals during the 1950s to determine how speculation about the nuclear battlefield shaped organizational thinking about the nuclear battlefield. This representative body of work, which together constituted the emerging theory of tactical nuclear warfare, defined the parameters of the debate about the use of nuclear weapons in the land battle for the remainder of the Cold War. Critical analysis of this text, in addition to that of other published work and unpublished typescripts, suggests an officer corps that possessed the intellectual capacity for organizational innovation. The chapter maintains that the intellectual reference points for thinking about future warfare reflected the culture of an officer corps bloodied in two world wars and struggling to find a role in a changing world.

Chapter 4 examines how the design and implementation of the curriculum at the Army Staff College, Camberley reflected organizational views about nuclear warfare. The chapter critically evaluates how the Army institutionalized learning on a subject about which very little was known, and that was politically sensitive and relied ultimately on abstract concepts untested in the crucible of war. It argues that the Staff College proved remarkably absorbent to new ideas and habitually incorporated the most fashionable thinking and latest doctrinal constructs into its syllabus. In this context, the development of Staff College curriculum mirrored the ebb and flow of NATO's changing strategic concepts, the maturation of BAOR's nuclear doctrine, and the Army's perceptions of its own place within national defence policy.

Chapter 5 examines how concepts for nuclear land combat were tested through tangible training regimes, war-games, and military manoeuvres to indoctrinate troops for fighting in a nuclear environment. It argues that Army operational research groups and training institutions made some headway into the practical challenges of preparing the service for nuclear ground combat, but that the results gained from these assessments highlighted some of the dilemmas inherent in planning for warfare using a new and untested weapon of unprecedented power. Objective analysis threatened to expose some of the Army's more fanciful ideas about future war and directly challenged its faith in its ability to successfully prosecute the surreal mission to which it had been assigned. While the Army claimed that the conclusions drawn from its operational research supported well-established beliefs and assumptions about the modern operating environment, its critics saw only wishful thinking and the erroneous use of scientific data. The uncomfortable realities exposed by these synthetic representations of nuclear war served only to entrench the Army's cognitive dissonance.

Chapter 6 assesses the evolution of the British Army's doctrine for tactical nuclear war. It challenges the orthodox narrative of an intellectually stagnant post-war British Army by demonstrating that the service was continually engaged with the development of new doctrine throughout the Cold War. In particular, the chapter draws attention to how formal written doctrine was influenced by two of the Rhine Army's most coveted, and controversial, commanders: Field Marshal Bernard L. Montgomery and Field Marshal Sir Nigel Bagnall. It argues that the post-war military thought of Montgomery was much more progressive than has hitherto been described by historians, and that the doctrinal reforms instigated by Bagnall in the 1980s were merely a logical progression of concepts articulated in the 1950s, calling into question the revolutionary nature of the reforms.

# 1

# British Thinking about Tactical Nuclear Weapons

The British attachment to nuclear deterrence as the best, and only, means of ensuring national security in the uncertain post-war world has been described as being born of a 'deterrence habit of mind'.[1] The ideational influences which shaped this nuclear monomania in Whitehall were the perceived unique vulnerability of the UK to attack with nuclear weapons (itself an extension of the inter-war fears of the proverbial 'bolt from the blue'); the identification of the Soviet Union as a threatening and immutable threat to the status quo, coupled with a faith in the commonality of interests between East and West to avoid nuclear war; the promise that nuclear weapons might abolish war in all its forms; and a symbolic attachment to nuclear power as a manifestation of Britain's autonomy and independence.[2] These powerful belief systems provided the logic justifying the rejection of 'graduated deterrence' as a viable alternative to the strategy of 'massive retaliation', which had become the cornerstone of British nuclear strategy by the end of the 1950s. The challenge posed by graduated deterrence to the strategic orthodoxy raised a number of fundamental questions about the practicalities and desirability of drawing distinctions in peacetime between nuclear weapons and their intended targets, whether the use of tactical nuclear weapons would precipitate a strategic nuclear exchange, and the credibility of a discriminate or 'escalatory' nuclear reaction to Soviet aggression.

In ruminating on these questions, the deterrence habit of mind established clear preferences about the role and functions of tactical nuclear weapons, which would go on to serve as the conceptual basis for Britain's interpretation of NATO's flexible response strategy in pure-deterrence terms during the 1960s and beyond. The elements of a pure-deterrence strategy have been described by Ivo H. Daalder as a denial of the existence of thresholds in war, particularly the one between conventional and nuclear war; a belief in the inevitability of escalation to general nuclear war between nuclear-armed adversaries; contrived ambiguity about the

---

[1] John Baylis and Kristan Stoddart, *The British Nuclear Experience: The Role of Beliefs, Culture, and Identity* (Oxford: Oxford University Press, 2015), pp. 16–41.
[2] Beatrice Heuser, *Nuclear Mentalities? Strategies and Beliefs in Britain, France and the FRG* (Basingstoke: Macmillan, 1998), pp. 3–52.

*Imagining Nuclear War in the British Army, 1945–1989.* Simon J. Moody, Oxford University Press (2020).
© Simon J. Moody.
DOI: 10.1093/oso/9780198846994.001.0001

nature of a nuclear response to aggression; and an attachment to the early use of tactical nuclear weapons which emphasizes their political rather than military effects.[3] This chapter locates the origins of the key tenet of the British pure-deterrence strategy—the impossibility and undesirability of pauses, firebreaks, or thresholds in war—with the denunciation of graduated deterrence in the late 1950s. Chapter 2 will show how the British deterrence habit of mind manifested in a preference for a pure-deterrence strategy for NATO.

## Towards a Strategy of Massive Retaliation

At the birth of the atomic age, visions of nuclear war embodied complex and diverse emotions. Popular fear, anxiety, and revulsion against the 'dark' science of nuclear power were tempered by celebration of the technical and industrial achievements of the Manhattan Project, which had helped to bring about an end to the brutal and costly conventional war-fighting in the Pacific.[4] British policy-makers were quick to understand the Janus-faced nature of nuclear power, which threatened to make the nation simultaneously more and less secure. An official memorandum prepared for Prime Minister Clement Attlee in September 1945 stated ominously that 'the new discovery makes the United Kingdom infinitely more vulnerable than ever before, both absolutely and as compared with larger and less centrally placed countries'.[5] Britain was perceived to be uniquely vulnerable to nuclear attack because it was a small, densely populated island which relied on shipping to import its vital strategic materials. Both the physical and human geography of the British Isles made it a perfect target for nuclear attack.

Beatrice Heuser describes how even before the advent of nuclear weapons, Briton's had become obsessed with the idea of direct attack from the air. The anxiety was validated by German air raids during the First World War, and reached their apogee during the course of the Second, when Britain was subjected to long-range missile bombardment by V-1 and V-2 flying bombs.[6] Although the much-feared 'bolt from the blue' failed to materialize, in part because of the practical and conceptual difficulties of waging offensive bombing campaigns with conventional munitions, the near instantaneous destruction of the cities of Hiroshima and Nagasaki by a single aircraft cast serious doubt on the ability of

---

[3] Ivo H. Daalder, *The Nature and Practice of Flexible Response: NATO Strategy and Theatre Nuclear Forces since 1967* (New York, NY: Columbia University Press, 1991), pp. 43–8.
[4] David K. Hecht, 'Imagining the Bomb: Robert Oppenheimer, Nuclear Weapons, and the Assimilation of Technological Innovation' in David H. Cropley (ed.), *The Dark Side of Creativity* (Cambridge: Cambridge University Press, 2010), pp. 74–6.
[5] Cited in Heuser, *Nuclear Mentalities*, p. 9.      [6] Heuser, *Nuclear Mentalities*, pp. 8–9.

Britons to ride out another blitz employing nuclear weapons.[7] If the world's major powers were ever again thrust into another global war, it might be that the theories of the inter-war airpower prophets such as Giulio Douhet, Billy Mitchell, and Hugh Trenchard would finally be vindicated—nuclear airpower might prove decisive, deciding the outcome of the conflict in a matter of weeks or days, perhaps even hours.[8]

Paradoxically, however, it was the appalling consequences of nuclear war that gave hope to British policy-makers that the possession of nuclear weapons could not only deter aggression, but abolish war in all its forms. Writing in the shadow of the mushroom clouds in 1945, the British military theorist Stephen King-Hall concluded that:

Total war—large scale national war—is at an end. It has vanished from the sphere of practical politics...physical violence as a continuation of political purposes will be limited to riots and large scale police action...Total War has reached its ultimate and absolute physical development, it has made political and economic nationalism a meaningless thing and so Total War has abolished itself.[9]

There were some observers who questioned whether a large-scale nuclear air offensive against a major power could in itself prove decisive since the weapons were so large that they had to be delivered to their target by piston-engine heavy bombers which were vulnerable to interception.[10] The emergence of thermo-nuclear weapons (which, theoretically, have no upper limit on the size of their yield) in the middle 1950s, coupled with delivery vehicles that could detonate them anywhere in the world, soon quelled any doubts about the strategic significance of nuclear power. It was still unclear how nuclear weapons might affect war on land, however, as little was known in Britain about the detailed technical characteristics of the bombs which had seemingly shocked Japanese leaders into

---

[7] For an excellent review of how the embedded theories of airpower have often proved difficult to translate into strategic effect in practice see Karl P. Mueller, *Air Power* (Santa Monica, CA: RAND, 2010), pp. 10–12.

[8] See, respectively, Giulio Douhet, *The Command of the Air*, trans. D. Ferrari (Washington, DC: Air Force History and Museums Programme, 1998); William Mitchell, *Winged Defense: The Development and Possibilities of Modern Air Power—Economic and Military* (Tuscaloosa, AL: University of Alabama Press, 2009); Phillip S. Meilinger, 'Trenchard and "Morale Bombing": The Evolution of Royal Air Force Doctrine Before World War II', *The Journal of Military History*, Vol. 60, No. 2 (April 1996), pp. 243–70. A discussion of the relationship between offensive bombing theory and nuclear strategy can be found in Beatrice Heuser, *The Evolution of Strategy: Thinking War from Antiquity to the Present* (Cambridge: Cambridge University Press, 2010), pp. 351–86 and Bernard Brodie, *Strategy in the Missile Age* (Santa Monica, CA: The Rand Corporation, 1959), pp. 3–144.

[9] Stephen King-Hall, *Defence in the Nuclear Age* (London: Victor Gollancz Ltd, 1958), p. 11.

[10] See, for example, the arguments by P. M. S. Blackett in *Military and Political Consequences of Atomic Energy* (London: Turnstile Press, 1948), p. 56.

an unconditional surrender.[11] Although the 'tactical' use of nuclear weapons in support of ground forces had been discussed by American military leaders during the deliberations in the summer of 1945 about a possible invasion of the Japanese home islands, small-yield nuclear weapons suitable for battlefield use had yet to arrive.[12] The general consensus at the dawn of the atomic age was that nuclear weapons were so expensive and laborious to manufacture that they were unlikely to be squandered on anything but the most valuable strategic targets. Even then, a strategic nuclear exchange would take place above the heads of the Army, and the service had little incentive to think in any meaningful way about the implications for its own operational plans. As the first post-war defence White Paper stated:

> The great strides made in the realm of science and technology, including the production of atomic bombs, cannot fail to affect the make-up of our forces. Time is wanted for the full effects of these startling developments to be assessed. But in the meanwhile... the question of fundamental reorganisation does not arise.[13]

Faith in nuclear weapons as the ultimate deterrent to aggression would assume greater significance against the backdrop of the burgeoning Cold War, as Britain sought new ways through which to achieve national security in the new world order at a time when defence budgets were rapidly shrinking. Investment in an independent strategic nuclear deterrent was deemed more economical than raising and maintaining the level of manpower that would be required to fight the type of prolonged conventional war which had been necessary to defeat Nazi Germany. At the same time, joining the nuclear club would allow Britain to remain at the high table of international politics at a time when its relative power and influence was waning.[14]

Although Britain had emerged from the Second World War a victorious power, it was virtually bankrupt and saddled with the largest external debt in history.[15] Such was the parlous state of the economy that a senior Treasury advisor, John Maynard Keynes, warned that 'a financial Dunkirk' may soon befall the nation.[16]

---

[11] Historians do not agree on the role played by nuclear weapons in bringing the war in the Pacific to an end. For a review of the historiography see J. Samuel Walker, 'Recent Literature on Truman's Atomic Bomb Decision: A Search for Middle Ground', *Diplomatic History*, Vol. 29, No. 2 (2005), pp. 311–34.

[12] Barton J. Bernstein, 'Eclipsed by Hiroshima and Nagasaki: Early Thinking about Tactical Nuclear Weapons', *International Security*, Vol. 15, No. 4 (1991), pp. 151–3.

[13] Cmd. 6743, *Statement Relating to Defence* (London: HMSO, 1946), p. 3.

[14] Baylis and Stoddart, *The British Nuclear Experience*, p. 32.

[15] G. C. Peden, *Arms, Economics and British Strategy* (Cambridge: Cambridge University Press, 2007), p. 245 and Alec Cairncross, *Years of Recovery: British Economic Policy 1945–51* (London: Methuen, 1985), pp. 3–7.

[16] Richard Toye, 'Churchill and Britain's "Financial Dunkirk"', *Twentieth Century British History*, Vol. 15, No. 4 (2004), p. 329.

Against this difficult economic background, Attlee's Labour government was confronted with the difficult task of funding its considerable overseas security commitments with depleted resources. In 1945, overseas expenditure came in at just over £700m. At this level, military spending could almost be held to account for the whole 1945 deficit of £800m.[17] Although the services laid claim to such high levels of funding to meet its short-term and long-term commitments, defence had to compete with social welfare programmes for a slice of the fiscal pie.[18] These popularly mandated programmes, which together established what came to be known as the Welfare State, required the nationalization of key industries and the better provision of health, welfare, and education for all.[19] The correct balance to be struck between national defence and social welfare created something of a dilemma. While Ministers were aware of the pressing need to restore the economic health of the nation, they also acknowledged that Britain could not simply abandon its global responsibilities. To do so, as the 1946 defence White Paper warned, would be to 'throw away the fruits of victory, and to betray those who had fought and died in the common cause'.[20]

All of this had ominous implications for the Army, which had been rapidly demobilized since the end of the war so that valuable manpower could be transferred from the fighting services into more profitable sectors of the economy.[21] Such was the pace of demobilization that the Army ran down from a strength of 3,000,000 (twenty-nine divisions and thirty-five brigades) in 1945 to 450,000 (three divisions and eight brigades) in all ranks in 1948.[22] In spite of this, British garrisons were still to be found in over forty countries, spanning every major theatre: in the North and South Atlantic, Europe, Africa, the Middle East, India, Burma, Hong Kong, Japan, Malaya, Singapore, and Indonesia.[23] In Germany and Austria, a significant number of soldiers were tied down with the myriad tasks associated with post-war occupation duties: the 1,894,000 German prisoners of war had to be processed; 2,233,694 displaced persons had to be repatriated; and communications, transport, and accommodation had to be repaired or developed.[24] Where Britain sought to defend contested commitments, the Army was drawn into prolonged counter-insurgency operations which required further boots on the ground. In Palestine alone, an effective Jewish

---

[17] Cairncross, *Years of Recovery*, p. 10.

[18] Anthony Gorst, 'Facing Facts? The Labour Government and Defence Policy 1945–1950' in Nick Tiratsoo (ed.), *The Attlee Years* (London: Pinter, 1991), pp. 190–1.

[19] Franklyn A. Johnson, *Defence by Ministry: The British Ministry of Defence, 1944–1974* (London: Duckworth, 1980), p. 17.

[20] Cmd. 6743, *Statement Relating to Defence*, pp. 2–3.

[21] Alan Allport, *Demobbed: Coming Home after the Second World War* (London and New Haven, CT: Yale University Press, 2009), p. 30.

[22] TNA, WO 32/16091, 79/GEN/3546/RD4(A), Rundown of the Army 1945–8, 13 July 1956.

[23] David Sanders, *Losing an Empire, Finding a Role: British Foreign Policy since 1945* (Basingstoke: Macmillan, 1990), pp. 49–50.

[24] TNA, CAB 128/1, CM(45)18, Review of Military Situation, 7 August 1945.

underground army had tied down 100,000 British troops before the United Kingdom passed its mandate over to the United Nations in 1947.[25] Later, the Army would fight a counter-insurgency campaign against Communist guerrillas in Malaya that would drag on for twelve years (1948–60) while simultaneously engaging in major combat operations against Mau Mau rebels in Kenya (1952–6) and EOKA independence fighters in Cyprus (1954–9).[26] These imperial security commitments placed an unwanted strain on Army resources at a time when it was engaged in high-intensity war-fighting operations on the Korean peninsula (1950–3) against a backdrop of escalating Cold War tensions.

The precarious balance of commitments and capabilities was exacerbated by fears of a hostile Soviet Union. In March 1946, the first detailed post-war assessment by the Joint Intelligence Committee (JIC) on Russian strategic interests and intentions painted a gloomy picture of how its policy might develop in the years to come. Exhausted by the war, it assumed that Soviet leaders would seek to obtain the highest levels of territorial integrity by extending the Soviet sphere of influence in Eastern Europe as a buffer against further attacks from the West. While Moscow would likely experiment with cooperation with its war-time allies, if it did not believe that London and Washington were sincerely collaborating, it would increase its military presence in Eastern Europe and sow the seeds of political unrest in many parts of the world through the exploitation of local Communist parties. The JIC concluded that the short-term aim of Russian policy was to avoid direct confrontation with the Western powers while it concentrated on the long-term goal of rebuilding the Soviet Union to a position of strength.[27]

The cooling of Anglo-Soviet relations through 1946, however, convinced the JIC of the Soviet's hostile intentions. The intelligence staff now believed that the writings of Lenin and Stalin should be regarded collectively as 'the *"Mein Kampf"* of the Soviet Regime' as they appeared to reveal how Soviet leaders were committed to the task of hastening the collapse of Capitalism in all parts of the world and replacing it with their own brand of Communism.[28] In the spring of 1947, the CIGS, Field Marshal Bernard L. Montgomery, told Army commanders at a War Office exercise that it was 'the religion of Communism operated by the Politburo which is dominating the country and forcing it down the garden path' to world domination.[29] Supporting this policy was a vast military machine, the pinnacle of which was a reported 175 army divisions and a well-equipped and well-armed

[25] Robert Self, *British Foreign and Defence Policy since 1945: Challenges and Dilemmas in a Changing World* (Basingstoke: Macmillan, 2010), pp. 42–6.
[26] Ibid., pp. 47–50.
[27] TNA, CAB 81/132, JIC (46)1(O), Russia's Strategic Interests and Intentions, Report by the Joint Intelligence Sub-Committee, 1 March 1946.
[28] TNA, CAB 158/1, JIC (47)7/1 Final, Soviet Interests, Intentions and Capabilities, Report by the Joint Intelligence Sub-Committee, 6 August 1947.
[29] TNA, WO 216/202, CIGS/BM/26/1241, War Office Exercise Spearhead, address on the world situation by the CIGS, The Staff College Camberley, 5–10 May 1947.

tactical air force. Yet, there was at least one chink identified in the armour of this seemingly impervious military behemoth. While the Red Army would be able to achieve rapid success on land, the strategic air situation remained averse to the Soviet Union in that she had no satisfactory answer to the West's atomic weapons and bomber forces.[30] This weakness would be exploited to the full in early British strategic planning.

Although military leaders feared the spread of Communism, directed by Moscow, throughout the world, major war against the Soviet Union was not viewed as imminent. In their 1947 report on 'Future Defence Policy' the Chiefs of Staff maintained that the likelihood of war within the next five years was small, but that the risk would increase gradually in the following five years, increasing more steeply thereafter as the rehabilitation of Russian industry gathered momentum.[31] Consequently, 1957 was set, for planning purposes, as the date at which the Soviet Union would be ready to embark on a major war. To combat this threat, the Chiefs of Staff articulated that the three pillars of British strategy should be the defence of the United Kingdom, the control of essential sea communications, and the maintenance of the Middle East as an offensive base. By protecting the home islands, the Middle East, and the sea lanes that connected them, Britain would be able to maintain a variety of strategically placed airbases from which offensive air campaigns could be launched against the Soviet Union in the event of a major war. It was taken for granted that this air campaign would be waged with nuclear weapons, with the Chiefs assuming that 'the knowledge that we possessed weapons of mass destruction and were prepared to use them would be a most effective deterrent to war itself'.[32] Therefore, 'it must be a cardinal principle of our policy to be prepared, equipped and able to use them immediately'.[33]

The embryonic deterrence strategy laid out in the 'Future Defence Policy' paper saw few meaningful roles for the Army, which was anyway in no position during the late 1940s to confront a first-class power organized and ready for war.[34] The feasibility of maintaining large conventional forces was further called into question when the decision was taken by the Treasury in 1947 to cap annual expenditure on the armed forces to £600m, with the Army's budget being reduced from £330m to £270m.[35] Although the War Office was against the proposed cuts, they were an inevitable consequence of the stark choices facing government about the

---

[30] TNA, CAB 158/1, JIC (47)7/2 Final, Soviet Interests, Intentions and Capabilities, Annex, 6 August 1947.
[31] TNA, CAB 21/1800, DO(47)44, Future Defence Policy, 22 May 1947.
[32] Ibid.    [33] Ibid.
[34] See, for example, reports by the Joint Planning Staff in DEFE 6/3, JP(47)97(Final), Position of the Armed Forces—Summer 1947, 8 July 1947 and the War Office in TNA, WO 216/244, CIGS/BM/29/1997, Some Notes on the Defence Problems of Britain, 30 December 1947.
[35] TNA, DEFE 5/5, COS(47)173(0), Future Defence Policy—Strength of the Armed Forces, 23 August 1947.

allocation of finite resources.[36] During a House of Commons debate on 27 October 1947, the Minister of Defence, A. V. Alexander, made clear his views on what he believed should be given priority in defence planning:

> In the light of the circumstances with which we are faced, my own view is that the first priority, which must not be interfered with, is defence research. The second, in the light of the present developing situation, must be to maintain the structure of the Royal Air Force, and its initial striking power. The third priority is for the maintenance of our sea communications, and, therefore, for the most efficient Navy we can get in the circumstances, and then we will do the best we can for the Army.[37]

There was no mistaking that the Minister of Defence viewed the Army and its expensive conventional forces as the lowest priority for defence spending. This was a view shared by the Navy and the RAF, who maintained that the only means by which the services could implement the strategy articulated in the 'Future Defence Policy' paper within the financial limit of £600m was to reduce radically the Army at the expense of the other two services.[38] Furthermore, the Chief of the Air Staff (CAS), Lord Arthur Tedder, argued that the Army would not require large conventional forces since in the event of an atomic attack there would be no role for the service except in aiding the civil powers in the United Kingdom.[39] Tedder even went as far as to suggest that the Army 'were not facing the changed type of warfare which modern weapons had already brought about'.[40] These views found sympathy with Prime Minister Attlee who appeared reluctant to maintain substantial land forces in Europe since 'previous experience had shown how continental commitments, initially small, were apt to grow into very large ones'.[41]

Events in the international arena during 1948–9 augured ill for the Chiefs' assumption that war should not be expected until 1957. The Communist coup in Czechoslovakia in February 1948, the Soviet blockade of Berlin from June 1948 to May 1949, the explosion of the first Russian atomic bomb in September 1949, and the Communist victory over Nationalist forces in the Chinese Civil War in December 1949 exposed a more aggressive and adventurous Soviet Union.[42] Finally, the outbreak of the Korean War in June 1950 appeared to validate the proposition that East and West were locked into a mortal ideological struggle.

---

[36]  TNA, DEFE 5/5, COS(47)185(0), Future Defence Policy—Strength of the Armed Forces, Note by the CIGS, 1 September 1947.

[37]  *Hansard*, House of Commons Debate, Vol. 443, Col. 652, 27 October 1947.

[38]  TNA, DEFE 6/3, JP(47)129(Final), Shape and Size of the Armed Forces, 11 November 1947, p. 39.

[39]  TNA, DEFE 32/1, COS(47)147, Shape and Size of the Armed Forces, 26 November 1947, p. 2.

[40]  TNA, DEFE 32/1, COS(47)143, Shape and Size of the Armed Forces, 19 November 1947, p. 4.

[41]  TNA, DEFE 4/10, COS(48)18, Minutes of Staff Conference held at 10 Downing St., 4 February 1948.

[42]  French, *Army, Empire, and Cold War*, p. 28.

A memorandum by the Chiefs of Staff in the summer of 1951 stated that the invasion of South Korea proved that Communism was inherently aggressive, a view which was confirmed by the intervention of Mao Zedong's Chinese forces in October 1950. The military Chiefs explained that the West was now in the curious position of being faced with 'Communist subversive and military action not amounting to total war, against a background of a threat of total war'. Therefore, the Allied Powers must 'expect further similar action in the future'.[43] This depiction of the Soviet threat as being an ambiguous combination of direct and indirect political and military confrontation shows that military leaders acknowledged that they were now operating in a unique international environment that would require a diverse range of capabilities to combat the full spectrum of potential threats to British interests.

The Chiefs of Staff incorporated all of the major changes that had occurred since their 1947 review, notably the formation of NATO and the emergence of a Russian bomb, into a new strategic planning document in 1950. The starting point for the 'Defence Policy and Global Strategy' paper' was that it would not be possible for Britain or the Continental European Powers to go it alone against the Russian threat without the support of the United States.[44] In a break with previous planning documents, it was not an articulation of an individual and independent national British strategy, but written within an alliance context. The Chiefs now argued that winning the 'cold war' was the primary requirement for the British armed forces, and that it was only through an adequate show of force that the Soviet Union could be deterred from embarking upon global war.[45] In the event of a 'hot war', the military aim would be to ensure the survival of the United Kingdom and bring the war to the speediest conclusion, without Western Europe being overrun, by 'bringing about the destruction of Russian military power'.[46] The Chiefs of Staff believed that the ability of the Western allies to achieve their aim without active hostilities depended 'largely on the threat of the atomic weapon'.[47] Nuclear weapons would not be a shortcut to victory, however, and the paper still called for a strong barrier of conventional forces, whose muddled role in alliance strategy will be discussed in Chapter 2. The 'Defence Policy and Global Strategy' paper was the clearest manifestation yet of the deterrence habit of mind which had gripped Whitehall after 1945, and the military Chiefs were in unison that 'the "Pax Atlantica" rests to-day on the atomic weapon as the Pax Britannica rested on the 19th Century on the British Fleet'.[48]

The concept of nuclear deterrence received even greater emphasis after Winston Churchill's Conservative party was swept into power in the 1951 General Election. Churchill sought to make fundamental changes to British defence policy

---

[43] TNA, DEFE 5/31, COS(51)353, Defence Policy and Global Strategy, 8 June 1951.
[44] TNA, CAB 21/3503, DO(50)45, Defence Policy and Global Strategy, 7 June 1950.
[45] Ibid.   [46] Ibid.   [47] Ibid.   [48] Ibid.

which was driven by two important considerations. First, Britain's deteriorating economic position required urgent savings to be made in the defence budget; and second, not enough emphasis was placed in British defence planning on the utility of nuclear weapons to deter Soviet adventurism.[49] The Chiefs of Staff were duly instructed to embark on a major review of British strategy that took note of these concerns—the result was the 1952 'Defence Policy and Global Strategy' paper.[50] The paper has been lauded by historians as 'one of the most significant documents in the history of post-war British defence planning' and an 'important innovation in military thought'.[51] While some scholars have questioned the revolutionary nature of the paper, many view the 'Defence Policy and Global Strategy' paper as 'a classic among military documents'.[52]

The central thrust of the 1952 paper was that nuclear weapons had revolution-ized the conduct of warfare and that the ability of the Western allies to resist Soviet aggression rested on the health of the Western European economies. Various developments had combined to undermine the economies of Britain and Western Europe, and the expensive rearmament programme initiated by the Attlee gov-ernment in response to the Korean War eighteen months previously could no longer be sustained.[53] The conclusion drawn from the Korean rearmament experience was that the maintenance of large conventional forces was not com-patible with the requirements of a healthy economy.[54] This view was compounded by the fact that the conventional fighting in Korea had proved to be prolonged, indecisive, and politically unpopular.[55] Furthermore, as recently as February 1952, NATO had agreed in the ambitious Lisbon force goals to build up a conventional strength of ninety-six divisions and 9,000 aircraft by 1954 to counterbalance the

[49]  Eric J. Grove, *Vanguard to Trident: British Naval Policy since World War II* (London: The Bodley Head, 1987), pp. 78–82.

[50]  TNA, CAB 131/12, D(52)26, Defence Policy and Global Strategy, 17 June 1952. The most recent analysis of the paper can be found in Baylis and Stoddart, *The British Nuclear Experience*, pp. 42–59.

[51]  Grove, *Vanguard to Trident*, p. 83 and R. N. Rosecrance, *Defense of the Realm: British Strategy in the Nuclear Epoch* (London: Columbia University Press, 1968), p. 171.

[52]  John Baylis and Alan Macmillan, 'The British Global Strategy Paper of 1952', *Journal of Strategic Studies*, Vol. 16, No. 2 (1993), p. 200. See, in addition, Ian Clark and Nicholas J. Wheeler, *The British Origins of Nuclear Strategy, 1945–1955* (Oxford: Clarendon, 1989), p. 170 and Alan Macmillan and John Baylis, *A Reassessment of the British Global Strategy Paper of 1952*, International Politics Research Papers 13 (Dept. of International Politics, University of Wales, Aberystwyth, 1993).

[53]  The rearmament programme, agreed in December 1950, raised the defence budget from a pre-Korean War total of £2,300 million to £4,700 million, 15 per cent of the GNP. Cmd. 8146, *Defence Programme: Statement made by the Prime Minister in the House of Commons on Monday, 29th January, 1951* (London: HMSO, 1951), p. 6. For further discussion see Jihang Park, 'Wasted Opportunities? The 1950s Rearmament Programme and the Failure of British Economic Policy', *Journal of Contemporary History*, Vol. 32, No. 3 (July 1997), p. 358.

[54]  Andrew J. Pierre, *Nuclear Politics: The British Experience with an Independent Nuclear Force, 1939–1970* (London: Oxford University Press, 1972), p. 87.

[55]  Lawrence Freedman, 'The First Two Generations of Nuclear Strategists' in Peter Paret (ed.), *Makers of Modern Strategy: From Machiavelli to the Nuclear Age* (Oxford: Oxford University Press, 1986), p. 739.

Soviet Union's manpower superiority in Europe.[56] However, because of fiscal limitations, it was becoming increasingly obvious to the Chiefs of Staff that Britain and her Continental allies would not be able to meet their scheduled contributions of land and air forces. Such was the deteriorating economic situation that the Chiefs feared that the Soviet Union could achieve a 'bloodless victory' should the Western European economies collapse.[57]

The solution to these two problems—how to successfully deter the Soviet Union whilst securing substantial financial savings in the defence budget— appeared to lie with nuclear weapons. The strength of the US Strategic Air Command was now believed to be so great that it could launch a devastating attack upon the USSR's vital centres to such an extent that 'she would be unlikely to survive it as a Power capable of waging a full scale war'.[58] The Chiefs of Staff hoped that the threat of 'immediate and crushing retaliation' with nuclear weapons would be a sufficient deterrent to Soviet aggression.[59] A posture based on deterrence through punishment would also obviate the requirement for large conventional forces, thus reducing expenditure on expensive manpower. As the CAS, Sir John Slessor, outlined in an internal Air Staff memorandum:

> The basis of the Chiefs of Staff Global Strategy Review is that the financial restrictions which will be imposed upon us in the coming years will be so severe that a complete re-shaping of the Armed Forces as at present planned must be considered. We have adopted a new strategic concept which puts more reliance on the Bomber offensive and assumes that the war will be a short one.[60]

The new strategic concept to which Slessor referred was 'massive retaliation'; that is to say, the threat that any act of aggression, *however small*, would be punished by a massive strategic nuclear bombardment against the belligerent's homeland. Slessor would become one of Britain's staunchest supporters of what he called the 'great deterrent', and published the massive retaliation thesis in book form shortly after his retirement from active military service in 1954. In the same vein as King-Hall, the overarching argument in *Strategy for the West* was that '*war has abolished itself* because the atomic and hydrogen bombs have found their way into the armouries of the world'.[61] Slessor was a disciple of the Trenchard school of thought which posited that offensive airpower was the *sine qua non* of modern warfare, and as an experienced bomber commander during the Second World War, he had witnessed first-hand the crushing effects of the Allied strategic

---

[56] TNA, CAB 129/49, C(52)49, The Report of the Temporary Council Committee of the North Atlantic Council, memorandum by the Secretary of State for Foreign Affairs, 19 February 1952.
[57] CAB 131/12, D(52)26.     [58] Ibid.     [59] Ibid.
[60] TNA, AIR 19/737, CAS 1118, Chief of the Air Staff to the Secretary of State for Air, 28 May 1952.
[61] John Slessor, *Strategy for the West* (London: Cassell & Co., 1954), p. 15 [emphasis in original].

bombing offensive upon the German war machine.[62] With the invention of atomic and thermonuclear weapons, Slessor was now of the view that nuclear airpower had abolished war as a meaningful tool of statecraft. Indeed, it was the horrific consequences of a massive nuclear retaliation that for Slessor made the deterrent so 'great'. Just as he and his colleagues on the Chiefs of Staff Committee had argued in the 'Defence Policy and Global Strategy' paper, deterrence and not defence should now be the primary aim of Western defence policy.

A. J. R. Groom has suggested that Slessor's tough, uncompromising resolution to use weapons of such appalling destructive power was not merely the reaction of a 'hard-boiled militarist, bloodied in the wartime raids on Hamburg or Dresden', but that his ultimate aim was 'the abolition of total or general war in the sense that his generation had twice known it'.[63] Although a noble objective, massive retaliation relied on the paradoxical logic that war could only be avoided by threatening to unleash it on a magnificent scale. In turn, the credibility of the threat was itself reliant on the hypothesis that nuclear weapons could indeed have a decisive impact on the course of a future war, and that this was accepted as such by decision-makers in the Kremlin. Narratives of nuclear war were therefore fundamental to the assumptions underpinning the 'Defence Policy and Global Strategy' paper. Yet, it was here where the Chiefs of Staff often arrived at muddled conclusions, stemming in part from the conflicting partisan views of the service Chiefs, each of whom advocated a different view of future war that was informed consciously and sub-consciously by vested interests and individual service preferences.[64]

The main points of contention between the Chiefs of Staff hinged on abstract considerations about the character of nuclear war, its intensity and duration, and whether there would be a period of conventional fighting after the initial nuclear exchange.[65] The Chiefs were all in agreement that the opening nuclear phase of a future war would be of 'unparalleled intensity' and that 'it seems certain that both sides, particularly Russia and the United Kingdom, will have suffered terrible damage'.[66] What would follow next proved to be much more difficult to imagine, and led to great ambiguity about the future character of conflict. For example, the Chiefs of Staff warned that 'it is both difficult and dangerous to forecast the length of another war', yet at the same time suggested that it may last 'only a few weeks'.[67] If the initial nuclear exchange did not bring about an immediate result, then the Chiefs claimed that there 'may be a long-drawn-out period of chaos with an

---

[62] William Jackson and Edwin Bramall, *The Chiefs: The Story of the United Kingdom Chiefs of Staff* (Washington, DC, New York, NY, and London: Brassey's, 1992), p. 278.

[63] A. J. R. Groom, *British Thinking about Nuclear Weapons* (London: Frances Pinter, 1974), p. 63.

[64] For a contemporary view of these issues see E. J. Kingston-McCloughry, *Global Strategy* (London: Jonathan Cape, 1957), pp. 154–5.

[65] John Baylis, *Ambiguity and Deterrence: British Nuclear Strategy, 1945–1964* (Oxford: Clarendon Press, 1995), pp. 143–145.

[66] CAB 131/12, D(52)26.        [67] Ibid.

intermittent struggle gradually spreading worldwide' in which 'all forms of enemy attack will be much reduced, though perhaps less at sea than elsewhere'.[68] This phase of fighting became known as 'broken-backed' warfare and was the concept favoured by the Navy since it justified the maintenance of a large conventional fleet at a time when politicians were desperately seeking to find economies in defence spending. Slessor would later claim that the idea of fighting a 'broken-backed' war was only entertained in the paper to appease the Chief of the Naval Staff (CNS), Sir Rhoderick McGrigor.[69] The 1952 strategic reassessment therefore presented two contradictory visions of nuclear war: a short war in which one or all of the belligerents would be destroyed during the initial nuclear exchange, and a longer war in which conventional forces would continue to fight in a second phase of uncertain duration.[70]

With a lack of practical experience of nuclear war-fighting, it could only ever be a matter of faith that a strategic nuclear attack could knock out a major power such as Russia, and that such a threat would prove a convincing deterrent to aggression. In this context, the strategy was a war against the Soviet imagination, and any attempts to undermine the horrific consequences of nuclear warfare were seen by the British defence establishment as reducing the overall deterrent effects of nuclear weapons. The 'deterrence habit of mind' was now well entrenched, and critics of massive retaliation would be silenced in the years to come.

## Distinctions between Nuclear Weapons

By the middle 1950s, developments in nuclear weapons technology were running amok, with designs for new rockets, missiles, artillery shells, mines, and even torpedoes. The successful test of the world's first hydrogen bomb by the United States in 1954 represented a thousand-fold multiplication in power compared to the original atomic bomb, but developments in explosive yields were also going in the opposite direction towards the production of atomic weapons of small size and limited power. These so-called 'tactical' nuclear weapons, which still possessed enough explosive force to destroy a small city, began to be deployed in increasing numbers to the European Continent as part of the Dwight D. Eisenhower administration's 'New Look' at defence policy, the military implications of which will be discussed in Chapter 2.[71]

---

[68] Ibid.

[69] Anthony Seldon, *Churchill's Indian Summer: The Conservative Government, 1951-1955* (London: Hodder and Stoughton, 1981), p. 335.

[70] A detailed critique of this aspect of the 1952 Defence Policy and Global Strategy paper can be found in Julian Lider, *British Military Thought after World War II* (Aldershot: Gower, 1985), p. 203.

[71] For the development of small-yield nuclear weapons see David C. Elliot, 'Project Vista and Nuclear Weapons in Europe', *International Security*, Vol. 11, No. 1 (Summer 1986), pp. 163–83.

The arrival of tactical nuclear weapons brought with it attempts by American policy-makers to try and define the new weapons in less drastic terms. For example, the US Secretary of State John Foster Dulles claimed at a press conference at the height of the First Taiwan Strait Crisis on 15 March 1955 that 'tactical atomic weapons' were now 'becoming conventional in the United States armed services'.[72] This was followed a day later with a statement by President Eisenhower in which he said that when used against strictly military targets, he saw no reason why 'these things [tactical nuclear weapons] ... shouldn't be used just exactly as you would use a bullet or anything else'.[73] This was the start of many attempts to try and conventionalize nuclear weapons in the minds of the public, both at home and abroad.[74]

The Eisenhower administration believed such messaging was increasingly essential since, as will be shown in Chapter 2, NATO had recently adopted a new strategic concept in MC 48 which tied its ground forces to the first use of tactical nuclear weapons in the event of Soviet aggression. Against this background, a diplomatic cable was sent from Washington urging its British allies to make distinctions between 'tactical' and 'strategic' nuclear weapons, including the suggestion that:

> Her Majesty's Government should also consider taking suitable opportunities to make clear the technical and moral justification of the tactical nuclear weapon with which allied forces are now being equipped.[75]

This was deemed a 'difficult and highly political question' by the Foreign Office,[76] and was subsequently referred to the Chiefs of Staff Committee for comment, who discussed the proposition at their meeting on 1 April 1955.

In addition to the regular members of the Committee, the Chiefs of Staff were joined by high-ranking government scientists and delegates from other interested departments of state. Sir William Penney, weapons developer for the recently established Atomic Energy Authority, opened the discussion by stating that technically speaking there could be every gradation of nuclear weapon between the smallest atomic bomb and the largest thermonuclear one, and that there could be no definitive dividing line between the two extremes. The CNS brought up the issue of targeting and attacked Dulles' remark about the use of tactical nuclear weapons against military targets, arguing that 'this led to the sterile argument of

---

[72] Cited in Dennis Merrill and Thomas G. Paterson (eds.), *Major Problems in American Foreign Relations, Volume II: Since 1914*, 7th ed. (Stamford, CT: Cengage Learning, 2010), p. 281.

[73] Ibid., p. 282.

[74] Simon J. Moody, 'Enhancing Political Cohesion in NATO during the 1950s or: How It Learned to Stop Worrying and Love the (Tactical) Bomb', *Journal of Strategic Studies*, Vol. 40, No. 6 (2017), pp. 826–827.

[75] TNA, DEFE 7/2340, Telegram no. 588, Washington to Foreign Office, 16 March 1955.

[76] TNA, DEFE 7/2340, Dean to Brownjohn, 30 March 1955.

what were military targets'. Furthermore, Vice-Chief of the Air Staff, Sir Ronald Ivelaw-Chapman, questioned the benefits of making public statements about the limited use of nuclear weapons, maintaining that it was essential that the Soviet leadership were under no illusion that any aggression on their part would be met immediately with the full weight of Allied nuclear capabilities. The Committee therefore agreed that it was not appropriate to try and make distinctions between tactical and strategic nuclear weapons, and that attempts to do so would undermine the deterrent effect of nuclear weapons.[77]

The nomenclature of nuclear weapons continued to evolve in tandem with the rapid pace of technological development, so that by the end of the 1950s, a vast vocabulary of loose expressions had emerged to describe nuclear weapons of varying ranges and yields, including 'weapons of mass destruction', 'tactical nuclear weapons', 'strategic nuclear weapons', 'fractional yield weapons', 'nominal yield weapons', 'megaton weapons', 'kiloton weapons', and 'sub-kiloton weapons'. The sheer variety of nuclear weapons now available, coupled with the challenges of defining accurately the tactical and strategic areas of operation, suggested that it would not be possible to classify weapons as 'strategic' or 'tactical' on the basis of their yield or means of delivery.[78] Furthermore, the Cabinet considered that even if it were practically possible to draw distinctions between nuclear weapons along the lines suggested by the Americans, it would be unwise to do so since:

> The possession by the West of a stock of nuclear weapons of all kinds and the ability to deliver them is at present the most important factor in achieving our aim of preventing war. An attempt to divide them into those which are small and therefore morally justifiable and those which are large and therefore immoral would inevitably reduce their deterrent value as a whole.[79]

British policy-makers therefore feared that attempts to try and conventionalize tactical nuclear weapons would serve only to diminish the frightful consequences of nuclear war, which were central to British conceptions of nuclear deterrence.[80] The Cabinet wanted to wage a war against the Soviet imagination, and this meant emphasizing the destructive power of *all* nuclear weapons, as this passage indicates:

> It would be fatal to give the impression that as long as no hydrogen bomb was dropped on Allied territory, none would be used against Russia, or that the only

---

[77] TNA, DEFE 7/2340, COS(55)23, NCDB/2/494, 1 April 1955. Moody, 'Enhancing Political Cohesion in NATO during the 1950s', pp. 827–828.

[78] TNA, DEFE 4/122, JP(59)123(Final), Nomenclature of Nuclear Weapons, 6 November 1959.

[79] TNA, CAB 129/74, C(55)95, Distinction between Large and Tactical Nuclear Weapons, 5 April 1955.

[80] Moody, 'Enhancing Political Cohesion in NATO during the 1950s', p. 828.

likely victims of nuclear weapons in a new global war would be the armed forces and not the civilian populations or centres of government and industry.[81]

Although the Cabinet remained cautious about making statements which could undermine its deterrent posture, in private, the Chiefs of Staff were adopting a more Dullesian tone when discussing the role of tactical nuclear weapons. At their meeting on 29 June 1955, they suggested that the rapid development of tactical nuclear weapons 'would tend perhaps within the next seven years to make the use of these weapons conventional'.[82] Consequently, the Chiefs could envisage using tactical nuclear weapons in a limited war without automatic escalation to the use of thermonuclear weapons. Indeed, it was the increase in the destructive power of nuclear weapons brought about by the H-bomb that would allow this to happen since 'the greater the power of the primary deterrent the less likely was it that the use of tactical atomic weapons in limited war would lead to global nuclear war'.[83]

There were important geographical distinctions to be drawn, however. A report produced by the Joint Planning Staff (JPS) at the behest of the Chiefs of Staff after their deliberations stated that:

We can envisage, therefore, a limited war involving the use of tactical atomic weapons taking place in the Far East or perhaps in the Middle East, but it would not be possible for a limited war to take place in Europe without developing into global war.[84]

The decision to use tactical nuclear weapons to support military operations would therefore reflect the character of the war being fought. While it was possible for the Chiefs of Staff to imagine the discriminate use of nuclear weapons in areas on the periphery of Europe against an enemy that had few or no nuclear capabilities with which to retaliate, the same could not be said for the European theatre itself because of the high strategic and political stakes involved. The most likely cause of war in the Middle East during the 1950s and 1960s, the Chiefs assumed, would stem from the ongoing Israeli-Palestinian conflict in which the United Kingdom, in view of her treaty obligations, would be immediately involved. It was believed that this conflict could be localized and that the employment of tactical nuclear weapons would be unlikely. Although every effort would be made in Africa and the Middle East to try and secure stability in the region with the minimum military effort and political turmoil, the conditions in the Far East would be different. If Communist China sought to fulfil her territorial gains in the region by resorting to war, the United Kingdom might be forced to go to war either to

[81] CAB 129/74, C(55)95.
[82] TNA, DEFE 7/963, COS(55)51, Long Term Defence Programme, 29 June 1955.
[83] Ibid.
[84] TNA, DEFE 4/78, JP(55)61(Final), Long Term Defence Programme, 8 July 1955.

protect her interests or to support her ally, the United States, who would in all probability use nuclear weapons in a tactical role.[85]

Field Marshal Sir John Harding, who had succeeded Sir William Slim as CIGS in 1952, also believed that the Far East was the only theatre in which a limited tactical nuclear war could be permissible and that the Army should prepare for nuclear operations in that region.[86] Indeed, by 1959, the severity of the threat posed by China, and to a lesser extent North Korea and Vietnam, was such that the JPS concluded that the only feasible military means of defeating the mass of Chinese ground forces would be through the use of tactical nuclear weapons. Such employment would still carry the risks of escalation, however, especially if nuclear operations were extended to include targets within China itself. The decision, therefore, to use nuclear weapons should always carry with it the risks of igniting a global war, and in the Far East, this meant assessing the extent to which the Soviet Union was prepared to support Chinese policies.[87] It was possible, however, that the use of tactical nuclear weapons in limited war might be more readily accepted by the international community as those weapons became more deeply entrenched within the framework of international security.[88]

No further statements were made by the United States on the issue of making distinctions between nuclear weapons until Dulles made reference in a speech on 6 December 1955 to 'selective retaliatory power', which suggested that the use of certain nuclear weapon systems might be limited to particular targets and situations.[89] The Foreign Office advised that government officials should say no more on the subject and instead refer to a recent statement made by the Chiefs of Staff, who had considered the issue further at a recent meeting.[90] The Chiefs' report reaffirmed the primacy of deterrence in British minds and recommended that any discussion on the subject should not go beyond a statement that:

> We were determined to resist aggression wherever it may occur and that we would use whatever weapons were appropriate to end the conflict rapidly and to prevent the war spreading.[91]

This statement suggests that the Chiefs of Staff were prepared to move, however tentatively, towards statements in public that tactical nuclear weapons could be

---

[85] TNA, DEFE 7/963, MISC/P(55)27, Long Term Defence Programme, 25 July 1955.

[86] TNA, WO 163/616, AC/M(55)7, The Long Term Defence Programme—National Service, 7 September 1955.

[87] TNA, DEFE 4/121, JP(59)110(Final), United Kingdom Force Requirements for Limited War, 14 October 1959.

[88] TNA, DEFE 4/121, COS(59)65, United Kingdom Force Requirements for Limited War, 20 October 1959.

[89] Moody, 'Enhancing Political Cohesion in NATO during the 1950s', pp. 828–829.

[90] TNA, FO 371/123118, ZE 112/56, Larger and Smaller Nuclear Weapons, 7 January 1956.

[91] TNA, DEFE 5/63, COS(55)341, The Effectiveness of Nuclear Deterrence, 16 December 1955.

used if their application achieved the required war aims without unnecessary escalation to the use of strategic nuclear weapons. However, by the beginning of 1956, the British defence establishment would come under increasing pressure to delineate clearly in public between different types of nuclear weapons. This time it was not from foreign allies but from within its own defence community. An alternative theory of nuclear strategy, destined to be known as 'graduated deterrence', emerged as a rival to massive retaliation and the whole notion of a national strategy based on massive nuclear retaliation was called into question.

## Graduated Deterrence and Limited Nuclear War

The most vocal critic of government nuclear strategy was Rear-Admiral Sir Anthony Buzzard, who held the post of Director of Naval Intelligence from 1951 until his retirement from active military service in 1954.[92] Buzzard was sceptical of the emphasis placed on the primacy of nuclear deterrence in British strategic appreciations and questioned the assumption that US strategic bombers would be able to deliver a knock-out blow against the Soviet Union with their nuclear payloads. Even if they possessed such capabilities, Buzzard enquired pessimistically, 'If we really believe that Russian morale will crack in six weeks, what are the prospects for this country?'.[93] Buzzard was correct to raise questions about the ability of the densely packed denizens of British cities to withstand attack from nuclear weapons. Little serious thought had been given to the effects of nuclear attack on morale, with defence planners assuming that the blitz-hardened population would be able to muddle through as they had during the last war. Buzzard would probably have been aware of a report produced shortly before his retirement by the Home Defence Committee Working Party on the initial phase of nuclear war which stressed that while it did not underrate the British capacity for 'taking it', it could not be assumed that all the millions of inhabitants of bombed areas would behave like the archetypal John Smith, 'who, with some sort of roof over his head, is ready to stay put if he possibly can and get on with his job'.[94] Ultimately, Matthew Grant concluded that morale was 'seen as a rhetorical stick to beat Ministers rather than a troublesome concept to be evaluated', a problem that would be reflected in the Army's own planning assumptions.[95]

---

[92] For further information on Buzzard's theories see John Baylis, 'Anthony Buzzard' in John Baylis and John Garnett (eds.), *Makers of Nuclear Strategy* (London: Pinter, 1991), pp. 136–152 and Baylis, *Ambiguity and Deterrence*, pp. 196–202.

[93] TNA, ADM 205/89, DNI 8529, Why Only Six Weeks for Our Priority Requirements?, 6 July 1953.

[94] TNA, CAB 134/942, HDC(WP)(53) 22 (Revise), Revised Draft Report on the Initial Phase, 30 June 1953.

[95] Matthew Grant, *After the Bomb: Civil Defence and Nuclear War in Britain, 1945–68* (Basingstoke: Palgrave Macmillan, 2010), p. 59.

As a devout Anglican, Buzzard was concerned with the moral implications of nuclear war, and lamented the fact that a strategy of massive retaliation would tie the United Kingdom irrevocably to the first use of strategic nuclear weapons against centres of populations and industry at the onset of a future war. After his retirement he worked closely with various defence and disarmament commissions for the World and British Councils of Churches where he facilitated dialogue between Christians and defence analysts on nuclear strategy.[96] By the middle 1950s, Buzzard had generated enough interest in his ideas from both clergymen and individuals in the influential 'Commentators Circle'[97] that his alternative theory of graduated deterrence was thrust into the public domain and Whitehall policy-making circles. Intimately linked with the use of small-yield nuclear weapons, the manner in which graduated deterrence was received and assessed by the British defence establishment reveals a number of assumptions about the role and functions of tactical nuclear weapons.

Foreseeing a period of pointed criticism of British nuclear weapons policy, the Royal Institute of International Affairs, Chatham House, hosted on 9 November 1955 a debate between Buzzard, Slessor, and the German political scientist Richard Lowenthal on the relative merits of massive retaliation and graduated deterrence.[98] Buzzard attacked the policy of massive retaliation as being too drastic and inflexible to deal with the myriad threats that Britain might face during the burgeoning Cold War, arguing that:

Increasingly we are getting into a position where, in effect, we shall be forced to threaten, and if necessary initiate, the destruction of civilization in the event of any measure of aggression too powerful for our small conventional forces to combat.[99]

Buzzard believed that the hands of the West were tied to either submitting to numerically superior Soviet conventional forces or else initiating thermonuclear war, with all of its horrifying consequences. Furthermore, with Soviet–US nuclear parity drawing ever closer, the Rear-Admiral was concerned that American decision-makers might be reluctant to unleash the Strategic Air Command because of the fear of retaliation in kind, and that therefore the Kremlin might call a bluff on the threat of massive nuclear retaliation.[100] Buzzard consequently

---

[96]   Baylis, 'Anthony Buzzard', p. 136.

[97]   This was the name given to an influential group of defence commentators in Britain that included important individuals such as Sir Basil Liddell Hart, John Slessor, Richard Crossman, George Wigg, John Strachey, and Anthony Buzzard. See Laurence W. Martin, 'The Market for Strategic Ideas in Britain: The "Sandys Era"', *American Political Science Review*, Vol. 56, No. 1 (March 1962), p. 34.

[98]   The debate was published in article form the following year in *International Affairs*.

[99]   Anthony W. Buzzard et al., 'The H-Bomb: Massive Retaliation or Graduated Deterrence?', *International Affairs*, Vol. 32, No. 2 (April 1956), p. 148.

[100]   Ibid., pp. 149–50.

proposed that his strategy of graduated deterrence might provide the West with an intermediate response capability to deal with those threats that were too large for Allied conventional forces to cope with but too small to warrant the strategic use of nuclear weapons. This response would rest on the tactical use of small-yield nuclear weapons to counterbalance the mass of Soviet manpower but, importantly, without recourse to the strategic use of nuclear weapons. In order to keep such a conflict limited and to reduce the risk of inadvertent nuclear escalation, Buzzard argued that distinctions between strategic and tactical nuclear weapons, and between different types of military and civilian targets, would have to be made in peacetime. By so doing, the West could exploit its tactical nuclear assets without the fear of provoking a retaliation by the Soviet Union with strategic nuclear weapons.[101]

It would not be until late 1955, however, that Buzzard's challenge to the strategic *status quo* caught the attention of government officials by way of an article he wrote for the *Manchester Guardian* outlining his new strategic theory. In it, he made public his views that graduated deterrence would not only benefit the West militarily, since it allowed the exploitation of its preponderance in tactical nuclear firepower, but that it was also morally superior to massive retaliation because it would limit wars (in weapons, targets, area, and time) with the minimum force necessary to deter or repel aggression, which might bring an adversary to the negotiating table without seeking total victory or unconditional surrender.[102] The moral dimension of graduated deterrence was one of the driving forces behind Buzzard's advocacy of the concept, and coloured all of his thoughts on the matter. The following month he wrote to the Editor of *The Economist* arguing that the adoption by the West of a policy of graduated deterrence would help to reduce the horrors of war and bolster the legitimacy of its defence posture in the eyes of allies and neutrals since 'we would be practising the moral principles we profess to defend'.[103] General Sir Nevil Brownjohn, Chief Staff Officer at the Ministry of Defence, informed the Chiefs of Staff of the disarmament articles, who agreed to examine them.[104] They were subsequently referred the following day to the JPS for further assessment and the preparation of a report.[105]

The aim of the paper, which took three weeks to complete, was to discover 'whether the Allied deterrent to war can be strengthened by any form of graduated deterrence'.[106] In the context of the ability of nuclear weapons to deter global war, the JPS argued that any declaration to limit the size or type of weapon for use in

[101] Ibid., pp. 148–9.
[102] Anthony Buzzard, 'Graduated Deterrence Instead of the Bomb Alone', *Manchester Guardian*, 31 October 1955, p. 6.
[103] Anthony Buzzard, 'Graduated Deterrence', *The Economist*, 19 November 1955, p. 647.
[104] TNA, DEFE 4/81, COS(55)95, Graduated Deterrents, 21 November 1955.
[105] TNA, DEFE 4/81, COS(55)96, Graduated Deterrents, 22 November 1955.
[106] DEFE 5/63, COS(55)341.

such a conflict would serve only to 'sow doubt in the Russian mind about our determination to use them if attacked and the deterrent value of these weapons would thereby be reduced'.[107] On the issue of limited war, the joint planners thought that Buzzard's thesis—that a threat to employ massive retaliation against limited acts of aggression could be taken as a bluff by the Soviet Union—appeared to be 'born of some confusion of thought'.[108] Rather, they believed that should the West use nuclear weapons against a Soviet satellite, for example, in the context of limited war, then the implied threat of H-bombing Russia proper if aggression continued would be enough to prevent the conflict from spreading. Furthermore, the JPS held practical objections to drawing distinctions between strategic and tactical nuclear weapons since the use of both would be necessary from a war-fighting point of view to halt a Soviet advance:

> A determined Communist drive would only be stopped by nuclear attack, not only on targets close to the front line of the land armies, but also on airfields, communication centres, bases and perhaps cities, many of them remote from the front line.[109]

It appeared, then, that graduated deterrence found little support from the military authorities. This is not surprising considering the lukewarm response to the American proposition to classify nuclear weapons as either 'tactical' or 'strategic' only a few years earlier. Buzzard appeared unfazed by the rebuff, however. A fervent Christian and regular churchgoer, Buzzard had promoted his ideas to the Bishop of Chichester, Dr George Bell, in an attempt to raise awareness of his dilemma and to advertise the benefits of his new strategic concept. Bell had challenged the morality of strategic bombing during the Second World War and was actively engaged in thinking about the ethics of nuclear war in this troubling new world.[110] He had recently contributed a chapter to a pamphlet published by the National Peace Council on the morality of nuclear war.[111] On 26 December 1955, the Bishop wrote to the newly appointed Foreign Secretary, Selwyn Lloyd, to say that he and Buzzard had been in 'close touch' on the matter of graduated deterrence and that he also wished to pass on an advanced copy of the National Peace Council pamphlet to the Foreign Office.[112] Akin to Buzzard, Bell argued against massive retaliation as a viable strategic concept for the United Kingdom on both strategic and moral grounds. He argued that since the West was bound to use

[107] Ibid.      [108] Ibid.      [109] Ibid.

[110] See, for example, one of the Bishop's diatribes in the House of Lords, *Hansard*, House of Lords Debate, Vol. 130, Cols. 737–45, 9 February 1944.

[111] John E. Roberts and George Bell (eds.), *Nuclear War and Peace: The Facts and the Challenge*, *Peace Aims Pamphlet No. 60* (National Peace Council: London, 1955). Church of England Synods and the British Council of Churches habitually issued statements critical of nuclear weapons and British nuclear strategy well into the 1980s. See Heuser, *Nuclear Mentalities?*, pp. 13–15.

[112] TNA, FO 371/123118, ZE 112/7, Bishop of Chichester to Foreign Secretary, 26 December 1955.

the minimum force necessary to achieve their objectives, it could never be right to use the H-bomb against predominantly civilian targets. Conversely, Bell believed that the use of tactical nuclear weapons against military targets might be justifiable and that the idea that such use in limited war would escalate to all-out strategic nuclear war should be repudiated.[113] The Deputy Under Secretary of the Foreign Office, P. H. Dean, replied to the Bishop's letter, stating simply that:

> We have these issues constantly in our minds when dealing with the immediate practical aspects of the problems posed by the existence of these weapons. They are not easy and I am very conscious indeed of what is at stake.[114]

The following month saw a flurry of activity by proponents of graduated deterrence, spurred on by an offer from Chatham House to provide facilities for Buzzard and a small study group to examine his theories. The other members of the group were Richard Goold-Adams, former editor of *The Economist* and a leading figure at Chatham House, the distinguished physicist P. M. S. Blackett, and Denis Healey, then Labour Party defence spokesman and future Secretary of State for Defence.[115] On 18 January, Buzzard articulated his thesis more succinctly than hitherto in a note which duly arrived at the Foreign Office shortly after. Buzzard began by saying that the recent rhetoric emanating from the Eisenhower administration throughout the previous year suggested that graduated deterrence was now *de facto* accepted in the United States. The Rear-Admiral argued, however, that more should be done publicly in peacetime, beyond the mere general statements being made by Dulles, to establish clear distinctions between tactical and strategic nuclear weapons.[116] Contrary to the views of the Chiefs of Staff and the Cabinet, Buzzard believed that drawing distinctions in peacetime between nuclear weapons would actually strengthen rather than diminish their deterrent effect, since:

> It is better for our deterrent to be *reasonably* unprofitable in its consequences to the aggressor, and *certain* to be applied, than for it to be *disastrous* in its consequences but *uncertain* to be applied.[117]

Thus, for Buzzard, the idea of a graduated response to aggression through the discriminate use of tactical nuclear weapons was simply more credible than a

---

[113] TNA, FO 371/123118, ZE 112/7, Confidential Minutes, 5 January 1956.

[114] TNA, FO 371/123118, ZE 112/7, Deputy Under Secretary to the Bishop of Chichester, 9 January 1956.

[115] Michael Howard, 'IISS—The First Thirty Years: A General Overview', *The Adelphi Papers*, Vol. 29, No. 235 (1989), p. 11.

[116] TNA, FO 371/123119, ZE 112/48, Should Distinctions between the Tactical and Strategic Use of Nuclear Weapons Be Established Publicly?, 18 January 1956, p. 1.

[117] Ibid., p. 3 [emphasis in original].

strategy which called for an immediate and overwhelming nuclear attack with strategic weapons at the first signs of Soviet aggression.

By 1956, graduated deterrence was beginning to enter public discourse on British nuclear weapons policy. In January of that year, Healey argued in another article for the *Manchester Guardian* that the value of the deterrent was gradually eroding as Soviet nuclear capabilities advanced. This raised questions about the willingness of the United States to use strategic nuclear weapons to annihilate Russian cities if that also meant risking a reply in kind. He even went as far as to say that since the indiscriminate use of thermonuclear weapons would involve grave dangers to the human race, 'no rational Government is likely to initiate it as a deliberate act of policy'.[118] Akin to Buzzard, Healey advocated drawing distinctions in peacetime between tactical and strategic nuclear weapons since this would convince the Soviet Union that:

> We are in a position to halt any military aggression she may contemplate by a form of retaliation which we shall not hesitate to employ, because its cost is proportionate to the importance of the issue at stake.[119]

Again, the emphasis was on instilling greater credibility in the nuclear-deterrent posture by providing decision-makers with the capabilities for a graduated response to armed aggression. Not all commentators agreed, however. Six days after the Healey article was published, Stephen King-Hall wrote to the editor of the *Manchester Guardian* arguing that Healey's arguments did not 'hold water'. King-Hall felt it was folly to attempt to distinguish in peacetime between the tactical and strategic use of nuclear weapons for practical reasons. Mirroring the argument made by Sir Rhoderick McGrigor during the Chiefs of Staff 1955 discussions on the subject, he believed it would be impossible to draw clear dividing lines between civilian and military targets since:

> Suppose an enemy advances westward against NATO troops and the latter use atomic weapons on the battlefield. Those troops are supplied through Antwerp and it is hard from a military point of view to deny that the base and lines of communication of troops are part of the battlefield. Would not the enemy naturally drop an H-bomb on Antwerp? This action would probably lead to an allied H-bomb descending on (say) an enemy oilfield.[120]

The concept of graduated deterrence had generated enough traction that even the Prime Minister, Sir Anthony Eden, was pressed on the issue by yet another man of

---

[118] Denis Healey, 'Can Warfare Be Limited? Small Bombs and Large', *Manchester Guardian*, 17 January 1956, p. 6.
[119] Ibid.
[120] Stephen King-Hall, 'The Tactical Bomb', *Manchester Guardian*, 23 January 1956, p. 6.

the cloth, this time the senior bishop of the Church of England, the Archbishop of Canterbury, Geoffrey Fisher. The Archbishop urged the government to take action in the field of disarmament and nuclear warfare so that the situation could be kept under 'moral control'. Fisher opposed the concept of massive retaliation with thermonuclear weapons, especially when the targeting of civilians was involved, and backed the Buzzard thesis that there should be made in public distinctions between the 'indiscriminate', 'suicidal', and 'universal' H-bomb and the tactical atomic bomb of 'limited' and 'localized' power. By so doing, he hoped that 'the evil of the H-bomb might be circumvented and finally forgotten and got out of mind'.[121] Eden replied to the Archbishop the next day stating matter-of-factly that the Cabinet had already discussed such difficult questions and had arrived at the conclusion that Britain must continue to possess the deterrent of the H-bomb.[122]

In private, however, Foreign Office officials poured scorn on Fisher's foray into nuclear issues. The Assistant Under Secretary of State for Foreign Affairs, I. T. M. Pink, believed that the Archbishop's desire to simply forget that the H-bomb existed and focus instead on tactical nuclear weapons of limited power was evidence of muddled thinking since:

It seems to me that the Archbishop is confusing the H-bomb with the Devil. But surely the continued existence of the H-bomb is as necessary to the Archbishop's thesis as the continued existence of the Devil is to the Church of England? For it is essential to the theory of 'graduated deterrence' that the H-bomb should remain in the background as the ultimate sanction. If so, it can by no means be forgotten or put out of mind.[123]

Pink also attacked Buzzard's suggestion that distinctions should be drawn in peacetime between tactical and strategic nuclear weapons, and reaffirmed the official view of the Cabinet and the Chiefs of Staff, which remained unchanged,[124] that this would serve only to undermine the deterrent:

The whole advantage of any deterrent, be it the H-bomb, hanging, the head-master's cane or the fear of hell-fire, is that you do not know what risks you are likely to run. It is the fear of the unknown which prevents many people from wrong-doing.[125]

---

[121]  TNA, FO 371/123119, ZE 112/39, Archbishop of Canterbury to the Prime Minister, 23 January 1956.
[122]  TNA, FO 371/123119, ZE 112/39, Prime Minister to Archbishop of Canterbury, 24 January 1956.
[123]  TNA, FO 371/123119, ZE 112/39, Confidential Minutes, 1 February 1956.
[124]  TNA, FO 371/123119, ZE 112/49, Nevil Brownjohn to P. F. Hancock, 23 January 1956.
[125]  FO 371/123119, ZE 112/39, Confidential Minutes.

This 'fear of the unknown' which Pink believed to be an essential criterion for an effective deterrent reinforces Beatrice Heuser's argument that British governments throughout the 1950s were purposely ambiguous regarding their nuclear targeting choices so as to keep the Soviet leadership in constant speculation as to what the primary strategic targets were—centres of power or cities.[126]

At the same time that the Foreign Office was discrediting the concept of graduated deterrence, an article written by Buzzard on the subject appeared in *World Politics*, which was the first time that the theory was articulated fully in written form publicly. In it Buzzard launched a broadside against massive retaliation, arguing that it did not meet the requirements of a rational defence policy since 'it threatens to destroy civilization as a result of any aggression too powerful for our small conventional forces to handle'.[127] Buzzard again made his clarion call for the Western powers to declare publicly, without waiting for Soviet agreement, distinctions between tactical and strategic nuclear weapons. This would allow the option, when threatened with limited aggression, of saying to the prospective aggressor:

> If you do attack, we will, if necessary, use atomic and perhaps chemical weapons against your armed forces. But we will not, on this issue, use hydrogen or bacteriological weapons at all, unless you do, and we will not use any mass destruction weapons against centres of population, unless you do deliberately.[128]

By pledging not to use more force than was necessary, Buzzard believed that graduated deterrence was not only morally superior to massive retaliation, but also more credible in that it provided for an intermediate nuclear response short of all-out thermonuclear war.[129] Buzzard maintained that both sides would gain enormously on an absolute basis from graduated deterrence because neither side could target the headquarter cities, communication centres, industry, and ports of the other, but that the West would enjoy relative gains since the Soviets would be unable to destroy the key ports on which the development and supply of so much of the Allied fighting potential depended.[130]

Despite this public promulgation of his theory, Buzzard's concept of graduated deterrence again failed to garner support in official government circles. The Conservative MP (Sutton and Cheam) Sir Richard Sharples wrote a concerned letter to his party colleague Anthony Nutting, the Minister of State for Foreign Affairs, arguing that the great advantage of the possession of the H-bomb was that it had made conventional war impossible because of the possibility that it might be

---

[126] Beatrice Heuser, *The Bomb: Nuclear Weapons in Their Historical, Strategic and Ethical Context* (London and New York, NY: Longman, 2000), p. 87.

[127] Anthony W. Buzzard, 'Massive Retaliation and Graduated Deterrence', *World Politics*, Vol. 8, No. 2 (January 1956), p. 228.

[128] Ibid., p. 229.    [129] Ibid., pp. 229–30.    [130] Ibid., p. 231.

used by either side, and that by surrendering such a deterrent, graduated deterrence again made war possible.[131] Nutting replied that Buzzard had indeed been 'badgering Ministers and officials in the Foreign Office and Ministry of Defence about his pet thesis of graduated deterrence for a very long time'. The Minister explained that the Foreign Office had given much thought to the Rear-Admiral's ideas but this had not changed their view, or that of the military leadership, that making distinctions between tactical and strategic nuclear weapons would undermine the deterrent effect of those weapons.[132]

The Minister of Defence, Sir Walter Monckton, attempted to lay rest to the issue during a defence debate in the House of Commons. He informed the House that it was possible to imagine circumstances where local aggression might be met with local retaliation with tactical nuclear weapons and that this would not necessarily lead to full-scale global thermonuclear war.[133] However, he reaffirmed the official line that it would not be practical policy for any government to state in peacetime the circumstances in which it would use some weapons and not others since:

Any attempt to make a definition of that kind in advance could hardly be to our advantage. Indeed, it might help others, who may be pondering on the question of whether they could take risks, to see how far they might go without bringing down upon them the ultimate deterrent. I think an attempt to define in advance and to lay down hypothetical cases is doomed to failure.[134]

After the debate Anthony Nutting wrote to Anthony Head, the Secretary of State for War, informing him that Monckton had now dealt fully with the issue and that Buzzard was to be told firmly that he should cease from continuing to discuss the matter with the Foreign Office.[135] Nutting duly informed Buzzard that:

We think that your papers are really a matter for the defence experts and we should prefer that you should go into this question with them rather than us. I realise that your proposals have political as well as defence implications, but as Harold Macmillan said in his letter, Ministers must be guided in these matters by the views of the Chiefs of Staff.[136]

The official government view was that it stood to reason that the Western powers would only use a proportionate amount of force and would not initiate

---

[131] TNA, FO 371/123118, ZE 112/30, Sir Richard Sharples to Anthony Nutting, 1 February 1956.
[132] TNA, FO 371/123118, ZE 112/30, Anthony Nutting to Sir Richard Sharples, 9 February 1956.
[133] *Hansard*, House of Commons Debate, Vol. 549, Col. 1035, 28 February 1956.
[134] Ibid.
[135] TNA, FO 371/123120, ZE 112/65, Anthony Nutting to Anthony Head, 1 March 1956.
[136] TNA, FO 371/123120, ZE 112/65, Anthony Nutting to Anthony Buzzard, 1 March 1956.

thermonuclear war unless forced to do so by military necessity. This was a view supported by Slessor, who stated in an article for *The Bulletin of the Atomic Scientists* that attempts by Buzzard and his disciples to draw distinctions between nuclear weapons in peacetime were 'not worth the paper they are written on'.[137] For both Slessor and Whitehall Mandarins, graduated deterrence would serve only to undermine the credibility of the 'Great Deterrent', making war more, and not less, likely. With the arrival of the H-bomb, the aim was now to abolish total war, not a method of waging it.[138] The Foreign Office noted that Buzzard had had this impressed upon him many times but that 'he is so dazzled by his theories as to be blind to other ideas'.[139] It was clear that officials were becoming impatient with Buzzard. The last part of Walter Monckton's speech was, according to one Civil Servant at the Foreign Office, 'specifically devoted to shooting down Admiral Buzzard's views', adding despairingly that he 'appears to be unsinkable'.[140]

Undeterred, Buzzard replied to Nutting's letter explaining that not only did he feel that his theory of graduated deterrence had political implications but that he also held deep concerns about the influence the Foreign Office was having on the formulation of defence policy.[141] He had published in the same month an article in *The Spectator* critiquing the government's recent defence White Paper on the lack of clarification about the role of tactical nuclear weapons in defence policy.[142] The Foreign Office was not pleased, however, with the Rear-Admiral's attack on its implied lack of coordination with the military authorities. A senior official thought that 'Foreign Office influence on Defence Policy is none of Sir A. Buzzard's business' and that he should be informed tactfully that the department did not wish to discuss the matter of graduated deterrence with him again.[143] Buzzard was subsequently told in April 1956 that the Foreign Office was indeed intimately concerned with the political aspects of defence policy and that 'you can rely on them to make their views known to the Ministry of Defence as necessary'.[144] He was advised to send all future correspondence to the military authorities.

This Buzzard did by sending a revised version of his theory of graduated deterrence to the Defence Department of the Foreign Office in August 1956 in which he argued that if the threat of 'mutual suicide' would deter either side from

---

[137] John Slessor, 'The Great Deterrent and Its Limitations', *Bulletin of the Atomic Scientists*, Vol. 12, No. 5 (May 1956), p. 144.
[138] Ibid.   [139] TNA, FO 371/123121, ZE 112/82, Confidential Minutes, 14 March 1956.
[140] TNA, FO 371/123121, ZE 112/82, Confidential Minutes, 15 March 1956.
[141] TNA, FO 371/123121, ZE 112/102, Anthony Buzzard to Anthony Nutting, 25 March 1956.
[142] Anthony W. Buzzard, 'Graduated Deterrence: The Next Step', *The Spectator*, Vol. 196, No. 6663 (March 1956), pp. 305–6. The White Paper in question was Cmd. 9691, *Statement on Defence* (London: HMSO, 1956).
[143] TNA, FO 371/123121, ZE 112/102, Confidential Minutes, 9 April 1956.
[144] TNA, FO 371/123121, ZE 112/102, D. S. L. Dodson to Anthony Buzzard, 18 April 1956.

using H-bombs against the other, as the government insisted, then the real challenge now was how to arrive at a common understanding with the Soviet Union on how to manage escalation should fighting break out.[145] He proposed sending a note to the Kremlin, which is worth outlining in full:

> We have between us, as yet, many unsettled local issues over which conflicts may well arise. Neither of us wants war, particularly global or total war, but war might break out unintentionally. We in the West will never be the first to initiate the use of the Hydrogen bomb, except for a truly vital issue and in the last resort. But if local war should break out between us, we might, in some circumstances, find ourselves forced to initiate the use of tactical atomic weapons against tactical targets. In order to ensure the best possible chance of such a tactical atomic local war remaining limited, and not spreading to the unlimited 'H' bombing of cities and global war, we propose that tactical nuclear weapons should be defined as 'so-and-so', and tactical targets as 'so-and-so'. We would like to negotiate and agree these definitions with you, but pending such agreement we, nevertheless, propose to establish them unilaterally in the hope that you and other countries will agree them in due course, and so that they are available for adoption if required, should a tactical atomic local conflict break out.[146]

Buzzard advanced the methods by which he thought tactical nuclear warfare could be kept limited at a defence conference held in Brighton between 18 and 20 January 1957.[147] In the ensuing discussion, which included the Bishop of Chichester and the original Buzzard group, the participants reached the conclusion that it would be unwise to impose any theoretical limitations on targets or weapons in advance of a situation arising and that the best hope of limiting any future tactical nuclear war was through limiting war aims.[148] One Foreign Office official, after consulting the conference proceedings, thought that Buzzard's arguments were 'not very impressive' and noted that it appeared that Denis Healey, who had previously supported graduated deterrence in its purest form, had now deviated to a view that was more akin to a policy of 'economy of force'.[149] This new thinking was enshrined in a June 1957 article by Buzzard, Healey, P. M. S. Blackett, and Richard Goold-Adams for the *Bulletin of the Atomic Scientists*. The authors argued that if, in theory, it was possible and practical to draw distinctions between

[145] TNA, FO 371/123132, ZE 112/269, Anthony Buzzard to G. L. McDermott, 4 October 1956.
[146] TNA, FO 371/123132, ZE 112/269, Defence Policy Reviewed, 8 August 1956.
[147] The conference led to the formation of the Brighton Conference Association which laid the foundations for the Institute for Strategic Studies. See Howard, 'IISS: The First Thirty Years', pp. 11–12.
[148] TNA, FO 371/129237, ZE 112/38, Report of the Defence Conference held at Brighton, 18–20 January 1957.
[149] TNA, FO 371/129237, ZE 112/38, Confidential Minutes, 9 April 1957.

nuclear weapons and their targets, such restrictions would only be possible in limited wars outside of the European theatre.[150] On the Central Front, a theatre of great strategic significance to both the Soviet Union and the Western Powers, peace would ultimately be maintained 'by virtue of the over-all thermonuclear stalemate'.[151]

Buzzard's parting shot on the subject was a note on the summary of his thesis which was passed to the Foreign Office in June 1957—clearly Buzzard thought that his theory required further consultation by the department. His overarching message was that the West should now shift its focus to preparing for limited wars since the possibility of global war had diminished radically because of the threat of mutual destruction through the use of thermonuclear weapons. Buzzard argued, however, that in order to emerge victorious in a limited war against the mass land armies of the Soviet Union, the West had no choice but to use tactical nuclear weapons as force multipliers, but that clear guidelines about their use must be promulgated beforehand. Buzzard argued that this would reduce the risk of escalation to the strategic nuclear level and would reassure public opinion at home and abroad that the West was prepared to restrain its use of force to only that which was morally justifiable.[152] The absence of a reply by the Foreign Office was telling, and speaks louder than words.

Although Buzzard's thesis was rejected wholesale by the establishment, similar ideas about limited nuclear options were being advanced by more influential writers, although these theories were likewise destined to reach an intellectual dead-end. Henry Kissinger is usually regarded as being the first to consider more flexible alternatives to the strategy of massive retaliation in his *Nuclear Weapons and Foreign Policy*, but this was not published until 1957, two years after Buzzard first debated his own theory with Slessor and Lowenthal at Chatham House. Kissinger had made his name as an academic nuclear weapons expert in the 1950s arguing that strategy in the nuclear age had become increasingly 'abstract, intangible, elusive' and difficult to translate into credible threats, a position he would maintain well into the 1970s as President Richard Nixon's National Security Advisor.[153] In 1957, Kissinger had arrived at the same conclusion as Buzzard that with US–Soviet nuclear parity drawing ever closer, 'a nation that relies on all-out war as its chief deterrent imposes a fearful psychological handicap on itself'.[154]

---

[150] Anthony W. Buzzard et al., 'On Limiting Atomic War', *Bulletin of the Atomic Scientists*, Vol. 13, No. 6 (June 1957), p. 220.

[151] Ibid., p. 222.

[152] TNA, FO 371/129246, ZE 112/237, Summary of Graduated Deterrence, 20 June 1957, pp. 1–2.

[153] See William Burr, ' "Is This the Best They Can Do?" Henry Kissinger and the US Quest for Limited Nuclear Options, 1969–1975' in Vojtech Mastny et al. (eds.), *War Plans and Alliances in the Cold War: Threat Perceptions in the East and West* (London: Routledge, 2006), pp. 118–40.

[154] Henry Kissinger, *Nuclear Weapons and Foreign Policy* (New York, NY: Harper & Brothers, 1957), p. 133.

Kissinger was motivated less by the moral implications of massive retaliation, and more by Realist concerns about the credibility of the threat:

> It requires us in every crisis to stake our survival on the credibility of a threat which we will be increasingly reluctant to implement and which, if implemented, will force us into the kind of war our strategy should make every attempt to avoid.[155]

If nuclear deterrence is a war against the imagination, then Kissinger worried that the West was increasingly turning it on itself. Akin to Buzzard, Kissinger believed that it would be possible to limit nuclear war, and that with proper tactics, it need not even be as destructive as conventional fighting.[156] This rested on the assumption that both sides shared a common interest in avoiding a thermonuclear holocaust and, as was demonstrated during the Korean War, would seek restraint and go to great lengths to communicate their limited intentions to the other. To avoid miscalculation and misinterpretation Kissinger similarly advocated the establishment of some concept of limitation of warfare mutually agreed in peacetime.[157] In 1957 Kissinger argued that there should be no inevitable progression from limited nuclear war to all-out thermonuclear war, and that limited nuclear war may even be less likely than conventional war to escalate into a strategic nuclear exchange.[158] This position was qualified in his 1960 work, *The Necessity for Choice*, where he was much more cautious about the risk of escalation since no theoretical model of how to limit war had yet won general agreement, fifteen years after the beginning of the nuclear age.[159]

In the same year, Basil Liddell Hart published a treatise on Western defence policy, *Deterrent or Defence*, in which he accepted that in theory the use of tactical nuclear weapons offered a better chance of confining nuclear use to the battlefield, thereby limiting the scale and scope of destructiveness compared to an all-out nuclear war.[160] In practice, however, Liddell Hart was much more pessimistic about the ability of military commanders to control the process of escalation. After a lifetime of writing and thinking about the conduct of war, he reached the conclusion that decentralizing nuclear decision-making from political control, which would be a necessary requirement for the expeditious 'tactical' application of nuclear weapons, would in all likelihood prove disastrous since:

> It is too risky to leave the decision to military commanders. For they will always tend to use every weapon available if it looks likely that their troops will be

---

[155] Ibid., p. 135.    [156] Ibid., p. 183.    [157] Ibid., pp. 183–9.    [158] Ibid., p. 192.
[159] Henry Kissinger, *The Necessity for Choice: Prospects of American Foreign Policy* (London: Chatto & Windus, 1960), p. 81.
[160] Basil Liddell Hart, *Deterrent or Defence: A Fresh Look at the West's Military Position* (London: Stevens & Sons, 1960), p. 81.

overrun. In that immediate concern they tend to lose sight of wider issues. By taking the narrow view they have often in the past marred the aims of higher policy. Now, they could wreck the world.[161]

Indeed, a number of officers who had held the post of Chief of the Defence Staff since its establishment in 1957 would go on to make public statements after their retirement conceding that the professional services they once represented would most likely have failed to control the use of nuclear weapons in any discriminatory or graduated manner.[162] For example, in a speech delivered to the Scientific Council of the Stockholm International Peace Research Institute in Strasbourg in 1979, Lord Mountbatten told the audience:

> I cannot accept the reasons for the belief that any class of nuclear weapons can be categorized in terms of their tactical or strategic purposes. In all sincerity, as a military man I can see no use for any nuclear weapons which would not end in escalation, with consequences that no one can conceive.[163]

Shortly after, Admiral of the Fleet, Lord Peter Hill-Norton, who was CDS from 1971 to 1973, wrote in a letter to *The Times* that he knew of no informed observer who believed that the idea of limiting war through the use of tactical nuclear weapons was credible.[164] Field Marshal Lord Michael Carver, who succeeded Hill-Norton as CDS, agreed during a House of Lords debate that few sensible military persons would now argue that the use of tactical nuclear weapons in warfare would not escalate into a strategic nuclear exchange.[165] In the same year, Marshal of the Royal Air Force, Sir Neil Cameron, informed an audience at the Royal Society of Arts in 1980 that 'so-called battlefield nuclear weapons are not means of winning victories ... the role of nuclear weapons is to deter war—all war, not just nuclear war, between East and West'.[166]

It is important to note that none of these military elites were arguing against the possession by Britain of an independent nuclear deterrent or that nuclear weapons did not play an important role in influencing the Soviet calculus of war. On the contrary, all were in agreement that strategic nuclear weapons remained an important insurance policy to protect the nation and its allies against armed aggression. These were, after all, men who had climbed to the top of their respective services and embodied the deterrence habit of mind which shaped

[161] Ibid., p. 96.

[162] See, Solly Zuckerman, *Nuclear Illusion and Reality* (London: Collins, 1982), p. 71.

[163] Louis Mountbatten, 'A Military Commander Surveys the Nuclear Arms Race', *International Security*, Vol. 4, No. 3 (Winter 1979–80), pp. 3–4.

[164] Zuckerman, *Nuclear Illusion and Reality*, p. 71.

[165] *Hansard*, House of Lords Debate, Vol. 408, Col. 843, 23 April 1980.

[166] Neil Cameron, 'Defence in the 1990s', *Journal of the Royal Society of Arts*, Vol. 128, No. 5289 (August 1980), p. 611.

British nuclear policy throughout the Cold War. As Cameron still hoped as late as 1980, nuclear weapons were supposed to have abolished all war. The arrival of tactical nuclear weapons had introduced unwelcome ambiguity into what was already a complex strategic debate. The idea that small-yield nuclear weapons might somehow release Western strategy from the increasingly incredible yoke of massive retaliation via an alternative strategy of graduated deterrence was dismissed, according to Zuckerman, as a 'confusing abstraction'.[167] Ultimately, the threshold for nuclear use cut across the most important threshold of all—that between war and no war.

## Conclusions

It is unclear the extent to which Buzzard's thinking helped to shape alternative theories about limited war in the nuclear age, but it is clear that neither he nor Kissinger nor Liddell Hart were able to bring about any change to government strategy. The British defence establishment remained stubbornly attached to its nuclear policies throughout the course of the Cold War, and the deterrence habit of mind refused to acknowledge the existence of thresholds in war, except for the most important threshold of all: that between war and no war. Suggestions to make distinctions in peacetime between strategic and tactical nuclear weapons were therefore anathema to Whitehall officials, who were convinced that this would serve only to undermine the deterrent effect of those weapons. So too was the proposal by proponents of graduate deterrence to devise a Queensbury Rules for nuclear war regarded as a dangerous proposition which would further erode the effectiveness of nuclear deterrence by removing the contrived ambiguity of response. The threat of massive nuclear retaliation to Soviet aggression in Europe remained the ultimate deterrent to war, and any attempt to make the consequences of that threat appear less catastrophic in the minds of the Soviet leadership was incompatible with the pure-deterrence strategy favoured by the political and military elite. The arrival of tactical nuclear weapons was viewed as an aberration to these entrenched beliefs, but the weapons could not simply be wished away. Indeed, the use of tactical nuclear weapons in a war-fighting role would assume great significance for the NATO alliance as it sought to find solutions to how its outnumbered conventional forces could defend the European Central Front against a Soviet attack. The role of tactical nuclear weapons and conventional forces within NATO defensive concepts is the subject of Chapter 2.

---

[167] Zuckerman, *Nuclear Illusion*, p. 78.

# 2

# Conventional Forces and Tactical Nuclear Weapons in NATO Strategy

The overarching parameters within which BAOR structured its thinking about tactical nuclear warfare were dictated by NATO's strategic concepts. The principal objective of NATO strategy remained constant throughout the Cold War: to preserve the political and territorial integrity of Western Europe by deterring Soviet aggression and defending the Central Front by direct military force if necessary. The most suitable military response to this threat, and the attendant force requirements, changed habitually throughout the years, however. In the first decade of NATO's existence, its strategic concept was revised three times in 1952 (MC 14/1), 1954 (MC 48), and 1957 (MC 14/2). The fourth and final change came in 1967 (MC 14/3) with the adoption of the ambiguous flexible response strategy. The evolution of NATO's strategic concept was driven by changing perceptions of the nature of the Soviet threat, the collective means available to counter it, and the unique strategic preferences of the Alliance's European and North American members, which were often divergent and at times incompatible.[1]

As a potential real war in the making, images of future war were fundamental to Cold War military strategy. In the British case, visions of nuclear war were inherently apocalyptic, which was consonant with the deterrence habit of mind which gripped policy-makers after 1945. According to this logic, nuclear war would be unprecedentedly destructive, difficult to control as a rational operation of war, and impossible to translate into political capital. For these reasons, Britain advocated the adoption of a pure-deterrence strategy for NATO, the key tenet of which was the assumption that deterrence of any war was best assured by accepting the invariable risk of escalation to general nuclear war.[2] This thinking manifested in two important ways with regards the role and functions of conventional and tactical nuclear forces in NATO strategy. The first was Britain's rejection of the notion that NATO's conventional shield force should be of sufficient strength to be able to fight a conventional battle for a prolonged period

---

[1] John S. Duffield, *Power Rules: The Evolution of NATO's Conventional Force Posture* (Stanford, CA: Stanford University Press, 1995), pp. 235–6.
[2] Ivo H. Daalder, *The Nature and Practice of Flexible Response: NATO Strategy and Theatre Nuclear Forces since 1967* (New York, NY: Columbia University Press, 1991), pp. 43–8.

*Imagining Nuclear War in the British Army, 1945–1989.* Simon J. Moody, Oxford University Press (2020).
© Simon J. Moody.
DOI: 10.1093/oso/9780198846994.001.0001

of time. The second was the insistence of British planners that the destruction wrought by nuclear war would be so terrific that it would be pointless to plan to conduct meaningful military operations during or after an initial strategic nuclear exchange.

Often described as the metaphorical 'shield' to the 'sword' of NATO's strategic nuclear weapon systems, the role of conventional forces and tactical nuclear weapons was open to a wide range of interpretations. 'Trip-wire', 'covering force', 'plate-glass window', and 'trigger line' were just some of the euphemisms coined by NATO planners to describe the roles and functions of its conventional ground forces, of which BAOR was an integral component. BAOR's principal fighting formation, 1(BR) Corps, was grouped together with Dutch, Belgian, and from 1957, West German army corps to form NORTHAG, which was tasked with defending a vulnerable 140-mile stretch of the North German Plain. To its south, the American-German Central Army Group (CENTAG) was positioned to defend the narrow invasion corridors leading to Frankfurt (Map 2). Together, the two army groups constituted the core of NATO's conventional ground forces, and were a vital element in the Allies' overall defensive posture on the European Central Front.

The specific functions of NATO's shield forces changed in relation to its overarching strategy, which articulated increasingly abstruse operational designs for war-fighting and war-termination through the application of tactical nuclear weapons. Victory conditions and the political ends of military operations became more ambiguous as the Cold War dragged on, as the proliferation of nuclear weapons on both sides of the Iron Curtain raised concerns about the military utility of nuclear weapons in rational military operations. 'Victory' in this particular future war rested on the ability of armies to conduct military operations in a manner they were culturally predisposed to find difficult—manage carefully their use of violence in a way that inflicted just enough pain on the enemy to force a political settlement, but not so much that it would provoke a response out of all proportion which, in the nuclear age, was of existential levels. This chapter focuses on British thinking about the role of conventional forces in NATO strategy. How well the Army understood the strategic context in which it was operating, and the extent to which it successfully incorporated military and political guidance into its organizational activities, is an important consideration when determining how well the service structured its thinking about tactical nuclear war.

## Tactical Nuclear Weapons as a Substitute for Conventional Forces

In the immediate post-war years, the Soviet threat was framed largely in political rather than military terms. As Chapter 1 has shown, British intelligence

**Map 2.** (06078-07). NORTHAG and CENTAG corps boundaries.

assessments of the late 1940s concluded that the likelihood of war was small, but that the Soviet Union would continue to rebuild its military strength while seeking to sow political unrest in Western Europe through the exploitation of local Communist parties. The immediate aim of the NATO alliance, therefore, was to enhance political cohesion in a manner that would facilitate the post-war reconstruction of Europe. In the short term, that objective could be achieved by coupling US military power to the Continent through the provisions of the North Atlantic treaty. Alliance planners hoped that American nuclear superiority would deter unwanted Soviet actions, and so there was little incentive to draw-up detailed military plans for a conventional defence, and little meaningful thought was given to the role of conventional forces in wider NATO strategy.[3]

Although armed aggression did not seem imminent, the Soviet Union nonetheless enjoyed a preponderance of military power. The most pessimistic appraisals of the situation at the end of the 1950s identified 175 fully manned, fully armed, and combat-ready Soviet divisions poised in Eastern Europe ready to strike the paltry sixteen divisions which could be mustered by the NATO alliance.[4] As European nations recovered from six years of world war, governments were unwilling to foot the enormous economic and political costs of raising land forces on the scale that would be required to mount a conventional defence of its territory. For these reasons, NATO's European members sought as much as possible to emphasize nuclear weapons in alliance strategic concepts as a cheaper alternative to raising mass conventional forces. Britain and France in particular were keen to minimize their conventional force contributions to NATO as both countries continued to maintain sizable forces overseas.[5] The result was a precarious military balance as outnumbered NATO forces looked to find ways to compensate for their numerical inferiority.

One of the ways in which the Alliance sought to offset its deficiencies in conventional manpower was through nuclear firepower, and NATO strategy became increasingly nuclearized as a result.[6] In this context, tactical nuclear weapons assumed a special significance as force multipliers that would allow NATO's slender shield forces to mount a forward defence of its territory. Forward defence, which was a pledge to defend NATO Europe as close to the inner-German border as possible, was a political necessity for the burgeoning alliance, but one that raised a number of operational and tactical problems. Not least, a forward defence required a surplus of standing manpower which could not easily

   [3] Duffield, *Power Rules*, pp. 236–7.
   [4] Richard A. Bitzinger, *Assessing the Conventional Balance in Europe, 1945–1975* (Santa Monica, CA: RAND, 1989), pp. 4–7.
   [5] Duffield, *Power Rules*, p. 244.
   [6] For further information see, Simon J. Moody, 'Enhancing Political Cohesion in NATO during the 1950s or: How It Learned to Stop Worrying and Love the (Tactical) Bomb', *Journal of Strategic Studies*, Vol. 40, No. 6 (2017), pp. 817–838.

be generated. The hope that tactical nuclear weapons might be able to compensate for inferior numbers of men proved to be much more complicated for the entangling alliance as competing views about the role of tactical nuclear weapons and the relationship between conventional and nuclear forces exposed a number of logical inconsistencies at the heart of NATO strategy.

BAOR's operational plans reflected the precarious strategic situation in which the Alliance found itself at the time of its creation. Undermanned, poorly equipped, and suffering from a lack of coordinated planning, the defence of Western Europe was accepted as a lost cause since BAOR would be unable to prevent a rapid overrunning of Northern Germany by superior Soviet forces. No attempt would be made to reinforce BAOR in the event of war. In April 1948, the CIGS, Field Marshal Montgomery, informed the military members of the Army Council that in the event of war, any available land forces based in the UK would not be sent to BAOR 'until it was quite clear that there would be a reasonable chance of fighting successfully on the Rhine'. Until that time came, which the CIGS believed would be no less than five years' time, the land forces based in Germany would be 'withdrawn North-Westwards to the UK' if an attack took place.[7] Because of this gloomy prognosis for the defence of Western Europe, priority in war-time would be given to reinforcing the Middle East Land Forces instead. This was consonant with the 'three pillars' strategy embodied within the 1947 Chiefs of Staff 'Future Defence Policy' paper, which stated that the essential elements of British defence policy were the defence of the United Kingdom, the control of essential sea communications, and the maintenance of the Middle East as an offensive base.[8]

BAOR's best hope if attacked was to conduct a hasty exit from the Continent in the hope of returning at a later date. Montgomery explained to the Chiefs of Staff Committee in June 1948 that if armed aggression did develop in Europe, then it would be of immense importance for the land forces of the West to hold it as far to the east as possible to prevent friendly territory from being overrun. BAOR's military weaknesses were such, however, that it would be forced to withdraw from its forward positions along the intra-German border to take up defensive positions on the River Rhine where it was expected to 'fight in Europe until they are pushed out'.[9] It was becoming increasingly apparent, however, that any plans to scuttle from the Continent in the event of war would be politically sensitive, and a bitter pill to swallow for Britain's Continental allies, who had pledged with the signing of the Brussels Treaty on 17 March 1948 a policy of defence and security cooperation. For those reasons, the British Chiefs of Staff agreed that even if it were

---

[7] TNA, WO 216/254, CIGS/BM/30/2235, Plans for Emergency Measures and for Mobilisation, 15 April 1948.

[8] TNA, CAB 21/1800, DO(47)44, Future Defence Policy, 22 May 1947.

[9] TNA, WO 216/261, Oral Statement by the CIGS to the Chiefs of Staff Committee, 1 June 1948.

operationally possible, BAOR could not leave its Western Union allies in the lurch, and it would have to stay and fight with what it had.[10]

Therefore, the River Rhine had to be held at all costs, and any reference to leaving the Continent in the event of war was quietly removed from British plans.[11] Subsequent defensive concepts, known collectively as CONGREAVE, envisaged an outnumbered BAOR mounting a fighting retreat across Western Germany to take up defensive positions on the best available natural obstacle, a 180-mile line astride the Rhine and Ijssel rivers (Map 3).[12]

The controlled withdrawal outlined in CONGREAVE would have been difficult to execute, and even then it was doubtful whether BAOR could have held the position.[13] For these reasons, there was a growing realization among senior staff officers that the object of Western Union defence policy should be to convince the Soviet leaders that war was unprofitable by giving tangible and unmistakable evidence that the Allies would fight to protect their vital interests and that they possessed the military capabilities to inflict serious damage on an attacker.[14]

The JPS determined that the Allies would need to field between fifty-seven and seventy-seven divisions by D+26 days in order to hold the river line, with a capacity to increase that strength to ninety divisions by D+6 months.[15] This would be a considerable undertaking that would require ready access to a vast pool of trained land forces along the lines of Montgomery's New Model Army.[16] The perceived weakness of Allied conventional forces meant that Anglo-American war plans, codenamed SPEEDWAY,[17] began to look to nuclear weapons as a technological solution to counterbalancing the Red Army's numerical superiority.[18] The problem appeared intractable, however, and by the summer of 1949 the JPS had pulled together the various strands of their thinking on European defence in their 'Overall Strategic Concept for War in 1957'. The report rejected the idea of

[10] TNA, PREM 8/1380, Minister of Defence to Prime Minister, 12 May 1948. Moody, 'Enhancing Political Cohesion in NATO during the 1950s', p. 820.

[11] TNA, PREM 8/1380, Minister of Defence to Prime Minister, 4 June 1948.

[12] TNA, AIR 20/10513, Joint British Army of the Rhine/British Air Forces of Occupation Appreciation for Exercise CONGREAVE, June 1948.

[13] TNA, WO 216/688, CIGS/BM/31/2524, The Situation in Western Europe and the British Army Problem Arising Therefrom, 27 July 1948.

[14] TNA, DEFE 6/6, JP(48)63(Revised Final), Western Union Defence Policy, 26 June 1948.

[15] TNA, DEFE 6/6, JP(48)64(Final), Defence of the Western Union, 20 September 1948.

[16] Montgomery's proposal for a New Model Army was an attempt to increase the availability of trained manpower that could be called upon to fight immediately at the start of a major war. This would be achieved by a steady flow of National Servicemen through the ranks of an expanded Territorial Army. See TNA, WO 216/205, Minutes of the Fifth Meeting of Home Army Commanders, 20 March 1947. TNA, WO 216/233, CIGS/BM/28/1774, The British Army, 8 September 1947; TNA, WO 216/233, CIGS/BM/28/1801, The British Army II, 23 September 1947; and TNA, WO 216/233, CIGS/BM/28/1807, The British Army III, 25 September 1947.

[17] The terms of reference for the studies can be found in TNA, DEFE 5/9, COS(48)209, Combined Planning, report by the Chiefs of Staff, 16 December 1948.

[18] TNA, DEFE 5/9, COS(48)210, Digest of Plan SPEEDWAY, memorandum by the Chiefs of Staff, 16 December 1948.

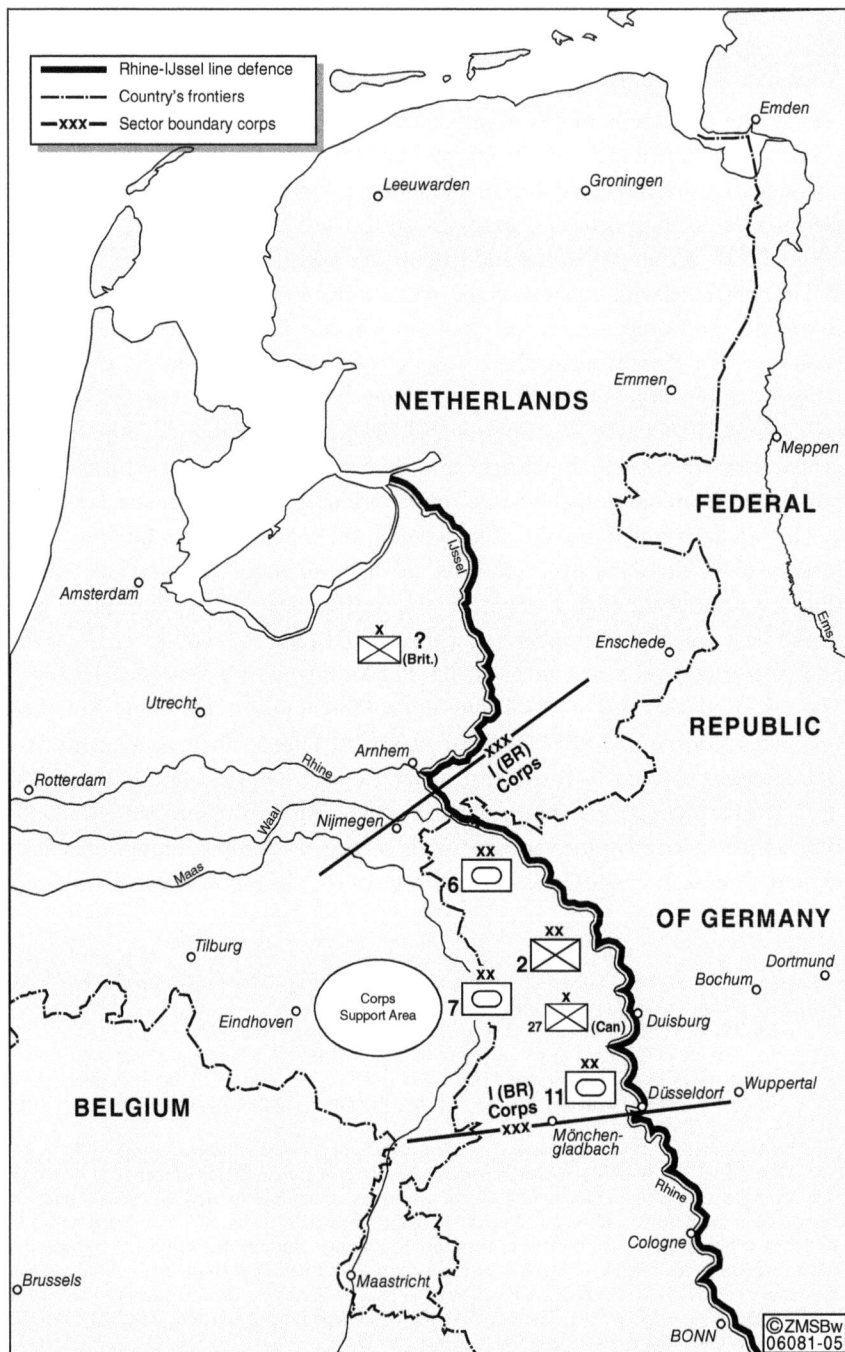

**Map 3.** (06081-05). 1(BR) Corps sector.

a land defence as a viable strategy for repelling a Soviet offensive in Europe since a strategy aimed at the destruction of the enemy's ground forces would be engaging the Soviet Union in the field most favourable to it. The JPS therefore concluded that the only possible means by which the Allies could prevent the Red Army from overrunning Western Europe was to launch an atomic air offensive against Soviet centres of control and communication at the outbreak of war.[19]

Therefore, the elementary consideration that faced Western defence planners at the end of the 1940s was how to defend a 4,000-mile-wide front in Central Europe against a numerically superior enemy in a manner that was both militarily effective and economically viable. In 1949, the first NATO strategy document to receive ministerial approval, DC 6/1, 'The Strategic Concept for the Defence of the North Atlantic Area', reflected this basic dilemma. It outlined the require-ment for NATO to mount a forward defence of its territory while recognizing its inferiority in conventional forces vis-à-vis the Soviet Union and its satellites. Reflecting the massive retaliation strategies of Britain and the United States, DC 6/1 maintained that one of the basic undertakings of its forces was to ensure the ability to 'carry out strategic bombing promptly by all means possible with all types of weapons, without exception'.[20] The ability to mount a forward defence as far to the East as possible was a political necessity for the burgeoning Alliance, and so ways had to be found to bolster Allied defensive capabilities whilst offsetting Soviet advantages.

As DC 6/1 hinted, nuclear weapons might provide a technological solution to some of these problems by offsetting Soviet numerical superiority and obviating the need for European nations to generate expensive conventional forces that they could ill afford. Indeed, NATO's defensive shield was already in a parlous state in 1950. The Federal Republic of Germany could not contribute manpower to its own defence because the question of re-armament had not yet been solved,[21] and according to Montgomery, the French Army 'would be laughable, if it were not pathetic'.[22] Compounding these deficiencies was the fact that it would be

[19] TNA, DEFE 6/6, JP(48)59(Final—Second Revise), Overall Strategic Concept for War in 1957, 20 July 1949.
[20] NATO, DC 6/1, The Strategic Concept for the Defence of the North Atlantic Area, 1 December 1949, p. 5.
[21] TNA, CAB 21/3503, JP(49)172(Final), Allied Defence Policy and Strategy, 3 March 1950. The main problems were that French objections to raising national German forces could not be overcome, Germany could not then be trusted politically, and any signs of a rearmed Germany within the Western camp may have provoked a Russian preventative war. However, the Attlee government had always realized that some form of West German rearmament was inevitable in the long run. By the early 1950s, with the heightening of Cold War tensions, German political and military integration was now seen as unavoidable if the West hoped to check Communist influence in Europe. See Spencer W. Mawby, 'Détente Deferred: The Attlee Government, German Rearmament and Anglo-Soviet Rapprochement 1950–51', *Contemporary British History*, Vol. 12, No. 2 (Summer 1998), p. 3 and Saki Dockrill, *Britain's Policy for West German Rearmament 1950–1955* (Cambridge: Cambridge University Press, 1991), p. 13.
[22] TNA, DEFE 32/1, WE/M/93, Western European Defence, 30 March 1950.

extremely difficult to dispatch reinforcements to Continental Europe in the event of war because of the vulnerability of Allied ports to attack from nuclear weapons.[23]

The outbreak of the Korean War in June 1950 would bring into sharp focus the weaknesses in NATO's defensive preparations to date. The Soviet-backed invasion of South Korea by Kim Il-sung's Korean People's Army suggested that Communism was on the march. Soviet aggression in Western Europe now appeared much more likely, and so visible preparations for the defence of the Central Front were deemed indispensable to deter a Soviet attack and reassure European nations.[24] Furthermore, the assumptions underpinning the strategic bombing concept articulated in DC 6/1 were called into question in the wake of the unexpected Soviet atomic bomb test in August 1949. This brought to an end the short-lived US monopoly on nuclear weapons, and raised concerns about the willingness of American leaders to initiate a nuclear retaliation if this meant making itself vulnerable to a reply in kind. All of this pointed towards the requirement for an increase in conventional forces in Europe. Although US nuclear weapons could still play a role in retarding Soviet military power, NATO planners calculated that in the Central Region the Alliance would need thirty fully ready divisions and a total of sixty-five divisions within a month of the outbreak of hostilities.[25]

This did not augur well for NATO's defensive posture on the Central Front, which was described by Montgomery, who was now Chairman of the Western European Union's Commanders-in-Chief Committee, as little more than a 'dogs-breakfast'[26] and unable to mount a forward defence.[27] Even if a German man-power contribution could be secured, the most pessimistic appraisals of the situation still predicted that NATO would only be able to contain a Soviet penetration east of the Rhine for a few days.[28] Yet, the official view of the British Chiefs of Staff was that if NATO did not commit itself to a forward strategy then this might fatally undermine the will and cohesion of the Alliance.[29] The problem would have to be confronted head-on.[30] If all else failed, BAOR and its allies would simply have to retreat into specially prepared bridgeheads in Europe from which a

---

[23] TNA, CAB 21/3503, DO(50)58, Ability of the Armed Forces to Meet an Emergency, 21 July 1950. Moody, 'Enhancing Political Cohesion in NATO during the 1950s', p. 822.

[24] Jack L. Granatstein, 'The United Nations and the North Atlantic Treaty Organization' in Gustav Schmidt (ed.), *A History of NATO: The First Fifty Years, Vol. I* (Basingstoke: Palgrave, 2001), p. 34.

[25] Duffield, *Power Rules*, p. 237.

[26] TNA, PREM 8/1154, FM/33, Field Marshal Montgomery to Minister of Defence, 10 October 1950.

[27] TNA, PREM 8/1154, FM/31, Western Europe Defence—some matters that give cause for alarm, Memorandum by Field Marshal Montgomery, 19 September 1950.

[28] TNA, PREM 8/1201, Address by Field Marshal Montgomery to the Senior Officers of the Brussels Treaty Powers, 5 May 1950.

[29] TNA, DEFE 5/31, COS(51)322, Defence of Europe in the Short Term, 31 May 1951.

[30] Moody, 'Enhancing Political Cohesion in NATO during the 1950s', p. 823.

counter-attack could be launched at a later date.[31] Even through the employment of 'strategic demolition munitions' and other ruses, it was likely that yet another British army would again be swept from the Continent at the beginning of a major European war.[32]

The adoption of a Rhine strategy by BAOR proved to be short-lived, however, since it was forced through Alliance politics to play its part in a forward defence, which necessitated occupying a defensive position even closer to the intra-German border. Suggestions for the development of operational plans to defend NATO territory west of the River Rhine were rejected by the Chiefs of Staff because of the serious effects that such a plan might have on the morale of Continental allies, especially France and West Germany, and that they should continue to try and sell the virtues of a forward strategy.[33] Although the JPS still considered 'unrealistic' the ability of BAOR to resist a determined Soviet attack with the forces then available, they nonetheless appreciated that 'for political reasons SHAPE [Supreme Headquarters Allied Powers Europe] cannot plan on anything less than the Rhine Strategy'.[34]

Manpower anxieties gripped the first Supreme Allied Commander Europe (SACEUR), General Dwight D. Eisenhower, who was as equally convinced as his British partners that a forward defence would need to be as close to the intra-German border as possible. Eisenhower wanted to mount a defence on the River Weser, but to achieve this he needed boots on the ground. In February 1952 the North Atlantic Council agreed to provide them with the ambitious Lisbon Force Goals to generate ninety-six divisions and 9,000 aircraft by 1954.[35] Soon after the Lisbon meeting, NATO adopted a new strategic concept in MC 14/1.[36] With an upward projection of conventional forces in Europe, the strategy laid out in MC 14/1 conformed to British views on the desirability of mounting a forward defence of NATO territory in stating that 'the concept for the defence of Western Europe is to hold the enemy as far to the East in Germany as is feasible'.[37] The operational concept in support of this aim was inherently offensive and described the conduct of an aggressive land battle 'making full use of local opportunities for offense [sic] and maintaining mobility wherever possible'.[38] MC 14/1 still reaffirmed the logic underpinning massive retaliation, however, and took no account of the effect that

    [31] DEFE 5/31, COS(51)322.
    [32] See TNA, WO 216/346, General Collins to Field Marshal Slim, 10 July 1950; TNA, WO 216/346, CIGS/BM/38/4074, Field Marshal Slim to General Collins, 13 October 1950; TNA, DEFE 5/31, COS(51)367, Demolitions in Germany, 15 June 1951.
    [33] TNA, AIR 20/10138, COS(50)244, North Atlantic Treaty Defence Plans—Preparation of Short Term Plan in Western Region, 10 July 1950; TNA AIR 20/10138, COS(50)111, Preparation of Short Term Plan in Western Region, 17 July 1950.
    [34] TNA, DEFE 6/19, JP(51)217(Final), SHAPE Emergency Defence Plan, 4 January 1952.
    [35] See the report of the Temporary Council Committee of the North Atlantic Council in TNA, CAB 129/49, C (52) 49, 19 February 1952.
    [36] NATO, MC 14/1 (Final), NATO Strategic Guidance, 9 December 1952.
    [37] Ibid., p. 17.     [38] Ibid., p. 14.

the arrival of the Soviet bomb might have on the willingness of American leaders to initiate strategic nuclear war.[39] Rather, a principal military requirement for the Allies was to concurrently carry out strategic air attacks promptly with all types of weapons in the face of Soviet aggression, the effects of which on the defensive battle 'will be cumulative and may be decisive'.[40] Ultimately, the overall strategic aim of the Alliance was 'to ensure the defense [sic] of the NATO area and to destroy the will and capability of the USSR and her satellites to wage war'.[41] In this context, Beatrice Heuser has described MC 14/1 as being 'the most far-reaching of any NATO strategy' in that it aimed not only to repel a Soviet offensive but also to exact a decisive defeat on the USSR.[42]

Almost as soon as MC 14/1 had been adopted, Britain was pushing for a new strategic concept which was more compatible with its own military potential and with that of the European NATO members more generally. As Chapter 1 has shown, the British Chiefs of Staff had concluded in their 1952 Global Strategy Paper that the Soviet Union was preparing itself for the 'long haul' and that winning the burgeoning 'Cold War' rested on the economic health of Western Europe. By this time it had become clear that fulfilling the conventional force goals agreed at Lisbon would be financially and politically impossible for the Allies. The Korean War rearmament effort had imposed tremendous strain on European nations, perpetuating economic weaknesses, and causing the standard of living to fall in some countries.[43] In any event, the absence of a Soviet attack after Korea combined with the death of Stalin in March 1953 implied a less menacing Soviet Union. The arrival of tactical nuclear weapons in Europe at this time also promised 'more bang for the buck' and the possibility of a downward revision of conventional force goals on the unproven assumption that those weapons could compensate for manpower shortages.[44] Gripped by a deterrence habit of mind, British policy-makers urged a greater reliance on strategic and tactical nuclear weapons to deter Soviet aggression, or if war broke out, to decide the battle in NATO's favour. It was hoped that the nuclear umbrella would provide military justifications for a reduction of expensive conventional forces which the nation could ill afford. These views found sympathy with the incoming administration of the erstwhile SACEUR, President Eisenhower, who was equally as keen to reduce US military expenditure in the long term by emphasizing nuclear weapons in both national and alliance strategy.

---

[39] Beatrice Heuser, *NATO, Britain, France and the FRG: Nuclear Strategies and Forces for Europe* (Basingstoke: Macmillan, 1997), p. 33.

[40] MC 14/1 (Final), p. 13.       [41] Ibid., p. 10.

[42] Beatrice Heuser, 'Victory in a Nuclear War? A Comparison of NATO and WTO War Aims and Strategies', *Contemporary European History*, Vol. 7, No. 3 (November 1998), p. 315.

[43] See, for example, Jihang Park, 'Wasted Opportunities? The 1950s Rearmament Programme and the Failure of British Economic Policy', *Journal of Contemporary History*, Vol. 32, No. 3 (July 1997), pp. 357–79.

[44] Duffield, *Power Rules*, p. 238.

Thus, on British insistence, SHAPE began work immediately on a new approach to defensive concepts which took note of the greater emphasis to be placed on nuclear weapons. The first extensive examination of the impact of new weapons on NATO forces requirements was submitted to the Standing Group by Eisenhower's successor as SACEUR, General Matthew M. Ridgway, in July 1953. Foreshadowing the British Army's own assessments on the use of nuclear weapons in field warfare, the report proved controversial since it suggested that a tactical nuclear war would require more, rather than fewer, men because of the expected high rates of attrition.[45] Soon after issuing the report, Ridgway was replaced by General Alfred M. Gruenther, who established a specialist planning cell known as the New Approach Group (NAG) to carry out further study, which was the first major special-study group to operate over an extended period of time within SHAPE. One of the defining features of the work conducted by the NAG was the possibility of incorporating tactical nuclear weapons into the Allied armoury and integrating those weapons within the broader operational concepts for the defence of Western Europe.[46] The work of the NAG would fundamentally change NATO strategy with significant implications for its ground forces.[47]

SHAPE submitted its completed studies on the new approach to the Standing Group in 1954, which were subsequently adopted by the Military Committee as a new strategic concept, MC 48 'The Most Effective Pattern of NATO Military Strength for the Next Few Years'.[48] MC 48 reflected British thinking on the primacy of nuclear weapons to deter a Soviet attack, and to blunt its effectiveness if deterrence failed, and had much in common with the Chiefs of Staff 1952 Global Strategy Paper.[49] Thus, the strategic concept articulated in MC 48 advised that NATO would be unable to prevent the rapid overrunning of Europe unless it employed nuclear weapons 'both strategically and tactically' at the onset of hostilities.[50] To achieve these aims on the ground, 'forces-in-being' would be required with an integrated atomic capability. The document acknowledged that the Soviets continued to enjoy a numerical superiority in field armies but emphasized that this advantage could be nullified because of the 'vulnerability of their tactical formations, transportation systems and lines of communication to continued atomic attacks'.[51] Mirroring the ambiguity contained in the Chiefs of Staff Global Strategy Paper, MC 48 described two phases to a future war. The initial

---

[45]  Ibid., p. 82.
[46]  Moody, 'Enhancing Political Cohesion in NATO during the 1950s', pp. 824–5.
[47]  Simon J. Moody, 'Was There a "Monty Method" after the Second World War? Field Marshal Bernard L. Montgomery and the Changing Character of Land Warfare, 1945–1958', *War in History*, Vol. 23, No. 2 (2016), p. 221.
[48]  NATO, MC 48 (Final), The Most Effective Pattern of NATO Military Strength for the Next Few Years, 22 November 1954.
[49]  Heuser, *NATO, Britain, France and the FRG*, p. 35.
[50]  MC 48, p. 3.      [51]  Ibid., p. 7.

phase 'would include an intensive exchange of atomic weapons', at which point the loser would probably capitulate, followed by 'a period of re-adjustment and follow-up leading to a conclusion of the war'.[52] It remained to be seen what 'conclusion' meant in this context as victory conditions were not explicitly articulated. Nonetheless, with the acceptance of MC 48, and the companion document MC 48/1,[53] SHAPE was granted the political authorization for planning the defence of Western Europe on the use of nuclear weapons, and the Europeans had achieved their aim of rejecting conventional parity with the Warsaw Pact as a goal for NATO.[54]

## Functions of the Shield Forces

The new nuclear emphasis contained within MC 48 was a welcome development for British policy-makers who had long sought to harmonize alliance strategic concepts with their own national military strategy. Britain remained anxious, however, to reduce its expensive conventional manpower in Europe so that it could divert scarce resources into its budding thermonuclear programme, which it was hoped would both deter the Russians and maintain influence with the United States. The new Prime Minister, Anthony Eden, who succeeded Churchill in April 1955, was acutely aware of the economic difficulties facing the nation and believed that Britain should now cut its coat according to its cloth, the implication being that there was little cloth left.[55] Consequently, the Minister of Defence, Selwyn Lloyd, informed his counterparts at a meeting of the North Atlantic Council in October 1955 that Britain and her allies were now engaged in a 'long haul' with the Soviet Union, and that long-term economic considerations must always be kept in mind.[56] In descending order of importance, Britain's defence priorities were now the strategic nuclear deterrent; the Cold War (including the new concept of 'secondary deterrents');[57] and preparations for global war. The development of the strategic nuclear deterrent and of guided missiles was where Lloyd believed the United Kingdom could make the most valuable contribution to the NATO alliance.[58] Conversely, those capabilities that would be needed to fight a

---

[52] Ibid., pp. 4–5.

[53] NATO, MC 48/1 (Final), The Most Effective Pattern of NATO Military Strength for the Next Few Years—Report No. 2, 9 December 1955.

[54] Heuser, 'Victory in a Nuclear War?', p. 318.

[55] Anthony Eden, Full Circle (London: Cassell, 1960), pp. 370–1.

[56] NATO, CR(55)44, Meeting of the North Atlantic Council, 11 October 1955.

[57] In this context secondary deterrents referred to those capabilities that would protect Britain in the event of nuclear war, such as air defence systems. The idea was that Russia might be deterred from launching a strategic nuclear attack if she believed that the United Kingdom would emerge relatively unscathed.

[58] NATO, CR(55)59, Meeting of the North Atlantic Council, 15 December 1955.

prolonged war were deemed to be the lowest priority, and where the largest savings could be found.[59]

Political leaders believed conventional forces should be the lowest priority since the latest intelligence assessments by the JIC had suggested that the threat of war with the Soviet Union had reduced considerably with the emergence of thermo-nuclear weapons and that such forces were now 'a relatively less important factor in world affairs'.[60] Conventional forces still had a role to play in British strategic concepts, but only in as much as they could act as a 'plate-glass window' or 'trip-wire' which would trigger a strategic nuclear attack when encountered by the enemy.[61] Therefore, the British government advocated for small and efficient forces equipped with tactical nuclear weapons in place of large conventional formations designed to fight a protracted war.[62] A telegram sent by Prime Minister Harold Macmillan, who had now succeeded Eden, to President Eisenhower in July 1956 best sums up official thinking on the utility of conventional forces:

It is on the thermo-nuclear bomb and atomic weapons that we now rely, not only to deter aggression, but to deal with aggression if it should be launched. A 'shield' of conventional forces is still required; but it is no longer our principal military protection. Need it be capable of fighting a major land battle?[63]

The downgrading of British conventional capabilities was enshrined in the 1957 Defence White Paper. The bulk of the defence effort would now go towards developing a cost-effective nuclear deterrent in the form of a lean manned-bomber force supplemented by ballistic rockets. National Service would be terminated in 1960, and the British Army of the Rhine would be reduced from 77,000 to 64,000, with similar reductions planned for the 2nd Tactical Air Force. The Army would be equipped with 'atomic rocket artillery' which was hoped would compensate for its loss of manpower.[64]

Although Britain sought to reduce NATO's reliance on conventional defence, ground forces still had an important role to perform, as a memorandum by the Standing Group articulated:

All military experience through the ages and including the most recent fighting in the world, clearly demonstrates that forces are required on the surface of the

[59] TNA, DEFE 7/963, MISC/M(55)69, Long Term Defence Programmes, 12 July 1955.
[60] TNA, CAB 134/1315, JIC(56)21(Final), Likelihood of Global War and Warning of Attack, report by the Joint Intelligence Committee, 1 May 1956.
[61] TNA, CAB 134/1315, PR(56)3, Policy Review, The Future of the United Kingdom in World Affairs, 1 June 1956.
[62] TNA, CAB 134/1315, PR(56)8, Policy Review, 19 July 1956.    [63] Ibid.
[64] Cmnd. 124, *Defence: Outline of Future Policy* (London: HMSO, 1957), pp. 4, 7.

land and the surface of the seas to prevent the overrunning of these areas by aggressors who are equipped with land and sea forces.[65]

A conventional shield of ground forces was therefore a basic necessity to prevent the Soviet Union from achieving a *fait accompli* in Central Europe. The size of such forces and the length of time it would be expected to fight were much more difficult to forecast, however, and would become the subject of fierce debate within the Alliance in the years to come. Although NATO planners accepted the logic behind the idea of shield forces performing the role of a nuclear 'trip-wire',[66] they were not regarded, as in the British case, as a mere 'plate-glass' that would shatter at first contact with the enemy. According to NATO's Standing Group Liaison Officer:

> It is not a static shield—it is a defence in time and space. For though it be dented and bent, it must hold until the atomic counteroffensive, which would be launched at the first alarm, has so damaged the invading forces, their avenues of approach, and their reserves of men and materials, that the attack will be brought to a halt. Having stopped the enemy and regained the initiative, the forces of the 'shield', profiting from the damaging blows inflicted by our air counteroffensive, will then eliminate any limited foothold he may have gained within NATO's borders.[67]

This dual role for conventional forces, which were still expected to fight after the initial nuclear onslaught, would be developed further in NATO's new strategic concept, MC 14/2.[68] Although this latest review was initiated by Whitehall in 1956 in an attempt to better align alliance strategy with British preferences, it did not conform to British expectations completely. Indeed, a larger role was emerging for conventional forces in MC 14/2 to allow for a greater range of military options available to commanders in the event of aggression. The need for greater flexibility in responses can be attributed to the growth of Soviet nuclear potential and the tremendous power of thermonuclear weapons, which were becoming available in large numbers. These two developments suggested that decision-makers in both Moscow and Washington would be mutually deterred from embarking on aggression, and that the Soviets might therefore seek methods short of global war to achieve their policy objectives in Europe.[69] Accordingly, MC 14/2 recognized the need for a non-nuclear response to aggression so that NATO could try to limit the

---

[65]   NATO, SGM/912/55, Requirement for Conventional Forces, 22 December 1955.
[66]   NATO, CM(56)121, Defence Planning—The Reappraisal, 22 October 1956.
[67]   NATO, RDC/328/56, Statement on the Need for 'Shield' Forces, 28 July 1956.
[68]   NATO, MC 14/2 (Revised) (Final Decision), Overall Strategic Concept for the Defense of the North Atlantic Treaty Organization Area, 23 May 1957.
[69]   Duffield, *Power Rules*, p. 239.

scope of military action below the nuclear threshold if required.[70] This would require an increase, rather than decrease, in conventional force contributions since the difficulties in reinforcing the Central Front in war-time necessitated a greater reliance on forces-in-being. MC 14/2 did satisfy Britain's desire, however, to see a closer integration of tactical nuclear weapons into the shield force by assigning it the role of generating 'appropriate targets for Allied nuclear weapons, exploiting terrain to create situations which will inflict maximum attrition on the enemy and halting his attack'.[71]

British military chiefs still worried that the new strategic concept did not account sufficiently for the havoc which would be wrought by nuclear bombardment on Soviet war plans,[72] and that too much emphasis was placed on the second phase of fighting, which described 'a period of reorganization, rehabilitation, and the assembly of residual resources to accomplish the remaining necessary military tasks leading to a termination of hostilities'.[73] According to the JPS:

> ...a nuclear war in Europe would result in such devastation that the integrity of the countries of Western Europe, as at present understood, would be meaningless. The only way to maintain their integrity therefore is to ensure that war is prevented by the existence of an effective deterrent and adequate shield force.[74]

This grim reminder of the consequences of a strategic nuclear exchange demonstrates Britain's unwavering faith in the ability of the great deterrent to prevent the outbreak of major war. Lip service was paid, however, to a combat role for land forces after the first nuclear phase of fighting:

> Although we do not deny that such forces, both on land and at sea, as survive the opening phases of nuclear war may attempt to pursue operations with the resources at their disposal, we do not believe that special provision to meet this situation (Phase II) should be made.[75]

Continuing in the tradition of his predecessors, the new Minister of Defence, Harold Watkinson, was adamant that emphasis should be placed on forces designed to deter war in all its forms rather than those configured to conduct military operations after a strategic nuclear exchange,[76] and that it was imperative

---

[70] MC 14/2 (Revised) (Final Decision), p. 11.    [71] Ibid., p. 18.
[72] TNA, DEFE 4/112, COS(58)86, Meeting with SACEUR, 7 October 1958.
[73] MC 14/2 (Revised) (Final Decision), p. 9.
[74] TNA, DEFE 4/122, JP(59)145(Final), Brief for the Western Summit Meeting: Possible Economies in NATO Defence Costs, 13 November 1959.
[75] Ibid.
[76] TNA, DEFE 4/125, JP(60)10(Final), NATO Defence Planning, 15 February 1960.

to influence NATO thinking at an early stage.[77] Watkinson was gripped by the deterrence habit of mind and was convinced that the use of any nuclear weapon would escalate uncontrollably into a strategic nuclear exchange since 'once the decision is taken, the freedom given to SACEUR is absolute and herein lies the danger of escalation'.[78] Furthermore, 'what they [the Soviet Union] get, they will give, and everything will be unleashed'.[79] For these reasons, Watkinson regarded NATO plans to fight a prolonged war for ninety days after a major nuclear discharge 'quite unrealistic' and that bottom priority should be given to requirements for this 'unreal stage of the war'.[80] In short, both the control of the nuclear weapons and the roles assigned to conventional and nuclear forces had to be subordinated to the ends of deterrence since 'we should all be destroyed in a major nuclear exchange and we should certainly be beaten in an all-out conventional war'.[81]

Concepts of victory and defeat in a future war became central to the UK's efforts to reshape NATO strategy during the 1960s. As early as 1958, the JPS had acknowledged that a state of nuclear sufficiency was slowly emerging on both sides of the Iron Curtain, and that this would serve only to validate further the primacy of deterrence in British defence policy.[82] There were now enough nuclear weapons deployed on the Central Front that they could reduce Europe to a 'radio-active wasteland'.[83] The battle then to be fought was one of 'survival'.[84] Furthermore, nuclear parity between the two power blocs meant that, for the first time, the Continental United States would be exposed to Soviet attack by ICBMs and short-range SLBMs. The conclusion drawn by the JPS in 1960 was that this new vulnerability actually strengthened the framework of strategic nuclear deterrence since 'as both sides face the possibility of nuclear devastation, a state of mutual deterrence has come about'.[85] This consideration served only to validate Whitehall's 'deterrence habit of mind' since the threat of mutual nuclear annihilation made the requirement to prevent war even more

---

[77]  TNA, DEFE 13/425, MO/13/1/16, Watkinson to Prime Minister, 5 October 1960.

[78]  TNA, DEFE 13/425, E20A, NATO Policy in Europe, 5 October 1960.

[79]  Ibid.        [80]  Ibid.        [81]  Ibid.

[82]  TNA, DEFE 4/104, JP(57)151(Final), The Effect of Nuclear Sufficiency, 27 January 1958. See the deliberations of the Chiefs of Staff on this issue in TNA, DEFE 4/104, COS(58)16, Nuclear Sufficiency, 18 February 1958 and TNA, DEFE 4/111, COS(58)77, Nuclear Sufficiency, 3 September 1958.

[83]  TNA, DEFE 11/221, 723/148, Annex to NATO Strategy and the Role of NATO Forces, 3 April 1962.

[84]  TNA, DEFE 4/137, JP(61)68(Final), NATO Strategy—Brief for Sir George Mills, 7 July 1961. These views were perceived to have been corroborated by the final report of the Von Karmen Committee which raised doubts about the practicalities of fighting a sustained conventional/tactical nuclear war in Europe and the fallacy of planning to mount military operations after the initial strategic exchange. See the Chiefs of Staff assessment of the report in TNA, DEFE 4/143, JP(61)163(Final), NATO Strategy—Final Report of the Von Karmen Committee, 15 February 1962.

[85]  TNA, DEFE 4/129, JP(60)63(Final), NATO Strategy, 26 August 1960.

important than it had during the days of a US nuclear monopoly. In this context, the Chiefs of Staff believed that:

> The effects of an all-out nuclear exchange would be so gigantic that the outcome of battles in Europe or the Atlantic would be insignificant by comparison; the time is coming when an all-out exchange would be likely to mean the end of life forms as they exist to-day. In consequence it is folly to spend on preparations for 'winning' an all-out war resources that could be spent on preventing it.[86]

Therefore, the idea of 'winning' a nuclear war in which thousands of megatons of nuclear armament were exploded on each side was at odds with a pure-deterrence strategy, particularly with regards to the utility of conventional ground forces who would be 'engulfed in this destruction'.[87] Indeed, the Chiefs of Staff concluded that SACEUR's plan to seek a meaningful military victory in such conditions was 'pure fantasy', since after a strategic nuclear exchange had taken place, 'what happens on the battlefields of Europe is irrelevant'.[88] Although the irrelevancy of maintaining major combat operations after H-hour featured prominently in UK official discourse during this time, policy-makers possessed enough insight to realize that to air such views openly in the forums of NATO would serve only to undermine the morale of the civilian populations and armed forces of the Alliance. It was accepted that discussing these issues with Allies would be difficult but that 'we shall only make matters worse if we go on concealing our real thinking ... since our alliances matter far more than any military impact we can have alone'.[89] Indeed, this logic was turned inwards by a suggestion from the Chiefs of Staff that:

> ... we cannot admit, even to ourselves, that we would not fight on after a nuclear exchange, nor that we should not attempt to defend as much as possible of the territory of our continental allies. In order to make our determination clear, both to friend and foe, we must organise, equip, train and supply our forces with these evident intentions in view. This is the premium which we have to pay to ensure that we achieve our primary objective, namely the prevention of war.[90]

Although accepting a need to display, at least at a superficial level, the intent to continue military operations on a battlefield that was quickly becoming in British minds like something lifted from a science fiction film, military leaders were also

---

[86]  TNA, DEFE 13/425, 13/1/16, The Reform of NATO Strategy: Memorandum for the Minister's Consideration, 31 August 1960.
[87]  TNA, DEFE 4/129, COS(60)55, NATO Strategy, 13 September 1960.
[88]  TNA, DEFE 13/425, COS/1200, Notes on United Kingdom Strategy, 13 September 1960.
[89]  Ibid.
[90]  TNA, DEFE 13/425, Annex to COS(60)256, NATO Strategy, 14 September 1960.

reluctant to accept that any length of conventional fighting could serve a useful strategic purpose. Although the Americans claimed that they had no practical thought of containing a Soviet attack indefinitely with conventional forces alone,[91] this was still anathema to the Chiefs of Staff who believed that any attempts to prolong the conventional battle in Europe beyond that required for political leaders to decide whether to authorize nuclear release would undermine the deterrent by implying that NATO was reluctant to cross the nuclear threshold to protect its vital interests.[92] They considered that the US assessment on the duration of conventional operations, which had been confirmed as between two and three weeks by the Secretary of State Dean Acheson in 1961,[93] did not appear to take into account the considerable pressure that would be exerted by the use of air forces in support of land operations to extend and escalate the scale of conflict. The fear was that the operational doctrines of the tactical air forces on both sides were such that deep interdiction campaigns against opposing air bases and associated installations would be necessary to achieve military effect, and that this would lead inevitably to a strategic nuclear exchange.[94]

The personal view of the UK military representative to NATO, General Sir Michael West, was that the UK ought to seek a change to SACEUR's mission to exclude any suggestion of defeating the Soviets in general war and that it should be confined to opposing any level of aggression from the very start with all the forces available—a key pillar of the pure-deterrence strategy. In his view, the reason was clear:

> General war is now in effect out of SACEUR's competence. It will be run from US and USSR and will result in the destruction of the northern hemisphere, including all the fighting forces in Europe.[95]

These views were aired forcefully at the 33rd meeting of the NATO Military Committee in Chiefs of Staff session in October 1964 by the Chief of the Defence Staff, Lord Mountbatten, who urged his French and German counterparts to reject the American concept of fighting a prolonged conventional battle in favour of a strategy which emphasized the immediate use of all available weapons in the event

[91] TNA, DEFE 11/221, Annex to COS 531/25/4/62, Washington to Foreign Office, 19 April 1962.
[92] TNA, DEFE 4/139, JP(61)83(Final), Briefs for Anglo/French Staff Talks, 15 September 1961. This was also a view shared by the German military authorities. See, for example, TNA, DEFE 13/721, 13/1/16, Assistant Chief of the Defence Staff to Minister of Defence, 6 November 1962.
[93] TNA, DEFE 4/135, JP(61)46(Final), Mr Acheson's Concept of Conventional Operations, 21 April 1961. See also TNA, DEFE 4/135, COS(61)27, Mr Acheson's Concept of Conventional Operations—United Kingdom Military Implications, 25 April 1961.
[94] TNA, DEFE 11/221, Annex to COS(62)119, NATO Strategy: Conventional Forces and MRBM's, 27 April 1962. See, in addition, agreement by the Deputy Chief of the Air Staff on this issue in TNA, DEFE 4/207, COS(66)58, NATO Strategy, 25 October 1966.
[95] TNA, DEFE 11/365, Annex to COS 2401/1/7/64, NATO Long Term Planning, 1 July 1964.

of a determined Soviet attack.[96] Mountbatten appeared satisfied that NATO's major commanders had been sufficiently convinced of the merits of the British pure-deterrence strategy, which he believed represented the first occasion on which the Committee had manifestly asserted its authority over the Supreme Commander in an 'acknowledged trial of strength which SACEUR clearly lost'.[97]

Mountbatten also made clear in unambiguous terms British thinking on the fallacy of planning to fight and prevail in a conventional/nuclear war during his valedictory address to SHAPE a year later. His starting point was that the destruction wrought by a strategic nuclear exchange would be such that civilization in the Northern Hemisphere would cease to exist, thus rendering the air/land battle irrelevant. For these reasons, he lamented the continued pressure by the United States to generate forces to conduct military operations after the strategic exchange, with all its terrifying implications. That this thought remained in anyone's mind, quipped Mountbatten, 'must surely frighten us', not least because:

> No sane person starts a war unless they think they will be in a better position at the end of it than at the beginning. The primary deterrent to all-out war is the certain knowledge that both sides would, in fact, be utterly destroyed in the process. What then would be the object in the few survivors rushing around shooting up everybody in sight, well knowing that their actions could achieve absolutely no rational military or political aim?[98]

The grim plight of the survivors appeared to be confirmed in a study by the major NATO military commanders, conducted in the wake of Mountbatten's address, which suggested that NORTHAG and CENTAG would only be able to contain a determined Soviet attack from between one and three days.[99] The conclusions confirmed to British military planners that a non-nuclear defence against a substantial Soviet conventional attack would not be possible without increasing considerably the size of NATO shield forces, which was politically and economically unviable for Britain and its European allies. For these reasons, staff officers due to attend HOSTAGE 66, a major Allied Forces Central Europe (AFCENT) command post exercise examining the operational difficulties of conducting military operations after a strategic nuclear exchange, were instructed that while it was deemed unpolitical to boycott the exercise, they should not encourage the assumptions that underpinned it.[100] Likewise, a briefing paper issued to

---

[96] TNA, DEFE 4/178, COS 3539/17/12/64, Report by the Chief of the Defence Staff on 33rd Meeting of the NATO Military Committee in Chiefs of Staff Session, 17 December 1964.

[97] Ibid.

[98] TNA, DEFE 4/186, COS 1918/21/6/65, SHAPEX 65—Valedictory Address by Chief of the Defence Staff, 21 June 1965.

[99] TNA, DEFE 4/186, DP 30/65(Final), SACEUR's Current Conventional Capability Appraisal (The Mountbatten Exercise), 26 May 1965.

[100] TNA, DEFE 4/196, COS 1266/2/3/66, Exercise HOSTAGE 66, 2 March 1966.

government ministers before the first Tripartite Talks in Bonn stated that UK war-games had demonstrated that a Soviet attack would advance much more rapidly than was implied in the Mountbatten Exercise, reaching the River Weser within twenty-four hours.[101] To achieve maximum effect, a decision to use tactical nuclear weapons would have to be taken within this time. What would happen next, the paper admitted, was a matter of 'speculation'.[102] If the first use of nuclear weapons did not convince the Soviets to withdraw, then it was assumed that they would reply in kind with their own tactical nuclear weapons:

> In this event there would be likely to be a large-scale tactical nuclear exchange...
> possibly running into hundreds—in order to inflict serious military casualties.
> Once such an exchange had started it would be very difficult to control and
> thus there would be a very high probability of escalation to a strategic nuclear
> exchange.[103]

The paper was particularly forthright in describing the consequences of the detonation of several hundreds of nuclear weapons along the Central Front:

> The devastation inflicted in the area of operations within the matter of a few days,
> or even hours, would be comparable to that caused over much wider areas during
> World War II by years of carefully planned strategic bombing, with the add-
> itional hazards of radiation and other side effects. Leaving aside the incalculable
> effects on morale, it is doubtful whether it would be physically possible for large-
> scale organised military operations to continue in such circumstances. In any
> case, if the principal centres of population and government on both sides of the
> Iron Curtain had by this time been destroyed in a strategic nuclear exchange, any
> residual military operations in Central Europe would be of very minor import-
> ance. With upwards of 100 million casualties in the USA and Western Europe
> only, the remaining inhabitants would be fully engaged in a grim struggle for
> survival and would be indifferent to the outcome of any sporadic military
> operations which might continue for a short time.[104]

For these reasons, there could be no question of a long period of 'broken-backed' warfare, and the UK delegation was duly instructed to impress upon its Allies that this served only to reinforce the national view that it was pointless to make preparations to mount 'impossible' military operations if tactical nuclear weapons

---

[101] In September 1966, West Germany, the United Kingdom, and the United States agreed to hold tripartite talks on all aspects of NATO's force posture. See TNA, DEFE 4/209, DP 74/66(Final), Briefs for the 37th Meeting of the Military Committee in Chiefs of Staff Session, 29 November 1966.
[102] TNA, DEFE 4/207, COS 2085/28/10/66, Tripartite Talks—Nature and Duration of War in Europe, 28 October 1966.
[103] Ibid.      [104] Ibid.

did not serve their purpose of disabusing the Soviets of their apparent miscalculation.[105]

## Political and Military Utility of Tactical Nuclear Weapons

The preference for a pure-deterrence strategy permeated all British thinking during the development and implementation of NATO's new strategic concept, which progressed rapidly in the wake of France's withdrawal from the Alliance's integrated military structure in March 1966. Political approval for a new strategy came a year later when NATO's Defence Planning Committee issued its guidance to the military authorities of the Alliance, which stated that:

> The overall strategic concept for NATO should be revised to allow NATO a greater flexibility and to provide for the employment as appropriate of one or more of direct defence, deliberate escalation, and general nuclear response, thus confronting the enemy with a credible threat of escalation in response to any type of aggression below the level of a major nuclear attack.[106]

The key feature of the new strategic concept that was evolving in 1967 was not just flexibility in response, which had long been acknowledged as desirable by most members, but the idea of escalation. In describing the role of tactical nuclear weapons within this framework, the document was clear that:

> Their primary purposes are to add to the deterrence of conventional attacks of any magnitude, and counter them if necessary, by confronting the enemy with the prospect of consequent escalation of the conflict; and to deter, and if necessary respond to, the use of tactical nuclear weapons by posing the threat of escalation to all-out nuclear war.[107]

As a piece of strategic direction, one would have to question the utility of such ambiguous political guidelines. The message being sent to NATO commanders, whose conventional and tactical nuclear forces were tasked with managing the precarious process of 'deliberate escalation', was the requirement for valid military plans that could apply nuclear firepower in order to deter or counter both conventional and nuclear attacks at any scale whilst still retaining the ability to be applied discriminately in order to transmit a political signal. In spite of the operational and doctrinal complexities that might arise from such ambiguous

---

[105] TNA, DEFE 4/207, COS 2039/17/10/66, Tripartite Talks, 17 October 1966.
[106] NATO, DPC/D(67)23, Decisions of Defence Planning Committee in Ministerial Session, 11 May 1967.
[107] Ibid.

strategic direction, staff officers in the British Defence Planning Staff (DPS)[108] raised no concerns during the collaborative consultation and drafting period, and instead welcomed the new developments as a 'new and realistic approach'[109] which was 'very much in accord with the United Kingdom's views on the possible nature and duration of a future war and on the deterrent concept which the alliance should follow'.[110]

On 16 September 1967, the Military Committee approved the new strategic concept, MC 14/3, which developed further the themes of escalation in officially committing the Alliance to a strategy of flexible response. If deterrence failed, the strategy paper outlined three types of possible responses available to NATO: direct defence, deliberate escalation, and general nuclear response. The first and last options are self-explanatory, and referred respectively to defeating conventional aggression on the level at which the attacker had chosen to fight, and massive nuclear strikes across the full spectrum of possible military and urban-industrial targets. It was the conceptually difficult intermediate course of action, however, which received the greatest attention in the paper, exposing the intellectual challenges that had plagued military thought since the inception of so-called tactical nuclear weapons. According to the new strategic concept:

Deliberate escalation seeks to *defend* aggression by *deliberately raising* but where possible *controlling*, the scope and intensity of combat, making the cost and the risk disproportionate to the aggressor's objectives and the threat of nuclear response progressively more imminent. It does not solely depend on the ability to *defeat* the enemy's aggression as such; rather, it *weakens his will* to continue the conflict. Depending on the level at which the aggression starts, the time needed for each escalatory action and reaction and the rate of success, escalatory steps might be selected from among the following examples provided they have not previously been used as part of a direct defensive system:

1. broadening or intensifying a non-nuclear engagement, possibly by opening another front or initiating action at sea in response to low intensity aggression;

2. use of nuclear defence and denial weapons;

3. demonstrative use of nuclear weapons;

4. selective nuclear strikes on interdiction targets;

5. selective nuclear strikes against other suitable military targets.[111]

---

[108] The DPS was the successor organization to the JPS, which was renamed in 1964 with the establishment of a unified Ministry of Defence.

[109] TNA, DEFE 4/214, DP 17/67(Final), Proposed Strategic Concept for the North Atlantic Treaty Organization, 8 March 1967.

[110] TNA, DEFE 4/214, DP 18/67(Final), Appreciation of the Military Situation as It Will Affect NATO Through 1975, 8 March 1967.

[111] NATO, MC 14/3 (Final), Overall Strategic Concept for the Defense of the North Atlantic Treaty Organization Area, 16 January 1968, p. 11 [emphasis added].

The language employed in this strategic concept exposes the confusing and often paradoxical nature of the concepts that had evolved to govern the employment of tactical nuclear weapons. It followed that forces equipped with tactical nuclear weapons at once had to *defend* against aggression, but at the same time *raise* and *control* escalation, with the view to *defeating* or *weakening the will* of the enemy. It now appeared that the traditional idea of military victory, as it was understood personally by senior NATO commanders just two decades earlier, was an anachronism. The companion document laying out the military requirements to implement the new strategic concept, MC 48/3, which was issued by the Military Committee on 8 December 1968, reflected British thinking on the fallacy of planning for a prolonged conventional battle in that it acquiesced to the known unknowns of nuclear war, stating that the 'nature and duration of military operations cannot be precisely forecast' and that once nuclear weapons have been introduced, 'the conflict may be very difficult to control'.[112]

If enhancing political cohesion is a primary function of alliances, then this was a case in point—by outlining in as ambiguous terms as possible its strategic guid-ance, MC 14/3 invited different interpretations of the concept, and NATO mem-bers happily obliged in light of their own strategic preferences. The differences of opinion centred upon the recurring question of how long the conventional shield should be able to hold a Soviet attack before the decision to authorize nuclear release was made.[113] For their part, British planners had always stressed the political rather than military functions of tactical nuclear weapons in relation to a limited Soviet attack which was too large for the shield forces to contain with conventional weapons alone. As early as 1960, the Ministry of Defence had described such nuclear use as a 'discriminate nuclear reaction', which was designed to convey to the Soviet Union that it could not gain any military advantage from the use of conventional force whilst at the same time minimizing the risks of escalation.[114] It had two objectives:

a. to demonstrate NATO's will to resist by being evidently prepared to use all the necessary force at its disposal;

b. to confront the enemy with the imminent choice between escalation and withdrawal.[115]

Thus, the theory of discriminate reaction assigned political rather than military utility to tactical nuclear weapons, whose use would signal to an aggressor that the strategic stakes for continuing an attack had been raised. By advocating the

---

[112] NATO, MC 48/3 (Final), Measures to Implement the Strategic Concept for the Defence of the NATO Area, 8 December 1969, p. 4.
[113] TNA, DEFE 4/236, DP 4/69(Revised Final), Interpretations of NATO Strategy, 10 March 1969.
[114] DEFE 13/425, 13/1/16.      [115] DEFE 11/221, 723/148.

selective use of nuclear weapons in a political signalling role, the concept of discriminate nuclear reaction bore an uncanny resemblance to the once ridiculed strategy of graduated deterrence which had been proposed by Anthony Buzzard just a few years earlier and rejected by the policy-making elite. However, the Ministry of Defence was reluctant to acknowledge any similarities to the Buzzard thesis, arguing that 'this proposal is not the same as the idea...that the West should announce in peacetime the way in which they would use first conventional and then nuclear weapons'.[116] What both concepts had in common was the acknowledgement that the intended meaning of NATO nuclear use should be understood clearly by the Soviet leadership.[117] This would make the requirement for robust command and control arrangements even more important.[118]

British strategists were therefore becoming increasingly aware of the requirement to understand Soviet intentions as a conceptual basis for NATO planning, in contrast to their American counterparts who were accused of being interested only in Soviet capabilities.[119] As Michael Quinlan reflected on his long career as a Civil Servant within the British nuclear state, escalation is neither a physical process like a chemical chain-reaction nor a sequence of random events, but is a matter of 'interactive choices by people' which have to be considered in 'human and political terms, not just a matter of military or technical mechanics'.[120] Within this light, UK planners viewed the Communist leadership as rational actors who understood clearly the horrifying consequences of general nuclear war as well as any Western leader. This perceived commonality of interests between British and Soviet leaders would be a hallmark of British thinking about nuclear deterrence,[121] and one that was reflected in the Mottershead Report of 1961, which concluded that NATO should seek to avoid forms of nuclear use which might lead to escalation, such as the targeting of Soviet cities.[122]

For British planners, the only path that would lead to a strategic nuclear exchange would be Soviet miscalculation. As the erstwhile Chief of the General

---

[116] Ibid.

[117] TNA, DEFE 13/425, MM/COS(60)11, NATO Strategy, 13 September 1960. Even as late as 1966, the Chiefs of Staff still expressed concerns about the 'misleading' definition of tactical nuclear weapons in this context. See TNA, DEFE 4/198, COS(66)17, Role of Tactical Nuclear Weapons in NATO, 29 March 1966.

[118] An examination of this issue can be found in TNA, DEFE 4/137, JP(61)84(Final), Military Aspects of the Control of Nuclear Weapons in NATO, 17 July 1961.

[119] TNA, DEFE 11/221, 10/B/5, NATO Strategy: Conventional Forces and MRBMs, Brief for the Minister of Defence, April 1962.

[120] Michael Quinlan, *Thinking about Nuclear Weapons: Principles, Problems, Prospects* (Oxford: Oxford University Press, 2009), p. 63.

[121] Beatrice Heuser, *Nuclear Mentalities? Strategies and Beliefs in Britain, France and the FRG* (Basingstoke: Macmillan, 1998), pp. 22–5.

[122] TNA, DEFE 4/135, JP(61)Note 11, NATO Strategy and Nuclear Weapons—Military Implications of the Mottershead Report, 28 April 1961.

Staff (CGS)[123] and now CDS, Field Marshal Sir Richard Hull, informed NATO's Military Committee, when the UK spoke of miscalculation, they did not mean war arising from mistake, but by a deliberate attack based on a miscalculation of NATO's willingness to fight.[124] Therefore, the only way to demonstrate a willingness to resist was to:

> Use nuclear weapons, of small yield and in very small numbers, as soon as the Russian intention to persist in the attack becomes apparent, in order to disabuse them of their miscalculation before they become too deeply committed.[125]

The accepted function of tactical nuclear weapons now appeared to be psychological in nature as the conceptual link between the shield forces and the strategic nuclear deterrent. The tactical use of nuclear weapons would represent a demonstration of intent to escalate the conflict and, therefore, should only be available in sufficient numbers for small-scale discriminate use, or for early support for ground forces. In this context, the psychological impact of nuclear weapon use was assumed to be 'out of all proportion' to the actual military damage to the Soviet Union, and so fewer numbers could be tolerated.[126]

That the function of tactical nuclear weapons was beginning to be seen increasingly as political and psychological rather than military reflected British fears about uncontrollable escalation. As later chapters will demonstrate, studies were beginning to show that in order to gain any military advantage from the use of tactical nuclear weapons, commanders would have to employ hundreds on each corps front in addition to longer-range high-yield weapons against interdiction targets deep in the enemy rear.[127] This destruction would be compounded, according to the US Secretary of Defense Robert McNamara, by the fact that the Soviet Union would most likely reply in kind to any NATO use of nuclear weapons.[128] The consequences of such an exchange would be the certain destruction of the country on whose soil the battle was fought. Although it was difficult to predict with any accuracy the exact length of time that a tactical nuclear war

---

[123] In 1964, the 'Imperial' was removed from the title of Chief of the Imperial General Staff, after which the office was known simply as Chief of the General Staff. Hull was therefore the last Chief of the Imperial General Staff and the first Chief of the General Staff.

[124] TNA, DEFE 4/210, Appendix 2 to Annex C to COS 2239/15/12/66, Statement by Field Marshal Sir Richard Hull to 37th MC/CS, 13 December 1966.

[125] DEFE 11/221, 10/B/5.

[126] TNA, DEFE 4/151, JP(62)110(Final), The British View of Strategy for the Defence of Central Europe, 17 January 1963.

[127] TNA, DEFE 4/153, JP 25/63(Final), Force Requirements to Meet the British View of Strategy for Central Europe, 26 March 1963.

[128] TNA, DEFE 4/153, COS(63)23, Force Requirements to Meet the British View of Strategy for Central Europe, 2 April 1963. The Chiefs of Staff did worry, however, that there was a school of thought amongst American officials that a prolonged conventional phase of fighting could indeed be contained without crossing the threshold to the use of strategic nuclear weapons. See TNA, DEFE 4/149, COS(62) 71, Escalation, 13 November 1962.

would rage in Central Europe, a week was considered sensible for both the conventional and nuclear phases of the conflict—much less than the thirty days NATO had agreed to be prepared to fight. Consequently, if tactical nuclear weapons were to have a place in British strategy for the defence of the Central Front, restraint would have to be shown while at the same time ensuring that their 'true role is clear'.[129] Only then could tactical nuclear weapon use satisfy the dual criteria in British thinking for both demonstrating NATO's will to resist and compelling Soviet leaders to consider the risks of escalation and call off its aggression.

Compellence would require both the will *and* capability with which to carry out the threat of nuclear attack, and the Chiefs of Staff agreed that tactical nuclear weapons should be available in sufficient numbers to 'implement valid military plans which would prevent the Soviets from achieving their aim'.[130] This meant that NATO should maintain a convincing fighting posture based on a sound military organization, modern equipment, and efficient training for the use of tactical nuclear weapons, and that tactical nuclear support must be available to all sectors of the NATO front.[131] Importantly, the numbers of tactical nuclear weapons should be limited to the numbers required to gain maximum time for taking a political decision on how to manage the extension of the conflict.[132] The new logic on the theory of escalation thus appeared to be that: 'A battle fought with some nuclear weapons is more likely to escalate than one fought with none; a battle using many is more likely to escalate than one fought with a few'.[133] This was a logical, if not a crude and common-sense, approach to conceptualizing the challenges of limiting the scope and scale of a future war where tactical nuclear weapons had been employed first by NATO. Although SHAPE continued to minimize the risks of escalation posed by tactical nuclear weapon use—after all, claimed one SHAPE special study on force planning, military history was replete with examples of conflicts that had not escalated unnecessarily—the UK remained firm in its conviction that the prime function of tactical nuclear weapons was to pose the threat of escalation, and not for the pursuit of military victory on the battlefield.[134] In the event that the Warsaw Pact sought to achieve their policy aims through the use of tactical nuclear weapons from the outset, a possible but unlikely course of action according to British planners, then this might lead quickly to negotiations or, in their default, one side or the other would be forced to choose

[129] TNA, DEFE 25/6, SZ/602/63, NATO Strategy—The UK View, 17 June 1963.
[130] TNA, DEFE 4/168, DP 33/64(Final), NATO Force Requirements Study, 26 March 1964.
[131] TNA, DEFE 4/208, COS 2101/2/11/66, NATO Strategy, 2 November 1966.
[132] TNA, DEFE 4/208, COS 2162/21/11/66, Tripartite Talks—Report of Working Group II on NATO Capabilities, 21 November 1966.
[133] DEFE 4/208, COS 2101/2/11/66.
[134] TNA, DEFE 4/212, DP 82/66(Final), Examination of the SHAPE Special Study on Defence Planning—1972 Onwards, 2 February 1967.

between initiating the strategic nuclear exchange and defeat.[135] The former decision, as has been shown, was tantamount to catastrophic defeat in British eyes.

There were modest changes, however, in British thinking about the character of future conflict by the late 1960s. The first was an acknowledgement that approval for the early release of tactical nuclear weapons could not be assumed, and therefore that the conventional phase of fighting might be more protracted than previously envisaged.[136] The second was a growing awareness that tactical nuclear weapons might possess a modicum of military utility. The brief for the 14th Anglo-German staff talks revealed this change in thinking in stating a tacit approval of the theory that if and when the decision was taken to use tactical nuclear weapons, the best way to achieve the political object of changing the enemy's mind was to kill a sufficiently large number of his forces and to disrupt his operations to the point of making them difficult to pursue without major new measures or an escalation of the conflict. The paper conceded that the UK believed this more modest interpretation of military effect was 'adequate and realistic'.[137]

This change of emphasis as regards tactical nuclear weapons should not be seen as a complete *volte-face* on an issue about which British planners had for so long sought to change. Indeed, UK and NATO views on strategy were now very close. What remained to be done was to further define and interpret the strategic concept,[138] which was the purpose of a detailed 1968 study by the DPS on the British contribution to NATO in the long term. The paper laid out with greater clarity the changing British view on tactical nuclear weapons. It argued that a purely token use of nuclear weapons not having a significant effect on the course of military operations would be unlikely by itself to persuade the enemy to cease hostilities and would merely invite a reply in kind. British thinking had now evolved to acknowledge that tactical nuclear weapons had a dual function but a single purpose. That purpose remained as it always had in British logic—to deter unwanted actions—but the functions by which this would be achieved were both political and military: political, because the decision to cross the nuclear threshold demonstrated a clear step up the escalation ladder, which might itself achieve the desired effect; and military, because of their actual effect on the conduct of operations.[139]

---

[135] TNA, DEFE 4/223, DP 90/67(Final), The Scale and Nature of Conflict in the Central Region of ACE, 28 November 1967.
[136] TNA, DEFE 4/228, DP 18/68(Final), Briefs for the Fourteenth Anglo/German Staff Talks, 4 June 1968.
[137] Ibid.
[138] For example, in stereotypical British fashion, even the nuanced meaning of individual words contained in MC 14/3 were brought into question, particularly 'sufficient' in the context of how long shield forces should be expected to hold a Soviet advance. See TNA, DEFE 4/232, DP Note 225/68, The NATO and European Situation, 24 October 1968 and TNA, DEFE 4/237, DP 6/69(Final), Briefs for the Eighth Anglo/Italian Staff Talks, 4 March 1969.
[139] TNA, DEFE 4/229, DP 7/68(Final), The British Contribution to NATO in the Long Term, 5 June 1968.

The document also revealed for the first time how British defence planners conceived the specific rungs of the escalation ladder. The starting point was that the process of escalation, i.e. a possible chain of events which could credibly result in a strategic nuclear exchange, was fundamental to deterrence. These steps were imagined as deliberate acts taken to demonstrate a readiness to take risks in the defence of vital interests, and to present to an enemy the necessity of taking greater risks. The DPS likened this logic to 'raising the stakes in a game of poker'.[140] The traditional British fear that the use of any nuclear weapon would result in uncontrolled escalation to a strategic nuclear exchange appeared to be diminished, however, with the conclusion that:

> On balance it seems credible that the steps in escalation could be controlled. Nevertheless the possibility of escalation getting out of control through misunderstanding exists, and since it is conceivable and must appear so to both sides it plays a significant part in deterrence. Furthermore response under pressure may not always be in accordance with a cool assessment of the consequences, and might even be irrational; these possibilities also play a part in deterrence.[141]

British views on the political functions of tactical nuclear weapons, in both escalatory and demonstrative roles, remained a feature of NATO strategy well into the 1980s. Although the adoption of flexible response had led to greater agreement on the function of conventional forces, there still remained ambiguity surrounding tactical nuclear weapons, with no clear guidance as to the role of, and objectives for, tactical nuclear forces within the strategic concept.[142] British views about these complex issues were advanced most forcefully by the Minister of Defence, Denis Healey, who had worked closely with NATO's Nuclear Planning Group (NPG) since its activation in 1966. The NPG was the official forum for discussing the unresolved tensions in NATO strategy of when, how, where, and for what purpose nuclear weapons would be used. The most significant and enduring study undertaken by the NPG was one establishing guidelines for the initial use of nuclear weapons, for which the UK and the Federal Republic of Germany (FRG) took the lead.[143]

The Anglo-German effort resulted in an influential paper known colloquially as the Healey-Schroeder paper, after the two countries' defence ministers, and bore the mark of the British pure-deterrence strategy. The paper emphasized early, but limited, use of tactical nuclear weapons to demonstrate NATO's resolve to resist aggression and to signal the dangers of escalation. In line with British thinking, the objective was not to erode Soviet military capabilities, but to reinforce deterrence.

---

[140] Ibid.      [141] Ibid.
[142] Daalder, *The Nature and Practice of Flexible Response*, pp. 69–70.
[143] Ibid., pp. 72–3.

As Healey argued, the 'purpose of nuclear weapons as we see them is to restore the credibility of the overall deterrent in a situation in which a large-scale conventional attack shows that the credibility has disappeared'.[144] After integration of numerous amendments, the Healey-Schroeder paper was adopted by the NPG in November 1969 as 'Provisional Political Guidelines for the Initial Defensive Tactical Use of Nuclear Weapons by NATO' (PPGs), which was approved by defence ministers in 1970. Reflecting British thinking, the PPGs concluded that:

> Given that any initial use of nuclear weapons would result in a qualitative change in the nature of warfare, such use by NATO should have a fundamentally political purpose. It should be designed to confront the enemy with the prospect of the risks of escalation consequent on a continuation of the conflict, with the aim of making him halt his attack and withdraw, thereby restoring the credibility of the deterrent.[145]

The PPGs went on to set out a number of ways in which NATO might introduce nuclear weapons into a conflict which included the demonstrative use of a single weapon not aimed at a military target; the use of atomic demolition weapons (ADMs); the use of nuclear weapons in an air defence role; battlefield use; use in an extended geographical area; and maritime use. The most appropriate term of initial use would vary according to the situation but, resembling the basic tenets of the Mottershead Report, it was generally regarded not to involve targets in the Soviet Union itself.[146]

In spite of the hard work conducted by the NPG, the NATO Allies never could reach a consensus on the military and political functions of tactical nuclear weapons.[147] The new CDS, Admiral Sir Peter Hill-Norton, informed the UK military representative to NATO in 1972 that these differences could only be resolved by a conscious process of education aimed at setting the 'tactical nuclear dilemma' in a more realistic context. The realistic context Hill-Norton had in mind was that of the concept of deterrence itself, arguing that divergent views had to be united in the proposition that:

> 'tactical use'—incidentally, like strategic use—is almost too beastly to contemplate but that we're all in business to be strong enough to ensure we don't have to. So don't lets frighten ourselves into fits and the Alliance into disarray by dwelling

---

[144] Charles Douglas-Holme, 'Healey Rebuts Nuclear War Criticism', *The Times*, 24 February 1970.
[145] Cited in Daalder, *The Nature and Practice of Flexible Response*, p. 77.
[146] TNA, PREM 16/1977, PM/78/73, Nuclear Weapons Policy, 31 July 1978.
[147] See, for example, the different national perspectives in TNA, DEFE 11/471, ACDS(Pol)/72/156, Nuclear Planning Group Meeting in Copenhagen, 1972.

on the detail of 'follow-on use' without the essentially deterrent nature of the exercise being uppermost at all times in the mind.[148]

The two decades following the adoption of flexible response saw no meaningful changes to NATO's strategic concept and the roles it assigned to conventional and tactical nuclear forces. Force levels remained stable, with the number of regular combat units rising slightly from approximately twenty-six divisions in 1969 to twenty-eight divisions in 1989.[149] The only challenge to NATO's strategic concept came from proponents of a no nuclear first-use doctrine, although this clarion call fell on deaf ears.[150] The formalization of strategic nuclear parity between the superpowers in the middle 1970s stabilized the balance of terror in Europe under the yoke of mutually assured destruction. At the same time, the effectiveness of conventional forces had steadily increased on both sides of the Iron Curtain as new technology and the introduction of more capable weapon systems enhanced the capacity for both attack and defence.

It was uncertain whether NATO or the Warsaw Pact would benefit the most from the new technology which was under development, which included improvements to the accuracy of delivery vehicles, communication systems, surveillance and target acquisition systems, and warhead design. Nor was it clear whether the new hardware would bring about fundamental change to NATO's assumptions about the utility of tactical nuclear weapons in defeating a Soviet attack. Hitherto, studies conducted by the NPG on the follow-on use of nuclear weapons (that is, a second nuclear use should the initial demonstrative use of nuclear weapons not have the desired effect) had indicated that if nuclear weapons were to be used in the numbers called for to achieve significant military effect, then this would result in unacceptable numbers of civilian casualties and collateral damage to the surrounding area. Furthermore, if the Warsaw Pact returned NATO's nuclear fire on a like-for-like basis, then military casualties on both sides would be high and NATO, with its assumed local conventional inferiority and lack of readily available reserves, would most likely be the first to capitulate. This led to the conclusion endorsed by defence ministers that NATO's nuclear weapons could not be counted on to redress the balance of conventional forces.[151]

As early as 1970, the Secretary General of NATO, Manlio Brosio, suggested that the development of smaller and cleaner nuclear weapons, coupled with more accurate delivery vehicles, could lead to a situation in which NATO political

---

[148] TNA, DEFE 11/471, 3095/5, CDS to General Sir Victor Fitzgeorge-Balfour, 18 September 1972.

[149] Duffield, *Power Rules*, p. 194.

[150] For an overview of the debate see John J. Mearsheimer, 'Nuclear Weapons and Deterrence in Europe', *International Security*, Vol. 9, No. 3 (Winter 1984–5), pp. 19–46.

[151] TNA, FO 41/1653, D/Studies/7/8/7, NPG—New Technology Study: Report by the Military Implications Team, 17 July 1975.

leaders could more easily authorize their military commanders to use nuclear weapons to repel a Warsaw Pact invasion. It was hoped that the expected decrease in collateral damage might lead to a more uninhibited use of tactical nuclear weapons on the battlefield, thereby helping armies in the field to redress any deficiencies in their conventional force posture.[152] Only five years later, improvements in weapons technology had provided, to some extent, the capabilities envisaged by Brosio.

The Americans, in particular, appeared to have 'rediscovered' tactical nuclear weapons with these developments, and there were a number of enthusiasts who saw immense possibilities in marrying the new guidance technology with even smaller warheads—so-called 'mini-nukes'.[153] Officials in Washington had often viewed with suspicion the negative conclusions of the NPG's work on the military utility of tactical nuclear weapons, which focused unwanted attention on the collateral damage caused by nuclear strikes against military targets, and who now saw an opportunity to correct what they had regarded as an injustice. This was of great concern to the Germans, who were wary of any moves which might be seen as blurring the distinction between conventional and nuclear warfare or suggesting that tactical nuclear weapons could provide the means to compensate for conventional inferiority.[154] Fears were that the ready access to such weapons would lower the nuclear threshold and encourage the possibility of a nuclear war between NATO and the Warsaw Pact 'fought to a finish in the cockpit of Europe'.[155] For their part, American representatives emphasized that new developments in nuclear weaponry were little more than the natural process of technological evolution, and that they would not be deployed with US forces in Europe without consultation with the other NATO members.[156]

Hopes for a new silver bullet which would solve NATO's defensive dilemmas for the 1970s and 1980s did not appear forthcoming, however. A report by the NPG's New Technology Study Military Implications Team concluded that although the greater accuracy of new technology systems would allow commanders to make the sort of strikes called for in the NPG studies with considerably reduced collateral damage, there was no evidence to suggest that their advent would contradict the general conclusion that nuclear weapons could not compensate for conventional weakness.[157] However, with an increase in the military effectiveness of ground forces, the land battle would be greatly intensified, shortening the time for conventional defence. The German delegation assumed that this would serve to reduce the 'time not later than', which was the window within

[152] TNA, FO 41/1434, D/Studies/7/8/6, Effect of Precision Guidance on Yields Needed in Nuclear Strikes, n.d. [c. 1974].

[153] TNA, FO 41/1434, DS12/15/45, NPG—New Technology Study, 18 September 1974.

[154] TNA, FO 41/1653, D/DS12/15/45, NPG New Technology Study—Military Implications Team, 28 August 1975.

[155] D/Studies/7/8/6.    [156] Ibid.    [157] D/Studies/7/8/7.

which political leaders would have to make the difficult decision whether to initiate the first use of nuclear weapons.[158]

British officials believed that certain aspects of the PPGs might need to be revised in light of the report. At the time when the PPGs were drafted, it was a self-evident proposition that the initial use of nuclear weapons by NATO would represent a basic qualitative change in warfare constituting a distinct and highly significant step up the escalation ladder. The prospect of using smaller and 'cleaner' nuclear weapons, which could destroy their target without causing undue collateral damage, raised concerns that such action would not communicate effectively to the Soviet Union that the stakes had been raised. In short, the British worried that the credibility of the use of nuclear weapons as a political signal would be undermined if decision-makers in the Kremlin did not understand the severity of the message that lay behind NATO's initial use. This suggested that the Alliance might, in certain circumstances, choose to employ the larger warheads of traditional tactical nuclear weapons in order to demonstrate a greater degree of political resolve.[159] The basic dilemma inherent within the concept of employing nuclear weapons in a demonstrative role, that of reconciling the use of nuclear weapons for primarily psychological purposes with the requirement that initial use should also have some military effect, was not resolved with the arrival of new technology.

British officials did acknowledge, however, that mini-nukes might provide an additional rung at the bottom of the escalation ladder linking conventional forces and traditional tactical nuclear weapons. By this time, the idea of creating a 'seamless robe' of nuclear weapons reaching from the immediate battlefield to deep strikes into Soviet territory was beginning to gain traction. The deployment of the SS-20 (Sabre), a highly mobile intermediate-range ballistic missile (IRBM), by the Soviet Union in 1976 brought into sharp focus NATO's aging tactical nuclear weapons. The SS-20 had sufficient range at 4,600km that it could strike any target in Europe, but could not reach the Continental United States. The Alliance did not have comparable long-range theatre nuclear forces (LRTNF) with which to respond to the SS-20, and so Europeans feared that this missing rung on its escalation ladder risked the US de-coupling itself from Europe in the event of a war breaking out in the theatre.[160] This would oblige NATO, according to the US Secretary of Defense Donald Rumsfeld at the 1976 meeting of the NPG, to think of deterrence in terms of a continuum and not fragment their thinking into '"strategic" and "tactical" or "flanks" and "central front"'.[161]

---

[158] TNA, FO 41/1653, X-21-08-3/3307/75, NPG—Technology Study: German Contribution to the Military Implications Team, 5 August 1975.

[159] TNA, FO 41/1653, WDN 24/5, NPG—New Technology: Political Implications, 10 April 1975.

[160] Kristan Stoddart, *Facing Down the Soviet Union: Britain, the USA, NATO and Nuclear Weapons, 1976–1983* (Basingstoke: Palgrave Macmillan, 2014), p. 82.

[161] TNA, DEFE 31/160, DS12/15/3, NPG Meeting: 14 and 15 June 1976, 16 July 1976.

The British supported the idea that NATO required a full spectrum of nuclear capabilities, which was put forward in a letter to the Americans by Sir Michael Quinlan in August 1977. This led to the formation of a US-led study group within NATO, which produced the 'Integrated Decision Document', which in turn formed the basis for the 'dual track' decision of December 1979. The dual track decision was a NATO resolution to modernize its LRTNF alongside assurances to the Soviet Union that this would be reversed if it withdraw its SS-20 missiles east of the Urals.[162] The Chiefs of Staff agreed that modernization of the Alliance's theatre nuclear forces was essential to ensure the credibility of NATO nuclear strategy, but warned that a British contribution should not come at the expense of conventional forces. The Chief of the Defence Staff, Sir Neil Cameron, believed that Britain should acquire a modest new force to replace its aging Vulcan medium bombers, as this would place London as a second centre of decision-making, distinct from Washington, in the event that NATO had to take the difficult decision of whether to initiate the first use of nuclear weapons against Soviet territory. Conversely, the military chiefs argued that Britain should instead offer to base modernized US LRTNF in the UK and channel all available resources into strengthening NATO's conventional forces, thereby 'raising the initial nuclear threshold rather than being used to fill a theoretical gap which probably has no counterpart in Soviet nuclear philosophy'.[163]

Although there were logical military justifications for the modernization of NATO's LRTNF, Britain's Foreign Secretary, David Owen, remained sceptical, arguing that it was simply irrational for NATO or the Warsaw Pact to plan for theatre nuclear war. In a passionate letter sent to Prime Minister James Callaghan in July 1978, Owen drew attention to what he regarded as the 'unreality' of some of NATO's current assumptions about the way in which nuclear weapons might be used. He did not believe, for example, 'that responsible political leaders in the West would ever contemplate using nuclear weapons for limited battlefield pur-poses'. For Owen, the initiation of nuclear war would represent such an awesome decision that no rational politician would contemplate it other than in circum-stances where the very survival of their country was at stake. Even then, Britain would probably encourage within NATO a demonstrative use against the Soviet Union itself, rendering the Alliance's large holdings of short-range nuclear weap-ons 'of no real use to us whatever'. For these reasons, Owen argued that Britain should phase out its national ability to conduct tactical nuclear warfare. This would save money and relieve some of the pressure on supplies of weapons-grade plutonium.[164]

[162] Beatrice Heuser and Kristan Stoddart, 'Difficult Europeans: NATO and Tactical/Non-Strategic Nuclear Weapons in the Cold War', *Diplomacy & Statecraft*, Vol. 28, No. 3 (2017), p. 461.
[163] TNA, DEFE 25/335, 1141/573(1), UK Contribution to a NATO Long Range Theatre Nuclear Force (LRTNF), 28 June 1979.
[164] PM/78/73.

Owen's reluctance to support LRTNF modernization ultimately became a moot point, however, as Callaghan's Labour government was toppled in the 1979 General Election by Margaret Thatcher's Conservative Party. Thatcher and her American counterpart, Ronald Reagan, were committed to facing down the Soviet threat from a position of military and economic strength. Thus, the 'dual track' progressed with the deployment in 1983 of ground-launched cruise missiles (GLCMs) in England and Pershing II IRBMs in the FRG. The arrival of these weapon systems ensured nuclear equipoise between East and West at each rung of the escalation ladder; the seamless robe of deterrence had finally been established. The second prong of the 'dual track' decision, that relating to arms control, did not come to fruition until the accession of Mikhail Gorbachev in the Soviet Union in 1985 and the signing of the bi-lateral Intermediate-Range Nuclear Forces Treaty (INF Treaty) two years later. The INF Treaty effectively reversed the 'dual track' decision, removing the SS-20, Pershing II, and GLCM weapon systems from Europe.[165]

## Conclusions

British thinking about NATO strategy revealed a number of assumptions about the character of future conflict. The first was the apocalyptic vision of nuclear war. Senior British officials were remarkably consistent in their conviction that nuclear war would be so catastrophically violent and unpredictable that it could serve no political purpose. Military 'victory' as traditionally understood would be unattainable, and words such as 'irrelevant', 'meaningless', and 'insignificant' were all employed to describe the role of land forces during or after a strategic nuclear exchange. For an organization whose *raison d'être* rests on its ability to fight and prevail in land combat, such a stark appraisal of the Army's traditional mission by its own political leaders raised fundamental questions about the use of force in the nuclear age. In this context, the utility of the Army in British strategic appreciations was in its ability, as part of NATO's shield force, to manage the process of escalation through the employment of force discretely and fluidly across the full spectrum of possible scenarios: from small-scale conventional resistance, through the discriminate employment of tactical nuclear firepower, to extensive nuclear operations designed to retard Soviet fighting power. This logic was enshrined in the strategy of flexible response, and was the overarching framework within which the British Army conceptualized the future operating environment from 1967 onwards. However, while the Army was cognisant of the broader political and

---

[165] A detailed analysis of the 'dual track' agreement can be found in Stoddart, *Facing Down the Soviet Union*, pp. 203–25.

strategic constraints stemming from the ambiguous guidelines of flexible response, the risks posed by escalation and the basic challenges of operating on a nuclear battlefield were not reflected in the service's theories of war, doctrine, or tactical concepts. How the Army approached these challenges is the subject of the following chapters.

# 3

# Military Publicists and Theories
# of Tactical Nuclear War

In a 1948 treatise on the patterns of wars throughout history, Lieutenant-General
Francis S. Tuker argued that with adequate foresight and imagination, and
through a thorough study of the 'military science', it would be possible for soldiers
to forecast the most likely character of a future conflict. This would require on the
part of the military organization intellectual progressivism in peacetime; only then
could it envision what the next war might look like and the types of forces that
would be required to fight it and prevail. Tuker attached great importance to the
role of service journals in providing a platform for officers to disseminate new
ideas and concepts, and to think critically about the profession of arms. Importantly, 'they must be prepared to take a line not necessarily in favour with those of
us who are at the top of the fighting forces'.[1] Against the backdrop of the uncertain
and rapidly changing military environment of the post-war years, this was a
clarion call for the younger, more enlightened and educated officers to step
forward and become the authors, both figuratively and literally, of the Army's
future: 'the "Yes-man" is more dangerous when he is the editor of a service
periodical than when he is a subordinate in the army itself . . . it is only by rubbing
our wits up against the wits of others who hold varying views that we can sharpen
them'.[2] This warning against intellectual complacency in peacetime would be
all the more important as nuclear weapons began to dominate thinking about
land warfare.

Tuker might have been pleased with the types of articles that eventually did
appear in the major service journals throughout the second half of the 1940s and
the 1950s. Between the years 1946 and 1957, the seven most popular journals
concerning Army matters—*The RUSI Journal*, *The RUSI Journal India*, *Army
Quarterly*, *British Army Review*, *Journal of the Royal Artillery*, *Royal Engineers
Journal*, and the *Royal Armoured Corps Journal*—published a total of ninety-four
articles relating to nuclear land combat.[3] Interest in thinking about the nuclear
battlefield rose steadily during the late 1940s, peaking in 1955 with thirty articles

---

[1] Francis S. Tuker, *The Pattern of War* (London: Butler and Tanner, 1948), p. 6.
[2] Ibid., pp. 6–7.
[3] This is to mean all articles that considered explicitly the impact that the tactical application of
nuclear weapons might have upon the future conduct of land warfare and on Army doctrine, tactics,
organizations, and equipment programmes. Also included in the survey are those articles that had been

*Imagining Nuclear War in the British Army, 1945–1989*. Simon J. Moody, Oxford University Press (2020).
© Simon J. Moody.
DOI: 10.1093/oso/9780198846994.001.0001

being published alone. The 1950s was the golden age of thinking about nuclear war-fighting. As Chapter 2 has shown, this was the period in which the West enjoyed a superiority in nuclear weapons, and NATO strategy was predicated on the assumption that tactical nuclear weapons could be used as a force multiplier to arrest a Soviet attack on the Central Front, safe in the knowledge that the Red Army could not reply in kind. The decade also witnessed the arrival of *bona fide* tactical nuclear weapon systems in Europe, and so the 1950s represented a paradigm shift in military thought in which nuclear weapons became the referent object of analysis.

Taken together, this body of work constituted the intellectual foundations of the theory of tactical nuclear warfare which would inform the Army's thinking into the 1980s. The intellectual reference points for thinking about the nuclear battlefield reflected the culture of a military organization bloodied in two world wars and desperate to prove its continued utility in a changing military environment. The Army's extensive corporate knowledge of conventional war-fighting provided an intellectual crutch for thinking through the imponderables of nuclear combat, and theories of tactical nuclear war themselves became a continuation of theories of armoured warfare which had been evolving steadily since the First World War. In this context, future operating constructs did not exist in stasis but were informed by, and contributed to, the wider professional debate about the profession of arms after 1945. The ideas promulgated within internally circulated professional service journals were to a large extent sealed off from outside influence, and there is no evidence to suggest that the early nuclear theorists were influenced by other narratives of nuclear war which were appearing in popular culture during the same period.

## Early Thinking about the Tactical Application of Nuclear Weapons

There were only five articles published in Army service journals during the late 1940s that considered the impact that nuclear weapons might have on the conduct of land warfare. For many officers, the arrival of the atomic bomb did not appear to be of immediate professional concern. The atomic bombings of Hiroshima and Nagasaki were understood as an extension of the Allied strategic bombing campaigns that had devastated the Axis powers during the course of the Second World War; because of the immense destructive power of those weapons and their relatively expensive production costs, a popular view, therefore, was that nuclear weapons would only be used against the most important of strategic targets.

reproduced from foreign service journals. Omitted from the survey are articles that related to the strategic use of nuclear weapons, nuclear weapon testing, and the science of nuclear energy.

Various studies conducted by the American defence establishment immediately after the end of the Second World War also suggested that the future battlefield would probably be fought with conventional weapons, for much the same reasons.[4] Furthermore, in Britain, technical information on the atomic bomb was simply not available to Army planners in the immediate post-war years, and this made it difficult to assess with any accuracy how nuclear weapons might affect war on land.[5] For these reasons, many of the articles that appeared in the immediate post-war years took two extremes and either sought to minimize the impact that nuclear weapons might have on future land campaigns or else painted an apocalyptic vision of a future war involving the use of nuclear weapons in which land forces would perform a supporting role.

Those officers who maintained that the advent of the atomic bomb did not require a radical revision of military thought wrote articles that were polemic in tone, defending the claim that nuclear weapons had made conventional land armies obsolete: 'the popular outcry that the atomic bomb has made everything else useless is a dangerous disease', wrote one officer in the *Journal of the Royal Artillery*, 'although we cannot completely disregard "the realms of fancy" we must base our decisions on what we know and not on prophecy'.[6] In the same issue, a Lieutenant-Colonel of the Royal Artillery believed that 'the saner view', to the suggestion that conventional weapons were now outdated, 'seems to be that for many years the atomic bomb will remain an accessory and not a substitute'.[7] Other authors argued that a particular branch or service specialism would remain largely unchanged in spite of nuclear weapons and would continue to play an important role in future land warfare. In an article on the future of armoured forces, a Captain of the Royal Armoured Corps maintained that while nuclear weapons would pose a great threat to army bases and centres of industry, they would be wasted on the actual battlefield. Therefore, tanks and armoured divisions would remain important features of armies in the years to come.[8]

A corollary of this view was that for the foreseeable future tactics, doctrine, and organizations would remain largely unchanged. This might well change in the

[4] See Robert A. Doughty, *The Evolution of U.S. Army Tactical Doctrine, 1946–76* (Kansas, MO: Combat Studies Institute, 1979), p. 2.

[5] This was not restricted to the military profession, however. The first page of British physicist P. M. S. Blackett's poignant 1948 study on nuclear energy warned that: 'It is always difficult to foresee the effect of an important new weapon on the art and practice of war … [and] especially difficult to foresee quantitatively the effects of atomic bombs, because of their technically revolutionary character'. P. M. S. Blackett, *Military and Political Consequences of Atomic Energy* (London: Turnstile Press, 1948), p. 1.

[6] R. C. Reynolds, 'The Future of Anti-Aircraft', *Journal of the Royal Artillery*, Vol. 73, No. 2 (April 1946), p. 99.

[7] S. M. Cleeve, 'Super-Heavy Artillery: The Problem in 1945', *Journal of the Royal Artillery*, Vol. 73, No. 2 (April 1946), p. 133.

[8] R. J. Sutherland, 'The Future of the Armoured Division', *Army Quarterly*, Vol. 53, No. 1 (October 1946), p. 92.

future if the destructive power of nuclear energy could be tamed, warned the editor of the *Royal Armoured Corps Journal*; if it did, the present conception of Army organization would become 'obsolete overnight'.[9] For the meantime, however, it appeared that nuclear weapons were too powerful and expensive to be squandered on the tactical battlefield and that the next war would begin on the same lines as the closing stages of the Second World War.[10] After all, outlined one observer in a private memorandum to Sir Basil Liddell Hart, the nominal 20kt atomic bomb would be wasted against small battlefield targets, resulting in misplaced energy comparable to 'shooting at flies with cannon'.[11] Other writers took a similar view, with one officer arguing that in its present form the atomic bomb could not be employed tactically since:

> The area of destruction is far too great besides the fact that there is a distinct possibility of the destroyed area remaining radio-active for a long time. No military commander dare risk taking his troops and equipment through such an area immediately after it has been subjected to atom bomb action, and expose them to the fatal effects of radio-activity.[12]

Such considerations reinforced the view that Army officers need not worry about the impact that nuclear weapons might have upon the profession of arms. The winner of the Bertrand Stewart Prize Essay for 1948 concluded his piece with a comforting message for those 'depressed Service officers' who might be worried that the Army had been rendered obsolete by the atomic bomb. He reminded his fellow soldiers that 'these weapons of mass destruction scarcely touch the fringe of tactics; the consideration of their effect can be left to the "Q Planners", to the organizers of large-scale convoys, and to the commanders of major battle fleets at sea. The regimental soldier ... can turn his attention back to conventional battle tactics'.[13]

---

[9] Editorial, 'Nuclear Fission', *Royal Armoured Corps Journal*, Vol. 1, No. 1 (July 1946), p. 8.

[10] See, for example, A. J. Wilson, 'The Future of Armour as the Arm of Mobility', *The RUSI Journal*, Vol. 91, No. 563 (1946), p. 396; M. E. Dennis, 'To-Day and To-Morrow', *Journal of the Royal Artillery*, Vol. 74, No. 1 (January 1947), p. 13; R. C. Hulbert, 'Silver Medal Essay 1946/47', *Journal of the Royal Artillery*, Vol. 74, No. 4 (October 1947), p. 374.

[11] LHCMA, Liddell Hart Papers, LH/15/5/443, The Description of an Imaginary Battle by Lieut.-Col. F. O. Miksche, unpublished typescript, n.d. [approx. 1948].

[12] C. L. Borve, 'Is There a Defence against the Atom Bomb?', *The RUSI Journal India*, Vol. 80, Nos. 338–9 (Jan–April 1950), p. 76.

[13] B. H. D. Barnes, 'Bertrand Stewart Prize Essay, 1948', *Army Quarterly*, Vol. 57, No. 2 (January 1949), p. 177. A few writers continued to argue throughout the whole period under review that nuclear weapons would not be used against troops in the field because of their financial cost and availability, or because of political constraints. See, for example, Editorial, 'The British Atomic Explosion and the New Warfare', *Army Quarterly*, Vol. 65, No. 2 (January 1953), pp. 130–1; C. N. Barclay, 'The Future of the Tank, Part I', *Army Quarterly*, Vol. 67, No. 1 (October 1953), pp. 45–6; W. G. A. Lawrie, 'The Years Between', *Royal Engineers Journal*, Vol. 69, No. 3 (September 1955), p. 219.

Despite the resistance by some sections of the officer corps to acknowledge the impact that nuclear energy might have upon the conduct of future land warfare, the destructive power of the atomic bomb could not be ignored completely. Although detailed information on the technical characteristics of Fat Man and Little Boy was sparse, there was a growing realization among the early nuclear prophets that conventional troop concentrations would become uniquely vulnerable to the immense blast, heat, and radiation kill mechanisms of nuclear weapons: 'No commander will in future be able to gather large forces for any sort of mass attack', began one 1949 article in the *British Army Journal*, 'without having to consider the possibility of atomic bomb attack ruining the bulk of his dispositions and plans'.[14] It was thought that the threat of nuclear attack would prevent force concentrations both in the forward areas and along the lines of communications in a theatre of operations.[15] Therefore, the traditional conception of the land offensive, employing a mass of armour and infantry supported by a panoply of supporting units, must, claimed one author, 'be considered as dead as the proverbial door nail' because such forces would invite wholesale destruction by a well-placed nuclear strike.[16] This suggested an end to concentration of force and massed attack,[17] and might place greater emphasis on tactical mobility.[18]

Thinking about the impact that increases in the lethality of firepower might have on the battlefield was not unique to the nuclear theorists, but has taxed the imagination of military intellectuals throughout history.[19] By the 1950s, military tactics had evolved to include three basic elements: firepower, protection, and mobility.[20] Both fire and manoeuvre are constant, tangible factors, and it is the

[14] Anon, 'The Atomic Bomb: What Every Officer Should Know', *British Army Journal*, No. 1 (January 1949), p. 12.

[15] H. L. G. Burlton, 'Gold Medal Essay 1946/47', *Journal of the Royal Artillery*, Vol. 74, No. 3 (July 1947), p. 241.

[16] Crystal-Gazer, 'Looking Ahead', *Royal Engineers Journal*, Vol. 65, No. 4 (December 1951), pp. 364-6.

[17] One Army Major came to the conclusion that this type of ground war would have more in common with guerrilla warfare than a traditional land battle. E. N. Ford, 'The Platoon Commander Training for War', *Army Quarterly*, Vol. 63, No. 1 (October 1951), p. 106.

[18] See, for example, Hoffman Nickerson, 'Atomic Military Theory: Some Reflections on Pre- and Post-Atomic Military Theory', *Journal of the Royal Artillery*, Vol. 73, No. 3 (July 1946), p. 221.

[19] For example, Antoine-Henry Jomini wrote in 1836 that 'the means of destruction are approaching perfection with frightful rapidity'. With the advent of the Congreve rocket and improvements in artillery, Jomini wondered whether infantrymen would again have to adopt armour as in the Middle Ages. Antoine-Henri Jomini, *Summery of the Art of War*, trans. G. H. Mendell and W. P. Craighill (Philadelphia, PA: J. B. Lippincott & Co., 1862), p. 48. Perhaps the most perturbing vision of the impact that increasingly lethal firepower would have on a future war came from the Polish banker I. S. Bloch in his famous work of 1897. Bloch believed that the momentous increase in the killing power of modern weapons would only lead to stalemate in war since there would be 'increased slaughter on so terrible a scale as to render it impossible to get troops to push the battle to a decisive issue'. I. S. Bloch, *Is War Now Impossible?* (London: Grant Richards, 1899), p. xvi.

[20] P. A. J. Cordingly, 'Armoured Forces and the Counter Stroke' in J. J. G. Mackenzie and Brian Holden Reid (eds.), *The British Army and the Operational Level of War* (Camberley: Tri-Service Press, 1989), p. 95.

relationship between the two that shapes the tactical environment on the battle-field. It follows that as technology advances, new weapons produce new forms of fighting and new forms of attack and defence. J. F. C. Fuller described this phenomenon as the 'constant tactical factor' in warfare: every improvement in weapon-power is eventually cancelled out by a counter-improvement, rendering the improvement obsolete. He conceptualized this as an evolutionary pendulum in weapon-power that swings from offence to defence in harmony with the speed of technological progress.[21] At times, the swing of the evolutionary pendulum might be such that one or two of the three elements of combat—firepower, protection, or mobility—appears to predominate over the other. Fuller argued that, historically, when the three elements were balanced equally, tactics flour-ished, but when that balance became too heavily weighted in favour of one element over the others, 'the art of war has either stood still or retrogressed'.[22]

Since nuclear weapons represented mankind's absolute mastery of firepower, the tactical pendulum appeared to have swung decisively in favour of firepower over mobility. One US Army officer identified this pattern and observed that the swing of the pendulum alternated with each major conflict, highlighting that during the First World War firepower defeated manoeuvre, whilst the reverse was true in the opening campaigns of the Second World War.[23] This suggested, then, that if nuclear weapons were employed tactically in a future ground war, firepower would dominate the battlefield since armies would not be able to protect themselves through the traditional means of digging in, building entrenchments, and constructing field fortifications, nor would they possess the necessary mobility to be able to circumvent the effects of an atomic explosion. The Czechoslovak Army officer Lieutenant-Colonel F. O. Miksche illustrated this problem vividly in his 1955 study of modern armies: 'As a result of the invention of atomic weapons, fire-power increased a thousand-fold. At the same time, the means of movement on the ground remain unchanged—lorries and tanks are used as in the last war'.[24] To solve the problem of the imbalance between the three elements of combat, British Army officers advanced extreme solutions in an attempt to restore the harmony between firepower, protection, and mobility. Consequently, the late 1940s and early 1950s witnessed the emergence of theories of war that advocated

---

[21] J. F. C. Fuller, *The Dragon's Teeth* (London: Constable & Co. Ltd, 1932), p. 213.

[22] J. F. C. Fuller, *The Foundations of the Science of War* (London: Hutchinson & Co., 1926), p. 153. In a similar vein, Lieutenant-General Martel wrote that if mobile warfare 'is carried out with success by one side, then great victories are achieved and a short and successful war results. If this mobile warfare does not lead to success, then a long drawn out war usually results'. IWM, Private Papers of Lieutenant-General Sir Giffard Martel, GQM 6/3c, Why All This Muddle, unpublished typescript, n.d. [approx. 1950].

[23] Clarence DeReus, 'Through the Atomic Looking Glass', *Military Review*, Vol. 35, No. 3 (June 1955), p. 11. See, for a similar argument, George B. Pickett, 'Squeeze 'Em an' Blast 'Em', *Military Review*, Vol. 35, No. 6 (September 1955), pp. 56–7.

[24] F. O. Miksche, *Atomic Weapons and Armies* (London: Faber and Faber Ltd, 1955), p. 17.

styles of warfare that fell on extreme ends of the tactical spectrum, with either mobility or protection being taken to their logical upper limits.

One of the first writers to offer a solution to the problem of fighting on a nuclear battlefield was one Colonel A. Jolly whose article, 'Armour and the Next War', appeared in the *Royal Armoured Corps Journal* in July 1946. This article advocated a style of manoeuvre warfare par excellence. Jolly wrote that in a future war involving the use of nuclear weapons, assembly areas, congested bridgeheads, headquarters, ports, and any bottlenecks that might see large troop concentrations, such as focal points in road communications, would become extremely vulnerable to nuclear attack. Therefore, if ground forces were to operate effectively in such an environment, they would most likely require the following characteristics: embarkation areas and overseas bases dispersed over wide stretches of coastline; amphibious assaulting armour; armoured protection for all personnel; cross-country mobility; and the ability to traverse water obstacles without the need for heavy bridging equipment. The article concluded by stating that the ideal land force for nuclear combat would be highly mobile, fully armoured, self-contained, and capable of maintaining independent combat operations as far as possible from conventional supply lines.[25] Jolly described this type of highly mobile army as having more in common with a naval fleet than a traditional ground force. The editor of the *Royal Armoured Corps Journal* highlighted that this would come naturally to tankers since speed, elasticity, and concealment were the ideals tactically, as they always had been, only 'the bomb would make their attainment more urgent'.[26] The analogy to fluid and highly mobile operations that was reminiscent of naval warfare was nothing new, however. One of the original pioneers of the theory of armoured warfare in Britain, Gifford Le Quesne Martel, outlined in a 1916 paper the concept of tanks operating like a fleet at sea.[27]

At the same time, however, other military theorists were offering competing visions of future war that not only emphasized protection over mobility, but warned against any kind of open movement on the battlefield. One of the first writers of this ilk was Lieutenant-General Francis S. Tuker whose article, 'Nuclear Energy and War', appeared in *The RUSI Journal India* just six months after the atomic bombings of Hiroshima and Nagasaki. Tuker's portrayal of a future nuclear land war was an apocalyptic narrative and reads at times more like a science fiction novel than a practical exposition of possible future trends in warfare. Tuker wrote that when a belligerent achieved the capabilities to be able to launch a surprise strategic attack using nuclear-tipped long-range rockets, 'the

---

[25] A. Jolly, 'Armour and the Next War', *Royal Armoured Corps Journal*, Vol. 1, No. 1 (July 1946), pp. 52–9.

[26] Editorial, 'Atomic Broadcasts', *Royal Armoured Corps Journal*, Vol. 1, No. 4 (April 1947), pp. 235–6.

[27] R. M. P. Carver, *The Apostles of Mobility: The Theory and Practice of Armoured Warfare* (London: Weidenfeld and Nicolson, 1979), pp. 22–3.

only safe place tomorrow is below the surface of the world'.[28] Tuker envisioned whole populations living in deep catacombs under the ground and under the sea within which all means of human sustenance would be provided. These 'Underneath's' would become an organic part of a wider self-sufficient fortress system which, in times of war, would provide defensive bastions akin to the stone-clad Medieval castles of old. From these fortresses, Tuker imagined, would be launched nuclear rockets and missiles, the sole aim of which was to smash the opposing side's nuclear potential by destroying its nuclear industries and means of production. If, at some point, it became necessary to send assault troops into the underground labyrinths of the opposition's fortress system to force an end to the nuclear exchange, then airborne forces would have to be relied on since the surface of the earth would be nothing but a radioactive no-man's land. In such a dystopian vision of future war, Tuker maintained that 'land armies as we know them to-day will be out of date'.[29]

Of course, this was a fantastical account of what a future nuclear war might look like and was completely detached from the realities of defence policy-making. Considering Tuker's dedication to stimulating debate and imagination within the officer corps, 'Nuclear Energy and War' was more than likely a means of stimulating professional discourse within the Army than an actual blueprint for future planning. However, Tuker's suggestion of the need in nuclear war for well-protected static defensive positions coupled with highly mobile airborne counter-attack units was one acknowledged by other military publicists. In a 1949 article in the *Army Quarterly* examining the defensive aspects of atomic land combat, the author argued that ground forces would still require secure bases, as they always had, and that these could best be provided by 'base fortresses' not unlike the ones advocated by Tuker, albeit on a smaller tactical scale. These would be self-sufficient defensive positions capable of defending a specific locality for an indefinite period of time. In this concept, the aim of the attacker or defender would be to lure the opposition away from its secure defensive sanctuaries and into pre-designated atomic 'killing-grounds' where it would be subjected to nuclear fires and counter-attacked by highly mobile strike forces.[30] The concept of mobile forces and static defensive positions mutually supporting one another was not new; it was as old as war itself. Indeed, the concept of nuclear 'killing-grounds' would become one of the pillars upon which the British Army's early doctrine for nuclear war would be built.

Articles of this type continued to appear into the early 1950s. The winner of the Bertrand Stewart Prize Essay for 1950 concluded that a future war would most

---

[28] F. S. Tuker, 'Nuclear Energy and War', *The RUSI Journal India*, Vol. 76, No. 322 (January 1946), p. 68.
[29] Ibid., p. 75.
[30] P. H. H. Bryan, 'Some Aspects of Defence in Atomic Warfare', *Army Quarterly*, Vol. 58, No. 1 (April 1949), pp. 49–55.

likely stagnate into a positional affair with high rates of attrition since tactical nuclear weapons, improvements in anti-tank guns, and greater precision of artillery would favour the defender against ground attack. Static defences would not be along the same lines as those of 1914–18, however, but would take the form of fortress positions from which mobile forces would operate, resembling 'position warfare of the Middle Ages, as it was understood and practiced by Marlborough and Saxe'.[31] Borrowing ideas from Tuker's 'Nuclear Energy and War', the author envisioned the world's surface being divided into 'Heartlands' (where raw material and industrial centres would be contained), 'Defended Zones' (the outposts of defence of the Heartlands), and 'Battle Zones' (a radioactive wasteland interspersed with fortresses where the actual fighting would take place). What political goals such a war would achieve is unknown, not least because it would impose almost universal suffering upon the world's population, raising concerns as to 'whether any potentate, fanatic even, let alone any democratic leader, would let loose such a dreadful holocaust upon the world'.[32]

In the early post-war years, then, certain assumptions had been made about the character of a future land war. If nuclear weapons were employed in a tactical role on the battlefield, then this would require a radical change in military thought as revolutionary as the weapons that had brought it about. It became clear to military theorists that mass would suffer most under nuclear conditions, and that this was the most immediate tactical problem to be solved. What the intellectual reference points should be for thinking about this dilemma—extreme trench warfare with its deep and elaborate earthworks, or mobile high-tempo armoured operations—was still unknown. It was these problems that occupied the minds of the atomic theorists throughout the 1950s.

## The Quest for Mobility

By the early 1950s, the caution that had been shown towards the arrival of nuclear weapons was swept away in the wake of a number of external developments in the nuclear field. As was shown in Chapter 2, NATO became committed to a nuclear defence of Western Europe in 1954 with the adoption of MC 48, and in the same year, Field Marshal Montgomery informed listeners during a much-publicized lecture to the RUSI that all operational planning at SHAPE centred on the employment of nuclear weapons in the land battle.[33] *Bona fide* tactical nuclear weapons were also, for the first time, being deployed to the European Central

---

[31] D. J. O. Fitzgerald, 'The Bertrand Stewart Prize Essay, 1950', *Army Quarterly*, Vol. 62, No. 1 (April 1951), p. 53.

[32] Ibid., p. 54.

[33] B. L. Montgomery, 'A Look Through a Window at World War III', *The RUSI Journal*, Vol. 99, No. 596 (November 1954), p. 508.

Front in the form of the M65 280mm atomic cannon and Corporal and Honest John missiles.[34] Hitherto, writers had referred to the tactical *application* of nuclear weapons; now the hardware was available, and 'tactical nuclear weapon' entered the lexicon of professional discourse. As will be explored in Chapter 5, the British Army was also beginning to investigate the potentialities of nuclear weapons in various war-games and military exercises. All of this quelled any doubts that tactical nuclear weapons would be used against ground troops in a future land war fought against the Soviet Union in Europe.[35] This was reflected in the service journals, with each subsequent issue offering at least one original study on the Army and the nuclear battlefield.

During the middle 1950s, military publicists focused increasingly on the problems raised by the vulnerability of troop concentrations to nuclear attack, which would become the primary conceptual challenge facing doctrine writers throughout the Cold War. Prophets of nuclear warfare took as their reference points the great land campaigns of the Second World War and imagined how they would have progressed under nuclear conditions. Common examples included: the Allied landings at Normandy in 1944, British troop concentrations during the 1942 battle of El Alamein (particularly the passing of armoured units through infantry formations), and the crossing of the Rhine in 1945.[36] Major-General Sir Harold Pyman recorded his thoughts on these operations in 1953 when he was commander of 11th Armoured Division in Germany:

> These few examples—and there are many others—show that heavy concentrations of land forces, particularly Armour and Artillery, make favourable atomic targets. All of these battles are worth studying again against a background of possible atomic support, and a threat of possible atomic attack.[37]

It did not take much imagination to picture the devastating effects that nuclear weapons would have had on the large and cumbersome armies of Second World War vintage concentrated for attack or defence. Pyman informed listeners during

---

[34] The 'Atomic Annie', as it was affectionately known, could project a 15kt nuclear shell up to a range of 18 miles. David C. Elliot, 'Project Vista and Nuclear Weapons in Europe', *International Security*, Vol. 11, No. 1 (Summer 1986), p. 173.

[35] For example, in July 1954 the editor of the *Royal Armoured Corps Journal* maintained that the use of tactical nuclear weapons would be a certainty in the next war. In the same month, the editor of the *British Army Annual* urged that they must now be considered 'conventional weapons'. Editorial, 'Editorial Notes', *Royal Armoured Corps Journal*, Vol. 8, No. 3 (July 1954), p. 113; Editorial, 'Atomic Warfare', *British Army Annual*, No. 1 (July 1954), p. 6.

[36] For example, L. O. Lyne, 'The Future of the Tank, Part II', *Army Quarterly*, Vol. 67, No. 2 (January 1954), p. 179; H. E. Pyman, 'Armour in the Land Battle', *Royal Armoured Corps Journal*, Vol. 8, No. 3 (July 1954), pp. 119–27; R. N. Gale, 'Infantry in Modern Battle: Its Organization and Training', *British Army Annual*, No. 1 (July 1954), p. 9.

[37] LHCMA, Pyman Papers, PYMAN 9/3, The Atomic Bomb as a Tactical Weapon on the Battlefield with Particular Reference to an Armoured Division, unpublished typescript, 15 October 1953.

a lecture at the Swiss Officers' Society in 1954 that whenever any threat of atomic bomb attack exists, force concentrations as were deemed necessary and acceptable during the last war would be 'foolhardy'.[38] Across the Atlantic, US Army officers had arrived independently at similar conclusions. For example, two articles typical of the period stated that 'if it is to escape from heavy casualties from tactical atomic weapons, the army must operate in a state of *great dispersion* both in defence and in the attack'[39] since 'greater dispersion makes troops less vulnerable to atomic attack by presenting to the enemy a less dense and hence less profitable target'.[40]

From this realization stemmed further questions to which few answers could be found. The problem was that the concentration of force had, historically, been an important positive factor in war. This had been recognized by a number of military thinkers and was most popularly expounded by Carl von Clausewitz, who, in his *magnum opus* on the theory of war, attached great importance to the concentration of superior forces in time and space for the successful outcome of military operations.[41] Clausewitz's contemporary, Antoine-Henri Jomini, believed this to be *the* fundamental principle of war, arguing that the primary aim of commanders at the strategic level was to throw the mass of an army upon the decisive point of a theatre of operations, and at the tactical level, against the most vulnerable point of the enemy position.[42] The legacy of these writings meant that concentration, or mass, became one of the most highly valued principles of war for many Western military organizations.[43] The principle of 'concentration' became codified in official British military doctrine with the publication in 1920 of the *Field Service Regulations* and has remained there ever since.[44] Yet, if mass would suffer most on the atomic battlefield, then, as Pyman highlighted above, decisive concentrations of force would be difficult, perhaps impossible. This was recognized by contemporary officers as having serious implications for the military art

---

[38] LHCMA, Pyman Papers, PYMAN 9/6, Armour—Lecture by Major-General H. E. Pyman to Swiss Officers' Society, unpublished lecture notes, March 1954.

[39] L. H. Landon, 'What Type of Army?', *Military Review*, Vol. 36, No. 12 (March 1957), p. 101 [emphasis in original].

[40] Edward L. Rowny, 'Ground Tactics in an Atomic War', *The Army Combat Forces Journal* (August 1954), p. 19.

[41] Carl von Clausewitz, *On War*, Book III Chapter VIII, Michael Howard and Peter Paret (eds. and trans.) (London, Toronto, and New York, NY: Everyman's Library, 1993), pp. 228–32.

[42] Jomini, *Summery of the Art of War*, p. 70.

[43] John I. Alger, *The Quest for Victory: The History of the Principles of War* (London and Westport, CT: Greenwood Press, 1982), p. 189.

[44] The eight principles of war listed in 1920 were: maintenance of the objective; offensive action; surprise; concentration; economy of force; security; mobility; and cooperation. War Office, *Field Service Regulations*, Vol. II, *Operations* (Provisional) (London: HMSO, 1920), pp. 14–15. Ninety years later, the Army's capstone doctrine still reaffirmed the continued significance of 'concentration' as a principle of war. Ministry of Defence, *Army Doctrine Publication: Operations* (Shrivenham: Development, Concepts and Doctrine Centre, 2010), pp. 2A–4.

that would most likely require a complete rethink of military tactics and techniques.

If mass would suffer most on the atomic battlefield, then the implication was that the basic aim of all commanders would be 'to force their enemies to concentrate sufficient forces to constitute an atomic target, while at the same time not offering one themselves'.[45] Indeed, it appeared to military theorists that tactics had turned full circle since the Second World War, as one writer highlighted: 'Whereas hitherto it was good tactics to prevent the enemy from concentrating his forces for attack or defence, now it will be our first aim to compel him to do so'.[46] Although this appeared both simple and straightforward, it did create a rather curious conundrum with regards to battlefield technique. The basic problem was one of forcing the enemy to concentrate while remaining sufficiently dispersed so as not to invite atomic attack.[47] This implied that armies would need to be able to switch rapidly between concentration and dispersion with ease. By so doing, this would allow ground forces to concentrate in time but not in space, denying the enemy a suitable target for atomic attack. The phrase 'concentrate to fight, disperse to live' was extremely popular and became the watchword of atomic military theorists throughout the 1950s.[48]

Dispersion in itself was not a new phenomenon for atomic-age military planners but had become, by the 1950s, a necessary battlefield technique in land warfare to circumvent the increased range, accuracy, and lethality of firepower. By the beginning of the twentieth century, the great strides that had been made in the effectiveness of battlefield firepower over the last hundred years had made combat a much more deadly pursuit, forcing armies to abandon the rigid close-order formations of antiquity in search of ways to mitigate the effects of enemy firepower through the development of new techniques, organizations, and force deployments.[49] Stephen Biddle referred to these innovations as 'the modern system' and posited that it was only through the employment of ground troops in a much more flexible manner that emphasized cover, concealment, dispersion, small-unit independent manoeuvre, suppression, and combined-arms integration that armies were able to overcome the challenges of operating on a battlefield

[45]  A. F. J. G. Jackson, 'Fighting Formations of the Future', *The RUSI Journal*, Vol. 100, No. 598 (1955), p. 231.

[46]  Wilkinson, 'Tactical Atomic Support of Ground Forces', p. 130.

[47]  G. G. R. Williams, 'Atomic Weapons and Army Training', *The RUSI Journal*, Vol. 99, No. 596 (1954), p. 572.

[48]  Andrew Bacevich attributed this slogan to a US Army officer who coined the maxim in a 1955 article for *Armor*. It is difficult to ascertain the British origins of this term and whether it was lifted from that article. See A. J. Bacevich, *The Pentomic Era: The U.S. Army Between Korea and Vietnam* (Washington, DC: National Defense University Press, 1986), p. 68.

[49]  See Michael Howard, 'Men against Fire: The Doctrine of the Offensive in 1914' in Peter Paret (ed.), *Makers of Modern Strategy: From Machiavelli to the Nuclear Age* (Oxford: Oxford University Press, 1986), pp. 510–26.

dominated by increasingly lethal firepower.[50] It was through the modern system of offence and defence that the stalemate and slaughter of trench warfare was finally overcome during the First World War. In the 1950s, military theorists looked towards the modern system approach to war-fighting as a means to conduct combat operations in a technological environment where powerful and long-range nuclear rockets and missiles suggested that 'battlefields may well become much larger and fixed fronts may give place to large areas of mobile fighting by small, fast columns'.[51]

If nuclear-age armies hoped to be able to switch rapidly between concentration and dispersion, then this would require high levels of tactical mobility. As Major-General Pyman acknowledged grimly, 'no land forces will survive for long in future warfare, unless they are capable of considerable mobility. Protracted static defence will literally be lifted off the face of the earth'.[52] There was a growing realization, then, amongst the military publicists that the Army needed to become much more flexible through increasing dramatically its means of mobility on the ground. Unsurprisingly, tankers were quick to seize the opportunity to promote their branch over other sections of the service. In a 1953 article in the *Royal Armoured Corps Journal*, the inter-war pioneer of mechanized warfare in Britain, Major-General J. F. C. Fuller, argued that the tank would become much more important in a future ground war involving the tactical application of atomic weapons since it would 'enhance the value of mobility, because rapid dispersions and concentrations, such as can be effected with cross-country vehicles, will become doubly necessary'.[53] This was a view shared by Pyman, a known tank enthusiast, who informed listeners at a lecture to the Royal United Services Institute (RUSI) that 'armour supported by atomics and atomics exploited by armour present a new means of ensuring true mobility on the battlefield in both offensive and defensive operations'.[54] Tanks were also believed to provide good

---

[50] Stephen Biddle, *Military Power: Explaining Victory and Defeat in Modern Battle* (Oxford and Princeton, NJ: Princeton University Press, 2006), pp. 28–51.

[51] D. S. Clarke, 'The Bertrand Stewart Prize Essay, 1953', *Army Quarterly*, Vol. 67, No. 2 (January 1954), p. 163.

[52] LHCMA, Pyman Papers, PYMAN 10/1, The Armoured Division, 14 December 1955, unpublished typescript. Another officer noted that if a static position was worth holding, it would be worth destroying by atomic fires. See 'Centaur', 'Some Thoughts on Nuclear War', *Royal Engineers Journal*, Vol. 69, No. 1 (March 1955), p. 85.

[53] J. F. C. Fuller, 'The Tank in Future Warfare', *Royal Armoured Corps Journal*, Vol. 7, No. 1 (January 1953), p. 40.

[54] Pyman, 'Armour in the Land Battle', p. 227. For similar arguments see T. A. Gibson, 'A Plea for the BAT', *British Army Review*, No. 1 (September 1955), p. 32 and J. W. Hackett, 'Panzer Battles', *British Army Review*, No. 3 (September 1956), p. 35. A report by the Army League asked whether tactical nuclear weapons would 'spell the end of the heavy tank, just as gunpowder spelt the end of the knight in armour?'. One officer agreed with this proposition, arguing that the slow-moving, heavy tank would become obsolete in nuclear war. *The Army in the Nuclear Age: Report by the Army League Sub-Committee* (London: St. Clements Press Ltd, 1955), p. 34; K. J. Mears, 'David or Goliath', *British Army Review*, No. 3 (September 1956), pp. 60–4.

protection against the effects of nuclear weapons, particularly radiation.[55] This renewed interest in mobile operations that tactical nuclear weapons had helped to bring about would, claimed one French observer, finally lead to that 'over-all mechanization, which the protagonists of armoured forces have been dreaming about since 1916'.[56]

Calls for greater mobility by nuclear military theorists did not occur in a vacuum, however, but developed in tandem with the wider debate during this period of how to foster greater mobility in the British Army more generally. The Second World War had witnessed the ascendancy of increasingly complex logistic systems to support frontline units, and champions of manoeuvre warfare lamented the way in which armoured divisions, in particular, had become anchored to their extremely cumbersome, road-bound, administrative tails, which had a tendency to restrict the mobility and flexibility that was so desired in mechanized formations.[57] As Chapter 5 will demonstrate, military exercises suggested that these exposed life-lines would become the Achilles heel of armies operating on the nuclear battlefield. Of particular concern was the vulnerability of advancing columns to attack from the air. This had been noted in the British Army as early as 1924 and proved to be a correct appreciation after the operational experiences of the Second World War had been digested.[58] In nuclear land combat, congested supply lines would serve only to invite destruction by the enemy's nuclear fires. Therefore, theories of tactical nuclear war contributed to, and were informed by, the wider debate on organizational transformation in the Army. Of course, since the inter-war period military intellectuals in Britain such as Fuller, Liddell Hart, and Martel had argued that the destructiveness of modern weapons would see the death of the mass land army of First World War vintage. In the nuclear era, the attainment of the tactical ideals of mobility and flexibility would become even more urgent than they had been in the 1920s.

Military publicists offered a number of solutions for fostering greater battlefield mobility. One was by streamlining the divisional structure. This in itself was not particularly innovative since many commentators were beginning to question the continued utility of the division as it was structured at the end of the Second

---

[55] See, Editorial, 'The Atom Bomb', *Royal Armoured Corps Journal*, Vol. 1, No. 3 (January 1947), pp. 169–70 and G. L. D. Duckworth, 'Tank Crews in Atomic Warfare', *Royal Armoured Corps Journal*, Vol. 9, No. 2 (April 1955), pp. 73–5.

[56] André Beaufre, 'Reflections on the Evolution of the Doctrine of the Employment of Armour', *Royal Armoured Corps Journal*, Vol. 8, No. 4 (October 1954), p. 176.

[57] See Giffard Martel, 'The Future of the Tank: Part III', *Army Quarterly*, Vol. 68, No. 1 (April 1954), p. 79; R. M. Ogorkiewicz, 'Armoured Formations: Past and Future', *Royal Armoured Corps Journal*, Vol. 10, No. 3 (July 1956), p. 100.

[58] David French, *Raising Churchill's Army: The British Army and the War against Germany 1919–1945* (Oxford: Oxford University Press, 2001), p. 25. This was reflected in 'airpower' becoming added to the British principles of war in 1945 at Montgomery's insistence.

World War.[59] In 1952 the standard British infantry division consisted of three infantry brigades, each of which was composed of a headquarters (HQ) and three battalions. Altogether, this amounted to 18,800 men and 3,300 vehicles. The armoured division was organized in a similar manner, consisting of a single armoured brigade composed of three armoured regiments, and a lorried infantry brigade of three battalions, totalling some 16,100 men and 3,500 vehicles. The organization in 'threes' in both the infantry and armoured divisions was adopted on the basis that it would give the division greater flexibility on the field since commanders could commit two battalions to combat whilst holding one in reserve or, if greater depth was required, one battalion could fight at the front with two in reserve.[60] The experiences of the Second World War had shown that the triangular division—as it was known—proved to be effective during the attack, but became rather cumbersome during defensive operations.[61] Military theorists believed that this type of organization would prove too inflexible to perform the type of operations envisaged for the atomic battlefield.

The major problem identified with the conventional division was that it required a glut of supporting units to keep it operationally effective in the field. For example, the large number of vehicles and heavy weapons organic to armoured divisions meant that although a good initial supply of war materiel and firepower could be carried into battle with it, subsequent maintenance requirements became extremely heavy.[62] Consequently, the administrative 'tail' of the division had, by necessity, bloated to impractical proportions. With the possibility that nuclear weapons might be employed on the battlefield, some Army leaders feared that the 'teeth' units on the fighting front might become easily located and subjected to nuclear attack.[63] Headquarter units were also perceived to be unnecessarily large and cumbersome for their function.[64] In a standard British armoured division of the middle 1950s the headquarters for the artillery element alone consisted of thirty-five vehicles and twelve trailers. This mass of transport, with the eighty men it carried, occupied around 10 acres of ground at normal

[59] For example, B. H. Liddell Hart, 'How to Quicken Manoeuvre and Gain Flexibility in Land Warfare', *Army Quarterly*, Vol. 60, No. 2 (July 1950), pp. 181–95; R. M. P. Carver, 'Tanks and Infantry: The Need for Speed', *The RUSI Journal*, Vol. 96, No. 3 (June 1953), pp. 452–6; W. N. R. Scotter, 'Streamlining the Infantry Division', *The RUSI Journal*, Vol. 98, No. 592 (1953), pp. 597–602; N. C. Baird, 'Economy of Infantry: Some Thoughts on Improving Flexibility', *The RUSI Journal*, Vol. 99, No. 595 (1954), pp. 439–42; R. M. Ogorkiewicz, 'The Organisation and Role of Armoured Formations', *Royal Armoured Corps Journal*, Vol. 11, No. 4 (October 1957), pp. 170–6.

[60] TNA, WO 279/765, Notes on the British Army, April 1952, pp. 23–4.

[61] Virgil Ney, *Evolution of the U.S. Army Division, 1939–1968* (Fort Belvoir, VA: Technical Operations Inc., 1969), p. 71.

[62] WO 279/765, Notes on the British Army, April 1952, p. 24.

[63] LHCMA, Pyman Papers, PYMAN 9/4, Address to the Royal Armoured Corps Conference, 1954, unpublished lecture notes, 1954. O. D. P. Ratnam, 'Atomic Warfare and Conventional Forces', *United Services Institute India Journal*, Vol. 85, No. 361 (October 1955), p. 336.

[64] R. W. McLeod, 'Some Elements of Mobility', *Army Quarterly*, Vol. 75, No. 1 (October 1957), pp. 50–7.

dispersion distances. Considering also that this HQ would have been sited along-side the myriad other supporting units of the Divisional Headquarters, it became clear that this would provide an easy and worthwhile target for enemy nuclear weapons.[65]

The infantry divisions were no more economical and at the height of active operations during the Second World War were consuming 400 tons of materiel per day (260 tons on petrol and ammunition and 140 tons on supplies, mail, engineering equipment, and ordnance stores). One means by which this consumption could be reduced would be by enforcing a harsh standard of living on the troops by cutting all essential items. This might reduce that consumption to 300 tons per day, but even then it was difficult to imagine that this still considerable amount could be transported to a theatre of operations where major ports and rearward bases would be subject to nuclear attack and transport by road would be extremely difficult.[66] For these reasons, some writers argued that in addition to relying on only a minimum number of mechanical transports and other heavy equipment, soldiers should be trained to exist on a low level of subsistence and forgo many of the luxuries that Western service personnel had become so accustomed such as chocolate, alcohol, and cigarettes. After all, high-lighted one Army Captain, 'it should be remembered that the Asiatic soldier...is accustomed to exist and fight hard on a ration scale which makes that of the British Army look like a six-course banquet'.[67]

Therefore, for military intellectuals thinking about the future nuclear battle-field, streamlining the divisional structure appeared to be of paramount import-ance. Field Marshal Montgomery told listeners at a lecture to the RUSI in 1955 that 'the day of the armoured division and of the infantry division *as we knew them in the late war* is past'.[68] This was echoed a year later by the Deputy Chief of the Imperial General Staff, Sir Dudley Ward, who wrote that 'in the long run it will be the force that can manage efficiently with the minimum tonnages to support it that will best be able to fight out the land battle'.[69] Cautious observers recommended solutions such as the 'standard division', which combined both infantry and armoured units, and were not too dissimilar to their Second World War counterparts, except for a slight reduction in support units. The more progressive nuclear theorists, however, suggested more radical concepts, arguing that the basic building block of future Army organizations should be the combined-arms battle-group—a unit in similar size to the conventional battalion,

[65] D. Young, 'New Look Artillery', *Journal of the Royal Artillery*, Vol. 81, No. 4 (October 1954), p. 290.
[66] P. N. M. Moore, 'Goose Eggs', *Army Quarterly*, Vol. 69, No. 2 (January 1955), p. 230.
[67] R. Wright, 'Docking the Tail', *British Army Annual*, No. 2 (March 1955), pp. 98–9.
[68] B. L. Montgomery, 'Organization for War in Modern Times', *The RUSI Journal*, Vol. 100, No. 600 (1955), p. 514.
[69] D. Ward, 'Divisional Organization', *British Army Review*, No. 3 (September 1956), p. 4.

which was self-sufficient with little or no administrative tail. Nuclear guns could supplant the myriad heavy artillery pieces that were normally attached to divisions, and infantry could be air-transported to their objectives, circumventing the need for inflexible road-bound convoys.[70]

Emerging technologies, such as the helicopter, also appeared to offer a solution to the Army's mobility problems. As light-infantryman Major J. L. L. Waddy acknowledged, 'if the communications on land have become an anchor to mobile operations, then supply and movement by air must become the means to achieve mobility'.[71] The helicopter had shown potential in a military role on the battlefields of Korea, where British servicemen would have witnessed US forces employ them to great effect in their role as troop transports and supply craft.[72] The Americans themselves were keen advocates of the use of air mobility to circumvent the hazards of the nuclear battlefield, and the US Army Chief of Staff, General Maxwell D. Taylor, published work habitually throughout the 1950s to promote his pet concept of 'sky cavalry'.[73] There were obvious benefits in the use of helicopters for tactical manoeuvre on the nuclear battlefield since they would be able to avoid congested supply routes on the ground and could transport soldiers over irradiated ground.[74] Some theorists believed that the use of airborne troops, as understood in the conventional sense, would play an important role in future nuclear land combat.[75] The speed and flexibility with which airborne troops could be deployed on the battlefield appeared to be well suited for exploiting and consolidating atomic attack.[76]

In addition, armoured personnel carriers (APCs) had the potential to provide infantry units with the necessary speed and flexibility to carry out high-tempo operations on the ground while offering them a degree of armoured protection against the effects of nuclear weapons.[77] Thus equipped, wrote Colonel J. D. Frost, infantry formations would be able to perform the types of operations that would

---

[70] 'Cygnus', 'Is My Regiment Really Necessary?', *Journal of the Royal Artillery*, Vol. 82, No. 3 (July 1955), pp. 219–24; Macksey, 'The George Knight Clowes Memorial Prize Essay, 1956', p. 171.

[71] J. L. L. Waddy, 'Helicopters for the Army', *Army Quarterly*, Vol. 69, No. 2 (January 1955), p. 194.

[72] For an overview on the use of helicopters during the Korean War see J. A. Stockfisch, *The 1962 Howze Board and Army Combat Developments* (Santa Monica, CA: RAND, 1994), pp. 7–12.

[73] See, for example, James M. Gavin, 'The Tactical Use of the Atomic Bomb', *Bulletin of the Atomic Scientists*, Vol. 7, No. 2 (February 1951), pp. 46–50; James M. Gavin, *Military Review*, Vol. 35, No. 12 (March 1956), p. 107; National Defense University, Washington D.C., Maxwell D. Taylor Papers [digitized collection], 'Mission of the United States Army', speech given by General Taylor in November 1956, p. 15. Although difficult to ascertain, it is likely that British officers would have read, or at least have been aware of, this literature.

[74] C. W. Dunbar, 'Airportability', *British Army Review*, No. 1 (September 1955), p. 71. See, in addition, P. S. Turner, 'Duncan Gold Medal Essay 1955', *Journal of the Royal Artillery*, Vol. 83, No. 2 (April 1956), p. 95.

[75] M. A. J. Tugwell, 'Future of Airborne Forces', *Army Quarterly*, Vol. 70, No. 2 (July 1955), pp. 155–8.

[76] 'Romulus', 'Future Employment of Airborne Forces', *The RUSI Journal*, Vol. 100, No. 598 (1955), p. 238.

[77] A. E. C. Bredin, 'Kangaroo Infantry', *Army Quarterly*, Vol. 62, No. 2 (July 1951), p. 211.

be required in atomic land combat since 'they can operate far more widely deployed than normal marching infantry; because they can be moved at speed to reinforce one another, to support one another, to counter attack another's position or to withdraw having inflicted the maximum possible delay on the enemy'.[78] Brigadier C. M. F. Deakin saw great opportunities in the adoption by infantry of APCs, especially in offensive operations, and painted a picture of future war which was 'one of comparatively small armour/infantry groups with RE [Royal Engineer] and monitoring teams and infantry in APCs, all probably wearing masks and protective clothing, penetrating to great depth behind a nuclear and electronic fire plan'.[79]

Thus, by the middle 1950s, military theorists had identified that the threat of nuclear attack would prevent force concentrations on the same scale as those that had been necessary to force a decision during the major land campaigns of the Second World War. Stemming from this realization was the idea that ground forces would need to be able to switch rapidly between dispersion and concentration, since the concentration of force in space would still be required, as it always had, only now it would only be possible for short periods of time before the risk of nuclear annihilation became too great. In turn, this indicated that the Army would need to attain high levels of battlefield mobility so that it could concentrate to fight and disperse to live. In this context, discourse about the future nuclear battlefield became an extension of the debates about mechanization during the 1920s and 1930s. As the inter-war prophets of manoeuvre warfare had predicted, the lethality and killing power of modern weapons appeared finally to have delivered the death knell to the cumbersome, manpower-intensive conventional formations of the first half of the twentieth century. In a similar vein to their spiritual predecessors, the nuclear theorists argued that the Army required improved command and control structures and streamlined organizations that exploited new technologies such as helicopters and APCs.

## The Atomic Land Battle

The general characteristics required for an army operating in a nuclear environment had been identified by the military theorists as being: small, self-contained units, possessing high levels of tactical mobility, with the ability to sustain independent combat operations divorced from higher command structures and conventional supply lines. There was still the question, however, of how the land

---

[78] LHCMA, Liddell Hart Papers, LIDDELL 15/5/283, An Organisation for Battle, unpublished typescript, n.d. [approx. mid-1950s].
[79] LHCMA, Liddell Hart Papers, LIDDELL 15/5/285, Address given by Brigadier C. M. F. Deakin to the Royal Armoured Corps Conference Bovington on Wednesday 4 December 1957, unpublished lecture notes, 1957.

battle would actually progress under nuclear conditions. It was unclear how the use of tactical nuclear weapons would affect the dichotomy of attack and defence, how troops would have to be deployed on the nuclear battlefield, and how battlefield techniques would have to change to exploit the power of the atom, but avoid its effects. The lack of empirical evidence on which to guide military thought created a number of conceptual difficulties in envisioning how future nuclear operations would progress, and many publicists again looked backwards into military history in the hope of finding clues for the future. Theorists also explored anew the principles of war in an attempt to locate an analytical framework for understanding the conduct of warfare in the nuclear era.

Principles of war provided a framework within which tactical nuclear weapons could be analysed. For example, one Captain of the Royal Tank Corps, K. J. Macksey, began his 1956 article for the *Army Quarterly* with the bold assertion that:

> *Presumably* it is not in dispute that the Principles of War remain unchanged even in the midst of the most violent technical and tactical revolutions. If this is so, then the land campaigns of the future will find the germs of their development in the lessons of the past.[80]

It was natural that some military publicists maintained that the principles of war were as true in the nuclear era as they had been during any other period of history. After all, claimed one writer, although preparations for nuclear land combat would tax the imagination of officers, 'it can only be sound to base all such training on the principles proved by centuries of war'.[81] Enunciated in such a way, the principles of war gave the professional soldier a tool by which the uncertain consequences of the atom could be dissected, and provided a convenient lens through which the changing military environment could be observed. Some writers advanced the notion that tactical nuclear weapons positively reinforced the significance of certain principles while adding a new twist to others. For example, some officers thought that principles such as 'Surprise', 'Mobility and Flexibility', and 'Morale' would gain greater relevance in nuclear land warfare, and that the principle of 'Concentration' might be modified to mean that it was equally important to force the enemy to concentrate in order to provide a suitable atomic target.[82]

---

[80] K. J. Macksey, 'The George Knight Clowes Memorial Prize Essay, 1956', *Army Quarterly*, Vol. 72, No. 2 (July 1956), p. 16 [emphasis added].

[81] R. S. Broke, 'For Which War?', *Journal of the Royal Artillery*, Vol. 82, No. 1 (January 1955), p. 53.

[82] P. J. Wilkinson, 'Tactical Atomic Support of Ground Forces', *Journal of the Royal Artillery*, Vol. 81, No. 2 (April 1954), p. 130; D. F. Wharry, 'Nuclear Fission and the Principles of War', *Journal of the Royal Artillery*, Vol. 83, No. 1 (January 1956), pp. 58–61.

However, with a lack of precedent on which to base assessments, it could only ever be a *presumption* that the principles of war would remain unchanged in the atomic era. It might be, as the editor of the *Royal Armoured Corps Journal* pondered, that for 'the first time in the history of war, experience gained in the immediate past fighting is going to be of little value to the future warrior'.[83] Some military intellectuals were more optimistic and maintained that the basic principles were still sound, but that they would require a slightly different application. After all, stated one observer, 'the physical effects of an atomic explosion are heat, blast, and radiation, the two former of which are not new to war'.[84] It was possible, then, Major-General Pyman maintained in an address to the RUSI, that the different branches of the Army would still perform their traditional functions.[85] This was not to say that all writers agreed that the principles of war would remain relevant in an age of nuclear plenty. In a fictional narrative written for the *British Army Review*, a Major of the Royal Artillery wrote about a future tactical nuclear war in which the main protagonist, a junior officer who was a product of the 1950s British Army, had been transposed into the forward headquarters of an Allied nation in a future nuclear land war. The character naïvely asked his commanding officer about the principles of war in the nuclear age:

'Principles of War!' hooted the general. 'Damme [sic], this is the most unprincipled war I was ever in. What about economy of effort when we use a bomb capable of devastating a town merely to destroy a battalion of infantry? Maintenance of the aim? What aim? If I have any principles left they are:

a) Never concentrate while the enemy has any missiles left.

b) Smash the enemy wherever he concentrates.

c) Ceaseless observation over the whole theatre.

d) Never let the enemy disengage.'[86]

Therefore, the re-examination of the principles of war by some officers failed to provide any conclusive insights into the conduct of the atomic land battle. Nonetheless, it was better to have an intellectual reference point that was tangential than none at all. After all, highlighted the editor of the *British Army Review*, the nuclear military theorists 'are on a good wicket because no one can *prove* by quoting past experience that they are wrong'.[87]

What was becoming clear to military publicists, however, was that ground forces, and their dispositions on the battlefield, would need to abide by the new

---

[83] Editorial, 'Editorial Notes', *Royal Armoured Corps Journal*, Vol. 9, No. 4 (October 1955), p. 169.

[84] M. F. Brogan, 'Tactics and Atomics', *Royal Armoured Corps Journal*, Vol. 9, No. 2 (April 1955), p. 63.

[85] H. E. Pyman, 'Armour in the Land Battle', *The RUSI Journal*, Vol. 99, No. 594 (1954), p. 223.

[86] A. C. McCloy, 'Wham!', *British Army Review*, No. 5 (September 1957), p. 24.

[87] Editorial, *British Army Review*, No. 3 (September 1956), p. 2.

'principles' of atomic land war—dispersion, mobility, and self-contained units. It followed that in offensive and defensive operations, ground forces should be deployed in a manner that allowed them to meet those requirements.[88] From this logic emerged the concept of a series of strongly defended localities, each capable of all-round defence, and so positioned as to dominate important communication centres and terrain features. Each of these positions would be no larger than the brigade-sized battle-group envisioned by military theorists. Gaps would be left between these positions with the object of luring in enemy formations where they would be destroyed by atomic weapons.[89] For that reason, the defended localities might be deployed in a 'chessboard' fashion, with a number of undisclosed strengthened positions, or 'back-stops', that would force the enemy to concentrate, providing a suitable target for nuclear fires.[90] An essential feature of this type of deployment was the requirement for mobile counter-attack forces attached to each locality that could rapidly concentrate to exploit the effects of atomic attack within the killing-grounds. The origins of this concept can be traced back as early as 1948 to the writings of Tuker and others.

The concept of 'islands of resistance' deployed in a 'chessboard' fashion dispersed across the battlefield was not an innovation pioneered by nuclear-age planners, but had been developed during the Second World War as a means to counter armoured forces.[91] In that conflict, various fire bases ('islands'), bristling with anti-tank weapons, were deployed in tank-proof country such as woods and villages. The battle-space had no flanks and each position had 360-degree protection. The ultimate aim was to canalize the attacking force into unfavourable terrain, which would leave it vulnerable to counter-attack.[92] Noticeably, a defence based on islands of resistance had the potential to work well during nuclear land combat. Forcing the attacker to concentrate would create profitable targets for friendly nuclear fires, whilst the dispersed positions of the defender would offer some degree of protection against the enemy's own nuclear weapons. Like many of the concepts pursued by the nuclear military theorists, there was nothing inherently new in this particular scheme, as Giffard Martel acknowledged:

> We are therefore back to our two types of forces, namely the armoured divisions in which every effort is made to increase mobility without losing the necessary

---

[88] Frederick Brundrett, 'Atomic Bombs and All That', *British Army Annual*, No. 2 (March 1955), pp. 7–8.

[89] W. Bate, 'Maintenance in Nuclear War', *British Army Review*, No. 3 (September 1956), p. 15.

[90] R. L. C. Dixon, 'The Bertrand Stewart Prize Essay, 1956', *Army Quarterly*, Vol. 73, No. 2 (January 1957), p. 169. See, in addition, the concepts outlined in N. B. M. Smithson, 'How Clear Is My Crystal?', Vol. 84, No. 3 (July 1957), pp. 222–4 and B. N. Majumdar, 'Logistical Concept for an Atomic War', *Army Quarterly*, Vol. 75, No. 1 (October 1957), p. 108.

[91] Theodore Mataxis and Seymour Goldberg, *Nuclear Tactics, Weapons and Firepower in the Pentomic Division, Battle Group and Company* (Harrisburg, PA: The Military Service Publishing Company, 1958), pp. 127–8.

[92] Miksche, *Atomic Weapons and Armies*, pp. 88–9.

hitting power, and the infantry divisions which must be capable of digging in at a very high speed and carrying out the more static role. It does not seem that the time has arrived to deviate from the age-old policy of these two types of troops.[93]

Indeed, what the nuclear theorists were advocating, consciously or unconsciously, was a classic mobile defence-in-depth that was reminiscent of the tactics developed by the German Army during the First World War to overcome the stalemate of trench warfare: on the defensive the enemy was expected and allowed to penetrate into the prepared defensive position. At first the attacker encountered only light resistance from outposts. As the attack progressed deeper into the defensive zone, resistance stiffened as the attacker encountered strong and entrenched machine gun positions that were capable of all-round defence. This resistance was designed to break up the momentum and cohesion of the attack. At that point the *coup de grace* was delivered by a powerful counter-attack force which advanced to the original frontline, thus encircling the attacker. On the offensive, small units organized for independent action used favourable terrain to bypass enemy strong points and penetrate into the depth of the enemy positions. Once they had broken into the defensive position proper, they advanced as quickly as possible into the defence. A successful penetration was immediately reinforced. The objective was not to attack enemy infantry—which was cut off, pocketed, and left for follow-on forces—but the enemy's rear areas, especially artillery positions and centres of command and control.[94] These were the first non-linear tactics, or 'modern system' of attack and defence, to use Biddle's phrase, and have remained the basis of manoeuvre warfare ever since. Akin to their German counterparts, British military theorists believed that a defence-in-depth that combined small, independent strong points and powerful mobile counter-attack forces would provide a solution to the problem of operating in a battlefield environment that was dominated by lethal and ubiquitous firepower.

One writer even suggested that this style of land warfare originated with the theories of the German military thinker Alfred von Schlieffen with its emphasis on small pockets of firepower covering wide gaps through which mobile forces could fall upon the flanks of the enemy.[95] Another writer traced this type of technique further through history, highlighting that this was the method by which the Romans had held Britain and the Crusaders had pacified Palestine, and in more recent memory, how the Germans had attempted to maintain themselves in

---

[93] IWM, Private Papers of Lieutenant-General Sir Giffard Martel, GQM 6/3d, Land Warfare, April 1955, unpublished typescript.

[94] William S. Lind, 'The Theory and Practice of Manoeuvre Warfare' in Richard D. Hooker (ed.), *Manoeuvre Warfare: An Anthology* (Novato, CA: Presido Press, 1993), pp. 6–7.

[95] G. C. Wynne, 'Pattern for Limited (Nuclear) War: The Riddle of the Schlieffen Plan—I', *The RUSI Journal*, Vol. 102, No. 608 (1957), pp. 498–9.

Russia in the early 1940s.[96] As always, there were a number of elements that were fundamental to the success of such a defence: the static defences had to be strong enough so as to force the attacker to concentrate forces which were disproportionately large, thus giving the mobile forces the initiative; the mobile forces had to be securely based so as to be able to concentrate or disperse as the occasion demanded; and the static defences must be so placed as to be able to provide mutual support. In nuclear land combat, these principles would remain the same; nuclear weapons would merely add a modern twist, mainly that the static positions would have to practise balanced dispersions so that a single atomic bomb would not be able to destroy more than one position in one fell swoop.[97] Captain R. L. C. Dixon of the Royal Tank Regiment believed that the level of dispersion between units in defence would be limited by two factors: 'the need to prevent conventional infiltration in force between them, and the need to make each locality strong enough to resist conventional attack in any strength less than that which would force the attacker to present a nuclear target'.[98] Of course, if the defensive positions could be overcome by conventional tactics without the use of nuclear weapons, they would be rendered useless.

Some commentators worried that over-insurance against atomic attack would reduce the combat effectiveness of the mobile troops during the crucial counterattack phase of the battle. Sir Harold Pyman touched upon this in a speech to 33 Armoured Brigade in 1955, warning that attempting to defraud the enemy of nuclear targets through dispersion would risk not being able to concentrate armoured units at the crisis point in battle, or even worse, by committing it in penny-packets. Such 'bad habits', cautioned Pyman, 'would lead to disaster in war'.[99] This risk was considered by US Army Officer Colonel M. A. Solomon who highlighted that dispersion is a *technique* and not a principle of war. He went on to say that 'obviously, dispersion does have some merit. It is an essential fundamental of military technique. However, dispersion is not the answer against atomic weapons. Battles cannot be won by dispersed forces'.[100] This viewpoint was echoed by his colleague Major J. H. P. Curtis who struggled to visualize how units could remain effective whilst operating in wildly dispersed formations.[101]

---

[96] D. S. Graham, 'The Great Misconception', *Royal Armoured Corps Journal*, Vol. 10, No. 4 (October 1956), p. 140.

[97] See F. Le. G. Whitting, 'Duncan Silver Medal Essay, 1954/55', *Journal of the Royal Artillery*, Vol. 82, No. 2 (April 1955), p. 83.

[98] Dixon, 'The Bertrand Stewart Prize Essay, 1956', p. 167. One writer believed that the key to solving this problem was to increase the number of anti-tank and automatic weaponry within infantry units. See 'Astrologer', 'Clouds in the Crystal', *Army Quarterly*, Vol. 70, No. 1 (April 1955), pp. 89–90.

[99] LHCMA, Pyman Papers, PYMAN 9/8, Speech to 33 Armoured Brigade, unpublished lecture notes, n.d. [approx. 1955]. For a similar view see William F. Train, 'The Atomic Challenge', *Military Review*, Vol. 36, No. 8 (November 1956), p. 6.

[100] M. A. Solomon, 'Dispersion Is Not the Answer', *Military Review*, Vol. 31, No. 3 (June 1951), p. 42.

[101] J. H. P. Curtis, 'The Army of the Future', *Military Review*, Vol. 37, No. 9 (December 1957), p. 43.

All of these problems pointed towards the need for a balanced or controlled dispersion on the battlefield. As one Lieutenant-Colonel explained in a 1957 article: 'the necessary dispersion to avoid nuclear destruction must therefore, on occasion, be balanced—as a calculated risk—against the concentration of force necessary to fight the tactical battle; as far as possible then, any lack of vital dispersion must be off-set by concealment and protection'.[102]

Even the idea of balanced dispersion was abhorrent to some theorists, however. A number of publicists associated with the Royal Artillery maintained that the heavy (atomic) gun would emerge as the Queen of the Battlefield, and that there would be no hope for any level of open troop concentrations on the battlefield. 'Dig or Die' became their motto, with proponents arguing that such was the unprecedented destructive power of nuclear weapons, any open movement on the battlefield would be suicidal, and that the humble shovel and a bit of luck would be the key to survival on the nuclear battlefield. One officer, in his rather unambiguously titled 1956 article, 'The Principle Weapon', envisioned a style of warfare which equated to an atomic gun duel—with armour and infantry reduced to the supporting role of protecting artillery crews in static defensive positions while opposing gunners worked to identify and destroy one another with atomic fires.[103] A Captain in the Royal Artillery suggested that this type of land war might resemble mobile chess, with various combinations of low-value columns trying to capture or destroy the Atomic Queen.[104] Another writer believed that the superiority of firepower over manoeuvre would see a return to a style of warfare that was more reminiscent of the First rather than the Second World War, with each side clinging to each other, sheltered by ever deeper and more elaborate earthworks.[105]

Other critics of the fortress and mobile striking force conception of defence maintained that individual static positions would simply be too vulnerable to nuclear attack and that 'even if every man were to devote all his energy to digging for hours, if not days, protection against the tactical nuclear weapon would still be inadequate'.[106] The assumption that men could merely dig a little deeper to avoid the effects of firepower had first emerged in the years leading up to the First World

[102] R. A. Barron, 'The Division in Nuclear War', *Royal Engineers Journal*, Vol. 71, No. 3 (September 1957), p. 249.
[103] J. H. P. Curtis, 'The Principle Weapon', *Journal of the Royal Artillery*, Vol. 83, No. 4 (October 1956), pp. 244–50.
[104] D. N. Howell-Everson, 'Are We Training for the Right War?', *Journal of the Royal Artillery*, Vol. 81, No. 4 (October 1954), p. 288.
[105] M. E. Bransby-Williams, 'Duncan Silver Medal Essay 1955', *Journal of the Royal Artillery*, Vol. 83, No. 3 (July 1956), p. 167.
[106] G. P. Crean, 'Death of a Dinosaur', *Army Quarterly*, Vol. 73, No. 1 (October 1956), p. 106; N. B. M. Smithson, 'To Be or Not to Be? Is That the Question?', *Journal of the Royal Artillery*, Vol. 83, No. 4 (October 1956), p. 288. See the thoughts of an infantryman on this matter in E. O'Balance, 'Thoughts of an Infantryman Under Nuclear Pressure', *British Army Review*, No. 2 (March 1956), pp. 50–3.

War, but as the grim fighting of that conflict testified, even the most formidable fortresses, bunkers, and fieldworks could, given enough time, be reduced to rubble through conventional artillery barrages.[107] Since the atomic bomb could deliver the equivalent of thousands of tons of conventional high explosives in an instant, rather than over a period of days, it appeared that this would be doubly true in nuclear combat. The dilemma was that if the defensive bastions were dispersed widely enough to mitigate the effects of nuclear attack, then this would render the whole defensive position vulnerable to conventional tactics.[108] Other publicists argued that history showed that any isolated defensive position with open flanks usually became surrounded and destroyed sooner or later and that 'few commanders would be happy about staunching the flow of an enemy through a twenty-mile gap between two insecure boxes, bastions or hedgehogs'.[109] Moreover, it was possible that the attacker would simply avoid entering the nuclear killing-grounds and bypass the static defences through wide flanking movements as was common in highly mobile operations.[110]

There were other means by which nuclear theorists believed that an opponent could be forced to concentrate without the need for prepared nuclear killing-grounds between dispersed defensive locations. One was by preparing defensive positions overlooking a natural or artificial obstacle, which would become one of the main tenets of Army doctrine, as Chapter 6 will show. Although this was not a new concept, since land forces have always sought to dominate terrain features that conferred a tactical advantage on the battlefield, obstacle belts would assume a new significance in tactical nuclear warfare by forcing an attacker to concentrate into a vulnerable nuclear target.[111] The techniques developed for defending an obstacle in conventional warfare would need modification for the nuclear battle-field, however, the most important of which was the use of mobile troops instead of static infantry positions.[112] Another means by which an opponent might be forced to concentrate was to exploit the radioactive properties of nuclear weapons and deny certain pieces of ground to the enemy, forcing it into congested areas of terrain where it could be canalized and destroyed.[113] In this context, the use of radiation to deny areas of ground favourable to the enemy would be analogous to the defensive use of gas during the First World War.[114]

---

[107] Biddle, *Military Power*, p. 30.     [108] Crean, 'Death of a Dinosaur', p. 106.

[109] D. S. Graham, 'The Future of the Regiment', *Journal of the Royal Artillery*, Vol. 84, No. 2 (April 1957), p. 108.

[110] V. P. Naib, 'Mobile Defence', *The RUSI Journal India*, Vol. 86, No. 364 (July 1956), p. 223.

[111] M. R. W. Burrows, 'Atomic Warfare and the Infantry Division', *Journal of the Royal Artillery*, Vol. 82, No. 2 (April 1955), pp. 118–21.

[112] M. R. W. Burrows, 'The Forcing of an Obstacle', *Journal of the Royal Artillery*, Vol. 82, No. 4 (October 1955), pp. 295–6.

[113] Brogan, 'Tactics and Atomics', p. 68.

[114] 'Musketeer', 'The Tactical Employment of Atomic Weapons', *Royal Armoured Corps Journal*, Vol. 7, No. 2 (April 1953), pp. 60–1.

In these types of conditions it was likely that engineers would play an increasingly significant role on the battlefield because of the specialist skills required to prepare obstacles for both offensive and defensive operations.[115] During the Second World War, 1,445 Baily bridges were built by 21st Army Group alone between 6 June 1944 and May 1945. In a future war in North West Europe it was likely that an even greater effort would be required. Since the maintenance of mobility would be paramount in nuclear war, formations would require close support from engineers with specialist bridging equipment.[116] Furthermore, the standard fortifications that were suitable for conventional war would require special treatment under nuclear conditions if they were to protect soldiers from nuclear blasts—they would have to be of considerable strength and able to be deployed in great haste, and would be required in high numbers throughout the theatre of operations.[117] This again would require engineers that were specially trained for nuclear conditions and equipped with advanced apparatus, including APCs.[118]

Another consideration for nuclear theorists, but one that appeared to emerge as an afterthought, was how soldiers would maintain their combat effectiveness in what would be an unprecedentedly violent and stressful operating environment. Not only would men have to fight in the shadow of instantaneous atomic annihilation, but the high levels of battlefield dispersion necessary to reduce that threat would mean that units and individuals would be isolated in the field. Senior officers acknowledged that this greater dispersion would place a premium on minor tactics and the superlative skill of junior commanders.[119] These small units, detached from other elements of the Army and the higher command, would also need to possess a high degree of morale and discipline if they hoped to be able to fight and survive on the nuclear battlefield.[120] The unique effects of nuclear weapons, particularly radiation, would pose a challenge to the individual will to fight like never before. As one writer noted, 'the radiation effects of nuclear weapons will be sinister and frightening for those who do not understand them.

---

[115] J. E. L. Carter, 'Engineering in Extremis', *Royal Engineers Journal*, Vol. 69, No. 1 (March 1955), p. 36.

[116] M. J. W. Wright, 'The Cooper's Hill War Memorial Prize Essay 1956', *Royal Engineers Journal*, Vol. 70, No. 3 (September 1956), pp. 225–6.

[117] G. N. Tuck, 'The Engineer Task in Future Wars', *Royal Engineers Journal*, Vol. 68, No. 2 (June 1954), pp. 114–15.

[118] M. L. Crosthwait, 'Speed and Surprise in an Atomic War', *Royal Engineers Journal*, Vol. 68, No. 2 (June 1954), p. 128; J. D. Goodship, 'Divisional Engineers in the Atomic Era', *Royal Engineers Journal*, Vol. 71, No. 2 (June 1957), pp. 125–30; R. L. France, 'Armoured Engineers', *Royal Engineers Journal*, Vol. 71, No. 3 (September 1957), pp. 239–45.

[119] M. R. Roberts, 'The Importance of Patrols in Nuclear Warfare', *The RUSI Journal*, Vol. 100, No. 60 (1955), p. 575.

[120] L. H. Landon, 'What Sort of Army?', *Journal of the Royal Artillery*, Vol. 82, No. 3 (July 1955), p. 216. These issues have been the perennial problems of greater dispersion. See Biddle, *Military Power*, p. 38.

It is impossible to see anything, to feel anything or to taste anything'.[121] In this context, one Colonel drew an analogy with the first use of gas during the First World War, arriving at the grim conclusion that: 'It seems that human beings are infinitely degraded by the close menace of some foul, lethal thing, immeasurably bigger than themselves, against which there is no defence. It revolts them and saps their very essence'.[122] How morale would remain intact under nuclear conditions remained one of the great unknowns in thinking about the nuclear battlefield. Although the Army acknowledged that this would present unique challenges for commanders at all levels, it made little effort to explore how the problem might be overcome.

## Conclusions

The professional soldier is often criticized in peacetime for planning for the last war. This statement becomes rather problematic when applied to the British nuclear theorists after 1945. The sheer volume of articles that appeared in professional service journals at the dawn of the nuclear age reveals an officer corps receptive to change and dedicated to the intellectual challenges posed by the arrival of tactical nuclear weapons. When viewed in isolation, individual articles might easily be dismissed as being the mere musings of interested soldiers discussing narrowly focused technical subjects specific to one particular branch or service specialism. Yet, theory is personal, and these were theories of war. When taken together, this considerable body of work can be seen to constitute the burgeoning theory of tactical nuclear warfare in Britain and provides a snapshot of the professional officer corps' thinking about the changing character of conflict. In this context, the Army had clearly entered the speculation phase of the process of military innovation, and the theoretical constructs developed in these formative years of the nuclear age would go on to influence the Army's official doctrine in the decades to come.

[121] J. N. W. Hearn, 'Nuclear Weapon Effects and Target Response', *British Army Review*, No. 5 (September 1957), p. 20.
[122] T. I. Lloyd, 'Nuclear Arms and the Service Man', *Royal Engineers Journal*, Vol. 68, No. 4 (December 1954), p. 354.

# 4

# Nuclear Instruction at the Staff College

In October 1950, an internal memorandum issued to all instructors at the Army Staff College, Camberley stated curiously that: 'I am planning to have an explosion at the end of Scene II. This will only be amusing if it is unexpected. Will all recipients please observe strict security!'.[1] The note was circulated by one of the Rawlinson Players, that 'gallant body of amateur actors' composed of members of the Directing Staff (DS), who performed demonstrations and playlets in the College's Rawlinson Hall to illustrate staff techniques and procedures in a lively and interesting manner.[2] The demonstration in question was on the challenges of civil defence, and the 'explosion' was in fact a recording of an atomic bomb blast broadcast via a clandestine gramophone hidden under a table in the centre of the lecture theatre. The audio was accompanied by the appearance of a cardboard cut-out of a mushroom cloud, which was superimposed on a map of Southampton with red blast roundels radiating from the city centre in one-mile increments. However crude and whimsical the demonstration appears in retrospect, the young Army officers seated in the Rawlinson Hall on that Tuesday morning witnessed one of the first attempts by the Staff College to introduce to its students a weapon system that would come to dominate thinking about land warfare in the decades to come.

The education and training of officers shines a revealing light on the professional ethos and organizational culture of the British Army as it attempted to find a new *raison d'être* in a rapidly changing world. As Brian Bond stated in the introduction to one of the rare examinations of the history of the Staff College, 'if there was a "Brain of the Army" capable of producing a "School of Thought" it was to be found at Camberley in the Staff College, and nowhere else'.[3] The Army Staff College was an historic institution established in 1858 to train Army officers in the administrative and staff aspects of their chosen profession, and continued until 1997 when it was merged, along with the other single-service staff colleges, into the new Joint Services Command and Staff College at Shrivenham. Before the First World War, few British Army officers wanted to attend Staff College, drawn as they were from the public school system that tended to value force of character

---

[1] Joint Services Command and Staff College Archives, Shrivenham [JSCSC], Staff College Course [SCC] 1950, Vol. 14, Demonstration Prometheus.
[2] F. W. Young, *The Story of the Staff College, 1858–1958* (Aldershot: Gale & Polden, 1958), p. 14.
[3] Brian Bond, *The Victorian Army and the Staff College, 1854–1914* (London: Eyre Methuen, 1972), p. 3.

*Imagining Nuclear War in the British Army, 1945–1989*. Simon J. Moody, Oxford University Press (2020).
© Simon J. Moody.
DOI: 10.1093/oso/9780198846994.001.0001

above intellectual attainment.[4] Indeed, some aspiring soldier-scholars were even accused of disloyalty to their regiment for wanting to spend two years in 'idleness' at Camberley.[5] The prejudice against Staff College was beginning to wane by the Edwardian period, and after the experiences of the Second World War had demonstrated beyond doubt the requirement in modern warfare for able staff officers and skilled divisional and corps commanders, ambitious officers realized that attaining the post-nominal 'psc' (passed staff college) was a prerequisite for promotion to the best jobs in the Army.[6]

The design and implementation of nuclear instruction at the Staff College after 1945 demonstrates how the Army perceived the changing character of conflict and its role in future war. How the Staff College institutionalized learning on a subject about which very little was known, that was politically sensitive, and that relied ultimately on abstract concepts untested in the crucible of war provides insights into how the Army structured its thinking about soldiering in the nuclear age. In this context, the education and training of the officer corps provides one of the few tangible means through which to analyse some of the conceptual challenges confronting military organizations when preparing to fight in an alien environ-ment. Changes to the curriculum of professional military education institutions have been identified by Thomas G. Mahnken as an indicator that military organizations are moving through the implementation phase of military innov-ation.[7] The history of the Cold War Staff College supports this hypothesis and represents a clear attempt by the Army to adapt its thinking to the new military challenges posed by the arrival of nuclear weapons.

## Evolution of the Curriculum

The Staff College curriculum evolved considerably between 1945 and 1989 and proved remarkably absorbent to new ideas by incorporating the most fashionable thinking and doctrinal constructs into its syllabus. The structure of the Army Staff Course itself, however, remained largely unchanged despite being subjected to almost continuous review and inquiry since the end of the Second World War.[8] The purpose of the course was to train officers in all of the skills required to take up second-grade staff appointments, and with further experience, command. The length

---

[4] David French, *Military Identities: The Regimental System, The British Army, and the British People c. 1870–2000* (Oxford: Oxford University Press, 2005), p. 145.

[5] Ibid., p. 153.    [6] Ibid., pp. 160–1.

[7] Thomas G. Mahnken, 'Uncovering Foreign Military Innovation', *Journal of Strategic Studies*, Vol. 22, No. 4 (1999), pp. 30–4.

[8] For an overview of the various attempts to reform the Army Staff Course see JSCSC, SCC 1984, Records, A Review of the Development of Staff Training Since the War and a Study of Future Trends, October 1984.

of the staff course was one year, and admitted 180 Majors (approximately twenty-nine years of age) in each cohort, of whom 140 were from the British Army and the remainder from other Commonwealth armies, the sister services, and the Civil Service. The students first attended a ten-week course at the Royal Military College of Science, Shrivenham as an introduction to the ways in which science and technology were shaping the character of conflict, before they were sent to Camberley for the staff course proper. The course progressed over three distinct phases organized into three, and later four, terms. The first, and most unpopular, element of the course provided the necessary grounding in English writing, administration, the minutia of staff duties, and the principles of war which 'were hammered into us like the Ten Commandments'.[9] One student recalled this time at Staff College as akin to 'going back to school again', denigrating it as merely 'clerks' work'.[10] The second element focused on the different phases of war—defence, withdrawal, attack, and advance—against the background of various limited and global war settings. The final element of the course was the most susceptible to change, and included the teaching of miscellaneous subjects including military history, psychological warfare, and nuclear operations.

Nuclear instruction was first incorporated into the Staff College curriculum in 1947, where the emphasis was on explaining the science and technology of atomic energy. The nuclear revolution had yet to take grip of Camberley, and the subject was approached tentatively and viewed more as an aberration to the profession of arms than as a military revolution that would force fundamental change on the Army. Addressing the new cohort of the class of 1947, the Commandant, Major-General Sir Richard Hull, informed students that 'In spite of the development of atomic energy there is no evidence to support a belief that the role of the Army will change. We must still be prepared for battle on land'.[11] And prepare for battle on land it did. The Staff College syllabus of 1947 would have been familiar even to those students who had graduated before the Second World War and was concerned with conventional tactics, administration, and rudimentary staff duties. The only change that might have signalled the dawn of a new era was the inclusion of four lectures on 'Atomic Energy' (delivered by Professor Sir Mark Oliphant— the energetic advocate for the peaceful use of atomic energy and original contributor to the Pugwash Conferences on Science and World Affairs), 'Atomic Research in the Forces', 'Eye Witness of Bikini Test', and, reflecting the idea that nuclear weapons were the preserve of strategic air forces, 'Atomic Research and Air Forces'.[12]

---

[9]  Michael Stuart Gray interview, 28362, Imperial War Museum Sound Archive.
[10]  James Michael Calvert interview, 9989, Imperial War Museum Sound Archive.
[11]  JSCSC, SCC 1947, Vol. 1, Precise of a Lecture given by the Commandant on 11 March 1947.
[12]  JSCSC, SCC 1947, Vol. 1, Outline Syllabus.

The only critical commentary to be found in the records from this period comes from the minutes of the Students' Committee, which felt strongly that 'we are perhaps "leaning too heavily" on the lessons of the last war and NOT paying enough thought to the future and whether the present scientific development of arms and [equipment] will seriously alter our tactical doctrine in the next war?'.[13] The frank reply from the Assistant Commandant was that:

> The CIGS has already laid down as a basis for military study that scientific developments are not likely to alter tactical doctrine for the next ten years. We do not originate doctrines here. I cannot therefore see what benefit is to be gained by a theoretical study of what war might be like in the distant future. Neither do I agree that any useful purpose would be served by lecturers from the IDC [Imperial Defence College] visiting us. At the moment they know no more about the effects of new weapons than we do.[14]

With the benefit of hindsight it appears that this rebuttal was too dismissive of the changes that were destined to occur: Army tactical doctrine did undergo a major revision in the ten years between 1947 and 1957; the Staff College would perform an increasingly important link in the doctrine development process when it became home to the Tactical Doctrine Cell (TDC) in the early 1980s; and the theoretical study of future war would consume much of the Army's intellectual energies in the decades to come.

The study of future war was formally introduced a year later in the form of lectures, syndicate room discussions, and written assessments, but the approach remained cautious, even defensive. The guidance issued to the Directing Staff explained that it was impossible to base all teaching at Staff College on 'modern weapons'—the euphemism for nuclear weapons—because of a lack of detailed technical information, and that instruction should therefore be based on the tactics and organizations of armies as they were in 1948. Nonetheless, it was deemed necessary to study future war if only to avoid the criticism often levelled at peacetime military forces that they prepare to fight the last war without looking sufficiently into the uncertain future.[15] To help guide thinking about 'modern weapons', students were issued a precis which began with a curious sketch, demonstrating the Army's propensity for gallows humour:

Scene in 1955
Nanny (in yellow oilskin): Johnnie, say your ABC
Johnnie: 'A' is atomic radioactivity,

---

[13] JSCSC, SCC 1947, Vol. 1, Report of Students' Committee: Third Tutorial Period.
[14] Ibid.
[15] JSCSC, SCC 1948, Vol. 1, Instructions to DS No. 9: Future War—The Shape of Things to Come.

'B' biologic bubonic proclivity,
'C' is for chemical warfare—that's gas,
If a boy don't look out for these three he's an ass.[16]

The precis was entirely technical in detail and was concerned not with the conduct of nuclear warfare, but with explaining the nature and effects of atomic explosions. The students were expected to digest this information alongside a close reading of the grim report by the British Mission to Japan on *The Effects of the Atomic Bombs at Hiroshima and Nagasaki*, which painted in vivid detail how the two cities sunk 'in an instant, and without struggle, to the most primitive existence', complete with photographs depicting the asphalt surface of roads which retained the 'shadows' of those who had walked there at the instant of the explosion.[17] In addition, the Staff College library was now well stocked with literature on both atomic energy and future war. Indeed, it could boast to have stocked twenty-two books and journal articles on future war, including A. Jolly's 'Armour and the Next War' and Francis Tuker's 'Nuclear Energy and War' (see Chapter 3); twenty-five titles, mainly American, on the subject of nuclear weapons; and scores of others concerned with rocketry and chemical warfare.[18] In 1948, this collection must have represented a sizable portion of all available academic studies on nuclear weapons that had emerged over the last three years.

Although early nuclear instruction at the Staff College was concerned primarily with the narrow technical aspects of nuclear science, the curriculum did begin to reflect a broader concern about the changing strategic environment and the future character of land warfare. Indeed, throughout the period under review, the Staff College demonstrated a remarkable aptitude to keep abreast of the latest developments in national and alliance strategic concepts. In 1949, instruction on future war was framed within the context of the 1947 'Future Defence Policy' paper, in which the Chiefs of Staff identified the three pillars of British strategy as the defence of the home base, control of sea lines of communication, and the protection of the Middle East.[19] Against this background, students were asked to consider broad strategic questions pertaining to the Army's most likely enemies (*de facto* the Soviet Union, although a large question mark was placed next to the words 'Germany' and 'Japan' in one set of student instructions), potential theatres of conflict, as well as more specific questions regarding the possible effects of new weapons on tactics, doctrine, and organizations.[20] Despite a greater grounding of

---

[16] JSCSC, SCC 1948, Vol. 15, Civil Defence Precis 2: Atomic Explosions.
[17] *The Effects of the Atomic Bombs at Hiroshima and Nagasaki: Report of the British Mission to Japan* (London: HMSO, 1946), pp. 4, 11.
[18] JSCSC, SCC 1948, Vol. 1, Appendix 'A' to Instructions to DS No. 9.
[19] TNA, CAB 21/1800, DO(47)44, Future Defence Policy, 22 May 1947.
[20] JSCSC, SCC 1949, Vol. 13, Future War: Divisional Discussion.

future war concepts within an established and understandable strategic context, students still felt that little benefit was obtained because of a general lack of knowledge on the development and effects of future weapons.[21]

News of the US commitment to build a hydrogen bomb, 'the latest development in man's inhumanity to man' according to one Staff College paper,[22] in the wake of the successful Soviet atomic bomb test in 1949 threatened to bring radical change to future operating concepts. Study on the future war phase of the course was therefore broadened in 1950 to include both strategic and tactical aspects. The former was included to provide a common understanding of the international context in which the Army would be operating since students had a tendency to 'drag their pet strategic theories into the later discussions'. DS were reminded when approaching the study of future war not to allow defeatism to take hold of the student body and to make sure that 'our larger (?) stock-pile of atom bombs is appreciated'.[23] The aim of the syndicate discussions on the tactical aspects of future war was to consider the possible 'tactical uses' of new weapons in a war in 1960 and any consequent changes required to tactical doctrine, organizations, and administration. This was the first time in which the tactical application of nuclear weapons was given serious thought at the Staff College, the conclusions of which conformed to broader thinking in the Army during this period—that although nuclear weapons could be employed profitably against troop concentrations, it was unlikely that they would be squandered on the tactical battlefield. Students were informed that the ultimate purpose of future war studies was to 'provoke thought and speculation about the future so that we should at least be mentally prepared for inevitable and possibly drastic changes'.[24] In contrast, the guidance issued to the DS on how to approach the problem was much more pessimistic:

> I am well aware that this subject causes dismay even to the most hardened DS. I hope that the following notes will provide material and talking points (as they are now fashionably called) to stimulate discussion. If, however, the students have really *thought* before the discussion, it should go quite well. On the other hand, should they not have done so, the barometer of the discussion will oscillate rapidly between 'very dry' and 'more wind'.[25]

However much students thought about the possible impact of nuclear weapons on future war, there remained a whiff of frustration about the general lack of

[21] JSCSC, SCC 1949, Vol. 1, Minutes of the Students' Committee Meeting held at Camberley on 22 July 1949.
[22] JSCSC, SCC 1950, Vol. 14, Future War.
[23] JSCSC, SCC 1950, Vol. 14, Future War—The Strategic Aspect.
[24] JSCSC, SCC 1950, Vol. 14, Future War—The Tactical Aspect.
[25] JSCSC, SCC 1950, Vol. 14, Future War—The Tactical Aspect [DS notes].

information on the development and effects of nuclear weapons,[26] and DS were forced to acknowledge that ultimately 'one man's guess as to what form future war will take is as good as another's'.[27]

In 1952, the Staff College decided to introduce a short exercise on the tactical employment of atomic weapons so that students could assess the possible effects of enemy employment against friendly troop concentrations preparing for attack.[28] This mirrored the greater attention paid to nuclear weapons within the new strategic concept articulated in the Chiefs of Staff 1952 Defence Policy and Global Strategy paper, which placed massive retaliation at the cockpit of British strategy.[29] However, no fundamental changes to tactical instruction were envisioned at this time. DS were encouraged, however, to obtain as much information as possible through US channels, with one instructor ordered to attend a short course on weapons of mass destruction at the Joint School of Chemical Warfare.[30] A new exercise, GOLIATH, subsequently appeared on the 1953 course in the form of a map discussion, but students again expressed dissatisfaction that nuclear weapons were merely grafted onto a previous conventional war exercise.[31] Such criticisms characterized feedback on the following course, where students felt that a 'false picture' was painted in certain exercises since 'concentration of troops as depicted in Exercise GORING would be inadmissible in a major atomic war'.[32] In a polemic riposte to this comment, the Assistant Commandant attempted to justify the continued relevance of conventional war tactics by demonstrating that the recent fighting in Korea and Indochina had been limited to the use of conventional weapons where traditional techniques such as river-crossings and break-in battles remained important.[33]

As the 1950s were coming to an end, any resistance towards the intrusion of mushroom clouds into the Staff College curriculum began to disappear from the official records as it became clear from both national and alliance strategic appreciations that a future high-intensity land war fought against the Soviet Union in Europe would be conducted in a nuclear environment. Major-General Michael Forrester recalled seeing the first signs of these innovations when, serving as a member of the Directing Staff between 1953 and 1955, he was instructed by the Commandant, General Sir Charles Jones, to rewrite an exercise which had been deemed outdated and not reflective of the current concept of operations in

[26] JSCSC, SCC 1949, Vol. 1, Minutes of the Students' Committee Meeting held at Camberley on 22 July 1949 and JSCSC, SCC 1950, Vol. 1, Recommendations by the Students' Committee: 5th Term 1950 Course.

[27] JSCSC, SCC 1949, Vol. 13, Future War: Discussion.

[28] JSCSC, SCC 1952, Vol. 1, Decisions from Assistant Commandant's Conference 3/52.

[29] TNA, CAB 131/12, D(52)26, Defence Policy and Global Strategy, report by the Chiefs of Staff, 17 June 1952.

[30] JSCSC, SCC 1952, Vol. 1, Decisions from Assistant Commandant's Conference 1/52.

[31] JSCSC, SCC 1953, Vol. 1, Recommendations by the Students' Committee.

[32] JSCSC, SCC 1954, Vol. 1, Recommendations by the Students' Committee.

[33] Ibid.

BAOR. The revised map exercise apparently had to account for greater frontages and better exploitation of mobility and firepower.[34] While not referencing directly the effects of nuclear weapons, it is clear within the military context that such considerations were underpinning this new outlook. By 1956, the effects of nuclear weapons were incorporated into the study of each phase of war—defence, withdrawal, attack, and advance—which had hitherto been restricted to the consideration of conventional weapons alone.[35] These developments were accelerated after the submission to Parliament in 1957 of Duncan Sandys' controversial defence White Paper, which threatened to impose radical change on the Army by terminating National Service and supplanting manpower in BAOR with 'atomic rocket artillery'.[36] This paved the way for the first major review of the Staff College curriculum in 1958 within which 'nuclear warfare' was added to the syllabus as one of the basic subjects to be studied on the course.[37] The rationale was that the value of BAOR to the strategic deterrent—the first priority in national defence policy—rested on its ability to convince the Soviet Union that it possessed a credible capability to be able to fight and prevail in nuclear land combat. Therefore, it was deemed essential that commanders and their staff should continue to study the 'art' of nuclear warfare.[38] This would entail a study of the latest War Office publications and doctrine pamphlets as well as a technical grounding in the characteristics of nuclear weapons employment, including their general effects and capabilities, the limitations of weapons systems, target analysis, post-strike assessment, and command and control arrangements.[39]

By the end of the 1950s, the Staff College curriculum reflected a growing awareness of the challenges posed by tactical nuclear weapons. These were incremental changes, however, and reveal an institutional reluctance to incorporate some of the more radical thinking about future warfare into the professional military education of the officer corps. As Major-General Michael Holme would later testify about his time as a member of the Directing Staff between 1952 and 1955, the syllabus and methods of instruction had changed little since his time as a student in 1948, nuclear exercises were interesting but unrealistic, and tactical methods were the same as they had been in the closing stages of the Second World War but with a greater emphasis placed on mobility.[40] This was confirmed by Field Marshal Montgomery who, after visiting the Staff College in 1958, wrote to the CIGS complaining that instruction was based on a 'mixture of the methods we used in the last war combined with some crystal gazing into the

---

[34] Michael Forrester interview, 27182, Imperial War Museum Sound Archive.
[35] JSCSC, SCC 1956, Vol. 1, Annex 'A' to Outline Syllabus.
[36] Cmnd. 124, *Defence: Outline of Future Policy* (London: HMSO, 1957), p. 4.
[37] TNA, WO 231/102, SCHQ 169, Review of Staff College Directive, 17 April 1958.
[38] Ibid.      [39] Ibid.
[40] Michael Walter Holme interview, 24897, Imperial War Museum Sound Archive.

unknown future'.[41] Speaking in his capacity as Deputy Supreme Allied Commander Europe (DSACEUR), he acknowledged the value of introducing students to 'nuclear theory', but thought that they would benefit little from the study of global nuclear war, or the 'Test Match' as he coined it, since such an eventuality he claimed had been 'indefinitely postponed'.[42]

The 1960s would bring yet more changes to the strategic environment as nuclear sufficiency on both sides of the Iron Curtain gave birth to the NATO strategy of flexible response and a new series of tactical doctrine. As Chapter 6 will show, *The Land Battle* series of pamphlets articulated clearly a new nuclear role for the Army, and so thinking about the unthinkable became a simple fact of life for Army officers enrolled at the Staff College. In 1964, the study of 'Nuclear War' occupied the whole of the fourth term of the Army Staff Course—a position it would occupy within the syllabus until the end of the Cold War. A precis issued to students outlining the importance of this new emphasis on nuclear instruction demonstrates an attempt to convey the changing role of the Army in national strategy:

First and foremost, we study the use of tactical nuclear weapons because they form part of the global war equipment of the Army and of our deterrent policy. However difficult it may be to imagine the tactical situations and the chaos which the use of these weapons may produce, we have a clear cut responsibility to consider the problems they create... There will undoubtedly be times when you will find it hard to accept the situations described to you, or which emerge from your exercise planning. When these occur, you should remember what our nuclear war studies are designed to do; they are to help you to appreciate the size of the problems and to stimulate new thought, whilst teaching the current British Army doctrine on the subject. By the contribution of constructive thought and argument you can help to develop that doctrine.[43]

Although the tone of the student precis was optimistic, the DS instructions again were much more pessimistic, containing the grim reminder that:

Using nuclear weapons against an Army of soldiers is like using sledge hammers against an Army of ants... we should not underestimate the enormous destructive power of these weapons, the complete devastation they will cause, the dazzle and shock effect, the fall-out and induced radiation, the mass casualties.[44]

---

[41] TNA, WO 231/102, DSAC 0900/1, Field Marshal Montgomery to Chief of the Imperial General Staff, 24 March 1958.
[42] Ibid.     [43] JSCSC, SCC 1964, Vol. 8, Nuclear War: Outline of Instruction.
[44] JSCSC, SCC 1965, Vol. 7, Annex 'A' to DS Notes to Outline Instruction: Bull Points from the Study of the Corps Nuclear Battle.

This statement was designed to 'eradicate right from the start any suggestion that nuclear war is merely conventional war with nuclear weapons added, or that nuclear weapons are just bigger bangs for the support of ground forces'.[45] In spite of this tentative acceptance by Staff College instructors of the ghastly reality of nuclear warfare, the Army nonetheless had to confront as best as it could the imponderables of nuclear warfare if it was to play an effective role in NATO's deterrent posture, since 'by being trained in the use of nuclear weapons and in all aspects of nuclear war we shall contribute towards the credibility of the deterrent'.[46]

Considerations of the wider utility of the Army to NATO's strategic deterrent posture in Europe began to be reflected in the Staff College curriculum by the early 1970s. Instruction in the fourth term now included the study of NATO strategy proper in addition to the tactics appropriate to land forces operating on the Central Front under the threat of nuclear, biological, and chemical weapons.[47] Instruction took the form of presentations, syndicate room discussions, indoor and outdoor exercises, and visits to both BAOR and the 7th US Army in Germany. Representatives from the Foreign Office and academics from various universities were invited to speak to students at the Staff College, and DS arranged for lectures and presentations on subjects such as Allied and Soviet bloc forces, NATO strategy, higher command, the philosophy of deterrence, and the strategic nuclear balance.[48] Although strategic studies had been a staple of Staff College curriculum since 1918, under the guise of 'Imperial Military Geography',[49] the 1972 cohort of students were sceptical of trying to adapt tactical concepts to a rapidly changing strategic environment. The Assistant Commandant was adamant, however, that a study of strategy must precede any discussion of tactics since 'the political, economic, and military constraints must be studied first in order to understand the evolution of the current tactical concept'.[50]

The political constraints that would likely be imposed on BAOR if it was ever to fight the war for which it was training increasingly bore their mark on the Staff College curriculum. By the end of the 1970s, the fourth term of the staff course looked very different to previous iterations with less emphasis placed on the teaching of nuclear tactics. This reflected NATO's latest strategic preference that the fighting on the Central Front should be limited to the use of conventional weapons for as long as possible before the general release of nuclear weapons was authorized. Indeed, the precis on nuclear fire planning issued to students on the 1978 course had as its epigraph 'ULTIMA RATIO'—the final argument. It

---

[45] JSCSC, SCC 1965, Vol. 7, The Tactical Concepts of Nuclear War [DS notes].
[46] JSCSC, SCC 1965, Vol. 7, Nuclear War: Outline of Instruction.
[47] JSCSC, SCC 1971, Records, Fourth Term Planning Directive.
[48] JSCSC, SCC 1972, Records, Fourth Term Panning Directive.
[49] French, *Military Identities*, p. 156.
[50] JSCSC, SCC 1972, Records, Minutes of the Students' Committee Meeting, Fourth Term 1972.

explained that the possible use of tactical nuclear weapons still remained an integral part of BAOR's doctrine, and that a general knowledge of their use, effectiveness, and the means of protecting troops in the field was a requirement for every staff officer. It still remained woolly, however, on what would happen once the final argument was in full swing, explaining ambiguously that:

> After General Release the tactical aim is likely to be to channel the enemy into areas where he can be held long enough to provide a nuclear target...once nuclear weapons have been used they will be the predominant weapon on the battlefield and all arms will operate in support of nuclear fire.[51]

The Staff College came as close as it ever did, however, in conveying the horror of nuclear war to students and the possible impact on morale. One 1979 precis on the land battle in general war stated that 'after the first exchange of nuclear fire, commanders and staff officers will find themselves involved in operations which are outside the experience of any fighting man. Conditions on the battlefield are likely to be nothing short of horrific'.[52] Likewise, Directing Staff were advised to stress to students that operations in general war may have to take place after nuclear and chemical strikes 'with all the hideous implications for soldiers, staff officers, and commanders'.[53]

This greater acknowledgement of the appalling consequences of nuclear war came at a time of growing scepticism on both sides of the Atlantic about the credibility of using tactical nuclear weapons in defensive operations. As Chapter 6 will show, the doctrinal reforms instigated by Field Marshal Sir Nigel Bagnall in the 1980s sought to recast the Army's operational concepts to place greater emphasis on the use of mobile armoured forces to arrest a Soviet offensive. Consequently, conventional defence supplanted nuclear warfare as the main theme for instruction in the fourth term by 1989. 'General War' vanished from the syllabus for the first time in decades, and all teaching material on nuclear warfare was condensed into four student precis on 'NBC Warfare', which were technical in nature and concerned primarily with personal protection against nuclear, chemical, and biological weapons. There was no instruction, for example, on nuclear targeting—which had been a Staff College staple since the early 1960s.[54] Emblematic of this change was the assigned reading accompanying the student precis 'Nuclear Warfare', which was a piece from *Jane's Defence Weekly* titled 'NATO Forced to Rethink Nuclear Battlefield'. No programmed activities

---

[51] JSCSC, SCC 1978, Vol. 10, Nuclear 1: Nuclear and Chemical Fire Planning in General War [student instructions].
[52] JSCSC, SCC 1979, Vol. 10, General War 1: The Land Battle in General War [student instructions].
[53] JSCSC, SCC 1979, Vol. 10, General War 1: The Land Battle in General War [DS notes].
[54] JSCSC, SCC 1989, Vol. 10, NBC 4: Nuclear Warfare [student instructions].

were specifically associated with this subject, effectively ending the study of nuclear combat as an operation of war at the Staff College.

## Exercise Settings and Assumptions

The evolution of the Staff College curriculum reveals how the Army perceived the wider strategic context within which it was operating and the value it placed on nuclear instruction in the professional development of its officers. In practical terms, this instruction involved the development of exercises designed to train students in the types of skills they would require to make effective commanders and staff officers on the nuclear battlefield. In turn, the exercise settings and assumptions that underpinned them expose in more narrow military terms how the Army intellectualized the challenges posed by nuclear weapons to the conduct of military operations. The first tactical studies conducted under nuclear conditions appeared at the end of the 1955 course with exercise BUFFALO, which was based on a corps and its divisions in the defensive battle under limited nuclear war conditions, and exercise SLING SHOT, which portrayed a divisional-level attack under unlimited nuclear war conditions.[55] The decision to categorize nuclear war as either 'limited' or 'unlimited' mirrored the prevailing assumptions of the Chiefs of Staff that although it might be possible to use nuclear weapons discreetly in a limited war in the Far East, it would be impossible to control the process of escalation once nuclear weapons had been employed in the European theatre.[56] The effects of these assumptions on teaching in the Staff College was that exercises involving the limited use of nuclear weapons were set in a theatre other than Europe, while exercises involving the large-scale use of nuclear weapons were set against the background of general war on the Central Front.[57] Consequently, it was decided that for both conventional and limited nuclear war the enemy should be based on the Chinese People's Liberation Army, the 'Vandals', rather than the Soviet Army, the 'Fantasians', which remained the opponent for unlimited nuclear war.[58]

---

[55]  JSCSC, SCC 1955, Vol. 1, Outline Syllabus.
[56]  See the views of the Chief of the Imperial General Staff on this issue in TNA, WO 163/616, AC/M (55)7, The Long Term Defence Programme—National Service, 7 September 1955 and TNA, DEFE 4/78, JP(55)61(Final), Long Term Defence Programme, 8 July 1955.
[57]  JSCSC, SCC 1955, Vol. 1, Exercise Settings.
[58]  JSCSC, SCC 1955, Vol. 1, Minutes of Assistant Commandant's Meeting 10/55, 30 August 1955. The 'Fantasian' armed forces were modelled on the Russian Army. The doctrine, organization, and equipment of the 'Fantasian' armed forces were revised habitually by the Director of Military Intelligence so that they were kept in line with the latest information on the Red Army. The 'Fantasian' army was the standard opposition in the Army's various exercises, manoeuvres, and war-games throughout this period. For further information see TNA, WO 231/86, 138/668/52/MI3(d), Notes on the Fantasian Armed Forces, 18 December 1952. The Army's pseudonym for the Chinese-style organization was originally the 'Franks' (the name of an ancient West European tribe who fought invaders from the

The earlier criticisms of the Students' Committee that nuclear weapons were merely grafted onto conventional battle tactics could similarly be applied to these later exercises, however, as there were clear limitations as to how far the threat of nuclear weapon use was allowed to interfere with the scenarios for each exercise. For example, a Directing Staff bulletin from 1956 stated that it was not necessary 'to attempt to paint a picture of the difficult situation which might exist after nuclear war had been in progress for some weeks or months'.[59] It is unclear whether the decision to ignore the consequences of general nuclear war was a reflection of the deterrence habit of mind which had gripped the policy-making elite—which refused to accept that any meaningful military operation could be conducted in such conditions—or of evidence of a cognitive dissonance in accepting the challenges posed by such an operating environment. Whichever it may be, the refusal to confront in any serious way how the Army might survive, let alone fight, during or after a strategic nuclear exchange became a remarkable feature of Staff College exercises throughout the following decades.

Demonstrating this disconnect between theory and practice was the generosity with which the Staff College allocated nuclear weapons for 'use' in exercises. For limited war settings in 1956, twelve to fifty tactical nuclear weapons were deemed sufficient for training purposes with yields from 2kt to 20kt delivered by the M65 atomic cannon and the Corporal surface-to-surface missile. Students could also call on nuclear air support from airfields out of theatre.[60] By 1958, the weight of nuclear firepower had increased, with students having to consider the 'tactical' employment of nuclear weapons ranging in yields of between 2 and 500kt and 1–5mt at a scale of eighty missiles per corps per week.[61] An assumption for certain exercises was that the 'Vandal' forces (by courtesy of the 'Fantasians') were capable of delivering nuclear weapons of various yields by gun, free flight rocket, guided missile, or air, and both sides would 'strive to attain nuclear superiority by immediate attacks on suspected nuclear ground launching sights'.[62] Although the idea of maintaining combat operations after a considerable nuclear exchange by both sides was fraught with conceptual and practical difficulties, instruction was based nonetheless on the assumption that commanders would enjoy access to a plethora of nuclear weapons in support of their missions.

With such vast levels of nuclear tonnage being 'employed' in exercises, a cognitive dissonance once again took hold as instruction sought to detach itself from some of the logical inconsistencies in planning for tactical nuclear war,

East), but was changed to 'Vandals', presumably because the newly activated NORTHAG had adopted a Frankish battle-axe as its insignia.

---

[59] JSCSC, SCC 1956, Vol. 1, DS Bulletin No. 5/56, February 1956.
[60] JSCSC, SCC 1956, Vol. 1, DS Bulletin No. 5/56, February 1956.
[61] JSCSC, SCC 1958, Vol. 1, DS Bulletin No. 2/58, Nuclear Instruction 1958.
[62] JSCSC, SCC 1957, Vol. 1, Limited War Setting for the Phases of War Exercises.

preferring to couch problems within established frameworks more readily under-stood by officers already advanced in their careers. For these reasons, the Staff College focused its students' thinking on the traditional pattern of the corps tactical battle while minimizing those elements that might prove an unwelcome distraction to soldiering in the nuclear age. For example, the political constraints that would certainly accompany any nuclear weapon use were completely ignored in the 1960s. Students were informed in 1965 that 'our nuclear exercises are given a fictitious setting in England rather than BAOR because we do not want to become involved in all the political factors which would inevitably play a major part in any real conflict'.[63] This practice of distancing students from the political realities of the contemporary operating environment continued into the 1970s, which was justified on the grounds that it would remind students that the Central Front presented its own peculiar political and military context.[64] Likewise, nuclear instruction did not consider the conduct of operations during or after a strategic nuclear exchange, nor did it account for the possibility that the Soviet Union might confront the West with a *fait accompli* by using nuclear weapons from the outset in a decisive blow. DS were informed in 1960 that for the purposes of nuclear exercises, this attractive alternative requires playing down, 'otherwise our exercises will be continuously bedevilled by it'.[65] This logic would continue well into the late 1980s, where a student precis on nuclear operations within a general war setting instructed them not to consider the political background of the conflict or of the politics that would inevitably shape the decision to authorize nuclear release.[66]

Part of the reason for this disconnect from strategic realities was that the Staff College did not always agree with the assumptions that underpinned BAOR's concepts of operations. As early as 1957, the Commandant, Major-General Nigel Poett, wrote to the Director-General Military Training, Major-General J. B. Churcher, challenging the notion then popular in Germany that a future European war would be nuclear from the outset. Poett believed this to be an unwarranted leap of faith, and argued that just because training in BAOR was predicated on the early use of nuclear weapons, this should not necessarily dictate what was taught at the Staff College since 'the conventional technique applied to European territory must continue to be studied and kept alive at any rate for the time being'.[67] Churcher replied that although he saw the value of conducting conventional warfare exercises in a European setting, the possibility

[63] JSCSC, SCC 1965, Vol. 7, Nuclear War: Outline of Instruction.
[64] See, for example, the introductory notes to Exercise BLACK TARQUIN in JSCSC, SCC 1972, Vol. 12, Exercise BLACK TARQUIN: Introduction to Exercise [DS notes].
[65] JSCSC, SCC 1960, Vol. 1, DS Bulletin No. 15/60, The Threat: Some Tactical Considerations, 3 August 1960.
[66] JSCSC, SCC 1983, Vol. 10, General War Map Discussion 4: Nuclear Ops [student instructions].
[67] TNA, WO 231/101, SCHQ 800/Trg, Major-General N. Poett to Major-General J. B. Churcher, 16 July 1957.

of non-nuclear war in Europe was so remote that it would be better not to conduct such exercises at the Staff College.[68] Accordingly, the Staff College was instructed to focus its exercises on nuclear war in Europe and limited and 'cold' war outside of Europe.[69]

Despite Poett's reluctance to base Staff College teaching completely on the new concepts currently being developed in BAOR, he was nonetheless anxious to establish a close liaison with the Rhine Army to help inform instruction of doctrine which his students, whether he liked it or not, would have to understand if they were posted to Germany upon completion of their studies. In June 1957, he wrote to the 1(BR) Corps Chief of Staff, Major-General John Anderson, offering an exchange of liaison officers between the two organizations.[70] Anderson agreed that it was important to keep in close touch on teaching about the tactical use of nuclear weapons and that BAOR was 'as up to date as anyone in the latest tactical thought on the subject'. He informed Poett that he had issued a standing order to the training branch instructing them to keep the Staff College informed of any exercises which might be helpful and welcomed the opportunity to send a liaison officer to observe the Staff College exercise OPEN DOOR—a counter-attack against an enemy penetration across a river line under nuclear conditions.[71]

Closer liaison with BAOR was deemed essential so that officers leaving Staff College for an appointment in Germany were cognisant of the latest operational and doctrinal concepts being developed.[72] For example, after a team visit to BAOR HQ in 1985, greater emphasis was placed on developing a better understanding at the Staff College of the significance, role, and handling of forces at the operational level. The Commandant, Major-General Patrick Palmer, reported that 'All exercises now include problems designed to stimulate greater independence of thought and action, to parallel the introduction of agile AFV's [armoured fighting vehicles] into the BAOR armoury and the associated move away from pedantic command and control procedures'.[73] Liaison between the Staff College and BAOR would continue unabated throughout the period under review, and was an essential link to ensure that instruction was based on the newest operational concepts.[74] By the 1980s, Staff College DS were in constant touch with BAOR

[68] TNA, WO 231/101, 43/SC/5897(MT 4c), Major-General J. B. Churcher to Major-General N. Poett, 19 August 1957.
[69] TNA, WO 231/101, Minutes of Commandant's Meeting with Assistant Commandant and GSOs 1, 2 September 1957.
[70] TNA, WO 231/101, SCHQ 800/Trg, Major-General N. Poett to Major-General J. D'A. Anderson, 1 June 1957.
[71] TNA, WO 231/101, B1002, Major-General J. D'A. Anderson to Major-General N. Poett, 4 July 1957.
[72] TNA, WO 231/102, SCHQ 169, Major-General Poett to the Under Secretary of State for War, 1 April 1958.
[73] JSCSC, SCC 1985, Records, Staff College Report for 1985.
[74] See, for example, the views of Major-General John Stanier in JSCSC, SCC 1977, Staff College Report for 1977.

HQ during the writing of new teaching material, and students were often sent to Germany to gain experience umpiring divisional-level field training exercises in BAOR. Such liaison activities were deemed a 'successful experiment' which helped to further the development of healthy working relationships between the Staff College and BAOR.[75]

This is not to say that all instructors at the Staff College agreed that BAOR's tactical concepts provided a sound basis for teaching the principles of nuclear land warfare. For example, one Lieutenant-Colonel W. J. Reed, who was a DS assigned to the nuclear war writing team in 1966, warned students that *The Land Battle* series of pamphlets should not be considered an 'Everyman's Guide to Winning Nuclear Battles' since they merely reflected thinking that was 'fashionable' in BAOR at the time of writing. He questioned the validity of a number of tactical techniques currently employed by BAOR, especially its laborious target acquisition procedures which often resulted in nuclear fires missing their targets. On that note, he even suggested that the popular children's game Battleships might be an equally realistic simulation of the type of guesswork required to successfully identify and strike a concealed enemy position.[76] In private, the teaching notes he sent to his colleagues were much more disparaging and accused *The Land Battle: Part 1* as being an 'apologia for the BAOR tactical concept of 1963'. The crux of Reed's criticisms was that students should be aware that there was not one single tactical concept or doctrinal construct that would be applicable to all situations, for which he offered this amusing limerick as a reminder:

> There was an old man who said 'Damn',
> It appears to me now that I am
> Just a being that moves
> In predestinate grooves,
> Not a bus, not a bus, but a tram
> We don't want to over-encourage rebels, but trams went out years ago![77]

Surprisingly, it appears that the playing of Battleships really did take off in Staff College and that the concept of striking with nuclear fires on the basis of 'guest-imation' was given serious thought, not least because apparently 'many people, including at least one past commander of 1(BR) Corps, consider that playing Battleships pays'.[78]

Part of the problem with teaching tactical concepts at the Staff College was due to the rapidly changing nature of NATO strategy and the different interpretations

---

[75] JSCSC, SCC 1982, Records, Staff College Report for 1982.

[76] JSCSC, SCC 1966, Vol. 9, Tactical Concepts.

[77] JSCSC, SCC 1966, Vol. 9, Nuclear 4 [DS notes].

[78] JSCSC, SCC 1967, Vol. 6, NBC 4 [DS notes]. For the briefing on how Battleships was to be played by syndicates see JSCSC, SCC 1967, Vol. 6, Battleships: Briefing Notes.

of the role of conventional and tactical nuclear forces within that framework. As the student introduction to the 'European Warfare' phase of studies explained, which was now the umbrella term used to describe the study of high-intensity land warfare against the Warsaw Pact in Europe, successive NATO strategies had been based up until that point on what it described as 'total deterrence', 'raising the threshold', 'flexible response', and 'playing for time', each of which had generated their own brand of tactics. Whereas in previous years the strategic and political context of future war had been all but shielded from students, by 1969 this was no longer the case since:

> A study of tactical doctrine without an understanding of the strategy from which it is derived is of little value. In its turn a strategy can not be understood without some knowledge of the political and economic factors by which it is determined.[79]

The tactical doctrine then being studied was derived from the new pamphlets cascading down from the Ministry of Defence (MoD) including *Guidance on the Conduct of Operations of a Battle Group in North West Europe* and *The Land Battle parts I, II, and IV*.[80] Although the three phases of battle contained in this doctrine—the covering troop's battle, the delaying battle, and the main defensive battle—would not conform to a tidy plan, students were encouraged to accept it as the only framework that could fulfil the political requirement for a flexible response to enemy aggression in Europe.[81] Likewise, DS were informed that although it would be unlikely that students would produce any fundamentally new concepts for the defence of the Central Front, 'they must not be allowed to produce suggestions that ignore the political realities, such as the indiscriminate use of ADM's and chemical mines'.[82] Although the political constraints of NATO strategy were beginning to be acknowledged to a greater extent than hitherto, the grim realities of nuclear war continued to be minimized, as the DS notes to a module on 'Command and Staff Duties in Nuclear War' in 1970 demonstrate:

> Many students (and DS!) may feel that NBC procedures are really idealistic stuff, fine in theory but hardly practicable in the emerging shambles of the 'nuclear holocaust'. In the interest of purposeful discussion, I suggest you counter this view by reminding students of the strong body of opinion that considers that the nuclear phase of general war will be introduced by a 'selective' rather than a 'massive' exchange of nuclear weapons and that the experience will be so

---

[79] JSCSC, SCC 1969, Vol. 6, European Warfare: Outline of Instruction.
[80] JSCSC, SCC 1969, Vol. 6, NBC 1: Basic Tactical Principles.
[81] JSCSC, SCC 1970, Vol. 6, General War 1: Tactical Concept [student instructions].
[82] JSCSC, SCC 1970, Vol. 6, General War 1: Tactical Concept [DS notes].

concerning to both sides that there will be a 'pause' in which it is hoped everyone will come to their senses.[83]

Although NATO planners had long acknowledged the immense conceptual and practical difficulties of controlling escalation in the tactical nuclear battle, the hope that nuclear weapons would be used selectively and that both sides would 'come to their senses' before a nuclear holocaust was unleashed on the Continent again demonstrates a cognitive dissonance about the unwelcome realities of nuclear war. Although exercise instructions acknowledged that it would be 'impossible to predict the state of the nuclear battlefield accurately' and that 'certainly little will go as planned',[84] the Staff College remained steadfast that strength of character would prevail and that through individual initiative, good leadership, adequate preparation, and training there remained a chance of 'maintaining some kind of order amid the chaos of a nuclear battlefield'.[85]

The strategic constraints dictating the Army's operational posture were drawn out even further in subsequent courses, the most important of which in the early 1970s were declared to be an increased determination by NATO to oppose aggression with conventional forces for as long as possible, and the requirement for a forward defence. The new emphasis on the conventional phase of fighting in NATO strategy was reflected in the Army's *Land Operations* doctrine, which formed the basis for tactical instruction at the Staff College. The change in concepts was explained to students as a 'classic example of a military commander having political and strategic limitations imposed upon him which requires him to take up a defensive position which is not as favourable as he would wish'.[86] Students were given a grounding in the principles of flexible response through lectures by the Commander-in-Chief Allied Forces Central Europe, General Jürgen Bennecke, and the historian Professor Sir Michael Howard. Students were also issued an extract from a book by Bernard Burrows and Christopher Irwin which championed mobile defence in depth as a means to counter a Soviet offensive without recourse to nuclear weapons.[87] The study of the application of nuclear weapons still remained important, even if nuclear war now appeared less likely than it had in the 1950s or 1960s, since 'without training in the use of such weapons and a knowledge of their effects the deterrent strategy loses its credibility'.[88]

---

[83] JSCSC, SCC 1970, Vol. 6, General War 2: Command and Staff Duties in Nuclear War [DS notes].

[84] JSCSC, SCC 1972, Vol. 12, Ex BLACK TARQUIN: DS Summing Up [DS notes].

[85] SCC 1970, Vol. 6, General War 2: Command and Staff Duties in Nuclear War [DS notes].

[86] JSCSC, SCC 1973, Vol. 10, General War 1: Tactical Concept [student instructions].

[87] JSCSC, SCC 1973, Vol. 10, General War 1: Tactical Concept [DS notes]. The book in question was Bernard Burrows and Christopher Irwin, *The Security of Western Europe: Towards a Common Defence Policy* (London: Charles Knight, 1972).

[88] JSCSC, SCC 1973, Vol, 10, Students' Guide to the Fourth Term 1973.

By the late 1970s, mobile defence became the new watchword for tactical instruction at the Staff College. The setting for general war instruction was now based primarily on a conventional defence under the *threat* of nuclear weapon use and reflected the new BAOR doctrine which envisaged three phases: Covering Force Action; Main Mobile Defence Battle; Corps Counter Moves. Although students received detailed information on this new doctrine, in true Staff College tradition, students were encouraged to 'avoid the use of ready-mixed pre-packaged tactical concepts and the use of jargon'.[89] Likewise, DS were reminded that tactics should not be considered a matter of 'rigid doctrine or dogma' and 'in tackling the problems set in this term students are encouraged to consider any solution that is based on sound [tactical] principles and not confine themselves to the 1(BR) Corps concept of [operations]'.[90] The 1977 course also introduced a number of new readings for students, including an extract from the script of a lecture on mobile defence by General Graf Kielmansegg, an Eastern Front veteran and Bennecke's successor at SHAPE, in which he illustrated the principles of a mobile defence with two historical examples from the *Wehrmacht*'s campaigns in Russia. This reflected the beginning of a renewed interest in the operational history of the German Army.[91]

In addition to mobile defence, considerations of the politics of war initiation and termination, nuclear thresholds, and targeting became central to Staff College instruction on the political realities of planning for war on the Central Front. The basic problem, as outlined in one student precis, was that 'because of the immensely destructive effects of nuclear weapons their use will always be subject to stringent political control and their initial use will, in addition, be subject to restrictions imposed at the highest political level'.[92] However, while students were taught about the long and laborious release procedures for initial use, follow-on use, and general nuclear response, the Staff College could not escape its preoccupation with allowing students to develop solutions to tactical problems free from political interference. A new computer-based war-game, SNOW GOOSE, was consequently added to the 1981 course which gave students the opportunity to test various defensive concepts free from the real-world constraints which hampered planning in 1(BR) Corps.[93]

The Staff College kept well abreast of new tactical and operational concepts throughout the 1980s. In part, this was facilitated by the activation at Camberley of the Tactical Doctrine Cell, which was a clearing house for ideas coming into and going out of the Staff College and was the formal link ensuring unity of doctrine between Camberley and the various arms schools. In this context, the SO1 Tactical

[89] JSCSC, SCC 1977, Vol. 10, General War 1: The Land Battle in General War [student instructions].
[90] JSCSC, SCC 1977, Vol. 10, General War 1: The Land Battle in General War [DS notes].
[91] JSCSC, SCC 1977, Vol. 10, General War 1: The Land Battle in General War [student instructions].
[92] JSCSC, SCC 1980, The Land Battle in General War [student instructions].
[93] JSCSC, SCC 1981, The Land Battle in Europe [student instructions].

Doctrine worked closely with the newly formed Directorate of Battle Doctrine, and became increasingly involved with the development of war-games.[94] An SO1 war-gaming post would ultimately be established in 1989 tasked with the evaluation, design, and development of war-gaming applications for all Staff College courses, making Camberley one of the leaders in the field.[95] Commandants recognized the potential of the Staff College to contribute to the development of tactical doctrine, but attempts by the MoD to find economies in the budget led to cuts in the number of DS, thereby limiting Camberley's potential for research and original work.[96]

## Approaches to Learning

As has been shown, the Staff College utilized a wide array of instruction methods to try and inculcate an understanding of the future nuclear battlefield including central lectures, syndicate room discussions, indoor and outdoor map exercises, TEWTs (tactical exercises without troops), war-games, and essay writing. A hallmark of the Staff College approach to learning was its emphasis on small-group teaching within syndicates, which had been pioneered by J. F. C. Fuller in the aftermath of the First World War, and was regarded as one of the great strengths of the Camberley system. Each syndicate of ten students was paired with a member of the College's Directing Staff, Lieutenant-Colonels on two-year appointments, whose job was not only to instruct didactically, but also to facilitate debate and to 'direct the flow of our inspired minds', as one former student described it.[97] Up until the early 1960s members of the Directing Staff could still be found with valuable war-time experience and were selected for the role because they demonstrated the potential to go far within their own individual branch of service. DS were not qualified teachers, however, and Major-General Sir David Thorne recalled that during his time as a student at Camberley in 1963 there was a greater emphasis on instruction, rather than critical thinking, with DS teaching rigidly to the curriculum.[98] Another student remembered his DS taking great pains to march his syndicate away from the prying eyes of the divisional Colonel during one outdoor exercise to inform them that the only advice they needed to take away from Staff College was that 'big fingers and small maps kills lots of chaps', which was a popular war-time slogan of the cynical frontline soldier.[99]

[94] JSCSC, SCC 1983, Records, Staff College Report for 1983.
[95] JSCSC, SCC 1989, Records, Staff College Report for 1989.
[96] JSCSC, SCC 1984, Records, Staff College Report for 1984.
[97] Julian Howard Atherden Thompson interview, 28361, Imperial War Museum Sound Archive.
[98] David Calthrop Thorne interview, 20320, Imperial War Museum Sound Archive.
[99] Alan Graham Wooldridge interview, 12551, Imperial War Museum Sound Archive.

That such aphorisms were apparently unfamiliar to student-soldiers of the 1960s exposes the dearth of operational experience within the Army officer corps as the Second World War faded into memory. The prospect of yet another continental land war, this time fought with new weapons of unprecedented power, further compounded the problem of how to prepare for future war. Although Staff College exercises were informed as best as possible through liaison with BAOR and a close reading of national and alliance strategy, there were clear limits to how well study in the classroom could prepare officers for the challenges of nuclear land combat. One of the ways in which thinking about an uncertain future could be framed was through a study of past experience, and so military history was instrumentalized to help uncover clues about the character of future war. Historical reference points were drawn from Second World War campaigns in Normandy and the Eastern Front and from the more recent Israeli experience in prosecuting armoured warfare during the Yom Kippur War.

The study of military history had been a feature of the Staff College syllabus since the days when Edward Hamley lectured students on military art and history in the 1850s in what was widely regarded by contemporaries as being 'the most useful and interesting part of the course'.[100] However, throughout the period under review, the post-war Staff College was never able to decide exactly how it wanted to teach military history and for what purpose. In 1948, the stated aim of the study of military history was the decidedly lacklustre one of 'broadening the officers' military education and fostering an interest in the subject'. Students were to study a past campaign with particular reference to the application of the principles of war and the sources of recruitment and standard of training of the soldiers who took part.[101] The students' reaction to their introductory lecture on 'How to Study Military History' apparently 'failed to achieve its object',[102] and students felt resentment at having to write a paper on the subject for syndicate discussion.[103] The situation seemed to improve by 1950 with the Students' Committee reporting that the study of military history had now 'achieved its purpose', with a number of students offering suggestions about which historical campaigns should be studied next.[104] Later, the scope of instruction would shift to a focus on the qualities of past commanders with a view to 'assessing the human factors which are likely to lead to success or failure in war'.[105] This was supported by

[100]  Young, *The Story of the Staff College*, p. 11.
[101]  JSCSC, SCC 1948, Vol. 1, Outline Syllabus.
[102]  JSCSC, SCC 1948, Vol. 1, Minutes of the Students' Committee Meeting held at Camberley on 11 May 1948.
[103]  JSCSC, SCC 1948, Vol. 1, Minutes of the Students' Committee Meeting held at Camberley on 8 July 1948. The requirement for individual military history papers was ultimately dropped in the 1954 course. See JSCSC, SCC 1954, Vol. 1, Minutes of Assistant Commandant's Meeting 9/54, 30 November 1954.
[104]  JSCSC, SCC 1950, Vol. 1, Recommendations by the Students' Committee: 4th Term 1950 Course.
[105]  JSCSC, SCC 1951, Vol. 1, Outline Syllabus.

Field Marshal Montgomery, who urged that teaching should focus more on the relationship between 'great' commanders and their staff, such as that between Napoleon and Berthier or, predictably, himself and de Guingand.[106]

The following decades saw military history drop in and out of fashion at the Staff College, where it occupied a token place on the syllabus. It would not be until Field Marshal Sir Nigel Bagnall's professional and personal interest in military history began to permeate the Staff College in the 1980s that the utility of the discipline for the lessons-learned process was effectively institutionalized to help inform thinking about mobile defence and counterstroke operations. For example, in 1984, students were issued a booklet entitled 'Operational and Tactical Lessons: War on the Eastern Front 1941–45'. Suggesting a greater awareness of the merits of military history, the booklet itself was inlaid with a well-known quote from Clausewitz's essay *Principles of War* (1812): 'Only the study of military history is capable of giving those who have no experience of their own a clear picture of what I have just called the friction of the whole machine'. The booklet contained a collection of essays on the operational history of the German Army deemed most pertinent to thinking about the conduct of a mobile defence on the Central Front. Subjects included 'Russian Combat Methods in WWII', 'German Defence Tactics against Russian Breakthroughs', 'Operations of Encircled Forces', and 'Tank Warfare in the West, East, and the South'. The purpose for this renaissance in military history at the Staff College was described thus:

> This handbook is an attempt to strike a balance between ignoring the problem of providing a common reference point and of being accused of 'spoon-feeding', by producing little more than a digest of the lessons of past campaigns. The examples are drawn from a limited period and deliberately deal almost exclusively with the Eastern Front. This is partly because they provide perhaps the most obvious parallels with the instructional theme for the Term, and also because, although the material has not been widely read, it is interesting, covers the span of command from Company to Army Group and...has the authority of being produced, shortly afterwards, by those most closely involved in the campaign.[107]

This is not to say that all observers believed in the merits of the study of military history to a modern military preparing to fight on the nuclear battlefields of Europe. A 1981 paper by the American historian Walter Millis argued that:

> The military professional who must today preside over the design, production and employment of the giant weapons of mass destruction cannot really learn

---

[106] TNA, WO 231/102, DSAC 0900/1, Field Marshal Montgomery to Chief of the Imperial General Staff, 24 March 1958.

[107] JSCSC, SCC 1984, Vol. 10, Operational and Tactical Lessons: War on the Eastern Front 1941–45.

much from Napoleon, or Jackson, or Lee, or Grant—who were all managers of men in combat, not of 'weapon systems' about which one of the most salient points is that they must never ... be allowed to come into collision ... it is not immediately apparent why the strategy and tactics of Nelson, Lee or even Bradley or Montgomery should be taught to the young men who are being trained to manage the unmanageable military colossi of today.[108]

However detached nuclear-age military planning appeared to be to the great land campaigns of the past, the study of military history provided one of the few means to communicate the realities of conflict to a student body which was increasingly without operational experience of its own. Whereas the majority of students in the early post-war years had seen active service in the Second World War, the Korean War, or in the myriad counter-insurgency campaigns in Palestine, Malaya, Cyprus, or Kenya,[109] a dearth of high-intensity war-fighting opportunities had a consequent impact on the practical soldiering skills of later cohorts. The Commandant's report for 1974 lamented that there was a general lack of experience, particularly amongst the infantrymen, of soldiering in Germany and that many students lack the 'feel' of a large-scale exercise.[110] Although by 1976, 100 of the students had at one time served in BAOR, there still remained a 'disturbing lack of experience and knowledge of mechanized operations in Europe, our primary role', according to the Commandant, Major-General John Stanier.[111] This lack of exposure to major exercises in BAOR meant that an unacceptable number of students were ignorant of arms other than their own and even lacked confidence in the operations of their own branch because of inexperience.[112] Things hadn't improved by the 1980s, with Major-General David Alexander-Sinclair observing that although many students had seen combat in Northern Ireland, the practical experience of mechanized and armoured tactics was poor and that 'those with operational experience have much to contribute to the course as a whole particularly when widespread experience of this sort is becoming rare in the British Army'.[113] By 1986, combat experience was so rare that in one particular division at Staff College, 41 per cent of students had no operational experience whatsoever.[114] For this reason, it was decided to continue to 'emphasise the importance of military history throughout the course, partly in order to restore it to its former

---

[108] Cited in Martin van Creveld, 'Thoughts on Military History', *Journal of Contemporary History*, Vol. 18, No. 4 (1983), p. 558.
[109] Young, *The Story of the Staff College*, pp. 17–18.
[110] JSCSC, SCC 1974, Records, Staff College Report for 1974.
[111] JSCSC, SCC 1976, Records, Staff College Report for 1976.
[112] JSCSC, SCC 1977, Records, Staff College Report for 1977. See, in addition, for a continuation of these problems, JSCSC, SCC 1980, Records, Staff College Report for 1980.
[113] JSCSC, SCC 1980, Records, Staff College Report for 1980.
[114] JSCSC, SCC 1986, Records, Staff College Report for 1986.

position as an essential part of an officer's education, and also to compensate for the lack of battlefield experience'.[115]

One of the ways in which the utilization of military history could help the Staff College communicate the realities of conflict to a student body increasingly detached from the experience of high-intensity land warfare was through the traditional staff ride to the battlefields of Normandy. Staff rides are an applied form of history that link historical narratives, classroom study, and the physical environment to produce a holistic analysis of the battlefield. With proper critical engagement with the process, staff rides can provide insights into many aspects of the human phenomenon of warfare including the dynamics of battle, the realities of conflict, the application of the principles of war, operational art, command and leadership, the relationship between technology and doctrine, morale, logistics, and countless other dimensions of war-fighting. The modern staff ride is most associated with the Prussian and German armies of the nineteenth and early twentieth centuries, where they featured prominently in the education and pro-fessional development of the officer corps in the Imperial Army, the *Reichswehr*, and the *Wehrmacht*.[116] The Staff College embarked on its first staff ride in 1907, when it took students abroad to study the battlefields of the Franco-Prussian War. After the First World War, students would revisit the battlefields of Mons, Le Cateau, the Marne, and Aisne, and with the conclusion of the Second World War in 1945, Normandy became the new destination for Camberley's annual tour.[117]

One operation in particular assumed special significance for the post-war British Army's staff ride—GOODWOOD—which saw an armoured charge by three British armoured divisions in July 1944 to capture vital ground south-east of Caen. The assault petered out, and appeared to demonstrate how relatively lightly armed infantry, properly deployed in depth, could blunt an overwhelming armoured offensive. The parallel to BAOR's predicament on the Central Front was clear, and as will be shown in Chapter 5, the operation was lauded as a blueprint for battle for the British Army in the 1970s. Thus, the Normandy staff ride not only provided students with numerous case studies on combined and joint operations, but also offered lessons that could be applied to the Army's thinking about the conduct of operations against the Red Army in Germany. Staff rides have limits, however, as to how much they can reveal about future trends, a critique made by Slessor when recalling the utility of the pre-war staff rides:

But tactics change, or should change, so quickly with the development of weapons that I am very doubtful whether there is anything to be gained—

---

[115] JSCSC, SCC 1987, Records, Staff College Report for 1987.

[116] For further information see David Hall, 'The Modern Model of the Battlefield Tour and Staff Ride: Post-1815 Prussian and German Traditions', *Defence Studies*, Vol. 5, No. 1 (2005), pp. 37–47.

[117] Peter Caddick-Adams, 'Footprints in the Mud: The British Army's Approach to the Battlefield Tour Experience', *Defence Studies*, Vol. 5, No. 1 (2005), pp. 22–3.

whether indeed there is not positive disadvantage—from detailed tactical study of past campaigns on the ground.[118]

A preoccupation with the narrow tactical details of an historic campaign was also a problem identified by Peter Caddick-Adams, who concluded that the Army's staff rides 'had very low expectations in learning outcomes, merely using the tour to bring out tactical decision-making and the "atmosphere" of war; the treasures of the terrain were often overlooked in favour of the story the speaker had to tell, and there was no attempt to interpret the history at the operational level'.[119] The staff ride (or 'bottlefield tour', as it was better known)[120] was remembered fondly by the students, however, who were very impressed with the way it was run and the 'lovely old figures' who accompanied them.[121] Those personalities were veterans, or 'Guest Artists' as they were described, who added atmosphere to the proceedings as they recalled their personal experiences fighting across the fields of France. Between 1947 and 1979, seventy-four veterans had addressed thirty-two tours, including famous personalities such as Major-General Pip Roberts, Major Bill Close, Hans von Luck, and Major John Howard of Pegasus Bridge fame.[122] As Caddick-Adams implies, the use of veterans was a double-edged sword. While students certainly benefited from hearing the personal testimonies of those who were there, the battle narratives became warped depending on which individual was speaking. This meant that DS had a tendency to plan the staff ride around the personal narratives of the particular Guest Artist who was available that year, rather than taking an objective look at what the historical record showed was important.[123]

The staff ride was subsequently discontinued, for financial reasons, and was replaced in 1980 with 'The Battlefield Stress Study'. The exercise was designed to replace some aspects of the staff ride and to permit students to study and discuss human behaviour under the stress of battle. Instead of just hearing the accounts of veterans, as was common during the tours of Normandy, the subject was now broadened to include insights from military historians, psychologists, and representatives from the Army Personnel Research Establishment. In 1982, the military historian was the renowned scholar Correlli Barnett, while the psychologist was Prof Norman Dixon.[124] Although there are no detailed records of the content of The Battlefield Stress Study, it would be interesting to ascertain how receptive

[118] John Slessor, *The Central Blue: Recollections and Reflections* (London: Cassell & Co., 1956), p. 93.
[119] Peter Caddick-Adams, 'Footsteps across Time: The Evolution, Use and Relevance of Battlefield Visits to the British Armed Forces' (PhD thesis, Cranfield University, 2007), p. 440.
[120] Charles Millman, *Stand Easy or the Rear Rank Remembers* (Edinburgh: The Pentland Press, 1993), p. 65.
[121] David Calthrop Thorne interview, 20320, Imperial War Museum Sound Archive.
[122] Caddick-Adams, 'Footsteps across Time', p. 438.
[123] Michael Stuart Gray interview, 28362, Imperial War Museum Sound Archive.
[124] JSCSC, SCC 1982, Records, Staff College Report for 1982.

students were to Dixon's approach to the subject in light of the publication of his controversial book *On the Psychology of Military Incompetence* (1976), which delivered a scathing critique of the psychopathology of the British Army and its members.

The 1970s also witnessed concerted efforts by the Staff College to forge greater strategic partnerships with civilian higher education institutions. For example, during the academic year 1973/74 eleven DS attended nine different university courses, including regular participation in the meetings of Reading University's Military and Policy in Society Group. Such visits were reciprocated in 1976 when thirty-six undergraduates from the University of London, Oxford University, and Reading University visited the Staff College to take part in syndicate discussions on 'The Place of the Student in Society'.[125] Major-General Hugh Beach, Commandant of the Staff College from 1974 to 1975, wrote in his annual report that 'the value of these contacts cannot be over emphasised' but that 'on balance this degree of involvement in university activities represents the limit that can be achieved without detriment to our own functions'.[126]

The Army's relationship with the scholarly community has always been something of a balancing act between the genuine requirement for officers to develop deep critical thinking and analytical skills through academic study, and the equally important necessity for those same officers to be trained in the practical skills required for regimental soldering. As the Director of Army Education concluded at a 1977 conference on the future of Army education, 'military skills are very specific and practical and best learned on the job or in special schools. Civilian agencies could only support such training with abstracted and generalised material'.[127] This is not to mean that the Army of the 1970s did not seek academic recognition for what was becoming an increasingly intellectual as well as technically demanding profession. As one Lieutenant-Colonel bemoaned:

> I sat in last year on a very large gathering of academics and leading industrialists at Birmingham University. It was fascinating to listen to academic after academic proclaiming in suitably polite language that service officers are really academic philistines because of the nature of their profession... Many of our civilian friends still see us in the less challenging but happier days of pre-war hunting 5 days a week![128]

The challenges, and desirability, of fostering greater intellectual curiosity in the officer corps can be seen in the debate about the possibility of establishing a

---

[125] JSCSC, SCC 1976, Records, Staff College Report for 1976.

[126] JSCSC, SCC 1974, Records, Staff College Report for 1974.

[127] TNA, DEFE 70/126, Presentation by the Director of Army Education at the Director of Army Training Conference, 3 February 1977.

[128] TNA, DEFE 70/126, Prince Philip's Proposal, 4 February 1977.

'military studies' degree for Army staff officers. The idea was floated by the Duke of Edinburgh during his keynote address at a conference organized by the Director of Military Training, where he stated that a degree in military studies would put non-technical graduate officers on the same academic level as teachers, parsons, lawyers, and economists, and that there was little evidence to suggest that such a degree should not 'rank below Anglo-Saxon poetry, business studies, or some of the more obscure sociological subjects for which universities seem prepared to offer degrees with such enthusiasm'.[129] A similar scheme to establish a degree-awarding Royal Defence Academy had been proposed in the late 1960s, in the wake of the Robbins Report and subsequent expansion of higher education in Britain, but was ultimately rejected primarily for financial reasons.[130] Prince Philip's proposal was also considered seriously, and reveals some candid observations about how the Army perceived itself as a learning organization in the 1970s.

One view was that the establishment of a military degree would be a valuable addition to the range of opportunities offered by the Army which, at a time of acute recruitment problems,[131] was an attractive proposition to confer greater recognition on the talents of career officers comparable to 'chartered' status in many civilian professions.[132] The Director of Army Training believed that the long-term benefits of a military studies degree would be increased by academic recognition of the military profession and the possibility of developing greater links between the service academies and mainstream higher education establishments.[133] This consideration was all the more important in light of a recent report on 'Attitudes to the Army' carried out by a market research firm which demonstrated firm evidence that many schoolboys thought the Army represented 'virtually the antithesis of intellectual effort'.[134] This view might have been unfair considering that the realities of soldiering after 1945 meant that officers could reasonably identify with 'other white-collar professionals in terms of the commitment that their duties required of them'.[135] In spite of the increasing professionalization of the service, some senior officers still clung to the archaic virtues of the Army as a gentlemanly institution. For example, General Sir Cecil Blacker,

[129]  TNA, DEFE 70/126, Conference: Wither Shrivenham, Address the Guests on a Military Science Degree, 3 February 1977.
[130]  J. C. M. Baynes, *The Soldier in Modern Society* (London: Eyre Methuen, 1972), pp. 126–9.
[131]  The Army had struggled to fill its ranks ever since National Service was phased out in 1963. Since then, the Army had relied on an intake of around 18,000 adult soldiers a year. 1973 represented a particularly bad year for recruiting with as few as 10,000 men joining the colours. Henry Stanhope, *The Soldiers: An Anatomy of the British Army* (London: Hamish Hamilton, 1979), p. 44.
[132]  TNA, DEFE 70/126, A/ULO/99 MISC (DAR 1d), DAT's Conference: 'Wither Shrivenham', 7 February 1977.
[133]  TNA, DEFE 70/126, A/43/Trg/HRH/1(AT4a), Military Studies Degree, 16 June 1977.
[134]  TNA, DEFE 70/126, A/43/HRH/1(AT4a), Major J. M. Lucken to Lieutenant-Colonel P. C. Harvey, 24 June 1977.
[135]  French, *Military Identities*, p. 322.

Adjutant-General and GOODWOOD veteran, maintained that officers should be concerned above all with learning how to become effective commanders and leaders—subjects not naturally suited to academic treatment or classroom examination. Furthermore, he argued that the status of a military studies degree would otherwise be regarded as 'suspect' by the academy since 'The Army is not, and should not pretend to be, a primarily academic institution'. From Blacker's point of view, the Army attracted 'doers' rather than 'thinkers', and so it should remain.[136]

Although there was greater awareness by the 1980s of the merits of raising the intellectual threshold of the Army staff course, not least because by now one-third of British officers had degrees and were expected to be able to discuss a variety of subjects intelligently with civil servants, MPs, and Allied officers, the Staff College was still wary of the detrimental impact this might have on its ability to mould its students into effective staff officers. As Major-General Alexander-Sinclair explained:

> Such an extension could enable the Army officer to progress... on an oily sea of theoretical discussions, seminars and papers of the 'Wither NATO?' or 'Third World War 1995' variety, without ever learning properly to write a Divisional Movement Order, run an operational staff cell, or master the Appreciation process. Such a generalized, wishy-washy course would no doubt give an opportunity to introduce more Civil Service, RN and RAF students and would provide employment for visiting academic lecturers. If we ever ignore the need for detailed, practical staff techniques in land forces our successors will again run the risk of being described as 'incompetent swine'.[137]

Finding the right balance between training and education is one of the perennial challenges of professional military education, and one that has confronted the Staff College throughout its history. Edward Smalley has concluded that the inter-war Staff College lacked clarity of purpose and failed to teach students how to undertake either routine staff duties or operations relevant to the type of continental warfare they would soon be called upon to fight, ultimately leaving graduates 'qualified, but unprepared'.[138] Graduates of the post-war Staff College never did embark upon the war for which they were trained, a war that would have been even further detached from reality than the Army could ever have imagined in the 1930s. As Field Marshal Montgomery wrote to the CIGS in 1958, at a time when he himself was planning for the defence of Western Europe in his role as

---

[136] TNA, DEFE 70/126, General Sir Cecil Blacker to the Duke of Edinburgh, 6 October 1975.

[137] JSCSC, SCC 1981, Records, Staff College Report for 1981.

[138] Edward Smalley, 'Qualified, but Unprepared: Training for War at the Staff College in the 1930s', *British Journal for Military History*, Vol. 2, No. 1 (2015), pp. 55–72.

DSACEUR, 'Can you "train for war" by academic study at a staff college? I very much doubt whether you can—but you can certainly study the techniques of command and staff work'.[139]

## Conclusions

The Staff College curriculum evolved considerably after 1945 and was demonstrative of the types of changes expected of a military organization moving through the implementation phase of the innovation process. The syllabus was remarkably absorbent to new ideas, and consistently incorporated the latest changes being made to Army doctrine, alliance strategy, and national defence policy. Beginning in 1950 with a playlet and a cardboard cut-out, instruction on nuclear warfare matured considerably over the decades, reaching its zenith in the 1960s with the teaching of BAOR's *Land Battle* series of pamphlets, before returning to a greater emphasis on conventional war-fighting in the 1980s when mobile defence and counterstroke operations came back into vogue. Such adaptations did not necessarily translate into more effective teaching, however, as many of the assumptions that underpinned the nuclear exercises were optimistic bordering on naïve, and failed to consider the more difficult questions about the realities of soldiering in the nuclear age. In this context, the Staff College reflected a wider institutional reluctance within the Army to confront in any meaningful way the severity of nuclear warfare and the types of challenges that future commanders would surely encounter. A more sympathetic appraisal might be that a lack of precedent on which to base assumptions about future war, coupled with a general lack of operational experience within the student body by the end of the Cold War, limited how far thinking about the unthinkable could progress without infringing on the other core function of Camberley—the development of skilled and able staff officers.

[139] TNA, WO 231/102, DSAC 0900/1, Field Marshal Montgomery to the Chief of the Imperial General Staff, 24 March 1958.

# 5

# Operational Research and the Nuclear Battlefield

In lieu of any practical experience of nuclear combat, operational research represented the only means through which the British Army could model or analyse in any systematic fashion the dynamics of the nuclear battlefield. As a war against the imagination, the simulation of nuclear conflict became itself 'a key battlefield of the Cold War' over which different groups of actors fought, for vested interests, to present their own imagined realities of the consequences of nuclear weapon use.[1] The Army was but another actor who constructed and wielded narratives of nuclear war for its own organizational needs. Faced with an almost impossible challenge unique in history, there were strong incentives for the service to prove that it could perform the surreal mission to which it had been assigned. These incentives were both external and internal to the organization. First, the credibility of NATO's deterrent posture was reliant on the ability of its shield forces to carry out the threatened punishment/denial mechanism in the event of Soviet aggression, i.e. that it possessed both the will and capability to fight with nuclear weapons in defence of the Central Front. In turn, this meant that the Army had to make reasonable attempts to demonstrate that it could operate effectively on the nuclear battlefield, in spite of the monumental challenges this would pose. Second, the audience for this optimistic narrative of nuclear war-fighting was not only Soviet decision-makers, but the Army itself. It was essential to the *esprit de corps* of the service, let alone for the morale of the individual soldier, to quell any doubts about its ability to fight and prevail in nuclear land combat.

Simulations of nuclear warfare therefore provided a means for the Army to validate its conceptions of future warfare. Although field exercises and war-gaming provided rare opportunities to 'rehearse' nuclear land combat, they also revealed limitations and contradictions in the Army's thinking. In this context, civilian operational researchers often came into conflict with military officers as the claim to knowledge of veteran soldiers, accrued through years of battlefield experience, appeared to be undermined by intuitions gleaned from synthetic

---

[1] Matthew Grant and Benjamin Ziemann, 'The Cold War as an Imaginary War' in Matthew Grant and Benjamin Ziemann (eds.), *Understanding the Imaginary War: Culture, Thought and Nuclear Conflict, 1945–90* (Manchester: Manchester University Press, 2016), pp. 3–4.

*Imagining Nuclear War in the British Army, 1945-1989.* Simon J. Moody, Oxford University Press (2020).
© Simon J. Moody.
DOI: 10.1093/oso/9780198846994.001.0001

representations of future war.[2] Objective analysis through operational research therefore threatened to expose some of the Army's more fanciful ideas about future war, and even cast doubt on the credibility of fighting a tactical nuclear battle as a viable operation of war. However, as with much of the Army's thinking about nuclear warfare, it again demonstrated a cognitive dissonance when faced with uncomfortable realities; while the Army claimed that the conclusions drawn from its operational research supported well-established beliefs and assumptions about the modern operating environment, its critics saw only wishful thinking and the erroneous use of scientific data.

## Early Exercises and the Atomic Bomb

Only a token effort was made during the immediate post-war years to assess how nuclear weapons might affect war on land. In comparison to the Navy and Air Force, who had vested interests in learning about the threat posed by weapons of mass destruction to port facilities, shipping convoys, and home bases, the Army had fewer strategic rationales for its own operational research into the use of nuclear weapons in field warfare.[3] In contrast, developments in conventional land warfare had developed apace during the course of the Second World War, and so the Army's military exercises were generally designed in the late 1940s and early 1950s to assess the effectiveness of existing forces structures and capabilities, especially those relating to armoured combat. That the Army appeared reluctant to turn its back on the art of conventional warfare so soon after the end of the war was reflected in the instructions to exercise EVOLUTION, which took place in the summer of 1946. The exercise was organized by the Chief of the Imperial General Staff, Field Marshal Bernard L. Montgomery, and sought to outline a new tactical doctrine for the Army.[4] The exercise instructions acknowledged the limitations to the study in stating that although 'the implications of the atomic bomb on strategy are now being studied...it is too early to make any deductions'.[5] Reflecting the prevailing view that nuclear weapons were too expensive and cumbersome to be squandered on the tactical battlefield, it went on to say that nuclear weapons

[2] Sharon Ghamari-Tabrizi, 'Simulating the Unthinkable: Gaming Future War in the 1950s and 1960s', *Social Studies of Science*, Vol. 30, No. 2 (2000), p. 164.

[3] Maurice Kirby and Matthew Godwin, 'Operational Research as Counterfactual History: A Retrospective Analysis of the Use of Battlefield Nuclear Weapons in the German Invasion of France and Flanders, May–June 1940', *The Journal of Strategic Studies*, Vol. 31, No. 4 (August 2008), pp. 636–7.

[4] See, Simon J. Moody, 'Was There a "Monty Method" after the Second World War? Field Marshal Bernard L. Montgomery and the Changing Character of Land Warfare, 1945–1958', *War in History*, Vol. 23, No. 2 (2016), pp. 213–214.

[5] TNA, WO 279/191, War Office Exercise: Evolution, papers issued personally by CIGS to all Commanders, August 1946.

would only be used in a future war against the most important strategic targets.[6] However, this did not mean that the Army would be relegated to a mere supporting role since:

> A revolutionary conclusion of this nature should not be accepted unless the evidence to support this is incontestable. No such evidence is yet available, nor may it be for many years. We must therefore be prepared, as in the past, for battle on land.[7]

It was in preparation for battle on land that the tactical implications of nuclear weapons were considered during exercise SPEARHEAD, which took place in May 1947 at the Staff College, Camberley.[8] The exercise was a re-run of the 1943 Salerno landings, only this time the Allies enjoyed nuclear fire support.[9] The exercise planners remained cautious, however, and warned that 'at the present stage of scientific development it is not possible to obtain a workable picture of the conditions of unrestricted atomic and bacteriological warfare' and that there was therefore a limit to the degree to which such weapons could be introduced into a military exercise. For these reasons 'only the fringe of the subject has been broached, and that in the widest sense the generally accepted battle technique of the past has not been superseded'.[10] The exercise did appear to confirm, however, the new principles of nuclear land combat identified by the military theorists: dispersion, organizational flexibility, and tactical mobility. Abiding by these principles would allow commanders to establish a large beachhead which could be pushed out as rapidly as possible to secure vital tactical ground and to prevent the enemy from counter-attacking with mobile forces.[11]

The conclusions reached as a result of this exercise were not too dissimilar to the ones reached by military publicists during the same period, for example in Colonel A. Jolly's article for the *Royal Armoured Corps Journal*, which was published a year earlier. As the theorists had prophesized, such was the immense destructive power that could be concentrated in time and space by the atomic bomb, dispersion and high tactical mobility would be essential. Addressing participants after the exercise, Montgomery stated that:

> Military thought and tactical doctrine must always be well in advance of the time; the Army must be prepared mentally for new types of weapons and for the

---

[6] Ibid.    [7] Ibid.

[8] Moody, 'Was There a "Monty Method" after the Second World War?', pp. 214–215.

[9] TNA, WO 216/202, War Office Exercise Spearhead, The Staff College Camberley, Introduction to the Exercise, May 1947.

[10] TNA, WO 216/202, Future Weapons and the Effect of Their Introduction into Exercise Spearhead, May 1947.

[11] TNA, WO 216/202, War Office Exercise Spearhead, The Staff College Camberley, The Army Outline Plan, May 1947.

changed conditions of war which they bring about. The need to avoid large concentrations of troops vulnerable to mass destruction weapons conflicts with the tactical need to concentrate superior forces to overwhelm the enemy at the select time and place. The need to concentrate to achieve success in the offensive battle will continue but, in view of the dangers, concentration must be carried out as secretly and as quickly as possible. The tactical battle must be won as soon as possible so that the danger period is kept short and the Army may again seek safety in dispersion as early as possible.[12]

The CIGS appeared encouraged by the exercise, writing to his war-time Chief of Staff, Francis de Guingand, that 'my Camberley exercise, Spearhead, was a tremendous success: quite the best thing I have seen for a long time'.[13] As Chapter 6 will show, so impressed was Montgomery with the conclusions drawn from SPEARHEAD that he established a committee to rewrite the Army's doctrine in light of the changes that would be required to operate in a nuclear environment.

The growing realization that the Army would need to attain greater mobility and flexibility in future war began to be reflected in War Office policy statements for equipment programmes. In the important field of armoured fighting vehicles, a statement on future tank policy articulated the requirement for cross-country mobility of the highest order since the Second World War had shown how inadequate all tanks had been in this regard. The statement went on to say that cross-country mobility would be of greater importance in the future since 'the increasing power of the air and rockets will certainly enforce the widest dispersion...thus making cross country movement essential'.[14] Although not stating explicitly the threat posed by the atomic bomb, the paper's acknowledgement of the 'increasing power' of modern air power and rockets implies that nuclear weapons were not far from the minds of the General Staff. Increased dispersion and cross-country movement would also mean improvements in communications would be necessary. Thus, a policy statement was issued in April 1948 which recommended the development of enhanced signal equipment and better integration of wireless communication devises. The justification for the statement was that:

Modern mass destruction weapons will compel the field army to greater dispersion, while more rapid and flexible transportation will enable it to effect higher speeds of concentration and movement. These combine to require longer range and more flexible means of communication.[15]

[12] TNA, WO 216/202, Exercise Spearhead, Final Address by CIGS, 10 May 1947.
[13] IWM, Montgomery Ancillary Collections 4, Montgomery to Francis de Guingand, 1 June 1947.
[14] TNA, WO 33/2575, General Staff Policy Statement No. 1, Tanks, 1 August 1947.
[15] TNA, WO 33/2575, War Office Policy Statement No. 25, Signal Equipment, 30 April 1948.

To better understand the challenges of employing conventional formations on the modern battlefield, two large-scale manoeuvres, AGILITY ONE and AGILITY TWO, took place in Germany in October 1949 to exercise the British Army of the Rhine and other Allied formations in the conduct of offensive and defensive operations. The 7th Armoured Division planned and executed an attack launched through an infantry formation, while the 2nd Infantry Division practised all manner of defensive techniques including night withdrawals and counter-attacks.[16] The exercises provided valuable insights into some of the challenges of deploying armoured forces in a nuclear environment. Summing up after the exercises, Commander-in-Chief (C-in-C) BAOR, Lieutenant-General Sir Charles Keightley, maintained that the exercises had demonstrated that the traditional practice of concentrating armoured formations for offensive operations would be unlikely to happen in future battles. This did not mean that armour would be committed in penny-packets, however—only that 'in modern war you do not want a mass of tanks sitting about in the open'. Tanks would therefore have to be adequately dispersed so as not to invite air attack, but should still be capable of massing force at the decisive point in the battle. This would be achieved through 'sound planning and good communication'.[17]

The exercises also highlighted the extent to which the administrative tail of the armoured division had bloated, which would be uniquely vulnerable to weapons of mass destruction. A 1950 report by the Standing Committee on Army Post-War Problems stated that the review of the organization of the armoured division must be conducted against the background of the conditions of the next war, which would be significantly different from those of the closing stages of the Second World War. Invoking the pessimistic language characteristic of the Chiefs of Staff at this time, the report suggested that it would be necessary to think of the first year of a future war in Europe as a 'battle for survival'. There would be a shortage of tanks and equipment, the battle itself would be conducted in an extremely adverse air situation, and the enemy would hold the initiative with a numerical superiority in both men and materiel. During this difficult opening phase British forces would be thrown on the defensive and 'the tactical role of the armoured division is assumed to be counter-attack with limited objectives'. Mobility and flexibility would therefore be of paramount importance if armoured forces were to remain 'both "handy" and hard-hitting'.[18]

Further opportunities to assess force compositions came in September 1951 when BAOR was exercised in mobile operations during BROADSIDE ONE and BROADSIDE TWO. The exercises were conducted upon the ground on which

[16] TNA, WO 216/594, Combined Exercises, Agility One and Agility Two, Exercise Instructions for Ground Forces, October 1949.

[17] TNA, WO 231/56, Combined Exercises, Agility One and Agility Two, Final Report, October 1949.

[18] TNA, WO 32/13858, ECAC/P(50)109, Organization of the Armoured Division, 9 November 1950.

BAOR expected to meet a Soviet offensive and were designed to practise ground manoeuvre in the face of enemy air superiority, particularly the techniques required to switch rapidly between concentration and dispersion.[19] This was a clear attempt to gain some insight into the challenges of fighting on a battlefield where enemy airpower would complicate movement on the ground. Nuclear weapons were not mentioned explicitly in the exercise instructions, but the emphasis placed on understanding the relationship between concentration and dispersion reveals that exercise planners believed this to be an important factor when conducting operations under the constant threat of nuclear fire. One important lesson drawn from the exercise was the utility of natural obstacles, especially river lines, during defensive operations. The post-exercise report stated that river lines must not be understood as something that needed to be held physically by troops, but as an aid to defeating the enemy. The real value of a river line was believed to be its ability to canalize the attacking troops into predesignated killing zones.[20]

The conceptual link between natural obstacles and the employment of nuclear weapons was made as early as 1949 when Field Marshal Montgomery, who was now Chairman of the Western Union Defence Organization Commanders-in-Chief Committee, asked the British Chiefs of Staff to initiate a study on the defence of a major water obstacle.[21] Montgomery was keen to ascertain whether there were any 'scientific devices', a euphemism for nuclear weapons, which could be exploited in order to help the outnumbered Western land forces under his command repel a Soviet attack across the Rhine.[22] A few months later, two army exercises, the Western Union exercise UNITY and the War Office exercise HORATIUS, appeared to demonstrate the validity of using nuclear weapons to prevent an attacker from crossing a river. As would soon become clear to NATO planners, the exercises showed that the small land forces expected to fight in a future war in Europe would not be able to hold off the Soviet masses 'without the use of mass destruction weapons...on the battlefield'.[23] Consequently, on 14 February 1951, the Chiefs of Staff invited the War Office to initiate a study on the tactical use of atomic weapons with a view to examining:

The types of target in the different phases of warfare against which it would be profitable to employ atomic weapons and how they would supplement, extend, or be used in substitution of existing methods of fire support both ground and air.[24]

[19] TNA, WO 231/59, Joint Exercises Broadside One and Broadside Two—Final Report (Army), December 1950.
[20] Ibid.        [21] TNA, DEFE 10/37, DRP(49)1, Defence of River Lines, 11 January 1949.
[22] TNA, DEFE 10/37, DRP(49)16, Defence of River Lines, 1 November 1949.
[23] TNA, DEFE 10/27, DRP(50)96, The Scientific Requirements for the Land Battle, 2 August 1950.
[24] TNA, WO 231/41, MO1/LM/21/4, The Tactical Use of Atomic Weapons, 15 March 1951.

That the tactical use of nuclear weapons was intimately linked to the defence of a major water obstacle is further evidenced by the fact that the key resource providing the foundations to the War Office nuclear study was a 1950 report by a working party activated by the Joint Chairmen of the Land/Air Warfare Policy Sub-Committee to assess the best methods of using atomic bombs in defence of a river line.[25] 'Defence of the River Line', by which the paper became subsequently known, was important according to the Chairman of the Defence Policy Research Committee, because 'for the first time it concentrated attention on the tactical use of the atomic weapon'.[26] The report was completed in June 1951 and concluded that nuclear weapons could be used profitably against large concentrations of troops and artillery and might be of 'outstanding importance in repelling an invasion or for breaking up a major assault on a river line'.[27] The tactical situation envisaged for this type of nuclear employment was the one constructed for 'Defence of the River Line' which anticipated an attack at four points across a river by an attacker who enjoyed a four-to-one superiority in manpower. It was believed that the simultaneous delivery of three air-burst atomic bombs against each of the assault points would be enough to paralyse the offensive. Ultimately, however, the report suggested that the effectiveness of nuclear weapons in a tactical role would be dictated by enemy deployments.[28] As Chapter 3 has shown, this was a point acknowledged by military theorists, who had reached the conclusion that heavy concentrations of troops would become uniquely vulnerable to nuclear attack. It was possible that greater mechanization might allow an attacker to deploy in less density while preparing to cross a river obstacle, but ultimately any attacker would be forced to concentrate in space in order to overcome the defence and maintain the momentum of the assault.[29]

Examination of the Army's own tactical mobility continued in 1951 with exercise COUNTER THRUST, which tested the ability of 1(BR) Corps to conduct mobile operations on wide fronts against superior enemy land and air forces on the plains of Northern Germany. Addressing participants after the exercise, General Sir John Harding stated that there were two main ways in which armoured formations could be employed during a mobile defence. The first was to position a mass of armour in a secure position and force the enemy to attack at a disadvantage. After the attack had lost momentum, the friendly armour could launch a decisive counter-attack against the enemy flanks. The second was to hold or check the enemy advance and then unleash a mass of armour in conjunction with other arms against the enemy position. Harding indicated that BAOR's armoured divisions were being trained in both of these techniques. The biggest

[25]  TNA, DEFE 5/25, COS(50)481, Best Method of Using the Atomic Bomb in the Defence of a River Line, 18 November 1950.

[26]  TNA, DEFE 10/37, DRP(50)23, Defence of River Lines, 17 October 1950.

[27]  TNA, DEFE 5/31, COS(51)344, Report on the Military Aspects of Atomic Energy, 6 June 1951.

[28]  Ibid.     [29]  Ibid.

problem hindering the use of such techniques in war was that the divisions were losing their mobility because there was too much transport on the road. Indeed, the Army appeared to be reaching the stage 'when there is so much transport that divisions cannot move at all'. Transport establishments would therefore have to be reduced and vehicle loads examined.[30]

Consequently, a few weeks later in England, SURPRISE PACKET exercised 6th Armoured Division and 3rd Infantry Division as part of a corps in mobile operations, with particular emphasis on 'speed in decision and manoeuvre and the development of offensive opportunism'.[31] The Chief Umpire's report was damning, however. In the early stages of the exercise, manoeuvre was handicapped by a lack of information and insufficient reconnaissance, and offensive opportunism was generally 'dormant'. Although the 'Fantasian' opposition enjoyed a five-to-one superiority in aircraft, as could be expected in a real war against the Soviet Union, there were still unreasonably high 'casualties' sustained from air attack. In part, this was due to a lack of air consciousness from the troops—such as a failure to practise basic anti-air drills and camouflage techniques—but was also due to the extremely high vehicle density on the roads. Furthermore, the technique for passing a formation rapidly over a water obstacle, which military theorists had predicted would hold a high premium in nuclear war, was still not understood, especially where armoured formations were concerned.[32]

The main lessons derived from both COUNTER THRUST and SURPRISE PACKET with regards to the handling of troops were that the bunching-up of transport would be most dangerous in light of the increased air threat and when confronted by superior enemy forces, and that armoured divisions required some form of obstacle to canalize the enemy strength.[33] Commenting on the manoeuvres over the last year, the SACEUR, General Dwight D. Eisenhower, reinforced the requirement to indoctrinate all ranks in the practice of camouflage, road discipline, and passive air defence. He also championed armour as the 'weapon of decision' and urged commanders to use it as such.[34]

The requirement in modern war for mobile forces that could switch rapidly between concentration and dispersion was confirmed in August 1953 with the Camberley exercise FOR AND ON. The report concluded that nuclear weapons might profitably be employed against tactical airfields, in the battlefield interdiction role, or in close support of ground troops. Underlining the fine balance to be

[30] TNA, WO 231/63, Joint Exercise Counter Thrust—Final Report (Army), November 1951. See, in addition, TNA, WO 32/13858, Commander-in-Chief Eastern Command to Under-Secretary of State, 18 February 1952.

[31] TNA, WO 231/65, Exercise Surprise Packet—Instructions for Spectators and Press, 1951.

[32] TNA, WO 231/68, Exercise Surprise Packet—Report by Chief Umpire, 18 October 1951.

[33] TNA, WO 231/69, Exercise Surprise Packet—Lessons Learned, 1951.

[34] TNA, WO 216/476, Comments on 1951 Manoeuvres—Land Forces, 27 December 1951.

struck between concentration and dispersion, the report stated that the aim of the attacker was:

> To make full use of the destructive and morale effects of the weapon to bring about conditions in which decisive exploitation will be possible, while at the same time avoiding the presentation of a profitable target to the enemy's atomic weapons.[35]

In order to exploit the shock effects of nuclear weapons, the troops allotted to this exploitation role would have to follow up the bombardment as quickly as possible. Because of the large kill radius of nuclear fires, and in order to present a less profitable target for enemy nuclear weapons, the troops should be deployed well back from the initial burst. This dilemma demonstrated further the requirement for rapid cross-country movement. Similar problems would confront a defender hoping to use nuclear weapons to break up an enemy attack during its preparation or execution. The aim here would be to deploy in depth while maintaining sufficient mobile reserves to seal off and destroy any penetrations and to make local counter-attacks. Again, the most difficult problem would be deciding what level of dispersion would be necessary to avoid crippling losses from atomic attack, whilst retaining sufficient strength on important tactical features to avoid being overcome through conventional battle tactics.[36]

It would not be until BAOR and its sister formations in NORTHAG exercised together in large NATO manoeuvres that the true horror of tactical nuclear warfare was revealed to the world. This came in September 1954 with the NATO-wide exercise BATTLE ROYAL, described by BAOR C-in-C General Richard N. Gale as a 'new look' exercise.[37] It was the largest of its kind to be conducted in Germany since the end of the war and involved 140,000 American, Canadian, Dutch, Belgian, and British troops in a simulation of nuclear land combat. The tactical concept was based on the assumption that a future land war against the Soviet Union would begin with an all-out enemy nuclear offensive and that the first few months would see the Allies fight a battle for survival. In this opening phase, NORTHAG's task was to defend the vital ground on which the delivery of SACEUR's counter-air offensive relied. The exercise was designed to test whether a Soviet armoured assault could be blunted by obstacle belts and 'stubborn' infantry formations and successfully counter-attacked by armoured forces in conjunction with airborne troops and supported by atomic artillery. The defensive forces were not expected to hold their ground indefinitely, but to try and

---

[35] TNA, WO 216/841, 43/Exercises/205(MT 10), The Tactical Use of Atomic Weapons, 25 August 1953.
[36] Ibid.
[37] NATO, CR(54)35, Meeting of the North Atlantic Council, 24 September 1954.

inflict unacceptable levels of attrition on the attacker.[38] To this end, 'tactics would be based on the atomic factor and not merely a number of divisions assisted by atomic missiles'.[39] Consequently, during the course of the exercise, a number of atomic shells were 'fired' against an advancing 'Fantasian' armoured column.

There were a number of problems with attaining realism and authenticity during BATTLE ROYAL, and resolving the effects of nuclear strikes proved to be a novel and challenging exercise for the umpires.[40] For example, the official report by NATO's Military Committee concluded that the simulation of aerial combat was entirely false, enemy representation was not realistic as to tactics, numbers, and organization, and the effect of tactical airpower on the land battle could not be accurately assessed.[41] Nonetheless, the Army was able to extract a number of helpful 'lessons' that informed thinking about the atomic battlefield.[42] Addressing British and Canadian officers after the exercise, the CIGS, Field Marshal Harding, said he was pleased with the progress that had been made in the general standard of training throughout the British Army of the Rhine, particularly in driving, maintenance of communications, concealment, and dispersion. Harding reinforced the traditional functions of land forces, arguing that vital ground would still have to be contested through 'hard and bitter fighting'. He stressed that on the atomic battlefield this could only be achieved through an improvement in tactical mobility and flexibility and urged commanders to study the problem realistically, objectively, and dispassionately. The solution to this problem would be essential for the future fighting efficiency of the Army. The CIGS believed this could not be solved by 'tinkering or pruning but only by major changes in outlook, in method, and in organisation'.[43]

BATTLE ROYAL was followed in 1955 by exercise CARTE BLANCHE which, as the name suggests, simulated the free play of tactical nuclear weapons directed against airfields and troop concentrations.[44] Predominately an air manoeuvre designed to test communications, command and control, air defence, and the tactical movement of troops on the ground, a remarkable 300 atomic bombs were

---

[38] Simon J. Moody, 'Enhancing Political Cohesion in NATO during the 1950s or: How It Learned to Stop Worrying and Love the (Tactical) Bomb', *Journal of Strategic Studies*, Vol. 40, No. 6 (2017), pp. 830–831.

[39] TNA, WO 231/97, Exercise Battle Royal—Planning and Narrative, 24 May 1954.

[40] The methods for umpiring an atomic strike were developed specially for BATTLE ROYAL. For the original directive see TNA, WO 231/99, Exercise Battle Royal—Directive on Atomic Umpiring, September 1954. Personal thoughts of the exercise from the Chief Umpire can be found in LHCMA, Pyman Papers, PYMAN 9/9, Notes to Director from Chief Umpire—Tactical Lessons, n.d. [*c.* October 1954].

[41] NATO, MC 43/3 (Final), NATO Exercise, 1955, 16 August 1956.

[42] For a detailed breakdown of the lessons learned during the exercise see TNA, WO 231/95, Exercise Battle Royal—Final Report, December 1954.

[43] TNA, WO 231/95, Exercise Battle Royal—Address by CIGS to British and Canadian Army Officers, n.d. [*c.* October 1954].

[44] Anon, 'Exercise Carte Blanche', *Flight*, Vol. 68, No. 2423 (1 July 1955), p. 32.

'dropped' by tactical aircraft in just two days of play.[45] Even without taking into consideration the long-term health issues associated with radiation poisoning, it was calculated that upwards of 1.3 million Germans would have died, with 3.5 million seriously wounded—more than five times the number of German civilian casualties sustained during the Second World War.[46] Both BATTLE ROYAL and CARTE BLANCHE served to demonstrate the sheer scale of destruction that would be wrought on the battlefield by the tactical use of nuclear weapons, which hardened opposition towards the deployment of tactical nuclear weapons in Europe. Unsurprisingly, the exercises caused something of a furore in the Federal Republic of Germany, on whose territory a tactical nuclear battle would be fought.[47] While the German Chancellor, Konrad Adenauer, had hoped that the accession of the FRG to NATO would lessen any impact of a future Third World War on his country, the 'new look' exercises had placed it firmly on the front line.[48] Thus, the first real attempts to simulate the dynamics of nuclear land warfare had exposed a number of inconvenient truths that would overshadow the Army's thinking about nuclear warfare in the years to come.[49]

## Nuclear Weapons and Operational Research

Field exercises provided only limited insights into the practical challenges of manoeuvring troops across the nuclear battlefield. If a more complete picture of nuclear war was to be found, then this would rely on a greater use of empirical data drawn from operational research. The Army had engaged with operational research since the opening stages of the Second World War, where groups of scientists were employed to conduct studies on early warning radar and anti-aircraft defences. By 1948 they had merged with other groups to form a new organization under the auspices of the War Office, known as the Army Operational Research Group (AORG), and from 1962, as the Army Operational Research Establishment (AORE).[50] AORE's function was to bring scientific minds and techniques to bear on the study of operational military problems through objective analysis. The types of generic problems regularly confronted

---

[45] Anon, 'Atomic Exercise Carte Blanche: The Practical Assessment of Future War', *Flight*, Vol. 68, No. 2424 (8 July 1955), p. 67.

[46] Lawrence Freedman, *The Evolution of Nuclear Strategy*, 3rd ed. (London: Palgrave Macmillan, 2003), pp. 104–5 and S. T. Cohen and W. C. Lyons, 'A Comparison of US-Allied and Soviet Tactical Nuclear Force Capabilities and Policies', *Orbis*, Vol. 19 (1975), p. 73.

[47] William W. Kaufmann (ed.), *Military Policy and National Security* (Princeton, NJ: Princeton University Press, 1956), p. 222.

[48] Beatrice Heuser, NATO, *Britain, France and the FRG: Nuclear Strategies and Forces for Europe, 1949–2000* (Basingstoke: Macmillan, 1997), p. 127.

[49] Moody, 'Enhancing Political Cohesion in NATO during the 1950s', p. 831.

[50] G. Neville Gadsby, 'The Army Operational Research Establishment', *Operational Research Quarterly*, Vol. 16, No. 1 (March 1965), pp. 5–6.

by operational researchers, such as the relationship between weapons, tactics, and doctrine, assumed a special significance when applied to tactical nuclear warfare.[51]

Thus, beginning in 1955, AORG embarked on a number of abstract and speculative studies to examine the operational use of nuclear weapons and the interactive nature of nuclear war. The first of these investigations was a retrospective analysis in which tactical nuclear weapon use was superimposed on eleven set-piece offensive operations conducted in Europe during the Second World War.[52] AORG scientists concluded that where heavy bombing had been used in direct support of the set-piece offensive operations studied, nuclear weapons could have feasibly been used to replace it, and might have been much more effective in neutralizing the target area, resulting in fewer casualties being suffered by friendly troops. Although in all of the operations studied nuclear weapons could have been used to replace heavy bombing in support of the original plan, the writers of the report suggested that this might not necessarily have been their best use. They suggested that given sufficient quantities and the means of delivering them, nuclear weapons could have been used to roll together the 'break-in', the 'dog-fight', and the 'break-out' phases of battle into one decisive operation, the 'break-through', the implication being that nuclear weapons could facilitate high-tempo mobile operations.[53]

The second investigation examined the use of nuclear weapons in critical defensive situations. It employed the German advance into France in 1940 as the operational background and attempted to ascertain how the Allied use of nuclear weapons might have affected the campaign.[54] It simulated the tactical use of nuclear weapons to destroy the bridges over which German forces advanced, as a substitute for air interdiction, and in a counter-attack role against German troop concentrations. The study confirmed the long-held assumption that natural obstacles such as river lines would play an important role in the nuclear land battle, not least because such a physical feature would act as a clear demarcation line between the opposing forces beyond which commanders could safely order nuclear strikes without fear of fratricide.[55] Nuclear weapons could also be used effectively to isolate the battlefield through the destruction of important towns and communication nodes. However, because of the quantity of bombs required to effectively retard the movement of enemy reinforcements, supplies, and materiel,

---

[51] R. W. Shephard, 'War Gaming as a Technique in the Study of Operational Research Problems', *Operational Research Quarterly*, Vol. 14, No. 2 (June 1963), pp. 120–2.

[52] TNA, WO 291/1498, Army Operational Research Group, Report No. 5/55: The Use of Atomic Weapons in Support of Set-Piece Offensive Operations, May 1955. The eleven operations included the capture of three ports, and one amphibious operation. Featured operations included: CHARNWOOD, GOODWOOD, COBRA, BLUECOAT, TOTALISE, TRACTABLE, VERITABLE, ASTONIA, WELL-HIT, UNDERGO, and INFATUATE.

[53] Ibid.

[54] TNA, WO 291/1502, Army Operational Research Group, Report No. 11/55: The Possible Use of Atomic Weapons in Critical Defensive Situations, November 1955.

[55] Ibid.

civilian casualties would be extremely high, with all of the political ramifications.[56] Ultimately, the dilemma facing the attacker was that if it wanted to defeat the defender, it had to move; if it had to move, then troops could not dig in; if troops could not dig in, then serious casualties could be expected in the face of nuclear attack. Thus, the attacker had to choose carefully when to move and when to dig. The equally delicate problem facing the defender was whether to use nuclear weapons against an attacker that was exposed on the move but dispersed and difficult to locate, or to employ a nuclear strike when the attacker had stopped moving but would probably be better protected in slit trenches.[57]

To allow a more accurate modelling of nuclear weapon effects in experiments, AORG and its sister organizations, such as BAOR's Operational Research Section, conducted further studies on the technical characteristics of nuclear weapons and their effects.[58] Although such experiments generated important scientific data for use in operational research, there were still limits as to how far realism could be attained in military exercises owing to a lack of battlefield exposure to nuclear weapons. This was not a problem unique to the Army, however. The training exercises of the Civil Defence Corps (CDC) at home during the same period, for example, have been regarded as more of a 'performance' than a realistic representation of post-nuclear attack Britain, owing to the fact that genuine nuclear bombs could, for obvious reasons, never actually be exploded. This 'deferred event' meant that the CDC's civilian volunteers, who occupied a curious insider-outsider position, merely 'rehearsed' nuclear war rather than 'lived' it.[59] As a potential agent of nuclear warfare, AORG sought to remedy this deficiency for the Army with two studies examining the value of nuclear 'indoctrination' in the service. This entailed exposing soldiers to a nuclear explosion, and then assessing the general level of nuclear knowledge within the Army.

The nuclear 'indoctrination' took place in September 1956, when 250 British and Commonwealth officers attended the first of the British BUFFALO nuclear

---

[56] Ibid.    [57] Ibid.

[58] See, for example, TNA, WO 291/1503, Army Operational Research Group, Report No. 12/55: The Protective Value to Personnel of Slit Trenches against the Thermal and Gamma Radiation Effects of Nuclear Explosions, December 1955; TNA, WO 291/1512, Army Operational Research Group, Report No. 8/56: Visual Incapacity Following Exposure to a Nuclear Explosion—Part I, Chorioretinal Burns, September 1956; TNA, WO 291/1515, Army Operational Research Group, Report No. 11/56: Visual Incapacity Following Exposure to a Nuclear Explosion—Part II, Flash Blindness, September 1956; TNA, WO 291/1628, Operational Research Section BAOR, Report No. 3/56: The Effects of Atomic Weapons on Forests in North West Europe, March 1957; TNA, WO 291/1519, Army Operational Research Group, Report No. 2/57: Optimum Burst Heights in the Tactical Use of Nuclear Weapons, March 1957; TNA, WO 291/1523, Army Operational Research Group, Report No. 6/57: An Estimate of Mortality Rates as a Result of Nuclear Weapon Attacks in the Field and an Analysis of Wound Types Amongst Surviving Casualties, June 1957; TNA, WO 291/1630, Operational Research Section BAOR, Report No. 4/57: The Use of Prepositioned Nuclear Weapons in Selected Sites in North West Europe, July 1957.

[59] Jessica Douthwaite, '… "what in the hell's this?" Rehearsing Nuclear War in Britain's Civil Defence Corps', *Contemporary British History*, advance online publication (2018), pp. 1–2.

weapon tests at Maralinga.[60] The object of the indoctrination was to provide the subjects with a deeper insight into the nature and possibilities of nuclear warfare than could be inculcated through lectures or 'fake' demonstrations. In order to ascertain whether any measurable change had occurred in the attitude of the indoctrinees towards nuclear weapons as a result of their experiences, AORG devised a pre-bomb and post-bomb questionnaire that was to be completed by the participating officers. The answers provide some fascinating insights into the minds of soldiers who had to ply their deadly trade under the looming shadow of the atom. After a short delay, during which time some of the more impatient officers were reported as being extremely 'browned-off', the indoctrinees were finally treated to not one, but two nuclear explosions. The yield of the first bomb was measured at 12.5kt, the second 10kt. In general, the officers appeared to be impressed by the flash and heat-wave of the nuclear explosion, but were underwhelmed by the noise and the blast from their viewing platform 5 ½ miles away.[61] The questions were designed to assess the indoctrinees' knowledge of, and attitudes towards, nuclear weapons. One of the questions asked was:

Lying down in the open on fairly flat ground, would you rather be:
a) 2 miles from a 20 KT bomb explosion
b) 400 yards from a 2000-lb HE bomb explosion
c) 50 yards from a 25-pr HE shell explosion
*Also, put a cross (x) under the one you dislike the most *

Unsurprisingly, the majority of the participants 'disliked' nuclear weapons much more after experiencing a nuclear explosion first-hand.[62] Another question asked:

If you were an Army Commander who required a blitz on an enemy concentration 4 miles behind their front lines, which would you prefer as the most likely to achieve your object:
a) An atomic missile
b) A HE bomb air attack of equivalent explosive force
c) Heavy artillery bombardment of equivalent explosive force

The answers from the pre-bomb questionnaire showed that 84 per cent of the officers would have chosen the atomic missile as the most suitable tool for the job, which rose to 94 per cent after the subjects had viewed a nuclear explosion.[63] This suggests at least an acceptance of nuclear weapons as valuable military instruments, although another set of questions from the post-bomb questionnaire

---

[60] TNA, WO 291/1526, Army Operational Research Group, Report No. 9/57: The Value of Live Indoctrination at a Nuclear Weapon Trial (Operation Buffalo), November 1957.
[61] Ibid.    [62] Ibid.    [63] Ibid.

revealed that the majority of officers believed that nuclear weapons would make war as an art 'very much more difficult'.[64]

The second study sought to assess the level of nuclear training within BAOR. It concluded that nuclear training was inadequate in several respects, and that this was represented by the generally poor attitude of officers towards the level and quality of nuclear instruction they had received. For example, radiation hazards, the subject most neglected in training, was regarded by most troops as the principal hazard in nuclear war.[65] Furthermore, the majority of men did not understand the basics of personal protection from nuclear attack. This resulted in the majority of subjects rating their chances of surviving a nuclear war much lower than in conventional war, which could have potentially grave implications for morale.[66] Although there appear to be no comparable studies in later years, the question of how morale might be maintained in nuclear war was never truly solved by the Army. One 1962 study on the treatment of morale in operational research suggested that 'there is no scientific and practicable basis for making quantitative or even qualitative predictive statements about differences in the general levels of morale of units and armies in hypothetical future situations'.[67] How troops might react to nuclear attack would remain ultimately unknown, but new approaches to operational research beginning in the late 1950s sought to model the interactive aspects of nuclear war-fighting to a greater extent than hitherto.

This new approach was a tactical nuclear war-game designed by AORG in 1956 as a tool to investigate some of the more complex problems arising out of the tactical application of nuclear weapons on the battlefield. Its creators believed the medium of war-gaming to be one of the most convenient and economic means for an experimental approach to this type of investigation.[68] The advantages of war-gaming over other approaches to operational research problems were that they enabled two-sided conflict to be studied through the interaction of 'Blue' and 'Red' commanders, they could be controlled to simulate any real or hypothetical operational situation, and they allowed extrapolation to future time. In theory, the interactive nature of war-gaming would provide insights into the relationship and interdependence between friendly weapons, equipment, and tactics and those of the enemy.[69]

---

[64] Ibid.
[65] TNA, WO 291/2436, Attitudes to Nuclear War and Knowledge of Nuclear Weapons and Their Effects, August 1959.
[66] Ibid.
[67] TNA, WO 291/2225, The Treatment of Morale in AORE War Gaming Studies of the Land Battle, July 1962.
[68] TNA, WO 291/2281, Army Operational Research Group, Occasional Note No. 10: AORG Tactical War Game, August 1956.
[69] WO 291/2281, AORG Tactical War Game.

The game represented a corps tactical battle between Red and Blue forces in North West Germany. Red was organized and equipped in accordance with the latest information on the Russian Army, and Blue mirrored that of the British Army of the Rhine. All elements of the land battle were represented at company level including infantry, armour, airborne forces, engineers, artillery (conventional and nuclear), anti-aircraft artillery, and tactical air support, with up to 1,200 individual units on the control board. The game was played on a relief model representing an area of some 150 x 90 km, with each game cycle representing one hour of battle time. During each cycle the commanders relayed orders concerning fire and movement to the umpires, who would assess the outcome. The controllers were bound by a book of rules and were only in very exceptional circumstances allowed to use their judgement, generally only to ensure that a correct military interpretation was given to the game situation that occurred. Commanders drawn from the regular Army were imported from outside AORG for each game, which was an important factor in ensuring that the game was realistic and did not become stereotyped. A game took approximately six weeks to play and was relatively inexpensive, costing approximately £40,000 per year.[70]

After a year of play, AORG published its first report in December 1957. It stated unequivocally that with the introduction of nuclear weapons to the land battle, new tactical concepts and organizations would be demanded. One of the first significant points to emerge was that the future pattern of land warfare would be dictated by how many nuclear weapons were made available. If only a few nuclear weapons were made available to field commanders, then operations in attack and defence would resemble those of conventional warfare, with nuclear weapons performing the role of more powerful conventional artillery. With a more plentiful supply of nuclear weapons, however, the pattern would change, and nuclear firepower would become the dominant factor in the outcome of battle. The role of conventional ground forces would then be to create and maintain the conditions needed to facilitate the most effective employment of nuclear firepower.[71]

If the land battle reached this critical nuclear phase, either gradually or from the outset, then another trend of considerable significance was identified by AORG researchers. As the nuclear potential of each side increased, it was found that pitched battles of a conventional nature decreased until they reached a stage where very few, if any, conventional engagements occurred. The reasons for this were clear. If the defender possessed enough nuclear weapons, it would seek to hold the attacker at a distance and destroy its forces by nuclear firepower without becoming locked in a potentially costly conventional battle. Likewise, the attacker would no longer be forced to attack enemy strong-points with conventional forces and

---

[70] Shephard, 'War Gaming as a Technique in the Study of Operational Research Problems', pp. 125–7.
[71] TNA, WO 291/2213, Army Operational Research Group, Memorandum No. H.15: The Land Battle in Nuclear Warfare: A Discussion of Tactical and Other General Trends, December 1957.

could simply use nuclear weapons to destroy any opposing forces that occupied the ground it wished to capture or pass over. The conclusion drawn from this assessment was that the strength of opposing forces would no longer be measured in terms of the size of the ground force, but by its nuclear potential.[72] This had obvious, and advantageous, implications for a ground force that was numerically inferior to its opponent. The report therefore concluded that if operational planning was to be based on the sustained use of nuclear weapons in the land battle, then the implications of that decision must be accepted and the necessary tactical and organizational changes made. If this did not happen, then 'the Army will find itself at a grave disadvantage if nuclear war is thrust upon it'.[73]

Subsequent war-games simulated both general war in Europe and limited wars elsewhere, with the object of giving guidance on the frequency and types of suitable targets for tactical nuclear weapons, and on their optimum organization and handling. Five games were played as part of the study: two in a limited war setting, in rolling desert-type country, with a restricted supply of nuclear warheads; one in a limited war setting with an unrestricted supply of warheads; and two against the background of general war in Europe, in medium-close country, with a restricted supply of nuclear warheads. In the limited war settings, the restricted supply of nuclear warheads was set at fifty per battlegroup, for operations lasting thirty days, with the unrestricted scenario adding an additional twenty warheads to the reserve. In the general war setting, the brief allowed forty warheads per battlegroup for ten days of fighting.[74]

The conclusions of the study revealed an insatiable appetite for nuclear use among battlefield commanders. The report stated that 'in any situation, commanders will tend to fire the maximum number of rounds allowed over any period in both attack and defence'. This perhaps predictable result was alternatively conveyed as evidence that 'Commanders will use all the fire-support they can get'.[75] The government's Chief Scientific Adviser, Solly Zuckerman, who had long been sceptical about the ability of nuclear weapons to influence the land battle in any meaningful manner, experienced the same phenomenon when working alongside generals and air marshals during the Second World War. This led him to conclude that escalation to all-out nuclear war was implicit in the concept of fighting a field war with tactical nuclear weapons, and that the only way in which a land battle might not go immediately nuclear would be if the psychological reactions of the commanding officers were 'the reverse of what has been the pattern in previous years'.[76]

---

[72] Ibid.    [73] Ibid.
[74] TNA, WO 291/2237, ARDE War Game—An Assessment of Sub-Kt Nuclear Weapons, August 1960.
[75] Ibid.
[76] Solly Zuckerman, *Nuclear Illusion and Reality* (London: Collins, 1982), pp. 68–9.

The more general findings of the study highlighted the problems posed by the inter-related factors of warhead yield, response times, and target acquisition accuracy; that if sub-kiloton warheads were to be effective in the close-support role, then they would need to be available in the same way, and at the same level of command, as conventional artillery; that the most useful employment of those weapons was against forming-up or hide areas; and that improvements in drills, communications, and release procedures would be essential in order to reduce response time to a minimum.[77] Even these early games were beginning to expose some of the uncomfortable truths about the military practicability of using nuclear weapons in defence of territory against an opponent equipped and prepared for armoured warfare. Zuckerman observed one such game between two divisional commanders summoned from BAOR for the purpose and confessed that 'the result was a shambles, with each "game" grinding to a disastrous halt. I watched in the umpires' hall, saying nothing'.[78]

With the Soviet Union rapidly closing the gap on the United States' lead in nuclear weapon systems by the late 1960s, further war-games confirmed Zuckerman's fears that tactical nuclear weapons would have to be employed in increasingly absurd numbers in order to affect the outcome of battle. In April 1966, R. W. Shephard of the Defence Operational Analysis Establishment (DOAE) presented the latest findings of the organization's war-games to the NATO Nuclear Policy Working Group. The conclusions were drawn from sample data taken from twenty-five games which had been played over the last six years in which 6,000 nuclear strikes had been analysed.[79] The analysis had shown that the attacker and defender could trade nuclear strikes with very little military pay-off for either side, as both would sustain similar rates of attrition. Therefore, if NATO hoped to rely on the use of tactical nuclear weapons to defeat a Soviet offensive, they would have to be used in overwhelming numbers.[80] For example, in one of the early games, in which the attack was assumed to come at a strength of eight divisions against a defending force of seven or eight brigade groups (a force ratio of 4:1), it was found that the defenders had to use 174 nuclear weapons against the attacker's seventy-seven in order to bring the attack to a halt. With such a force ratio, the rate of the advancing Red forces was still very high (reaching the River Weser within fifteen hours) and Blue forces, to achieve any military effect, had to use nuclear weapons very early in the battle.[81]

The implication of these results was that there was no net advantage, and no reason to suppose that nuclear weapons were inherently more valuable to the defender than to the attacker. It was in part for these reasons that NATO adopted

[77] ARDE War Game.
[78] Solly Zuckerman, *Monkeys, Men and Missiles* (London: Collins, 1988), p. 295.
[79] Digital National Security Archive, Response to Denis Healey's Letter on Tactical Nuclear Escalation, 20 March 1969.
[80] Ibid.    [81] Ibid.

the new strategic concept of flexible response in 1967, which reframed the role of tactical nuclear weapons as tools of escalation rather than weapons with which to fight a prolonged land campaign. The situation looked even worse when both sides had access to the same number of nuclear weapons. For instance, in one game Red and Blue forces each were assigned 180 nuclear weapons with the now standard 4:1 conventional force ratio. After just twenty hours of battle, a total of 286 nuclear strikes had been made. At the end of all this, the Blue force was relatively worse off than it was to begin with, losing 30 per cent of its force compared to 20 per cent losses for Red, and its defensive position had been decisively breached. In short, tactical nuclear weapons gave Blue no net dividend, even if hundreds were exploded within the corps area.[82] Aside from the purely military considerations, DOAE assessed that such a 'tactical' action would result in the destruction of 2,300 square kilometres of territory, rendering it indistinguishable, for the countries involved, from strategic nuclear attack. Under these conditions of unparalleled violence, 250,000 civilian casualties could be expected, with the same number becoming instantly homeless.[83] In under three days of war, devastation could be inflicted comparable to that sustained by Germany as a result of strategic bombing during the course of the Second World War.

War-games continued to be of interest to the Army throughout the 1970s, not least because they were a relatively cheap method to practise command and evaluate new ideas, equipment, and doctrine without deploying men and vehicles to training facilities which were in increasing demand. Furthermore, as Chapter 4 has shown, because of the growing lack of combat experience within the Army, even among senior officers, war-gaming remained an important tool for simulating the types of decisions that would have to be made in high-intensity warfare. This was even more important in the context of operations on the Central Front, in which the opening hours and days of a future conflict might well dictate the final result.[84] By 1979, the Army could boast to have developed and utilized routinely a plethora of war-games, from the flexible and fast-paced 'free kriegspiel'-type games employed at the Royal Military Academy Sandhurst, to the stylized combat modelling approach to war-games of the Directorate of Combat Development, and the research-led 'learning' and 'teaching' war-games of DOAE.[85]

War-games were also used as a tool in the 1970s to test emerging ideas for the defence of the Central Front. One such series was the Battlegroup War Game, which was based on the German defensive plan during Operation GOODWOOD, and envisaged the use of non-mechanized infantry to defend mutually supporting

---

[82] Ibid.    [83] Ibid.
[84] TNA, DEFE 70/464, TDRC 5003/1679, War Gaming in the British Army, 29 October 1979.
[85] TNA, DEFE 70/464, D/DAT/16/22/1(AT1b), War Gaming in the British Army, 30 September 1979.

positions located in woods and villages during the 1985–2005 timescale.[86] The game was played on two separate terrain models, one characterized by undulating farmland with a mosaic of small villages, the other being heavily wooded and interspersed with four or five large villages. Incorporating some of the new technology which was entering NATO armouries, Blue forces were composed of an infantry battalion with an enhanced scale of MILAN anti-tank guided missiles, a squadron of tanks, close reconnaissance troops, and a company of mechanized infantry. Red forces consisted of a standard Russian motor rifle division of three motor rifle regiments and a tank regiment with all of its supporting elements.[87] As can be seen by this order of battle, the game was designed to reflect similar force ratios to the historic Operation GOODWOOD, where a relatively light infantry force of German defenders stunted a British armoured assault of three divisions. Likewise, akin to the tactics employed by German infantry during GOODWOOD, Blue forces were widely dispersed throughout the area with orders to engage Red's main body in the flanks and rear only, with the aim of inflicting maximum casualties and delay on the attacker.[88]

This was the first brick on which the development of the concept was built, and although certain important aspects of the battle were inadequately represented, such as air power and electronic warfare, the suppressive nature of Red's artillery fire, and morale, the war-games appeared to validate the concept. The report stated that there could be no doubt that Blue forces could delay Red's advance and cause casualties when employing the tactics of the 'village concept', as the GOOD-WOOD concept was known colloquially. Theoretically, and with no opposition, Red forces could be expected to move through the area simulated by the game in one hour. With the new defensive concepts employed by Blue forces, however, delays of up to twelve hours were achieved—a considerable dividend for a future war in which every minute and hour that could be saved might provide time for a political settlement, or for the difficult decision to be made about the release of nuclear weapons.[89]

The Battlegroup War Game was therefore the first step towards an analysis of the 'village concept' and the basic idea of using non-mechanized infantry in the main defensive battle. The aim of the series was not only to develop the concept further, but also to indicate whether it had sufficient validity to proceed to further trials. In this context, the series did appear to add credibility to the concept, and suggested that it played to British strengths and Soviet weaknesses. For example, the concept demanded high levels of junior leadership, a field in which the British had for so long set the standard. Conversely, it was assumed that the Soviet officer

---

[86] TNA, DEFE 70/464, D/DCD(A)/17/2/3, Battle Group War Game Series 33—Final Report, 17 August 1979.
[87] TNA, DEFE 70/464, MAB/3/090, Final Military Report Part 8: Battle Group War Game Series 33, The Village Concept, June 1979.
[88] Ibid.      [89] Ibid.

would struggle to practise mission command because of the highly centralized command philosophy of the Red Army. The survivability of the German defence at GOODWOOD against armoured attack also provided hope that in a similar situation the non-mechanized infantry battalions of BAOR would be able to fight and prevail against what would undoubtedly be an armoured onslaught of epic proportions.[90] Further games were planned for the 1980s, which hoped to provide further insights into how the concept would affect the corps battle as a whole.[91] Unfortunately, this material has not yet been released to the public.

## Cognitive Dissonance and War-Gaming

The questionable results of the Army's war-games generated friction between the service and its civilian masters regarding its ability to prosecute a tactical nuclear war in a rational manner. Future war scenarios are rarely neutral, and the end-state is usually determined in advance by the scenario planners, who invariably have an agenda. As Mary Kaldor has stated, in an imaginary war, military exercises are able to 'test out the war effort in the imagination. But what is judged to contribute to victory or defeat . . . is ultimately subjective and depends on the predilections of military planners and politicians and on the institutional environment'.[92] The Army had clear motives to demonstrate that it could operate effectively on the nuclear battlefield, and in spite of evidence which suggested that the practical challenges of fighting with nuclear weapons might be insurmountable, the Army continued to claim that its operational research confirmed that it could not only fight a tactical nuclear war, but emerge 'victorious'.

Because of a lack of precedent, it could not be proved conclusively that the Army's conceptions of future war were incorrect. Nonetheless, sceptics of the idea that tactical nuclear war could fulfil a meaningful military or political function wielded as evidence the Army's war-games to cast doubt on the whole concept. One such critic was Sir Solly Zuckerman, who was determined to expose some of the fallacies inherent in the Army's operational research in his attempts to influence government nuclear policy and NATO strategy in the 1950s and 1960s. In his opening address to the Canadian Defence Research Board Symposium in December 1961, he warned his listeners that it was folly to place too much faith in the ability of nuclear weapons to redress the balance of forces on the Central Front, since war-games had shown that the number of weapons that

---

[90] TNA, DEFE 70/464, D/DCD(A)/17/2/3, Battle Group War Game Series 33—Final Military Report, 5 November 1979.

[91] TNA, DEFE 70/464, D/DCD(A)/17/2/3A, Battle Group War Game Series 33—Final Military Report, 19 November 1979.

[92] Mary Kaldor, *The Imaginary War: Understanding the East–West Conflict* (Oxford: Basil Blackwell, 1990), p. 213.

would be required to destroy or halt an enemy on a corps front in depth would be not three, four, or five, but hundreds.[93] For Zuckerman, the sheer destruction that would be wrought to the battlefield by thousands of tonnes of nuclear armament would be such that the secondary effects of the destruction caused would far outweigh any military effects that might be achieved. As the Scientific Director of the British Bombing Survey Unit during the Second World War, Zuckerman had witnessed first-hand the damage caused to German cities by conventional bombing, and it did not take much imagination to transpose this experience into a future war fought with nuclear weapons:

> We must see it as a zone of devastation in which all but the strongest buildings would have been utterly destroyed; in which roads would have been blocked and bridges made impassable; in which forests would have been razed; in which extensive fires would be raging; and over which vast numbers of civilian casualties would have occurred... Many a nuclear battle of the kind that the war gamers have analysed imply the equivalent of an average of one to two tons of conventional explosive on every acre over which the battle raged.[94]

Even if only fifty, and not 500, 20kt bombs were employed on a single corps front, then this would still result in devastation on a scale far more extensive than anything that had hitherto been experienced in warfare. As Zuckerman felt compelled to inform his Canadian audience, it took four years for the RAF to drop one megaton of explosives on Germany during the war; the same weight of attack could now be delivered in less than an hour.[95] In an effort to impart a modicum of reality to the picture, Zuckerman designed two studies in 1960, the first to show what would happen to the city of Birmingham if it was struck by a single 1mt thermonuclear bomb, and the second to demonstrate the fate of the small town of Carlisle if it was hit by a 20kt atomic warhead.[96] The results were horrendous, indicating that both Birmingham and Carlisle would have been reduced to mere smithereens, after which the surviving inhabitants might well envy the dead. Surprisingly, there were no other comparable studies being conducted at the time, and Zuckerman's findings had to be used in a United Nations report entitled *Effects of the Possible Use of Nuclear Weapons*.[97]

It would not be until the publication of General Sir John Hackett's future history, *The Third World War*, in 1978 that Zuckerman's study on the effects of a nuclear attack on a major city would unintendedly enter the public domain. In a

[93] TNA, WO 32/20384, Field Warfare in a Nuclear Age, 13 December 1961.
[94] Ibid.    [95] Ibid.
[96] Zuckerman, *Monkeys, Men and Missiles*, p. 280.
[97] Thant, *Effects of the Possible Use of Nuclear Weapons and the Security and Economic Implications for States of the Acquisition and Further Development of these Weapons* (New York, NY: United Nations, 1968).

well-known chapter of the book, the Soviet leadership authorize the destruction of Birmingham as a coercive step up the escalation ladder after its initially successful offensive in Western Europe has been repelled by a NATO counter-attack.[98] The chapter was written by Lieutenant-Colonel David W. Williams (the book was a collaboration of multiple authors), who was then serving as the Directing Staff member responsible for Nuclear, Biological, and Chemical Warfare at the Royal Military College of Science, Shrivenham.[99] The description of the destruction of Birmingham was almost identical to that contained in Zuckerman's then still classified study, and it is a reasonable assertion that Williams had encountered the report during the course of his professional duties and appropriated it for the book. Akin to the language used by Zuckerman to paint the image of nuclear destruction for the Canadian Defence Research Board, *The Third World War* described how:

> Within a second or so of the detonation the blast-wave hit the city centre beneath the fireball. The enormous pressures had the effect of instantly crushing all buildings below it so that what remained was only a levelled mountain of rubble. The blast-wave then roared and crushed its way outwards from the centre utterly destroying everything in its path. No structures above ground level were able to withstand the tremendous pressures and the coincident wind speeds resulting from the blast. Within three kilometres of Winson Green nothing survived, every building and structure being reduced to rubble and strewn across the roads so that the entire area looked like a gigantic rubbish heap.[100]

The Army was never called upon to fight in such conditions in *The Third World War*, as a like-for-like attack by NATO on the city of Minsk brought about the collapse of the Soviet regime before tactical nuclear weapons might have been introduced into the battle for the Central Front. The book was a polemic promoting the idea of strengthening NATO's conventional force posture, and so the portrayal of a militarily futile and politically questionable operation of war would not have served well the generally optimistic tone of the narrative.[101] Although it was a commercial success, *The Third World War* did not have the intended effect of changing British defence policy since, as Chapter 2 has shown, British conventional forces actually declined during this period. Perhaps Hackett and the Army were both guilty of deliberately avoiding the logical inconsistencies which would arise from any scenario employing the extensive use of nuclear weapons in land warfare.

---

[98] John Hackett, *The Third World War: August 1985* (London: Sidgwick & Jackson, 1978), pp. 287–303.
[99] Jeffery H. Michaels, 'Revisiting General Sir John Hackett's *The Third World War*', *British Journal for Military History*, Vol. 3, No. 1 (2016), p. 91.
[100] Hackett, *The Third World War*, pp. 291–2.
[101] Michaels, 'Revisiting General Sir John Hackett's *Third World War*', p. 95.

It was these inconsistencies, and the assumptions which underpinned them, that Zuckerman sought to expose in his attempts to influence the thinking of the Chief of the Defence Staff, Lord Mountbatten. One such attempt was his 1962 essay on 'Twenty Propositions' on conventional and nuclear warfare, which had been requested by the new Minister of Defence, Peter Thorneycroft, as a personal view, but circulated amongst the service chiefs at the request of Mountbatten.[102] In the first proposition, Zuckerman rejected outright the idea, which had been popular in the short years when the United States enjoyed overwhelming nuclear superiority, that tactical nuclear weapons might be used akin to conventional artillery to compensate for inferior numbers of men. Zuckerman considered this notion a product of blind faith, and not proper scientific analysis. Referencing the war-games of the previous years, he argued that they had consistently demon-strated that in a future land war on the Central Front, between 200 and 250 nuclear strikes of an average yield of 20kt could be expected to be exploded within a few days in an area 50 kilometres by 50 kilometres. This, Zuckerman claimed, would 'render the whole idea of mobile or any form of warfare meaningless'.[103] Another proposition was that escalation to general nuclear war was implicit in the concept of field warfare fought with tactical nuclear weapons, since war-games showed that a field commander would always wish to use more and more nuclear weapons if it became apparent that a previous weight of attack had not had the desired military effect.[104] This observation was in part informed by another proposition regarding the maintenance of morale in a nuclear land battle. Zucker-man claimed that:

> Once nuclear weapons started exploding on the scale assumed in war-games, it is inconceivable that troops or their commanders would continue to behave as rational members of a military organisation. Faced with the choice between having their position overrun by the enemy or letting off any nuclear weapons still in their possession it is possible that they would take the second alternative— regardless of any overall moratorium that may have been imposed by higher authority.[105]

Mountbatten, who had hitherto not given much thought to the problems of using tactical nuclear weapons on the battlefield,[106] obviously took heed of Zuckerman's propositions and rolled them out verbatim in an address given to SHAPE at the command post exercise SHAPEX 62. Mountbatten ended the address with the rhetorical question: 'What form of mobile field warfare can be carried out in an

---

[102] Zuckerman, *Monkeys, Men and Missiles*, p. 294.
[103] TNA, DEFE 13/721, SZ/794/62, Zuckerman to CDS, 7 September 1962.
[104] Ibid.        [105] Ibid.
[106] Zuckerman, *Monkeys, Men and Missiles*, p. 278.

area of say 50 kilometres by 50 kilometres after 200 Hiroshimas have taken place?'.[107]

Although the CDS appeared enamoured with Zuckerman's propositions, the CIGS, Field Marshal Sir Richard Hull, was not. In a private memorandum to Mountbatten, Hull warned of the dangers of allowing the propositions to become dogma, and in a slightly barbed comment suggested that Zuckerman's paper was 'written from an emotional and humanitarian point of view rather than from that of pure scientific advice on defence'.[108] Zuckerman would later claim that while he did have humanitarian instincts, his real concern was that 'the army planners were living in a wonderland. They did not seem to realize what a mess nuclear explosions would make of a battlefield'.[109] In contrast, Hull demonstrated the cognitive dissonance that had taken grip of the Army officer corps by claiming that war-games had shown that:

> tactical nuclear weapons can be used effectively and that although damage in the battlefield would be extensive, it would not be such as to prohibit completely the conduct of operations. Games have also shown that the defenders can success-fully disrupt and halt the Russian attack even though both sides used tactical nuclear weapons.[110]

It is unsurprising that Hull took a more favourable view of the data drawn from the war-games as there were a number of self-imposed limitations placed on the exercises which screened out some of the more uncomfortable realities of using tactical nuclear weapons in field warfare. On 23 November 1962, the Permanent Secretary of the MoD, Sir Robert Scott, visited AORE at Byfleet, where the games were being played, and sent a short report to Zuckerman highlighting the unreal-ity of the Army's exercises. He revealed that certain factors were being deliberately ignored, such as events on neighbouring fronts, escalation, and psychological factors. There was apparently no formal umpiring, the control system allowed for no exercise of choice by the controller, and decisions were taken by a system of random computing. There were also issues with the assumptions underpinning the scenarios themselves, which routinely saw Blue commanders tasked with the mission of physically defending the Rhine and other important terrain features.[111] As Chapter 2 has shown, by the early 1960s, the Chiefs of Staff had acknowledged that the real value of tactical nuclear weapons lay in their deterrent, rather than war-fighting, functions. However, the type of battles described in the AORE

---

[107] TNA, DEFE 11/472, 10/B/5, Talk on Tactical Nuclear Weapons Given at SHAPEX 62, 24 May 1962.

[108] TNA, DEFE 25/6, CIGS/PF/499, Tactical Nuclear Weapons, 18 September 1962.

[109] Zuckerman, *Monkeys, Men and Missiles*, p. 294.

[110] TNA, DEFE 25/6, Annex to CIGS/PF/499, 2 October 1962.

[111] TNA, DEFE 25/6, RHS/773/62, The Tactical Nuclear War Game, 26 November 1962.

war-games, involving the use of hundreds of tactical nuclear weapons, was in fact 'a battle directed solely at the retention of territory'. This juxtaposition between official policy and exercise scenarios led Zuckerman to conclude that 'to plan for tactical nuclear battle on this scale is to plan for the "almost certain" defeat of our whole policy'.[112]

The essence of the argument between Hull and Mountbatten/Zuckerman was that the CIGS regarded the AORE war-games as evidence supporting an already defined War Office view that tactical nuclear weapons could play a useful role in field warfare, whereas Zuckerman and Mountbatten were convinced that tactical nuclear weapons were not weapons in the ordinary sense, and certainly not weapons which could be used in battle on the scale envisioned by the Army. In his scientific assessment of the AORE studies, Zuckerman conceded that in lieu of any practical experience, the war-games were an 'interesting and instructive method of investigating some of the possible features of tactical nuclear field war', but that the number of studies yet made were so few that the data they provided must be approached with care.[113] He also questioned the significance of the results on the grounds that:

> A war game is a useful technique for study, but it is not a scientific experiment. In a good scientific experiment, every effort is made to remove human influence and random effects, so that if the experiment is repeated, the original result is again obtained. In a war game, on the other hand, human influence is deliberately introduced through the commanders; and random effects are deliberately built in through such factors as weapon inaccuracy, equipment reliability, meteorological conditions, and so on. This adds realism to the game and is desirable from this point of view. But it is then essential to realise that the results of a single game, or of a small number of games, are of little general significance.[114]

Zuckerman worried that War Office thinking on the future character of conflict was based almost entirely on this limited data and that 'the War Office seems to have accepted the results of the AORE games without the critical study they merit, and without a proper appreciation of the limitations of war-gaming in general'.[115] Indeed, he would later claim that 'when I read the available reports, I got the feeling that no-one had thought the matter through' because of a number of negative assumptions which underpinned the exercise scenarios.[116] The first was that an operation, in which hundreds of nuclear weapons would be used, would be restricted to a single corps front, as opposed to spreading to the flanks. The second was that such an operation, even if confined to a single corps front, would be

---

[112] TNA, DEFE 25/6, SZ/660/63, Zuckerman to CDS, 12 July 1963.
[113] TNA, DEFE 25/6, SZ/671/63, Tactical Nuclear Weapons, 29 July 1963.
[114] Ibid.        [115] Ibid.        [116] Zuckerman, *Monkeys, Men and Missiles*, p. 272.

unaccompanied by deep interdiction strikes on both Allied and enemy territory. The third assumption was that the hundreds of thousands, or even millions, of collateral civilian casualties would not make a difference to the conduct of the battle. The final negative assumption was that field operations and troop move- ment would be possible over terrain completely transformed by hundreds of nuclear explosions.[117]

Part of the problem was that there was still considerable confusion and ambi- guity about the role and functions of tactical nuclear weapons. As Chapter 2 has shown, BAOR had to operate within the context of NATO's strategic concept for the defence of the Central Front, which was predicated on the idea that the use of tactical nuclear weapons could compensate for shortages in conventional man- power. Since BAOR did not possess sufficient strength to defeat a Soviet attack with conventional weapons alone, it had little choice but to rely on the tactical application of nuclear weapons. The Army was, therefore, in something of a conundrum, as Sir Robert Scott observed:

> On SACEUR's instructions under current agreed NATO military policy, BAOR is expected to defend territory using tactical nuclears [sic] if necessary. This is the setting for the army war games, the results of which the War Office showed us. Ministry of Defence studies have however shown the absurdity of a tactical nuclear land battle in conditions of chaos and confusion and with a high risk of escalation ... unless BAOR get very large conventional forces or the number of nuclear weapons they assess are needed, they cannot discharge their mission of stopping a strong Russian attack. We could not provide the conventional forces required, and the Ministry of Defence studies have shown the fallacy of planning to use large numbers of tactical nuclears [sic] as weapons. BAOR are therefore in a dilemma so long as their present instructions stand.[118]

On 29 July 1963, the Chiefs of Staff Committee met with Zuckerman for an informal discussion on tactical nuclear warfare to try and reconcile the differences of opinion on the viability of the concept in light of the AORE war-games. As far as policy was concerned, all agreed that tactical nuclear weapons were required for deterrence; that escalation was not inevitable in all circumstances; and that shield forces in Europe must have a tactical nuclear capability in order to pose a retaliatory threat, which would require an adequate armoury of weapons, the necessary plans to use them, and a tactical doctrine on which training could be based.[119] With regards to the operational implications that this policy would have

---

[117] SZ/671/63.

[118] TNA, DEFE 13/734, RHS/498/63, R. H. Scott to CDS, 16 July 1963.

[119] TNA, DEFE 25/141, Record of Informal Discussion on Tactical Nuclear Warfare between CDS, CIGS, CAS, and CSA, 1 August 1963.

for the Army, however, there was still disagreement on the extent to which it might be possible to fight a land battle employing a significant number of nuclear weapons. Zuckerman's pessimistic appraisal on the fallacy of planning to mount meaningful military operations on a nuclear battlefield was now well known, but Hull appeared more optimistic, and dogged, as ever. The CIGS explained that although he had been sceptical about the ability of the Army to operate under nuclear conditions, the results of the war-games had now convinced him otherwise, and that until he received further evidence to disprove the AORE conclusions, he would continue to hold the view that tactical nuclear warfare could serve a military function.[120] Indeed, Hull wrote privately to Mountbatten to say that he doubted it could be proved that movement on the nuclear battlefield would be impossible, and that he had little choice but to 'plan on both the enemy and ourselves being able to move'.[121] The CIGS also attempted to defend AORE from Zuckerman's accusation that they had not considered the activities of adjoining corps sectors by arguing that the nuclear battle on one corps front would not necessarily spread to, or be repeated in, another.[122] This was refuted by the CAS, Sir Thomas Pike, who said that it would prove virtually impossible to limit nuclear air operations to the geographical area of a single corps front once battle had commenced; attacks across the whole front, in addition to battlefield interdiction in depth, were the standard operating procedure for both Allied and Soviet air forces, and should be expected.[123]

One important point to arise from the meeting was Hull's fear that 'disparaging talk' about the ability of BAOR to carry out its mission, or the purpose of so doing, would serve only to 'undermine the morale of Senior Commanders and soldiers alike'.[124] Furthermore, the CIGS confided in the CAS his concerns that the Army might lose faith in its ability to deal successfully with a Soviet attack, and that morale in Germany would suffer a critical blow if it was decided to denude the forces in the field a tactical nuclear capability.[125] However, according to Wing Commander Tony le Hardy, 'every Army officer I have talked to agrees that if Tactical Nuclear Weapons are in fact used in the numbers required to achieve a Tactical result then there won't be much left of the battlefield'.[126] While this suggests that the officer corps shared some of Zuckerman's scepticism, the dilemma for the Army remained the deterrent aspect of its task. According to le Hardy:

It will/always be difficult to put across to the average soldier that he is required to train for a battle which not only cannot be 'won' but which cannot even be

[120] Ibid.        [121] TNA, DEFE 25/6, CIGS/PF/499, CIGS to CDS, 31 July 1963.
[122] Record of Informal Discussion on Tactical Nuclear Warfare.
[123] Ibid.        [124] Record of Informal Discussion on Tactical Nuclear Warfare.
[125] TNA, DEFE 25/6, le Hardy to CDS, n.d.        [126] Ibid.

'fought' as an operation of war. This will be a challenge to the commanders of the future but it should not prove impossible.[127]

Another visitor to BAOR in November 1965 reported that one of the lessons being learnt by senior commanders through playing war-games was the 'unreality of expecting to fight any protracted campaign once [tactical nuclear weapons] were being used'.[128] Although the war-games were beginning to highlight the dangers of conceptualizing tactical nuclear war within the same parameters of conventional military operations, many officers believed that they had a further use as a tool to test the viability of new dispositions and organizations. The war-games were apparently 'held in high esteem in NATO circles', and if they could be used to show how BAOR could be made more efficient, then this might convince allies that any future changes to 1(BR) Corps were being made by virtue of military, as opposed to budgetary, considerations.[129] Not only did war-games provide 'much of the framework for the development of the United Kingdom philosophy on the tactical nuclear battle',[130] but they also became a vehicle for British defence engagement within NATO. In 1963, the SACEUR, General Lyman Lemnitzer, ordered that a representative from AORE should initiate an enquiry into how war-gaming could help inform planning at SHAPE,[131] which was supported by Mountbatten as a means to influence SACEUR's thinking.[132] Plans were also put in place in 1966 to collaborate on the conduct of war-games with the FRG, and to train German staff officers, inventors of the modern *kriegsspiel*, in the British war-gaming 'tradition' at Byfleet.[133] Thus, for all their flaws, the Army's war-games continued to be an important tool for practitioners thinking about the unthinkable.

## Conclusions

The narrative of nuclear war which the Army sought to portray through its operational research was one of optimistic familiarity: while a tactical nuclear war would be ultraviolent, it would not be such as to prohibit completely the conduct of military operations, and the challenges of operating on a nuclear battlefield could be overcome through sensible changes to tactics and procedures. Early exercises paid lip-service to the threat posed by nuclear weapons and

---

[127]   TNA, DEFE 25/6, le Hardy to CDS, 19 July 1963.
[128]   TNA, DEFE 25/8, Visit of Head of DScl to BAOR and 2 ATAF, 19 November 1965.
[129]   Ibid.
[130]   TNA, DEFE 4/244, DP Note 215/69, Central Region Study—Second Progress Report, 13 November 1969.
[131]   TNA, DEFE 25/8, SZ/855/63, CSA to CDS, 9 October 1963.
[132]   TNA, DEFE 25/8, CDS to CSA, 20 January 1964.
[133]   TNA, DEFE 25/8, Collaboration in War Gaming with the FRG, 25 May 1966.

reflected the prevailing view at the time that nuclear weapons were too important to be squandered on the tactical battlefield. The Army was more concerned in the late 1940s and early 1950s with its ability to prosecute armoured warfare more effectively in the context of conventional operations, and many of its early exercises were designed to enhance its tactical mobility and flexibility. The possibility that destructive nuclear weapons might be introduced to a future battlefield served only to add a new urgency in the quest to learn the lessons of the Second World War as they applied to mechanized combat. As the Cold War progressed, however, operational researchers had developed increasingly sophisticated methods of modelling the effects of nuclear weapons in military exercises. In particular, the Army became pioneers in the art of war-gaming in the nuclear era, which revealed new insights into the interactive aspects of nuclear war-fighting. Yet, this increased knowledge about the nuclear battlefield exposed limitations in the Army's own thinking about its future mission. The data generated through operational research appeared to demonstrate beyond doubt that the scale of destruction that would be unleashed during the type of nuclear battle being prepared for by the Army would be out of all proportion to any military benefits such a campaign might have. In light of this evidence, the Army was unable, for reasons relating to organizational morale and the deterrent functions of its mission, to accept that its assumptions about the character of future war might be flawed. If the Army was guilty of harbouring a cognitive dissonance about its ability to prosecute nuclear land combat, then this is a case in point.

# 6

# The Evolution of Nuclear War-Fighting Doctrine

The purpose of military doctrine is to provide a cohesive body of thinking to guide preparations for that most unpredictable and constantly changing business of war-fighting. The speculative nature of peacetime doctrinal development means that it is fraught with risk and can spell disaster for the military organization that draws faulty assumptions about the future character of conflict.[1] The writing of effective doctrine in peacetime requires military organizations to identify suitable lessons from previous conflicts, assess the present character of warfare, and peer into the future to predict the types of forces that will be required to fight and prevail.[2] In short, one of the inherent tensions of writing peacetime military doctrine is harmonizing past, present, and future conceptions of warfare.[3] Traditionally, the British Army had taken a *laissez-faire* attitude towards official written doctrine, preferring to rely more on stated principles than prescriptive dogma.[4] This approach had its merits, however, for a military organization such as the British Army, which could be called upon to fight almost anywhere in the world. With the lack of a master 'template' to guide the development of a standard army-wide set of doctrinal instructions, the Army had historically been wary of the risk of preparing to face the wrong enemy at the wrong time and in the wrong place.[5]

With the emergence after 1945 of the Soviet Union as the Army's only peer-to-peer threat, much of the uncertainty about where the Army would fight in the future, and against whom, was therefore diminished. Military planners understood the organization, tactics, and doctrine of the Red Army and could foresee

---

[1] See the conclusions drawn by Barry R. Posen in *The Sources of Military Doctrine: France, Britain, and Germany Between the World Wars* (New York, NY: Cornell University Press, 1986).

[2] Charles Grant, 'The Use of History in the Development of Contemporary Doctrine' in John Gooch (ed.), *The Origins of Contemporary Doctrine*, The Occasional No. 30 (Swindon: Strategic and Combat Studies Institute, 1997), p. 9.

[3] This problem is discussed further in Paul Latawski, *The Inherent Tensions in Military Doctrine*, Sandhurst Occasional Papers No. 5 (Camberley: Royal Military Academy Sandhurst, 2011).

[4] David French, *Raising Churchill's Army: The British Army and the War against Germany, 1919–1945* (Oxford: Oxford University Press, 2001), p. 279 and David French, *Military Identities: The Regimental System, the British Army, and the British People c. 1870–2000* (Oxford: Oxford University Press, 2005), pp. 344–5.

[5] Hew Strachan, 'Introduction' in Hew Strachan (ed.), *Big Wars and Small Wars: The British Army and the Lessons of War in the 20th Century* (Oxford: Routledge, 2006), pp. 3–5.

*Imagining Nuclear War in the British Army, 1945–1989*. Simon J. Moody, Oxford University Press (2020).
© Simon J. Moody.
DOI: 10.1093/oso/9780198846994.001.0001

how a Soviet land offensive might develop in a future war. Furthermore, with the British Army of the Rhine a permanent fixture in Central Europe, commanders had time to study the local terrain and plan how a defensive battle might be fought. The result was that, as far as the Rhine Army was concerned, there was now a specific scenario for which tactical doctrine could be developed. The Army's nuclear war-fighting doctrine evolved over three distinct phases. The first phase, covering the first post-war decade, was a cautious approach to the writing of doctrine in which nuclear weapons were grafted onto concepts already established for the conduct of conventional warfare. The second phase witnessed the evolution of a *bona fide* nuclear war-fighting doctrine during the 1960s against a background of changing NATO strategy. The final phase saw Army doctrine come full circle with a return to conventional, mobile defence within the context of the Bagnall reforms of the 1980s.

## Confronting the Conventional–Nuclear Dichotomy

The first post-war review of Army doctrine came in 1948, in the wake of the Camberley exercise SPEARHEAD, in which the simulated use of tactical nuclear weapons had suggested that ground forces were now required to operate with greater dispersion, cross-country mobility, and flexibility.[6] These new insights had led the CIGS, Field Marshal Montgomery, to establish a committee under the chairmanship of General Sir John Crocker to ensure that military thought and tactical doctrine were being kept well in advance of the time.[7] Montgomery's critics claim that his legacy cast a long, debasing shadow over the post-war officer corps, saddling the Army with an outdated, over-centralized, and stagnant military doctrine which was ill suited to the types of threats it might face in a rapidly changing military environment.[8] However, Montgomery's 'corrupting' influence on Army doctrine during his tenure as the professional head of the service was perhaps less marked than the historiography suggests.[9] As David French has shown, the three publications to emerge from the Crocker Committee were far

---

[6] TNA, WO 216/202, Exercise Spearhead, Final Address by CIGS, 10 May 1947.

[7] See Douglas E. Delaney, *Corps Commanders: Five British and Canadian Generals at War, 1939–1945* (Vancouver: University of British Columbia Press, 2011), p. 169.

[8] John Kiszely, 'The British Army and Approaches to Warfare since 1945' in Brian Holden Reid (ed.), *Military Power: Land Warfare in Theory and Practice* (London: Routledge, 1997), pp. 183–7 and Colin McInnes, *Hot War, Cold War: The British Army's Way in Warfare, 1945–95* (London and Washington, DC: Brassey's, 1996), pp. 53–6.

[9] See Simon J. Moody, 'Was There a "Monty Method" after the Second World War? Field Marshal Bernard L. Montgomery and the Changing Character of Land Warfare, 1945–1958', *War in History*, Vol. 23, No. 2 (2016), pp. 210–29.

from being outmoded, and actually contained greater elements of 'modern' manoeuvrist thinking than has previously been believed.[10]

Crocker was the ideal candidate to facilitate a review of the Army's doctrine, having spent much of his career working on the conceptual challenges of how to effectively employ armoured forces in deep manoeuvre operations, most notably during his secondment to the Royal Tank Corps Centre at Bovington during the 1930s. The capstone publication of Crocker's enquiry was *The Conduct of War* (1950), and although it remained rooted firmly to those concepts usually associated with conventional war-fighting, it spoke to both attrition *and* manoeuvre.[11] The Army was understandably sceptical of turning its back completely on the vast body of corporate knowledge it had attained through decades of conventional war-fighting because of the sudden appearance of a weapon system unproven in battle. The Army's counterparts in the Canadian and US armies had arrived independently at similar conclusions, both of which were producing conservative military doctrine at the same time.[12] Thus, we see in the preface to *The Conduct of War* a cautious appraisal by Field Marshal Bill Slim, who had succeeded Montgomery as CIGS by the time of publication of the pamphlet, warning that although weapons and methods of war were changing constantly, the basic principles of war remained the same.[13] He went on to remind readers that although the lessons of the past were important, it was essential to guard against the danger of letting past experience carry too much weight.[14] At the same time, the doctrine did reflect a greater awareness of the utility of ground manoeuvre on the modern battlefield, stating that the 'higher commander who can prevent the enemy from moving and who possesses mobility himself will always be successful' and that an army with high mobility would always beat one that was based on numerical superiority.[15] It also advocated a manoeuvrist approach to operations, which would result in greater battlefield efficiency:

> The enemy will be defeated with greater ease if he can be attacked on a flank or if a mobile force strong in armour can be loosed against his rear. The battle must

---

[10] David French, *Army, Empire, and Cold War: The British Army and Military Policy, 1945–1971* (Oxford: Oxford University Press, 2012), p. 85.

[11] Moody, 'Was There a "Monty Method" after the Second World War?', pp. 215–216.

[12] Andrew B. Godefroy, *In Peace Prepared: Innovation and Adaptation in Canada's Cold War Army* (Vancouver: University of British Columbia Press, 2014), pp. 73–4; Ingo Trauschweizer, *Nuclear Weapons and Limited War: The U.S. Army in the 1950s* (Florence: European University Institute, 2009), pp. 1–4; Robert A. Doughty, *The Evolution of U.S. Army Tactical Doctrine, 1946–76* (Kansas, MO: Combat Studies Institute, 1979), p. 2.

[13] War Office, *The Conduct of War* (London: War Office, 1950), p. ii. The stated principles of war were: selection and maintenance of the aim; maintenance of morale; offensive action; security; surprise; concentration of force; economy of effort; flexibility; co-operation; administration.

[14] Ibid., p. 3.     [15] Ibid., p. 12.

therefore never be allowed to become or remain static. It will always be the aim of the commander to keep the battle open and to gain scope for manoeuvre.[16]

In spite of the emphasis placed on manoeuvre in *The Conduct of War*, contemporary observers such as J. F. C. Fuller, Sir Basil Liddell Hart, and Sir Giffard Martel claimed that the Army had taken a retrograde step in its doctrinal evolution. Often, this condemnation was directed at Montgomery personally on the charge that it was his apparent preference for fighting tidy, teed-up, and methodical battles that forced the Army to reject a more modern approach to European defence in favour of a doctrine which they saw as little different to that which had served 21st Army Group in Normandy: 'what caused us after the war to turn our backs on all this great progress that was being made in the art of war, and to return to position warfare?' wrote Martel in 1950.[17] For that well-known champion of mobile warfare, the answer was clear, arguing that since 'the Field Marshal is a very great expert on Position Warfare . . . [and] does not believe much in mobility', he was compelled to demand 'large old fashioned manpower armies to hold the Elbe or the Rhine in position warfare'.[18] This is a somewhat unfair assessment of strategic realities. What Montgomery's detractors had failed to account for sufficiently were the political and strategic constraints which shackled the Northern Army Group to the intra-German border. As long as NATO was committed to a forward defence, BAOR was required to physically defend the territorial integrity of the Alliance, and a tactical doctrine which emphasized the attrition of enemy forces was entirely appropriate for the unique military context of the Central Front.

The companion documents to *The Conduct of War* also advocated a blend of attrition and manoeuvre. For example, while *The Infantry Division in Battle* (1950) reaffirmed the importance of the 'tidy' battlefield and the requirement to destroy the enemy through 'hard and prolonged fighting',[19] it simultaneously urged commanders to take risks, exploit success with vigour, and abandon the more methodical methods to achieve decisive results, especially during the 'breakout' battle.[20] Likewise, *The Armoured Division in Battle* (1952) described the unique characteristics of armoured divisions as being that of mobility, flexibility, and hitting power.[21] It warned that the armoured division would lose much of its

[16]  Ibid., p. 17.
[17]  IWM, Private Papers of Lieutenant-General Sir Giffard Martel, GQM 6/3b, Modern War, unpublished typescript, n.d. [approx. March 1950].
[18]  IWM, Private Papers of Lieutenant-General Sir Giffard Martel, GQM 6/3b, Vital Questions and Suggested Answers, unpublished typescript, March 1950. Martel believed that part of the problem was that Montgomery had surrounded himself with 'Yes Men'. IWM, Private Papers of Lieutenant-General Sir Giffard Martel, GQM, 6/3b, What Has Gone Wrong at the War Office, unpublished typescript, n.d. [approx. 1950].
[19]  War Office, *The Infantry Division in Battle* (London: War Office, 1950), pp. 21–2.
[20]  Ibid., p. 45.
[21]  War Office, *The Armoured Division in Battle* (London: War Office, 1952), pp. 10–11.

power if deployed in a static supporting role and that 'so long as a higher commander can keep his mass of armoured firepower mobile on the battlefield, so long will he hold the advantage'.[22]

The matter of Army doctrine was discussed in detail at the Generals' Convention at Warminster in April 1952. With regards to the tactical doctrine laid down in *The Infantry Division in Battle*, Lieutenant-General Sir Richard N. Gale said that since it was concerned with a specific tactical problem, it should not be read as official doctrine. Gale stressed that what was required was a flexible tactical doctrine that could be adapted to various local situations since it was impossible to predict with complete accuracy how each particular battle would play out.[23] Field Marshal Slim concluded the discussion by warning against the adoption of too rigid a doctrine. He reminded his commanders that the British Army was still liable to be sent to all sorts of 'funny places' and that it would be unwise to produce a doctrine that was first-class for operations in Central Europe but was unsuited to desert or jungle warfare.[24] Here can be seen the perennial problem with the British Army's relationship with written doctrine. Although a large proportion of the Army was located in Germany, preparing to wage high-intensity land warfare against a modern military power, many more divisions were committed to operations in support of Britain's large portfolio of overseas security commitments. Thus, the Army high command was understandably wary of expending too much energy on the production of a tactical doctrine which was only suitable for a particular military environment.

For the British Army of the Rhine, however, it did have a clearly defined enemy in Central Europe and an assigned operational role within NORTHAG. The major challenge for doctrine writers in the early 1950s was overcoming the lack of detailed information on the technical characteristics of nuclear weapons. For example, when Sir Frederick Brundrett, the Deputy Scientific Adviser to the Ministry of Defence, attended a BAOR staff conference in Germany in the spring of 1952, he reported to the Vice-Chief of the Imperial General Staff, Lieutenant-General Sir Nevil Brownjohn, that he had been rather disturbed to find that the attitude towards atomic warfare 'appeared to be so restrictive that even the mention of the word atomic was regarded as rather insecure'. Brundrett explained that in a future Continental land war, BAOR would be fighting alongside the Americans, who would certainly be using nuclear weapons in a tactical role on the battlefield. That being the case, he suggested that it was of the upmost importance to get the Chiefs of Staff to agree to instigate some kind of special training in

[22] Ibid., p. 12. Moody, 'Was There a "Monty Method" after the Second World War?', pp. 216–217.
[23] TNA, WO 216/778, Generals Convention at Warminster, verbatim reports: Item 1, Tactical Doctrine—Defence, April 1952.
[24] Ibid.

atomic warfare and to publish some information on the subject at a much lower level than had hitherto been permitted. Brundrett highlighted that books on atomic warfare were already freely available to purchase from bookshops, and that the three British services were lagging behind in disseminating information throughout their ranks.[25]

Brownjohn discussed the issue briefly with the Commander-in-Chief of the British Army of the Rhine, General Sir John Harding, who thought it premature to think about the problem in too much detail at that time.[26] After further discussions, it was agreed to wait until further exercises had been conducted before embarking on the process of developing a new tactical doctrine and training regime.[27] Brownjohn wrote back to Brundrett, assuring him that passive defensive measures against nuclear attack were being studied and that a training pamphlet would be published very soon.[28] The Camberley exercise FOR AND ON subsequently took place in August 1953, the main conclusions of which underlined the delicate balance to be struck between concentration and dispersion on the nuclear battlefield. After a short delay because of complications in providing a scientific appendix, the Army's first training pamphlet for nuclear warfare was finally released in October 1954.[29]

*Notes on Atomic Warfare* represented the most thorough assessment yet by the Army on the tactical application of nuclear weapons. As stated in its introduction, however, these notes were only meant to provide a background for future training and study, and did not represent official doctrine. Greater knowledge of recent scientific developments and further nuclear training exercises were required before 'correct organisations can be fixed or firm doctrine on future tactics, possibly involving considerable changes in techniques, laid down'.[30] Thus, it underlined that whatever character a future war adopted, land battles and campaigns would still be a struggle for ground and victory would only be won 'after hard and bitter fighting'. Both sides would still have to defend or seize important terrain features such as airfield complexes and their associated radar systems, ports and coastlines, missile sites, and industrial areas. Consequently:

> To do this there will always be ground that must be held or gained, and ground that is in dispute can only be held or gained by fighting for it. It is with this fighting that these notes are concerned.[31]

---

[25] TNA, WO 216/644, Brundrett to Brownjohn, 27 June 1952.
[26] TNA, WO 216/644, Vice-Chief of the Imperial General Staff to Deputy Chief of the Imperial General Staff, 28 June 1952.
[27] TNA, WO 216/644, Vice-Chief of the Imperial General Staff to DSA, 14 July 1952.
[28] TNA, WO 216/644, Brownjohn to Brundrett, 1 August 1952.
[29] TNA, WO 231/95, BM/404(MT 10), Brigadier J. A. W. Ballard to Major-General B. Daunt, 14 October 1954.
[30] War Office, *Notes on Atomic Warfare* (London: War Office, 1954), p. 3.       [31] Ibid.

*Notes on Atomic Warfare* therefore still conformed to traditional conceptions of conventional war-fighting. Indeed, it described in great length how the ten principles of war as enunciated in *The Conduct of War* still remained relevant in the nuclear era. The main difference from conventional war-fighting was simply one of the scales of firepower available to commanders in the field.

The Army's *Notes and Information on Training Matters*, which were published habitually by the Director-General of Military Training (DGMT), displayed an equally cautious tone. The March 1955 edition merely directed its readers to external sources of information while encouraging officers to 'keep themselves abreast of informed opinion and original thought' by engaging with suitable literature on nuclear matters. It provided a list of relevant service publications such as the *British Army Annual*, the *Army Quarterly*, and *The RUSI Journal*, in addition to advertising essay writing competitions and the publication of new books on the theory of nuclear warfare.[32] The next edition of *Notes*, which was published six months later, was equally restrained, and stated that although questions relating to nuclear warfare were the subject of much thought and discussion in the Army, it is 'important to ensure that the whole subject is kept in a proper perspective'.[33] It warned against the risk that thinking about future war might obscure the vital task of training for war with the weapons that were then available since 'changes are likely to take place slowly, as a study of military history will show; the process is one of evolution rather than revolution'.[34]

The October 1956 edition of *Notes and Information on Training Matters* reflected a subtle change in tone, however, when discussing nuclear weapons, suggesting that 'nuclear weapons must be considered as normal weapons at the disposal of a higher commander in the event of total war'.[35] It is unclear whether this statement represented the official War Office view, or was merely mimicking the public announcements being made by the US Secretary of State John Foster Dulles at this time (see Chapter 1). Whichever it was, the pamphlet outlined that the training priorities for the Army would now be to improve camouflage and deception techniques; to learn how to dig more deeply and quickly; and to practise the techniques required to be able to switch rapidly between concentration and dispersion.[36] The extreme physical strain placed on soldiers under nuclear conditions suggested that special steps needed to be taken to ensure that troops possessed the necessary endurance to operate in such abnormal conditions. Such skills included the ability to:

---

[32] War Office, *Notes and Information on Training Matters: Number 10* (Surrey: War Office, 1955), pp. 13–15.

[33] War Office, *Notes and Information on Training Matters: No. 11* (Surrey: War Office, 1955), p. 6.

[34] Ibid., p. 7.

[35] War Office, *Notes and Information on Training Matters: No. 13* (Surrey: War Office, 1956), p. 16.

[36] Ibid., p. 17.

Cover long distances across country on foot at fair speed, then to fight and dig in at the end of it; to overcome obstacles such as rivers, demolitions, hills; to continue enduring with little sleep.[37]

How the Army might prepare men to perform such difficult feats on the nuclear battlefield of the future was curiously missing from the training pamphlet. Although the service retained an impressive level of corporate war-time knowledge of the battlefield conditions in conventional war, it had no practical experience of fighting with nuclear weapons. Thus, while *Notes on Atomic Warfare* and its attendant training pamphlets represented the clearest promulgation yet of how the Army envisaged operating in a nuclear environment, the intellectual reference points for thinking about future war were rooted firmly in recent experience, and nuclear weapons were almost grafted onto existing modes of thought. Andrew Godefroy demonstrates that this was an affliction suffered by the Canadian officer corps in the same period, with senior commanders relying heavily on their Second World War experiences when approaching the formulation of new tactical doctrine.[38]

Indeed, the first two BAOR commanders forced to consider seriously the challenges of fighting on the conventional–nuclear battlefield both rose to prominence in the crucible of the last war. The first was General Harding, who did not serve in North West Europe through 1944–5 and, by his own admission found Germany an 'entirely new' and 'strange' environment.[39] Harding took command of BAOR in 1951 and was confronted immediately with the tricky business of planning for a forward defence of Western Germany in an unfavourable strategic and operational context. Harding had few opportunities to implement innovative operational concepts since his command was preoccupied with how to ensure that an understrength Rhine Army could not be knocked off-balance by a surprise Soviet attack. Consonant with early British concepts for the defence of Germany, he would achieve this by developing plans which would allow BAOR to safely fall back to prepared defensive positions on the Rhine-Ijssel line where it was hoped that the enemy could be held at bay.[40] The operational plans of Harding's successor, General Gale, invoked the memory of the Second World War in that they were based on the *Wehrmacht*'s mobile defence concepts as employed in operations on the Eastern Front.[41] Amongst the lessons that the British extracted

---

[37] War Office, *Notes and Information on Training Matters: No. 14* (Surrey: War Office, 1957), p. 5.
[38] Godefroy, *In Peace Prepared*, p. 147.
[39] John Harding interview, 8736, Imperial War Museum Sound Archive.
[40] TNA, WO 106/6051, Appreciation by Gen. Sir John Harding C-in-C BAOR of the Situation, 17 January 1952.
[41] For an account of the US Army's attempts to learn from the German experience see Kevin Soutor, 'To Stem the Red Tide: The German Report Series and Its Effects on American Defense Doctrine, 1948–1954', *Journal of Military History*, Vol. 57 (1993), pp. 653–89 and James A. Wood, 'Captivated

from that theatre was that the Soviets had struggled to overcome carefully prepared delaying measures and were vulnerable to sudden counterattacks by armoured forces, and that its commanders found it difficult to cope with the unexpected.[42] This pointed towards the need for a manoeuvrist approach to the conduct of operations when dealing with the Soviet masses. Indeed, this was a notion that Martel supported, who as Head of the Military Mission to the Soviet Union during the Second World War had witnessed first-hand Soviet reactions to German mobile operations. Martel wrote in 1950:

> So long as we are content with killing Russians and have no intention of occupying any large part of Russia, then there seems to be no necessity for any large number of normal formations [infantry divisions] in addition to the armoured divisions...I wish more people could have had the opportunity, which I had, of hearing from the Russian commanders the tremendous effect of large scale operations by really mobile armoured forces, which they had to face in 1941.[43]

Martel conveyed this thinking to General Gale, pressing the requirement for the British Army to conduct mobile operations against the Soviet Union in a future war rather than static or semi-mobile operations.[44] Gale replied by stating that this was in fact the official view of the Army and that the philosophy of mobile warfare was stressed continually in its teaching. Gale illustrated to Martel the commitment of the Army to mobile operations by highlighting that by the end of November 1951 there would be no fewer than three armoured divisions in Germany to one infantry division.[45]

The early composition of 1(BR) Corps was therefore geared towards conducting mobile operations. Indeed, because it lacked the sufficient quantity of men and material, BAOR had no choice but to fight a mobile battle at the tactical level and to employ many of the techniques associated with manoeuvre warfare. The wide frontages of NORTHAG's sector, coupled with Soviet numerical superiority, meant it would have been impossible to fight a static battle of attrition with the forces that were available. The problem was that a positional defence under these circumstances would leave gaps uncovered by fire between the defensive positions, which could easily be exploited by Soviet forces to infiltrate the position and

Historians, Captivated Audiences: The German Military History Program, 1945–1961', *Journal of Military History*, Vol. 69 (2005), pp. 123–48.

---

[42] French, *Army, Empire and Cold War*, p. 94.
[43] IWM, Private Papers of Lieutenant-General Sir Giffard Martel, GQM 6/3b, The Handling of an Armoured Corps Against Russian Forces, unpublished typescript, July 1950.
[44] TNA, WO 216/408, Notes on Mobile Armoured Forces, 20 July 1951.
[45] TNA, WO 216/408, Gale to Martel, 27 July 1951.

destroy formations piecemeal.[46] This predicament explains why 1(BR) Corps was top-heavy in armour, as Slim explained to senior officers in 1951:

> I do not know whether any of you have noticed, but the composition of the British Army of the Rhine, for which I am afraid I am responsible if you do not like it, is at the moment one infantry division and three armoured divisions because I thought there were going to be a lot of gaps.[47]

Although BAOR's dispositions were geared towards a mobile defence, Gale was nonetheless tied to a forward defence of Western Germany for primarily political reasons. Militarily, SACEUR's strategic concept relied on the preponderance of nuclear airpower to retard a Soviet offensive, which in turn relied on the use of certain bombing and navigational aids located in Western Germany. This meant that BAOR had to assist the US Strategic Air Command and UK Bomber Command by holding those stations for the period required for the initial air offensive. Gale's plan was to deploy the minimum troops necessary to protect the communication nodes for forty-eight hours, after which they would make a clean break for the main defensive position on the Rhine-Ijssel. With the slender forces available to Gale, it was important that the covering forces be extricated quickly after the forty-eight hours so as not to risk insufficient strength on the Rhine by becoming bogged down in a running battle.[48]

By this time, 1(BR) Corps was reorganizing its traditional divisional structures into leaner and more agile formations better suited to the types of operations envisaged by military planners. A new outline organization for BAOR's infantry and armoured divisions had been proposed as early as 1956 by the DCIGS, General Sir Dudley Ward.[49] From this investigation emerged a new organizational concept destined to be known as the 'brigade group'. Brigade groups were designed from the ground up to be able to operate in a nuclear environment and were designed as self-contained units, capable of sustaining independent combat operations with high levels of tactical mobility and flexibility.[50] The War Office consulted all overseas commands on the proposal,[51] which was accepted unanimously as the most suitable formation for prosecuting BAOR's unique mission.[52]

---

[46] TNA, WO 216/778, Generals' Convention at Warminster, 1951.    [47] Ibid.

[48] TNA, WO 216/888, Appreciation by General Sir Richard Gale Commander-in-Chief BAOR and Commander Northern Army Group, 29 September 1955.

[49] TNA, WO 163/641, AC/P(56)1, Reorganisation of the Division: A New Outline Organisation for the Armoured and Infantry Division, 14 January 1956. Ward outlined further his vision for the new divisional structures to his NATO colleagues. See NATO, AC/100-VR/3, Defence Planning—Multilateral Discussions, Army Divisional Organization, 22 February 1956 and NATO, AC/100(WG-1)R/1, Defence Planning—Multilateral Discussions, Military Working Group on Points Arising from Item C, 24 February 1956.

[50] TNA, DEFE 7/1682, The Brigade Group as the Basic Fighting Formation, n.d. [c. 1957].

[51] TNA, DEFE 7/1682, Brigade Group Organisation, 25 July 1957.

[52] TNA, DEFE 7/1682, Sir Richard Powell to John Hare, 26 August 1957.

Infantry brigade groups in BAOR were composed of three infantry battalions, an armoured regiment, and a field artillery regiment. The armoured brigade groups consisted of three armoured regiments, an infantry battalion, and a regiment of self-propelled guns. A Major-General's headquarters commanded two or more brigade groups.[53]

How the brigade groups would be employed in war-time was exemplified by the plans of General Sir Harold Pyman, who was the GOC 1(BR) Corps between 1956 and 1958. Pyman planned to delay a Soviet advance by deploying his infantry brigade groups adjacent to likely crossing points across the River Weser, whilst keeping his two armoured brigade groups in reserve for the counter-attack. Since 1(BR) Corps would be required to defend large expanses of ground, Pyman instructed his officers never to attempt to hold it physically everywhere, but to 'dominate' the ground through a combination of strongly held areas, stop-lines, and reserve formations positioned to give great depth.[54] However, as per the NORTHAG policy for defensive operations, the intention would not be to prevent the enemy from crossing the river, but to force the attacker to concentrate so it could be decimated by nuclear fires.[55] Pyman believed that 'the power of the infantry brigade group, supporting the corps atomic artillery, will be immense'.[56] When the opposing sides made contact, 1(BR) Corps would rely on the tactical application of nuclear weapons to annihilate the enemy and bring the attack to a halt, as Pyman illustrates:

> Every time the enemy makes to cross the River Weser I shall break up his concentration on either side of the river with atomic artillery and I shall attack with my infantry brigade groups any of his elements which cross the river... should the enemy obtain a major concentration west of the River Weser, I shall screen it until such time as it presents me with an opportunity to destroy it with atomic artillery, or possibly air atomic support supported by one or both of my armoured brigade groups operating on ground of my own choosing.[57]

The use of infantry brigade groups to provide a screen adjacent to a major river line became known colloquially as 'watch and ward'. Their role was to dig in well dispersed along the banks of a river to observe and report on enemy forces attempting to cross the obstacle. Any elements that did penetrate into the defensive position would be counter-attacked with armoured forces and nuclear fire as per Pyman's corps plan. Brigadier James Cowan reckoned the 12th Infantry

---

[53]   TNA, WO 163/634, AC/P(57)18, The Brigade Group Concept, 20 March 1957.

[54]   LHCMA, Pyman Papers, PYMAN 11, 1 (British) Corps Training Directive, 29 October 1956.

[55]   LHCMA, Pyman Papers, PYMAN 11, Directive on the Tactical Handling of Armoured Car Regiments, 3 October 1957.

[56]   LHCMA, Pyman Papers, PYMAN 11, 1 (British) Corps Training Directive, 12 November 1957.

[57]   LHCMA, Pyman Papers, PYMAN 17/6, 1 (British) Corps Plan, n.d. [c. 1956–8].

Brigade Group, of which he was Brigade Major between 1958 and 1960, became the experts in this particular form of warfare, but formations throughout BAOR became extremely adept at the techniques required to effectively 'watch and ward'.[58] For example, Major-General David Thorne recalled his time as a young officer in Germany 'digging bloody great trenches' up to seven or eight foot deep as protection against Russian nuclear weapons during those long nights in the forest.[59] As the war rolled over them, the screen forces could expect to hold their positions for days rather than weeks, after which they would have to perform the difficult task of weaving their way back through the advancing enemy to reach friendly lines.

## The Nuclear Queen of the Battlefield

The sheer levels of firepower that were available to corps commanders by the middle 1950s was such that a fundamental change in military thinking was required. This consideration had encouraged the US Army to incorporate new thinking on the tactical application of nuclear weapons in its 1954 Field Service Regulations,[60] while the Canadian Army formulated a new written doctrine for nuclear warfare after the conclusion of its 'Gold Rush' series of exercises in 1955.[61] In Britain, the War Office published the first army-wide official doctrine for nuclear war in 1958 under the title *The Corps Tactical Battle in Nuclear War*. The preface stated boldly that:

> The time has now arrived when the quantity and quality of nuclear weapons becoming available on the battlefield impose a necessity for completely new tactical methods...we shall not find the solutions to the problems of nuclear battle by adapting ideas which were successful in conventional war because we shall not experience those conditions again if nuclear weapons are used.[62]

It reaffirmed the importance of tactical mobility in attack and defence, and assumed that a high proportion of the infantry would be mounted in armoured personnel carriers.[63] Although the doctrine sought to distance itself from those concepts that had been successful in conventional war, gunners were once again

---

[58] James Alan Comrie Cowan interview, 18802, Imperial War Museum Sound Archive.
[59] David Calthrop Thorne interview, 20320, Imperial War Museum Sound Archive.
[60] Doughty, *The Evolution of U.S. Army Tactical Doctrine*, p. 14.
[61] Godefroy, *In Peace Prepared*, p. 125. See, in addition, Peter Kasurak, 'Canadian Army Tactical Nuclear Warfare Doctrine in the 1950s: Force Development in the Pre-Professional Era', *Canadian Military Journal*, Vol. 11, No. 1 (2010), pp. 38–44.
[62] War Office, *The Corps Tactical Battle in Nuclear War* (London: War Office, 1958), p. iv.
[63] Ibid., p. 1.

crowned Queen of the Battlefield as they had been in the First World War, since 'nuclear artillery will become the predominant arm on the battlefield with armour and infantry in support of it'.[64] In a break with previous thinking, the significance of ground- and terrain-based objectives had diminished since nuclear weapons could destroy or neutralize any position, however strong.[65] Conversely, the importance of natural and artificial obstacles to defensive operations had increased, as they could be used to canalize a Soviet advance where it could then be subjected to nuclear fires and counter-attacked by mobile armoured forces.[66] This counter-attack was conceptualized as a corps-level 'counter-stroke', which would be appropriated by Field Marshal Sir Nigel Bagnall some thirty years later as the capstone concept in the Army's new operational-level doctrine. For the first time in British written doctrine, *The Corps Tactical Battle in Nuclear War* also considered the influence that the 'awe inspiring effects of enemy nuclear explosions' and high levels of nuclear attrition, which might be sustained instantaneously, might have on morale. It concluded rather flippantly that discipline would be maintained through commanders' 'understanding, sympathy and common sense' and morale would depend on a 'frame of mind induced by a mixture of anger, hope, and confidence'.[67]

With officers showing a greater interest in nuclear matters after the publication of the new doctrine, the War Office decided in 1959 to publish a bi-annual series of pamphlets, *Notes on Tactics and Weapons*, under the auspices of the DGMT to disseminate information on the latest developments in technology, tactics, and concepts. This new series of pamphlets, which supplanted *Notes and Information on Training Matters*, was concerned primarily with the interactions between firepower, mobility, and tactics. This was a difficult equation to solve, but would be crucial if the Army hoped to be able to operate effectively on the nuclear battlefield. The basic problem, as the 1960 *Notes on Tactics and Weapons* articulated, was that advancements in both firepower and mobility since 1950 had seen the former outstrip the latter. Tanks, for example, were no more mobile in 1960 than they had been in 1945, yet firepower had increased a thousand-fold with the arrival of tactical nuclear weapons. As long as road-bound vehicles were still employed, efforts to achieve a degree of mobility in harmony with the immense firepower now available would fail. It was hoped that 'the flying platform type vehicle should eventually revolutionise the concept of war, just as did the advent of motor vehicles'.[68] It is unclear to what the 'flying platform type vehicle' referred, but it is almost certainly the Hiller VZ-1 Pawnee, a unique direct-lift rotor 'aircraft' then in development in the United States, which utilized large fans for lift within a platform upon which the single pilot shifted body weight for

---

[64] Ibid., p. 4.    [65] Ibid., p. 4.    [66] Ibid., p. 7.    [67] Ibid., pp. 17–18.
[68] War Office, *Notes on Tactics and Weapons: No. 2* (London: War Office, 1960), p. 6.

directional control.[69] Other futuristic inventions bandied around combat development teams on both sides of the Atlantic were flying tanks and jeeps, crewless tanks operated by remote control, and a plethora of novel amphibious vehicles.[70]

In December 1960, the series became the responsibility of the Director of Combat Development (DCD), which was a new directorate tasked by the Army Council to keep it abreast of future policy and concepts since 'changes must not be thrust upon us; we must anticipate them and be ready to meet them'.[71] One such policy consideration was the wider role of the Army in national and alliance strategy, and how a nuclear armed BAOR might contribute to NATO's deterrent posture. As early as 1959, it had been acknowledged that *The Corps Tactical Battle in Nuclear War* had been developed in the context of fighting and winning a general war, and that it might be ill suited for use in a limited war setting where nuclear weapons existed only as a threat.[72] The 1962 edition of *Notes on Future Tactics and Weapons* justified the offensive and unlimited approach to nuclear war-fighting enshrined in current doctrine on the grounds that if BAOR was to make a meaningful contribution to the deterrence of general war in Europe, then it should be capable of 'waging nuclear war for a very limited time without reinforcement'.[73] In short, if the Army hoped to present a credible deterrent to Soviet aggression, then it had to demonstrate that it possessed both the will and capability to fight and prevail in nuclear land combat.

The next tranche of Army doctrine, *The Land Battle* series published between 1961 and 1964, was a showcase for the Army's continued appetite for offensive military operations. Focused solely on war-fighting and command and control, it was brazen in its disregard of political or strategic constraints, stating simply that 'the pamphlet is concerned with tactical doctrine and takes no account of political considerations'.[74] There was no reflection on the course of events leading up to the difficult political decision to authorize nuclear weapon use and it assumed that 'the authority to use them has been given to the military commander'.[75] Indeed, if all mention of nuclear weapons was redacted from *The Land Battle, Part 1*, one could be forgiven for assuming that this was a tactical doctrine for conventional war-fighting on the Second World War model. Brigades of infantry and regiments of armour still performed their traditional functions, airborne forces would conduct daring drops behind enemy lines, and tactics in the attack and defence

---

[69] Mike Rogers, *VTOL Military Research Aircraft* (New York, NY: Orion, 1989), pp. 74–8.
[70] See Kenneth J. Comfort, *National Security Policy and the Development of Tactical Nuclear Weapons, 1948–1958* (Cohoes, NY: Public Administration Institute of New York State, 2005), p. 74 and Andrew J. Bacevich, *The Pentomic Era: The U.S. Army between Korea and Vietnam* (Washington, DC: National Defense University Press, 1986), p. 96.
[71] War Office, *Notes on Future Tactics and Weapons: No. 3* (London: War Office, 1960), p. 4.
[72] War Office, *Notes on Tactics and Weapons: No. 1* (London: War Office, 1959), p. 4.
[73] War Office, *Notes on Future Tactics and Weapons: No. 4* (London: War Office, 1962), p. 14.
[74] Ministry of Defence, *The Land Battle Part 1: Tactics, Nuclear Operations in Europe* (London: Ministry of Defence, 1964), p. 1.
[75] Ibid., p. 1.

progressed along familiar lines. Victory would still be achieved, as it always had, through the destruction of enemy forces since 'the outcome of a nuclear battle will depend upon the ability of a commander to destroy the enemy with nuclear firepower while avoiding the destruction of his own force'.[76] This nuclear fire-power would be applied liberally with no consideration as to the physical damage this would surely cause to the battlefield. Confirming Solly Zuckerman's fears about the Army's reluctance to accept the risks of uncontrolled escalation if nuclear weapons were employed outside of the immediate battlespace, *The Land Battle, Part 1* envisaged that 'at the start of the battle, nuclear weapons will probably be used under corps control for interdiction tasks' and that as soon as the pattern of attack had been revealed, 'a series of nuclear attacks on specified targets over the whole front is probably the most effective method of disrupting the enemy'.[77]

The very nature of the Army's nuclear war-fighting doctrine, and the assumptions on which it was based, generated something of a controversy after the Head of the UK Defence Staffs, General Michael West, saw how it had influenced a memorandum drawn up by the American-British-Canadian (ABC) Armies group on 'Tactical Concepts 1971–80' while in Washington. West, quite rightly, thought that the current tactical concept of nuclear operations gave the impression that nuclear land combat was merely an extension of conventional operations but with 'bigger bangs'. Challenging the orthodoxy that permeated Army doctrine, he claimed that:

> ... the aim of a commander, since the world began, has been to win. But in the nuclear age this is no longer true. The problem of getting commanders to do a total re-think and accept this sort of thing is a major one—as evidenced with my talks with SACEUR—but certainly one way not to do it is to have a nice, uncontroversial and old-time concept as per TEAL VIII.[78]

Although it has not been possible to locate the complete document in the official records, the introduction survives, which outlines the assumptions on which the ABC Armies' tactical concept was based. The main thrust was:

> In order to deter effectively, the forces of the Alliance must be seen to be capable of conducting effective tactical operations and, if nuclear weapons are used, of inflicting unacceptable damage on the enemy. This implies demonstrating clearly to them that the price of aggression would, in fact, be unacceptable ... To face the Soviets with the choice between withdrawal and escalation—and to ensure that the Soviets realise that they will have to face this choice—clearly requires the

---

[76] Ibid., p. 11.   [77] Ibid., p. 36.
[78] TNA, DEFE 4/175, COS 3101/19/10/64, ABC Armies' Operational Concept, 19 October 1964.

provision of a tactical nuclear, as well as a conventional, capability. It also means that there must be well-trained, well-equipped, highly mobile and properly balanced land and air forces in adequate strength and the plans to use them in an emergency.[79]

The major concern was that the document had been circulated down to divisional commanders in the British Army and within the armies of the US, Canada, and Australia without official approval of the Chiefs of Staff—indeed, it had not even been seen by the Committee. This raised fears that British officers would think that the tactical concepts contained within the document had been endorsed by the Service Chiefs and that those outside the UK would assume it to be a reflection of official views on tactical nuclear warfare.[80] The problem was that certain aspects of the tactical concept, such as the idea that airborne forces could be employed in a vertical envelopment during an offensive battle in Europe under conditions of general nuclear war, were deemed 'far-fetched' by the Chief of the Defence Staff, Lord Mountbatten.[81]

In contrast, the Army itself believed it was being rather progressive. A 1967 report by the Committee on the Future Structure of the Army was confident that the service had largely been successful in adapting its approach to modern warfare and that the 'sentimental attachment to outdated methods which sometimes inhibited progress in tactical techniques before the Second World War has now wholly disappeared'.[82] It recognized that regimental and corps loyalties still remained an established and valuable feature of Army life, but when sectional interests conflicted with those of the organization as a whole, 'the former will have to give way'.[83] It urged for greater encouragement of creative ideas and the requirement for officers to think broadly and imaginatively. It offered the German *Reichswehr* of the 1920s as a model for the British Army of the 1970s, both of which were small, professional armies, limited by treaty to 100,000 men, and confined to its own country. The Committee proposed the activation of experimental formations on the lines of the inter-war Experimental Mechanized Force so that the Army would not be 'stifled by attachment to outworn practices simply because they are traditional'. This would require a better educated officer corps in order to defeat the arch enemies of 'narrow mindedness and intellectual indolence'.[84]

Within this new atmosphere of intellectual curiosity, the Army's nuclear doctrine for the late 1960s finally began to consider seriously the challenges, and

[79] TNA, DEFE 11/366, Introduction to the ABC Armies' Operational Concept 1971–80, n.d. [*c*. 1964].
[80] TNA, DEFE 11/366, Le Hardy to CDS, 23 November 1964.
[81] TNA, DEFE 11/366, CDS to CGS, 11 November 1964.
[82] TNA, WO 163/692, 20/General/7237, Committee on the Future Structure of the Army: Second Report, June 1967, p. 5.
[83] Ibid.          [84] Ibid., p. 13.

the political and military utility, of fighting a tactical nuclear battle. The *raison d'être* of the service was reframed to emphasize its contribution to the strategic deterrent. The starting point for *Land Operations*, which superseded *The Land Battle* series in 1968,[85] stated that 'with the consequences of unrestricted nuclear war appearing so catastrophic, it is almost inconceivable that war between the major powers which possess nuclear weapons should break out by design'.[86] The pamphlet accepted that war might break out through miscalculation, but for the first time in written doctrine, the Army acknowledged that Central Front forces could become embroiled in a 'process of escalation over which they had incomplete control'.[87] Reflecting the new strategic context in which BAOR was operating as a result of NATO's adoption of flexible response, *Land Operations* conceived the Army as a vital link in the escalation process through its ability to produce sufficient threat of force to deter aggression or, if deterrence broke down, to respond appropriately with conventional and/or tactical nuclear forces. Although this doctrine was much more aware of the modern subtleties and nuances of conducting military operations across the conventional–nuclear spectrum, there were still hangovers from previous doctrine. For example, the ten principles of war, unchanged in eighteen years, were exulted as having 'stood the test of time',[88] and the traditional virtue of 'offensive spirit' remained the ultimate factor in the pursuit of victory.[89]

The fourth volume of *Land Operations*, which dealt with the nuclear battle, reaffirmed that the Army's contribution to deterrence rested on its 'demonstrable ability to take part in tactical nuclear operations at any time considered politically expedient'.[90] According to the pamphlet, nuclear war could start in one of three ways: the aggressor decides to attack from the outset with nuclear weapons, forcing the Army to use its own nuclear weapons to avoid capitulation; the aggressor attacks initially with conventional weapons but resorts subsequently to the use of nuclear weapons, again compelling the Army to reply in kind; or the Army initiates the first use of nuclear weapons because the aggressor attacks with an overwhelming conventional superiority.[91] In all of these scenarios, the doctrine envisaged that 'escalation will continue until a pause in hostilities is achieved by military or diplomatic means or until all out nuclear exchange takes place'.[92] The conditions prevailing after an all-out nuclear exchange are noted for their absence,

---

[85] The Army issued a provisional doctrinal pamphlet in the interim between the publication of *The Land Battle* and *Land Operations*. See Ministry of Defence, *Guidance on the Conduct of Operations of a Battle Group in North-West Europe (Provisional)* (London: Ministry of Defence, 1969).

[86] Ministry of Defence, *Land Operations: Volume I—The Fundamentals* (London: Ministry of Defence, 1968), p. 2.

[87] Ibid., p. 3.       [88] Ibid., p. 6.       [89] Ibid., p. 8.

[90] Ministry of Defence, *Land Operations: Part IV—Nuclear Operations; Part 1—Nuclear Firepower* (London: Ministry of Defence, 1970), p. 1.

[91] Ministry of Defence, *Land Operations: Part IV—Nuclear Operations; Part 2—Tactics* (London: Ministry of Defence 1971), p. 3.

[92] Ibid.

the implication being that such horrors did not warrant putting pen to paper. Nonetheless, there were attempts to articulate tactical concepts for a limited phase of nuclear war-fighting. Here, nuclear firepower still remained Queen of the Battlefield as it had in *The Corps Tactical Battle in Nuclear War*, with all other arms in support of its application. BAOR would fight a mobile defence in depth, whereby an attacker would be canalized by various natural and artificial obstacles through distinct 'zones'—the covering force zone, the aggressive delaying zone, and the main defensive zone—where it would finally be checked, contained, and then destroyed by a combination of nuclear strikes and deliberate counter-attack by armoured forces.[93]

Thus, despite a greater awareness of the wider deterrent purpose of the Army's mission in Germany, *Land Operations* still ultimately subscribed to the recognizable pattern of conventional warfare. A critic might argue that this is merely confirmation of the reluctance of military organizations to embrace change, preferring to plan to fight the last war. However, a more balanced appraisal should consider the requirements of deterrence, which are inherently paradoxical. If BAOR was to effectively perform its primary mission—deterring an attack across the North German Plain by denying the Soviets a quick or easy victory—then it had to demonstrate that it possessed the capabilities to carry out the threat. By developing an offensive tactical doctrine which emphasized the destruction of the enemy army as the shortest path to victory, the Army was communicating the credibility of its posture. In this context, what mattered more was that the Army possessed a clear theory of victory, and not whether certain ideas were outmoded or, as General West suggested, an extension of conventional war but with bigger bangs.

## A Return to Conventional Defence

Almost as soon as the *Land Operations* series of pamphlets had entered circulation, the seeds of later reforms to the Army's doctrine were being sown by Sir Nigel Bagnall when he became Director of the Royal Armoured Corps in 1971. Bagnall was a staunch critic of NATO's tactical nuclear posture, and rose to prominence within a general atmosphere of increasing scepticism on both sides of the Atlantic about the military utility of nuclear weapons. Over an eighteen-year period, during which time Bagnall was promoted to General Officer Commanding (GOC) 4th Armoured Division in 1975, Assistant Chief of the Defence Staff (Policy) in 1978, GOC 1(BR) Corps in 1981, C-in-C BAOR/NORTHAG in 1983, and Chief of the General Staff in 1985, he sought to add greater credibility to

---

[93] Ibid., p. 22.

the Army's doctrine by increasing its capacity for conventional defence through new operational concepts. Under this vision, the military utility of tactical nuclear weapons was considered to be 'just about nil'.[94]

That the value of tactical nuclear weapons appeared to have diminished was in part due to technological developments in conventional weapon systems. Signs that a technological revolution might allow for a more effective conventional defence began to appear during the Yom Kippur War (1973) where Israeli armour had been mauled by Egyptian infantry firing wire-guided anti-tank missiles, and manned aircraft had been shot out of the sky by powerful surface-to-air missiles. These developments suggested that modern weapons favoured the defensive over the offensive in land warfare. Although claims that the tank had finally been driven off the battlefield proved unfounded, since countermeasures such as 'active' armour had nullified any decisive advantage, it was clear that the conventional battlefield had become much more lethal.[95] Indeed, such was the awe with which Soviet military commanders regarded US conventional weapons by the 1980s that they feared NATO might be able to achieve its war aims through the use of conventional weapons only.[96]

NATO doctrine was indeed beginning to display a greater emphasis on conventional war-fighting methods during this period. In 1982, the US Army adopted a new doctrine, dubbed 'AirLand Battle', which sought to exploit the greater tactical mobility, firepower, and survivability of the new generation of armoured fighting vehicles and attack helicopters to engage advancing Warsaw Pact forces deep in the rear and the flanks through manoeuvre and massed fires.[97] This new doctrine was conceived as an antidote to Soviet offensive concepts which imagined using Operational Manoeuvre Groups (OMGs), which harked back to the Red Army's mobile group concept of the Second World War and were introduced into Warsaw Pact planning in 1978, to make deep penetrations into NATO's defensive positions to disrupt its command and control and bring about a psychological collapse of the organization.[98] After an analysis of such use of OMGs in a Warsaw Pact military exercise, the SACEUR, General Bernard W. Rogers, was convinced that NATO should now plan to attack all 'follow-on' forces, including second-echelon and reserve units. The concept was agreed by

[94] Nigel Bagnall, 'The Central Region: A Strategic Overview' in Brian Holden Reid and Michael Dewar (eds.), *Military Strategy in a Changing Europe* (London: Brassey's, 1991), p. 241.

[95] Hew Strachan, 'Conventional Defence in Europe', *International Affairs*, Vol. 61, No. 1 (Winter 1984–5), p. 28.

[96] Beatrice Heuser, 'Warsaw Pact Military Doctrines in the 1970s and 1980s: Findings in the East German Archives', *Comparative Strategy*, Vol. 12, No. 4 (1993), pp. 447–8.

[97] Diego A. Ruiz Palmer, 'The NATO-Warsaw Pact Competition in the 1970s and 1980s: A Revolution in Military Affairs in the Making or the End of a Strategic Age?', *Cold War History*, Vol. 14, No. 4 (2014), p. 566.

[98] Christoph Bluth, 'Offensive Defence in the Warsaw Pact: Reinterpreting Military Doctrine', *Journal of Strategic Studies*, Vol. 18, No. 4 (1995), p. 63.

Ministers in 1982 and enshrined in a revision of NATO's land force tactical doctrine in 1985.[99]

It was not only improvements to conventional weapon systems that were changing perceptions about the military utility of tactical nuclear weapons, as the final decade of the Cold War witnessed heightened fears about the consequences of nuclear war. Already in 1977, the Soviet premier, Leonid Brezhnev, had proposed a bilateral 'no-first-use' policy between the superpowers, which was indicative of growing confidence in the ability of the Red Army to achieve its war aims through the OMG concept. This was reiterated again in 1982 as a unilateral pledge.[100] At the same time, four distinguished American defence experts (McGeorge Bundy, George F. Kennan, Robert McNamara, and Gerard Smith) similarly called for NATO to adopt a 'no-first-use' policy because the nuclear strength of the opposing power blocs was now deemed so great that a nuclear war could not fail to be a 'ghastly catastrophe for both sides'.[101] The catastrophic consequences of nuclear use were brought into sharp focus a year later with the publication of a seminal article in *Science* on the potential global and atmospheric consequences of nuclear war.[102] The ominous hypothesis of the study, that multiple nuclear explosions might lead to environmental conditions resembling a 'nuclear winter' which would destroy most natural life on the planet, garnered much attention in the scientific communities of the United States and the Soviet Union. The realities of the damage caused by radioactive contamination were illustrated vividly after the Chernobyl accident in 1986, which added a new impetus for rethinking military strategies for a war in Europe.[103]

Talk of 'no-first-use' policies on both sides of the Iron Curtain led to fears within the British Army's high command that political leaders might not authorize the use of nuclear weapons at the critical stage of battle, either because the nations concerned could not reach a consensus, or because the centres of decision-making had been rendered inoperable.[104] As has been shown, the Army's nuclear doctrine of the 1950s and 1960s began with the assumption that nuclear use had been authorized by political leaders, with no consideration of the tactical and operational implications if that authority did not come in a timely fashion, or at all. This was a weakness which Bagnall sought to remedy. Furthermore, unlike many of his predecessors, Bagnall was acutely aware of the challenges of maintaining control of a battle in which nuclear weapons had been

[99] Ibid., p. 68.

[100] Heuser, 'Warsaw Pact Military Doctrines in the 1970s and 1980s', p. 440.

[101] McGeorge Bundy et al., 'Nuclear Weapons and the Atlantic Alliance', *Foreign Affairs*, Vol. 60, No. 4 (1982), p. 754.

[102] R. P. Turco et al., 'Nuclear Winter: Global Consequences of Multiple Nuclear Explosions', *Science*, Vol. 222, No. 4630 (1983), pp. 1283–92.

[103] Bluth, 'Offensive Defence in the Warsaw Pact', pp. 66–7.

[104] Sangho Lee, 'Deterrence and the Defence of Central Europe: The British Role from the Early 1980s to the End of the Gulf War' (PhD thesis, King's College London, 1994), pp. 97–8.

introduced, and the consequent risk of escalation to the use of strategic nuclear weapons.[105]

A key pillar to the intellectual foundations of Bagnall's reforms was his practice of drawing lessons from history to inform thinking about contemporary problems. Bagnall drew his reference points primarily from the German experience in the Second World War, particularly its mobile defence operations on the Eastern Front. He was known as an intellectual and an avid reader of military history, authoring books during his retirement on the Punic Wars and the Peloponnesian War.[106] Furthermore, his ability to communicate well in the German language facilitated fruitful conversations with Generals Hermann Balck and Friedrich von Mellenthin, whose counter-stroke operations against the Red Army in Russia were further inspiration for Bagnall's own mobile defence concepts.[107] Bagnall also sought to draw lessons from the Israeli experience in armoured warfare, and as a Defence Fellow at Balliol College, Oxford, during 1972–3, he made a visit to Israel where he was able to gain insights into the use of mobile armoured forces to counter a numerically superior enemy.[108]

An example of Bagnall's early thinking can be found in a 1975 paper delivered at the Staff College on 'Defence Concepts for AFCENT', in which he drew a number of lessons from the recent Yom Kippur War which were deemed pertinent to BAOR's predicament on the Central Front. Bagnall deducted that the high rate of munition expenditure and reliance on the regular replenishment of armoured vehicles experienced by the Israelis made logistics networks increasingly important in modern war; if NATO could increase its relative invulnerability to logistic disruption in relation to the Soviets, then this could result in a major operational advantage. Thus was born the kernel of a new concept for the conduct of the land battle which envisaged the defeat of a Soviet attack by disrupting their rear areas, rather than attempting to meet them head on in direct and unequal confrontation. Bagnall also found inspiration for the counter-stroke, which has become synonymous with his doctrinal reforms, in General Ariel Sharon's encirclement of the Egyptian Third Army, which he proclaimed exemplified a more modern approach to war-fighting which pitted strength against weakness through complex ground manoeuvre against the enemy's rear. The concept called

---

[105] Ibid., p. 101.

[106] Nigel Bagnall, *The Punic Wars: Rome, Carthage, and the Struggle for the Mediterranean* (New York, NY: Thomas Dunne Books, 2005); *The Peloponnesian War: Athens, Sparta, and the Struggle for Greece* (New York, NY: Thomas Dunne Books, 2006).

[107] Balck and Mellenthin were both distinguished German generals who gained considerable command experience in combat against the Russians on the Eastern Front during the Second World War. Towards the end of the Cold War they were invited to participate in a number of conferences and seminars in the United States to share those experiences considered most relevant for NATO in Central Europe. See, for example, the proceedings of such a conference in William DePuy, *Generals Balck and von Mellenthin on Tactics: Implications for NATO Military Doctrine* (McLean, VA: The BDM Corporation, 1980).

[108] Lee, 'Deterrence and the Defence of Central Europe', pp. 80–3.

first for relatively lightly equipped but mobile reserve forces (Bagnall suggested these be provided by the West Germans) designed to operate in depth against Soviet lines of communication from the urban and wooded areas which interspersed the Central Front. The second requirement was general-purpose forces of greater self-sufficiency capable of fighting a mobile battle, free from conventional lines of communication, for a longer period than Soviet formations.[109]

Other historical campaigns were also invoked in an attempt to find a conventional antidote to a Soviet armoured assault. One operation of particular relevance to BAOR's situation on the Central Front was GOODWOOD, which appeared to demonstrate how stay-behind parties of light infantry armed with powerful anti-tank weapons could successfully arrest a powerful armoured assault. This blueprint for battle had been identified by General Sir William Scotter who, as Vice-Chief of the General Staff from 1975–6, had sought to find ways in which non-mechanized infantry could be deployed to provide enough elasticity and depth in the main defence to absorb the momentum of a major Warsaw Pact thrust. Scotter recalled how the reference point was selected:

We searched the history of modern armoured warfare for a parallel to our circumstances in Europe today; a parallel in terms of terrain, comparative strengths of airpower, fire power and density of deployment. We looked at recent examples of armoured warfare such as Korea, Yom Kippur and the Indo-Pakistan conflicts, but in none was the ground or circumstances sufficiently similar to the likely battle in Europe. We finally arrived at a classic operation in Normandy in 1944 in which a weak German regimental group held the assault of three British armoured divisions concentrated on an eight mile front... We know the Operation as Goodwood.[110]

Although this was the method through which BAOR had successfully held the North German Plain in General Hackett's 1978 fictional account of a Third World War,[111] some observers cast doubt on the viability of a defensive concept based on the lessons of GOODWOOD. For example, Charles J. Dick claimed that GOODWOOD was an anomaly in the annals of history and that the blunting of the British armoured attack was due less to the nature of the German defence, and more to special circumstances and British errors, which were unlikely to be replicated by a Soviet adversary.[112]

---

[109] JSCSC, SCC 1975, Vol. 10, Seminar at the Staff College: Defence Concepts for AFCENT, 28 April 1975.
[110] William Scotter, 'A Role for Non-Mechanised Infantry', *The RUSI Journal*, Vol. 125, No. 4 (1980), p. 59.
[111] John Hackett, *The Third World War: August 1985* (London: Sidgwick & Jackson, 1978), p. 236.
[112] Charles J. Dick, 'The Goodwood Concept: Situating the Appreciation', *The RUSI Journal*, Vol. 127, No. 1 (1982), p. 23.

To help sift through the various doctrinal concepts being promulgated at this time, the Army Board agreed in 1979 to establish a new post of Director-General Army Training (DGAT) at three-star level to be responsible for training policy and the coordination of combat development and tactical doctrine throughout the Army. A subsequent examination of the staffs of the DGAT and the various Arms Directors then involved in tactical doctrine led to the formation in 1982 of an arms executive (ARMEX), the Army's own forward-looking 'think-tank', tasked with improving the coordination of all-arms views on tactical doctrine, operational research, and combat development.[113] The primary role of the ARMEX organization was to formulate tactical doctrine up to twenty-five years ahead of time and assume responsibility for editorship of all-arms tactical doctrine pamphlets. ARMEX would also sponsor all-arms trials, studies, and experiments required for the development of doctrine and concepts, including war-gaming at the Royal Armament Research and Development Establishment and appropriate conceptual studies at the DOAE.[114]

The first DGAT, Lieutenant-General Sir Robin Carnegie, was keen for ARMEX to discredit Erwin Rommel's infamous barb that although the British Army wrote excellent doctrine, few officers bothered to read it, stating that:

> If our work is to be successful not only must our doctrine and advice be wise but it must be understood and accepted. Army documents however brilliant in judgement or foresight which remains unread or fails to influence those for whom it was written is a waste of time and effort. The Army as a whole must have confidence in our work and to achieve this we must avoid giving the impression that ARMEX is beavering away in an ivory tower unrelated to realism.[115]

To achieve these aims, Carnegie encouraged new ideas from whatever source, civilian or military, and pledged to consult the wider Army on all matters relating to the formulation of tactical doctrine. The CGS, General Sir John Stanier, who had extensive experience serving in BAOR, instructed ARMEX to concentrate on the problems of fighting in North West Europe as the most urgent requirement.[116] 1982 did prove to be an important evolutionary period for British tactical doctrine with a fresh corps concept of operations and the exploratory work of the new tactical doctrine team at ARMEX. Interestingly, we see in a loose minute the first attempt to conceptualize and define the operational level of war, which would become the cornerstone of *British Military Doctrine* published seven years later.

[113] TNA, DEFE 70/718, ECAB/P(82), DGAT—The Way Ahead, n.d. [*c*. 1982].
[114] TNA, DEFE 70/718, D/DASD/8/7/17/1 (ASD1), The Arms Executive, n.d. [*c*. 1982].
[115] TNA, DEFE 70/718, D/SAG(A)/7/14, ARMEX Organization, 17 March 1982.
[116] Ibid.

Here, it was conceived as 'the concept and conduct of operations at higher formation level where the tactical battles fought by lower formations are controlled and coordinated'.[117] It also defined the counter-stroke as follows:

> A counter stroke is mounted at formation level by concentrated armoured troops against enemy forces that have achieved a penetration and are either still on the move or temporarily halted. They will not have taken up defensive positions. A counter stroke can not be planned in detail in advance since the situation is likely to be too fluid. The aim is to destroy the enemy, the recovery of lost ground being only an indirect consequence. The key to success of the counter stroke is the correct choice of ground and timing. The most favourable circumstances are when the whole enemy is on the move. The availability of an anti-tank screen to protect the flank of a counter stroke is vital.[118]

In 1983, ARMEX moved to St Christopher House in London from its previous home at Old Sarum, so that it could better influence Army policy. It was renamed the Directorate of Battle Doctrine (DBD) and was to be led by a two-star officer.[119] In spite of the apparent demotion of the organization to the level of a Major-General's command, it continued in the vein in which it had started, sponsoring a number of novel initiatives. In April 1983 it commissioned a number of studies which reflected the Army's increasing interest in counter-stroke operations, the use of reservists, and the utilization of military history in the lessons-learned process.[120] Indeed, it became a leader in what the Army described as 'non-technical research', and identified a number of areas of enquiry including: comparative analysis of the doctrine, training philosophy, and procurement procedures of foreign nations including the Soviet Union; historical research on the changing character of conflict; research into contemporary sociological and psychological factors affecting the recruiting, motivation, morale, discipline, and battle effectiveness of soldiers and officers; geopolitics; human behaviour; and economics. The DBD intended to engage with external bodies such as the RUSI, IISS, and civilian universities in the hope that this would offset the tendency to study doctrine through mathematical analysis, with potentially fruitful benefits.[121]

At the same time as ARMEX was activated, Bagnall established his own think-tank in the form of the TDC when he became COG 1(BR) Corps in 1982. The TDC was initially made up of twelve members from different arms and branches

---

[117]  TNA, DEFE 70/719, D/ARMEX/66/TD, All Arms Tactical Doctrine, March 1983.
[118]  Ibid.
[119]  TNA, DEFE 70/719, D/DASD/8/7/17/1(ASD 1e), The Direction of Army Training, 6 May 1983.
[120]  TNA, DEFE 70/719, Annex 'A' to D/DASD/8/7/17/1(ASD 1a), Non-Technical Research Coordination and Programme for FY1983/4, 27 April 1983.
[121]  TNA, DEFE 70/719, D/ARMEX/62/5, Non-Technical Research, 26 April 1983.

of the Army who shared Bagnall's vision for doctrinal reform. The meetings would typically involve debates on the latest operational concepts, tactics, and training policy in addition to discussions about current affairs affecting the Army. Careful consideration was given to allowing the questioning and contribution of ideas by junior officers, some of whom were still Majors. The unorthodox approach of the TDC was not without its critics, however, who levelled charges of elitism against the new group. The exclusion of many senior officers was also perceived to be a threat to the chain of command and of creating an unwelcome faction within the officer corps. Nonetheless, the TDC was instrumental in allowing Bagnall to garner support for the implementation of his emerging operational concepts.[122]

The cornerstone of these new ideas was the use of a mobile defence in depth to halt a Soviet offensive on the Central Front, which Bagnall showcased in a lecture to the RUSI in 1984 in his capacity as C-in-C BAOR/NORTHAG. Bagnall lamented the lack of an agreed concept for operations between the various national corps in NORTHAG and what he believed to be an over-literal inter- pretation of forward defence and the defensive nature of the Alliance. This, Bagnall claimed, had historically manifested in static, linear defensive disposi- tions, with each national contingent hermetically sealed within its own corps boundaries, without any direction as to the overall design for battle.[123] This was anathema to the scholar of manoeuvre warfare, who urged for operational flexi- bility within the political guidelines, which would enable NORTHAG to take the initiative at an early stage. Bagnall believed there was no alternative to NATO attempting to seize the initiative against the Red Army since NORTHAG 'would inevitably be ground down in a battle of attrition which we could never hope to win'.[124] Quoting Clausewitz on the importance of gaining local superiority in numbers at the decisive point in defensive operations, Bagnall urged for a more mobile battle so that NORTHAG could achieve a concentration of force at the critical juncture.[125] This would call for the timely commitment of corps reserves to manoeuvre against Soviet thrusts. Tactical nuclear weapons were left firmly out of the equation, but then this is what the emerging operational concept sought to achieve, since:

> If we can achieve this coordination, and develop an operational concept which
> avoids us being ground down in a battle of attrition but which instead aims to
> dislocate Soviet plans and force them to react to us, then I believe we can greatly

---

[122] Lee, 'Deterrence and the Defence of Central Europe', pp. 222–6 and Eitan Shamir, *Transforming Command: The Pursuit of Mission Command in the U.S., British, and Israeli Armies* (Stanford, CA: Stanford University Press, 2011), p. 113.

[123] Nigel Bagnall, 'Concepts of Land/Air Operations in the Central Region: I', *The RUSI Journal*, Vol. 129, No. 3 (1984), p. 60.

[124] Ibid.    [125] Ibid., p. 62.

extend our conventional defence capability and in so doing, raise the nuclear threshold.[126]

Thus, there was little that was truly revolutionary in Bagnall's concept of operations, which called merely for the sensible coordination and allocation of resources between the cover force, the main defence force, and reserve force so that NORTHAG could better react to Soviet moves. Indeed, General Sir Martin Farndale, who succeeded Bagnall as GOC 1(BR) Corps in 1983, conceded in a subsequent address to the RUSI that the use of a counter-stroke with mobile reserves to unbalance an attacking army 'is as old as warfare itself'.[127] What defined Bagnall's conception of the counter-stroke, however, was the level of war at which it would take place—the operational level. Although the importance of operational art had long been acknowledged by Russian military theorists, this was a new concept for the British Army of the 1980s which would require different skill sets from the corps and divisional commanders who were tasked with prosecuting this potentially decisive move on the battlefield. It would call for bold leadership from the front, the use of initiative, flexibility of mind, and the abandonment of rigid phase lines and axis of advance. Farndale accepted that this would require a new ethos in the officer corps since:

> The counter stroke is not a typically British operation, as we tend to be too cautious. We must learn how to overcome this caution when it is necessary. We must develop initiative and confidence and the right mental attitude in our commanders so that when the opportunity comes all are capable of the execution. Commanders at each level must all understand the concept and become used to thinking two levels up and down so that they place their own forces correctly as part of the whole concept.[128]

What Farndale described is the command philosophy now known to the British Army as mission command, although even this had been a key tenet of the German Army's way of warfare fifty years earlier, known then as *Auftragstaktik*. Ultimately, operational art, the counter-stroke, and mission command became the holy trinity of BAOR's emerging defensive concept. The TDC, which Bagnall had established in 1982, had fostered these ideas and was the body tasked with writing the British Army's first operational-level doctrine, *Design for Military Operations: The British Military Doctrine*, which was published in 1989 under the auspices of the Staff College, thereby codifying Bagnall's thinking in written form.

---

[126] Ibid., p. 62.
[127] Martin Farndale, 'Counter Stroke: Future Requirements', *The RUSI Journal*, Vol. 130, No. 4 (1985), p. 6.
[128] Ibid., p. 8.

*British Military Doctrine* was in many ways fundamentally different, both in content and presentation, to previous doctrinal pamphlets. The foreword, written by the new CGS General Sir John Chapple, was a riposte against those critics, real or imagined, who might have claimed that laying down doctrine in such a comprehensive manner 'is not the British way' since 'the modern battlefield is not a place where we could hope to succeed by muddling through'.[129] It then moves on to a meta-analysis of the purpose, functions, and levels of doctrine, why it is important, and how it is developed. This section is festooned with quotes from Liddell Hart and Fuller which counsel the reader about the importance of critical thinking.[130] Indeed, the voices of famous captains from history can be heard on every page and, personifying Bagnall's respect for the discipline, even a brief precis by Professor Michael Howard on best practice in the utilization of military history.[131] As noted, the introduction of operational art into the lexicon of British military doctrine was a cornerstone of the booklet, in which it was defined as:

> The vital link between the setting of military strategic objectives and the tactical employment of forces on the battlefield...The skilful execution of the operational level of command is described as 'Operational Art'. That art embraces both decisions taken at the operational level *and* the outcome of those decisions, often tactical activity but bearing on the strategic level.[132]

A deep understanding of the operational level of war would be essential if 'the Army is to be capable of using manoeuvre to effect against a powerful enemy also employing manoeuvre techniques'.[133] To help explain the conceptual link between operational art and manoeuvre, the same principles of war which had served the Army for thirty-nine years were invoked.[134] A sound appreciation of these principles would enable the commander to conduct a mobile defence through the execution of deliberate manoeuvre operations including envelopments, turning movements, and encirclements, which would set the conditions for the exploitation phase.[135]

What was noticeable by its absence was any reference to tactical nuclear weapons, despite the fact that if the counter-stroke operation failed, then commanders would have little choice but to revert to the use of nuclear weapons as dictated by the strategy of flexible response.[136] The improved defensive concept outlined in *British Military Doctrine* still possessed a deterrent function, but this was to be achieved through denial (by making the costs of a conventional attack prohibitively costly) rather than through punishment with nuclear or conventional

---

[129] Ministry of Defence, *Design for Military Operations: The British Military Doctrine* (London: Ministry of Defence, 1989), p. vii
[130] Ibid., pp. 3–5.   [131] Ibid., p. 65.   [132] Ibid., p. 39.
[133] Ibid., p. 49.   [134] Ibid., pp. 67–9.   [135] Ibid., pp. 74–84.
[136] Lee, 'Deterrence and the Defence of Central Europe', pp. 202–3.

retaliation. As Bagnall outlined in the preface to *The British Army and the Operational Level of War* shortly after his retirement in 1989:

> ... deterrence, if it is to have any meaning, requires a visible capacity to wage war if it fails. Although it is not always fully appreciated, of equal importance and complementing nuclear deterrence, is the conventional capability to make it credible, as well as deterring the adventurism of a quick grab.[137]

Although this attempt to inject greater credibility into NATO's deterrent posture was reflective of the general attitude in the 1980s of the requirement for greater reliance on conventional forces, some contemporary observers theorized that a deterrent posture based purely on a denial strategy was inherently much weaker than one that combined both denial and retaliation.[138] For example, Samuel P. Huntington argued that such was the balance of power on the Central Front that a Soviet conventional offensive in Europe would inevitably be at least a partial success, making a purely denial strategy ineffective.[139] Thus, a conventional deterrence could only be credible if it incorporated a retaliatory component, which would be best served by making provision for, in the case of a Soviet attack, a prompt retaliatory offensive into Eastern Europe.[140]

Critics of conventional deterrence argued, however, that even the most militarily effective conventional forces could not match the deterrent value of nuclear weapons; as ghastly as conventional war may be, it could never be as terrifying as nuclear war. According to this logic, without the threat of nuclear escalation, the superpowers might contemplate fighting a conventional war in Europe since 'it is vastly more alarming to contemplate the destruction of one's society than to envision the failure to gain a victory on a conventional battlefield'.[141] This could be a potentially disastrous thought-process for NATO and the Warsaw Pact, since it would be prudent to assume that no alliance armed with nuclear weapons would accept major defeat on the battlefield without first using its nuclear power. Evidence suggests that Soviet operational concepts of the 1980s, which sought to inflict conventional defeat on NATO by rapidly overwhelming its forward defence before the decision to use tactical nuclear weapons could be made, would in all probability have triggered a strategic nuclear response from the Alliance. This was

[137] J. J. G. Mackenzie and Brian Holden Reid (eds.), *The British Army and the Operational Level of War* (London: Tri-Service Press, 1989), p. vii.

[138] Fred Charles Ikle, 'NATO's "First Nuclear Use": A Deepening Trap?', *Strategic Review*, Vol. 8, No. 1 (Winter 1980), pp. 18–23 and Henry Kissinger, 'The Future of NATO' in Kenneth A. Myers (ed.), *NATO: The Next Thirty Years* (Boulder, CO: Westview Press, 1980), pp. 3–19.

[139] Samuel P. Huntington, 'Conventional Deterrence and Conventional Retaliation in Europe', *International Security*, Vol. 8, No. 3 (Winter 1983–4), pp. 38–9.

[140] Ibid., p. 40.

[141] John J. Mearsheimer, 'Nuclear Weapons and Deterrence in Europe', *International Security*, Vol. 9, No. 3 (Winter 1984–5), p. 25.

reflected in the NPG's General Political Guidelines for the use of theatre nuclear weapons, which replaced the PPGs in 1986, and which stated that nuclear release should be authorized in the event of 'the loss of the cohesion of NATO's conventional defenses [sic]'. Farndale would later confirm that had NORTHAG expended all of its operational reserves and still lost the battle against the Warsaw Pact, then nuclear use would have been the only option left to avoid catastrophic mission failure.[142] Of course, Bagnall's concepts never were tested in the crucible of war, but as the 1981 Statement on the Defence Estimates warned, 'non-nuclear war between East and West is by far the likeliest road to nuclear war'.[143]

## Conclusions

With the publication of *British Military Doctrine*, the Army's concepts for how it planned to fight a future land war had come full circle from complete reliance on tactical nuclear weapons in the 1960s, to a complete rejection of their utility and a return to conventional defence in the 1980s. Army doctrine in the immediate post-war years was cautious and incorporated many of the lessons that had been learnt fighting conventional battles in North Africa and Normandy. However, even this conservative military doctrine contained the kernels of ideas that would become fully formed in the 1980s. In this context, the innovative nature of the Bagnall reforms can be brought into question. For example, the importance of manoeuvre and tactical mobility had been a feature of Army doctrine since the Crocker Committee published *The Conduct of War* in 1950, while concepts of counter-stroke operations first appeared in *The Corps Tactical Battle in Nuclear War* in 1958, and as an adjunct to nuclear strikes in *The Land Battle* in 1964. Bagnall and his disciples were also not the first to consider the wider deterrent function of the Army's role in Germany, since the operational requirements to threaten and control escalation were enshrined within the *Land Operations* series of pamphlets of the late 1960s and 1970s. Nor can the reforms instigated by Bagnall claim to have constituted an intellectual revolution in the Army through the institutionalization of military history. Since the early days of the Cold War, the Army sought to learn valuable lessons from the Second World War, and this naturally involved enquiring about the German experience of employing mobile forces to counterbalance Soviet numerical superiority on the Eastern Front. This interest in German combat techniques also pointed towards the requirement for better command and control, with an emphasis on independent thought and high levels of morale among the junior ranks of the officer corps. While *British Military Doctrine* stated explicitly the merits of mission command at the operational level

---

[142]  Palmer, 'The NATO-Warsaw Pact Competition in the 1970s and 1980s', pp. 570–1.
[143]  Cmnd. 8212-1, *Statement on the Defence Estimates 1981* (London: HMSO, 1981), p. 13.

of war, this had been acknowledged long before the assumed doctrinal awakening of the British Army in the 1980s. Although the doctrinal reforms outlined in *British Military Doctrine* constituted a more effective means of employing NORTHAG's available combat power, it is less clear whether they could have solved the defence equation on the Central Front.

# Conclusion

Although BAOR was never called upon to fight the war for which it was trained, the Army's approach to thinking about its surreal mission reveals much about the service's capacity for organizational innovation, the evolution of military thought after 1945, and the role of land forces within the wider matrix of Cold War deterrence strategies. It is difficult, if not impossible, to prove positive deterrence, but prudence must surely account for the role that BAOR and its sister formations in NORTHAG and CENTAG played in shaping Soviet perceptions about the utility of war for furthering their policy objectives in Europe. That BAOR found itself astride the inner-German border for more than forty years was more a result of political rather than military considerations; it was the political string which tied Britain to its collective security obligations in Europe. Thus, by its very presence, BAOR served an important function in demonstrating NATO's resolve to resist Soviet aggression, even if the military aspects of that mission appeared at times to be an illusion. It is within the wider context of NATO's deterrent posture on the Central Front that the Army's attempts to imagine nuclear warfare must be understood.

Even a cursory glance at the Army's activities after 1945 demonstrates that the service possessed the intellectual capacity for organizational adaptation, and the BAOR which saw out the final years of the Cold War was almost unrecognizable to the field army which had occupied Germany at the end of the Second World War. The officer corps understood the significance of the nuclear revolution and arrived at logical conclusions as to how tactical nuclear weapons might affect land warfare. Its ability to think critically about the challenges posed by nuclear weapons calls into question the traditional narrative of the post-war British Army as an anti-intellectual organization, tied to out-of-date methods and a stagnant military doctrine. The Army clearly progressed through the three phases of military innovation described by Thomas G. Mahnken as speculation, experimentation, and implementation. The net result was organizational innovation of the type defined by Kimberley M. Zisk as 'a major change in how military planners conceptualize and prepare for future war'.[1] However, just because the Army demonstrated both the intellectual capacity for change and the organizational

---

[1] See Kimberley M. Zisk, *Engaging the Enemy: Organization Theory and Soviet Military Innovation, 1955–1991* (Princeton, NJ: Princeton University Press, 1993).

*Imagining Nuclear War in the British Army, 1945–1989.* Simon J. Moody, Oxford University Press (2020).
© Simon J. Moody.
DOI: 10.1093/oso/9780198846994.001.0001

flexibility to implement it does not mean that it arrived at the correct conclusions about the future character of land warfare. Its assumptions about future war reflected how well the Army was able to make an objective analysis of past, present, and future conceptions of war, the manner in which it structured its thinking, and what the limits of that thinking were. It is here where the Army might have been left wanting.

In spite of the tangible changes which occurred within the conceptual component of the Army's fighting power, there were clear limits as to how far the service was willing, and able, to think about the unthinkable. Some of the most difficult questions pertaining to nuclear warfare were left unanswered, and there was no doubt a number of unknown unknowns about the realities of nuclear war-fighting which the Army did little to uncover. In this context, the Army displayed a cognitive dissonance when conceptualizing important aspects of future war relating to the practicalities of operating in an arena of unprecedented violence, and for what political purpose 'victory' on the nuclear battlefield would serve. This cognitive dissonance supports Elizabeth Kier's theory that the professional culture of an officer corps is destined to screen out some parts of reality while magnifying others.[2] Thus, for all the major changes to how the Army conceptualized and planned for future war, there was also significant ambiguity, contradiction, and parochialism.

It is perhaps unsurprising that aspects of the Army's thinking about future war suffered from a lack of clarity considering that British nuclear strategy has invariably been described in a similar fashion.[3] In the great strategic debates which gripped the NATO alliance throughout the Cold War, the pure-deterrence strategy favoured by British policy-makers relied for its credibility on a vision of nuclear war which was inherently apocalyptic. Within this narrative, the role of land forces in general war was consistently denigrated as being meaningless, irrelevant, and insignificant. Such pessimistic appraisals of the utility of land power in the nuclear age could not have failed to leave its imprint on the Army's own perceptions of its role within wider national and alliance strategy. Indeed, it was this insecure bureaucratic environment which first stimulated speculation about future war as officers sought desperately to find a new theory of victory in a rapidly changing military environment. Service journals not only provided a means to disseminate new ideas, but also became a polemical platform to promote the continued existence of the organization at a time when only nuclear weapons appeared to matter.

---

[2] Elizabeth Kier, *Imagining War: French and British Military Doctrine between the Wars* (Princeton, NJ: Princeton University Press, 1997), p. 28.
[3] See, for example, the conclusions drawn by John Baylis in *Ambiguity and Deterrence: British Nuclear Strategy, 1945–1964* (Oxford: Clarendon Press, 1995).

That the Army continued to understand its *raison d'être* as the service which fought campaigns and won wars was embodied within its written doctrine. Although the tactical concepts and operational techniques contained within it had evolved considerably between 1945 and 1989 in response to the external environment, it nonetheless gave the impression that nuclear land combat was merely an extension of conventional operations with more powerful forms of artillery. This logic was most pronounced in how the Army's doctrine conceptualized the relationship between military effect and policy objectives, or rather, its inability to do so. Effective military doctrine should be utilitarian, by providing a conceptual guide for thinking about the conduct of military operations, and instrumental, in that that thinking should move measurably towards a clearly articulated end-state. The end of conventional military doctrine is usually victory on the battlefield through the destruction or paralysis of the enemy army. In the nuclear age, however, such were the risks of mutual annihilation that war could no longer be understood in zero-sum terms. It was here that the Army's doctrine appeared out of step with the new logic of strategic theory. For example, the Army's doctrine consistently reinforced the virtues of offensive spirit and the idea that military victory could be achieved through the destruction of the enemy forces. The changes brought about by the Bagnall reforms equally did little to address the question of how success in the land battle could be translated into political capital without escalating into a catastrophic nuclear exchange. Although Bagnall rejected the military utility of tactical nuclear weapons, the decisive counter-stroke operations contained in *British Military Doctrine*, if successful, might have been just the mechanism to force the Kremlin to resort to their own use of nuclear weapons in order to avoid conventional defeat on the battlefield.

The Army's operational research had sought to model and analyse what such an exchange of tactical nuclear weapons might look like, but it was here that its cognitive dissonance about the realities of nuclear warfare was the most pronounced. The Army was guilty of avoiding the inconvenient truth that the hundreds of tactical nuclear weapons that its war-games had showed would be necessary to defeat a Warsaw Pact offensive would have resulted in a level of collateral damage far exceeding any military effects that might have been achieved. In spite of strong criticism for its *laissez-faire* attitude about the practicalities of fighting a tactical nuclear land war, the Army stubbornly maintained that it could indeed operate effectively on a battlefield where hundreds of Hiroshima-sized bombs had been exploded with millions of civilians killed, wounded, or displaced. It would be unfair, however, to suggest that the scores of officers involved in the Army's nuclear exercises were somehow delusional about the consequences of tactical nuclear war. In this context, Mary Kaldor proposed that 'although scientists and military planners knew objectively what would happen if nuclear weapons were employed, even if only a few, they had somehow not internalized the

awesome nature of these weapons'.[4] This process certainly appears to be confirmed *ex post facto* by those who lived the military fantasy. For example, General
Sir Garry Johnson, who spent his formative years as a Cold Warrior as a staff
officer in the Ministry of Defence, recalled that:

> ...in the early 1970s, the nuclear aspect dominated our exercise thinking, our
> field training exercises. There were nuclear killing zones. It was very much going
> to be how we were going to survive a fight on a nuclear battlefield. By the early
> 1980s, nobody believed in that anymore...we were practicing manoeuvre war,
> and after five to six days of exercises, when we believed we would have held the
> first echelon, and [the Warsaw Pact] second echelon would have been coming
> forward and we had no second echelon, at that stage the nuclear became
> important and at that stage the exercise stopped.[5]

That the exercise stopped before the introduction of nuclear weapons highlights
the increasing scepticism by the end of the Cold War about the viability of the
Army's mission in Germany. Other contemporary observers were even more
pessimistic than their British counterparts about the ability of armies to conduct
meaningful military operations on a battlefield completely destroyed by nuclear
fires. Lieutenant-General William E. Odom, who served as the military assistant to
US national security advisor Zbigniew Brzezinski in 1979, believed that:

> First, armoured forces probably could operate successfully on a nuclear battle-
> field, but the vicissitudes of nuclear targeting, fallout, residual radiation, tree
> blow-down from airbursts, which I didn't understand before, the effects on
> forests and a number of other such effects promised a great deal of uncertainty.
> Second, these effects, if misestimated, could create more obstacles to effective
> combat operations than they could provide advantages. Third, managing logis-
> tics in the rear areas seemed almost an impossible challenge without very long
> intervals between nuclear use, such as days and weeks. And in exercises, we
> weren't allowing for those kinds of intervals.[6]

It was not only NATO forces, however, who would struggle to maintain major
combat operations in a nuclear environment. Years of regimental soldiering in
Germany had led some senior British officers to question seriously the martial
prowess of the Warsaw Pact and its prospects for a successful invasion of NATO

---

[4]  Mary Kaldor, *The Imaginary War: Understanding the East-West Conflict* (Oxford: Basil Blackwell,
1990), p. 193.
[5]  Jan Hoffenaar and Christopher Findlay (eds.), *Military Planning for European Theatre Conflict
during the Cold War: An Oral History Roundtable, Stockholm 24–25 April 2006* (Zurich: The Centre for
Security Studies, 2007), p. 86.
[6]  Ibid., p. 128.

territory. Reflecting on his service as Chief of Staff for 1st Armoured Division in the early 1970s, Lieutenant-General Sir Michael Gray reached the conclusion that the disposition of Soviet formations was such that their ability to fight their way to the Rhine in seven days was simply not tenable:

> ...their lines of communication were enormously stretched, and getting that number of tanks that we envisaged coming over the borders would have been an absolute nightmare for any logistician, indeed almost impossible, and therefore assessments of the threat I began to realise were overdone.[7]

While it was possible for some officers to look back in retrospect at what was becoming an almost impossible military situation, the Army was seemingly alone in its convictions that it would be possible to fight and prevail in a future war involving the use of tactical nuclear weapons. A consideration about which the Army's detractors could have been more sympathetic was how the constraints of national and alliance strategy forced BAOR into a surreal military environment. Since the Army was denied, for political and economic reasons, the manpower required to mount a conventional defence of Western Europe, BAOR had little choice but to rely on tactical nuclear weapons to stop a Warsaw Pact offensive. In turn, it was essential to the *esprit de corps* of the service, let alone for the morale of the individual soldier, to quell any doubts about the ability of the Army to fight, and win, the war for which it had been trained.

How exactly morale could be maintained in nuclear war remained one of the great unknowns, and the Army consistently failed to portray in its doctrine, operational research, or professional military education how the human face of war would react to the introduction of nuclear weapons to the battlefield. There were veiled references to the challenges of maintaining morale and command and control in what would be an unprecedentedly violent and chaotic arena, but there was no real effort to analyse how this might be achieved. At the times when the Army did try and articulate how soldiers might perform whilst operating under nuclear attack, it predictably sought solace in the moral qualities and strength of character of the officer corps, which it worked so hard to instil. Operational research could do little to uncover the human face of nuclear war, and so faith in the traditional fighting qualities of the Tommy would have to suffice. Although the Army's doctrine had, by the 1970s, made attempts to harmonize the conflicting requirements of devolving authority for nuclear release to sub-unit commanders whilst ensuring tight control over the Army's nuclear assets, this again proved unsolvable. It might be, as David French has suggested, that 'British doctrine was trying to strike an impossible balance

---

[7] Michael Stuart Gray interview, 28362, Imperial War Museum Sound Archive.

between flexibility and centralization'.[8] With the stakes so high, it opted for centralization, which served only to raise further difficult questions about what would happen should political leaders not authorize nuclear release in a timely fashion, or at all.

One could be forgiven for thinking that the Army's cognitive dissonance about the contradictions and limitations in its thinking about a future nuclear war was evidence that it was planning to fight the war it wanted to fight, rather than the one it was most likely to fight. There is no doubt that, with a lack of precedence on which to base planning assumptions, the Army fell back on the corporate knowledge it had attained through decades of conventional war-fighting. Furthermore, the Army's organizational behaviour might have been predicted considering the wider political and bureaucratic context in which it was operating. Faced with an almost impossible challenge unique in history, the Army had a vested interest in proving that it could perform the surreal mission to which it had been assigned.

Furthermore, BAOR's primary function was not war-fighting, but deterrence, and the requirements of deterrence call for special consideration when assessing how well the Army conceptualized and prepared for future war. Nuclear deterrence is, in many ways, fundamentally irrational because the threat is carried out after the forbidden action has been taken. Once the forbidden action has been taken, it is not always appropriate, or logical, to carry out the threat—especially if the punishment or denial mechanism risks escalation to an unrestricted strategic nuclear exchange. If this logic is applied to the Central Front scenario, then one must contemplate whether there would have been any military rationale for BAOR to initiate tactical nuclear war if the Warsaw Pact invaded the North German Plain. Most observers would agree that the millions of tons of TNT equivalent which would have been exploded on the battlefield over the course of a tactical nuclear war would have served only to destroy, rather than protect, the territory which NATO had pledged to defend. Although it is impossible to predict what course of action would have been taken by the political authorities had NATO failed to deter an invasion of Western Europe, it is unlikely that BAOR's war-plans could have restored the situation on favourable political terms. Of course, one of the prerequisites for any effective deterrent posture is that its underpinning threats are credible; that is, that the deterrer has the will and capability to carry it out if the unwanted action is taken. In this context, it mattered less whether BAOR's concepts for nuclear war were realistic, and more that those concepts displayed with some credibility the intellectual foundations of a theory of victory.

David French has described the post-war British Army as a Potemkin army—generating just enough combat capability that it could present a plausible front to

---

[8] David French, *Army, Empire, and Cold War: The British Army and Military Policy, 1945–1971* (Oxford: Oxford University Press, 2012), p. 210.

both friend and foe that more lay behind it.[9] If this was true for the physical component of the Army's fighting power, it was equally true for the conceptual component. While the Army had to make reasonable attempts to try and solve the conceptual challenges of how it intended to fight and prevail on a nuclear battlefield, the prospect of tactical nuclear warfare appeared so removed from rational military planning that it needed only to communicate that it had sufficiently adapted its force structures and doctrine so as to make a good account of itself in the unlikely event that the Soviets did embark on aggression in Europe. This Potemkinism in the Army's nuclear war-fighting philosophy was entirely compatible with Britain's pure-deterrence strategy, where operations designed to take place after an initial nuclear exchange were viewed intrinsically as having little military value. It may be, as Matthew Grant has argued with regards to Civil Defence training, that by simply supporting the 'façade' of readiness, the Army was bolstering Britain's overall deterrent strategy.[10]

The likelihood that war would break out on the Central Front became increasingly remote as the Cold War dragged on, and by the late 1970s, it had become clear on both sides of the Iron Curtain that any plan to fight a tactical nuclear war was all a fallacy. For example, Brigadier James Cowan recognized that his brigade in Germany was highly capable but ultimately 'trained for a war which most people believed wouldn't happen'.[11] Revealing the Potemkinism in the Army's thinking, he went on to say that 'the whole thing was deterrence, and we had to make it look as though it would work, that was the important thing, it had to look as though it would work'.[12] Cowan would later concede that the reliance on nuclear weapons seemed to be 'iffy', and that with the benefit of hindsight, 'the whole thing was unreal . . . but that is the way everyone was thinking at the time'.[13] Cowan's erstwhile opponents across the Iron Curtain also harboured doubts about the feasibility of fighting a tactical nuclear war. Professor Vitalii Tsygichko, who worked as an analyst for the Russian General Staff Headquarters in the 1960s, recalled that:

> Starting from approximately 1965, or 1966, we assessed the consequences of the use of nuclear weapons in Western theatre of war. All these estimations showed that it was pointless from any point of view to start such an operation, provided that at least one third of all tactical weapons that had been accumulated at that time would have been used . . . provided that both sides applied the weapons, there would have been total destruction: millions of tons of soil would have been

---

[9]  Ibid., p. 301.
[10]  Matthew Grant, *After the Bomb: Civil Defence and Nuclear War in Britain, 1945–1968* (Basingstoke: Palgrave Macmillan, 2010), p. 198.
[11]  James Alan Comrie Cowan interview, 18802, Imperial War Museum Sound Archive.
[12]  Michael Stuart Gray interview, 28362, Imperial War Museum Sound Archive.
[13]  James Alan Comrie Cowan interview, 18802, Imperial War Museum Sound Archive.

thrown into the atmosphere, and the result would have been an ecological catastrophe and the destruction of almost all population in the territory from Western Europe to the Urals.[14]

This sense of hopelessness at the prospect of using nuclear weapons in an operational role was also confirmed by one Polish staff officer, Tadeusz Pióro, who remembered that 'we really considered those operational plans to be science fiction, meaning that in reality, they would have been impossible to implement, especially with the use of nuclear weapons'.[15] Pióro also claimed that the Polish General Staff Headquarters suffered from a similar cognitive dissonance to their British counterparts since:

> [we] did not think about whether it was possible to implement such actions in reality; we just did not think about it. We planned and tried to fulfil the plans, as if it was possible to carry out such plans in the real world. We did not consider the results of what could have happened in the future.[16]

Although the fallacy of planning for nuclear war had become readily apparent by the closing stages of the Cold War, military cultures possess a remarkable ability to continue with their mission in spite of conceptual and practical difficulties. General Johnson admitted there was a sense of unreality about the thought of nuclear war in the British Army, but that this was tempered with a real sense of preparation to do it correctly if it had to be done.[17] Ultimately, Johnson recalled that:

> We knew that we had enough destructive capability to make people think before they really did something where our national security was involved. We took it rather like car insurance. You don't pay more than you have to and you hope you never have to use it. For most of our military the nuclear business was the province of swivel-eyed fanatics. The rest of the military got on with their game. The army had understood that battlefield tactical nuclear weapons were not the game.[18]

Professor Tsygichko also encountered such 'swivel-eyed' fanatics in the East:

> I would like to point out that many people fully understood that this idea of retaliation would result in a catastrophe. Among politicians as well as the military, there were a lot of crazy people who would not consider the consequences of a

---

[14] Hoffenaar and Findlay (eds.), *Military Planning for European Theatre Conflict during the Cold War*, pp. 64–5.
[15] Ibid., p. 92.    [16] Ibid., p. 93.    [17] Ibid., p. 110.    [18] Ibid., p. 156.

nuclear strike. They just wanted to respond to a certain action without dealing with the 'cause and effect' problems. They were not seeking any reasonable explanations, but used one selective response to whatever an option was. I know many military people who look like normal people, but it was difficult to explain to them that waging nuclear war was not feasible. We had a lot of arguments in this respect. Unfortunately, as far as I know, there are a lot of stupid people both in NATO and our country.[19]

As these testimonies demonstrate, the British Army was not unique in its inability to confront some of the more difficult aspects of nuclear war. In a world in which war really did appear too serious a matter to be entrusted to military men, the generals had responded with a mental avoidance to the consequences of nuclear war, and a cognitive dissonance had taken hold of operational planners on both sides of the Iron Curtain. Tactical nuclear war was not unthinkable, but it was certainly difficult to think about.

---

[19]  Ibid., p. 161.

# Bibliography

## 1. Unpublished Primary Sources

The National Archives, Kew

Admiralty: ADM 205
Air Ministry: AIR 19, AIR 20
Cabinet: CAB 21, CAB 81, CAB 128, CAB 129, CAB 131, CAB 134, CAB 158
Foreign Office: FO 41, FO 371
Ministry of Defence: DEFE 4, DEFE 5, DEFE 6, DEFE 7, DEFE 10, DEFE 11, DEFE 13, DEFE 25, DEFE 31, DEFE 32, DEFE 70
Prime Minister's Office: PREM 8
War Office: WO 32, WO 33, WO 106, WO 163, WO 216, WO 231, WO 279, WO 291

NATO Archives, Brussels

Defence Committee: DC 6/1
Military Committee: MC 14/1, MC 14/2, MC 14/3, MC 43/3, MC 48, MC 48/1, MC 48/3
North Atlantic Council: AC, CM, CR, RDC
Standing Group: SGM
Supreme Headquarters Allied Powers Europe: AG, DSAC, OT

Joint Services Command and Staff College Archives, Shrivenham

Army Staff College Course: 1947 (Vol. 1), 1948 (Vols. 1, 15), 1949 (Vols. 1, 13), 1950 (Vols. 1, 14), 1951 (Vol. 1), 1952 (Vol. 1), 1953 (Vol. 1), 1954 (Vol. 1), 1955 (Vol. 1), 1956 (Vol. 1), 1957 (Vol. 1), 1958 (Vol. 1), 1960 (Vol. 1), 1964 (Vol. 8), 1965 (Vol. 7), 1966 (Vol. 9), 1967 (Vol. 6), 1969 (Vol. 6), 1970 (Vol. 6), 1971 (Records), 1972 (Records, Vol. 12), 1973 (Vol. 10), 1974 (Records), 1975 (Vol. 10), 1976 (Records), 1977 (Records, Vol. 10), 1978 (Vol. 10), 1979 (Vol. 10), 1980 (Records), 1981 (Records), 1982 (Records), 1983 (Records, Vol. 10), 1984 (Records, Vol. 10), 1985 (Records), 1986 (Records), 1987 (Records), 1989 (Records, Vol. 10).

Liddell Hart Centre for Military Archives, King's College London

Captain Sir Basil Liddell Hart
General Sir H. E. Pyman
Sandys White Paper on Defence Conference [audio cassette]
Major-General P. N. White

Imperial War Museum Department of Documents

Lieutenant-General Sir Giffard Martel
Field Marshal Viscount Montgomery

Imperial War Museum Sound Archive

James Michael Calvert
James Alan Comrie Cowan

Michael Forrester
Michael Stuart Gray
John Harding
Michael Walter Holme
Julian Howard Atherden Thompson
David Calthrop Thorne
Alan Graham Wooldridge

National Defense University, Washington, DC
Maxwell D. Taylor Papers [digitized]

Digital National Security Archive
Nuclear History II, 1969–76


# 2. Published Primary Sources

## Official Publications and Manuals

Cmd. 6743, *Statement Relating to Defence* (London: HMSO, 1946).

Cmd. 7042, *Statement Relating to Defence* (London: HMSO, 1947).

Cmd. 8146, *Defence Programme: Statement made by the Prime Minister in the House of Commons on Monday, 29th January, 1951* (London: HMSO, 1951).

Cmd. 9691, *Statement on Defence* (London: HMSO, 1956).

Cmnd. 124, *Defence: Outline of Future Policy* (London: HMSO, 1957).

Cmnd. 8212-1, *Statement on the Defence Estimates 1981* (London: HMSO, 1981).

Joint Chiefs of Staff, *Dictionary of Military and Associated Terms* (Washington, DC: Department of Defense, 2008).

Ministry of Defence, *Army Doctrine Publication: Operations* (Shrivenham: Development, Concepts and Doctrine Centre, 2010).

Ministry of Defence, *Design for Military Operations: The British Military Doctrine* (London: Ministry of Defence, 1989).

Ministry of Defence, *Guidance on the Conduct of Operations of a Battle Group in North-West Europe (Provisional)* (London: Ministry of Defence, 1969).

Ministry of Defence, *Land Operations: Part IV—Nuclear Operations; Part 1—Nuclear Firepower* (London: Ministry of Defence, 1970).

Ministry of Defence, *Land Operations: Part IV—Nuclear Operations; Part 2—Tactics* (London: Ministry of Defence 1971).

Ministry of Defence, *Land Operations: Volume I—The Fundamentals* (London: Ministry of Defence, 1968).

Thant, *Effects of the Possible Use of Nuclear Weapons and the Security and Economic Implications for States of the Acquisition and Further Development of these Weapons* (New York, NY: United Nations, 1968).

*The Effects of the Atomic Bombs at Hiroshima and Nagasaki: Report of the British Mission to Japan* (London: HMSO, 1946).

War Office, *Field Service Regulations*, Vol. II, *Operations* (London: HMSO, 1920).

War Office, *Notes and Information on Training Matters: Number 10* (Surrey: War Office, 1955).

War Office, *Notes and Information on Training Matters: No. 11* (Surrey: War Office, 1955).

War Office, *Notes and Information on Training Matters: No. 13* (Surrey: War Office, 1956).

War Office, *Notes and Information on Training Matters: No. 14* (Surrey: War Office, 1957).
War Office, *Notes on Atomic Warfare* (London: War Office, 1954).
War Office, *Notes on Future Tactics and Weapons: No. 3* (London: War Office, 1960).
War Office, *Notes on Future Tactics and Weapons: No. 4* (London: War Office, 1962).
War Office, *Notes on Tactics and Weapons: No. 1* (London: War Office, 1959).
War Office, *Notes on Tactics and Weapons: No. 2* (London: War Office, 1960).
War Office, *The Armoured Division in Battle* (London: War Office, 1952).
War Office, *The Conduct of War* (London: War Office, 1950).
War Office, *The Corps Tactical Battle in Nuclear War* (London: War Office, 1958).
War Office, *The Infantry Division in Battle* (London: War Office, 1950).

## Hansard

House of Lords Debate, Vol. 130, 9 February 1944.
House of Lords Debate, Vol. 408, 23 April 1980.
House of Commons Debate, Vol. 443, 27 October 1947.
House of Commons Debate, Vol. 545, 25 October 1955.
House of Commons Debate, Vol. 549, 28 February 1956.
House of Commons Debate, Vol. 549, 29 February 1956.

## Memoirs

Eden, Anthony, *Full Circle* (London: Cassell, 1960).
Millman, Charles, *Stand Easy or the Rear Rank Remembers* (Edinburgh: The Pentland Press, 1993).
Slessor, John, *The Central Blue: Recollections and Reflections* (London: Cassell & Co., 1956).
Zuckerman, Solly, *Monkeys, Men and Missiles* (London: Collins, 1988).

## Newspaper Articles

Buzzard, Anthony W., 'Graduated Deterrence', *Economist*, 19 November 1955.
Buzzard, Anthony W., 'Graduated Deterrence Instead of the Bomb Alone', *Manchester Guardian*, 31 October 1955.
Douglas-Holme, Charles, 'Healey Rebuts Nuclear War Criticism', *The Times*, 24 February 1970.
Healey, Denis, 'Can Warfare Be Limited? Small Bombs and Large', *Manchester Guardian*, 17 January 1956.
King-Hall, Stephen, 'The Tactical Bomb', *Manchester Guardian*, 23 January 1956.

## Journal Articles

Anon, 'The Atomic Bomb: What Every Officer Should Know', *British Army Journal*, No. 1 (January 1949), pp. 7–14.
Astrologer, 'Clouds in the Crystal', *Army Quarterly*, Vol. 70, No. 1 (April 1955), pp. 87–96.
Bagnall, Nigel, 'Concepts of Land/Air Operations in the Central Region: I', *The RUSI Journal*, Vol. 129, No. 3 (1984), pp. 59–62.
Baird, N. C., 'Economy of Infantry: Some Thoughts on Improving Flexibility', *The RUSI Journal*, Vol. 99, No. 595 (1954), pp. 439–42.
Barclay, C. N., 'The Future of the Tank, Part I', *Army Quarterly*, Vol. 67, No. 1 (October 1953), pp. 42–51.
Barnes, B. H. D., 'Bertrand Stewart Prize Essay, 1948', *Army Quarterly*, Vol. 57, No. 2 (January 1949), pp. 161–77.

Barron, R. A., 'The Division in Nuclear War', *Royal Engineers Journal*, Vol. 71, No. 3 (September 1957), pp. 246–62.

Bate, W., 'Maintenance in Nuclear War', *British Army Review*, No. 3 (September 1956), pp. 14–19.

Beaufre, André, 'Reflections on the Evolution of the Doctrine of the Employment of Armour', *Royal Armoured Corps Journal*, Vol. 8, No. 4 (October 1954), pp. 173–7.

Borve, C. L., 'Is There a Defence Against the Atom Bomb?', *The RUSI Journal India*, Vol. 80, Nos. 338–9 (Jan–April 1950), pp. 72–6.

Bransby-Williams, M. E., 'Duncan Silver Medal Essay 1955', *Journal of the Royal Artillery*, Vol. 83, No. 3 (July 1956), pp. 161–71.

Bredin, A. E. C., 'Kangaroo Infantry', *Army Quarterly*, Vol. 62, No. 2 (July 1951), pp. 208–15.

Brogan, M. F., 'Tactics and Atomics', *Royal Armoured Corps Journal*, Vol. 9, No. 2 (April 1955), pp. 63–70.

Broke, R. S., 'For Which War?', *Journal of the Royal Artillery*, Vol. 82, No. 1 (January 1955), pp. 50–4.

Brundrett, Frederick, 'Atomic Bombs and All That', *British Army Annual*, No. 2 (March 1955), pp. 5–8.

Bryan, P. H. H., 'Some Aspects of Defence in Atomic Warfare', *Army Quarterly*, Vol. 58, No. 1 (April 1949), pp. 49–55.

Burlton, H. L. G., 'Gold Medal Essay 1946/47', *Journal of the Royal Artillery*, Vol. 74, No. 3 (July 1947), pp. 231–46.

Burrows, M. R. W., 'Atomic Warfare and the Infantry Division', *Journal of the Royal Artillery*, Vol. 82, No. 2 (April 1955), pp. 118–30.

Burrows, M. R. W., 'The Forcing of an Obstacle', *Journal of the Royal Artillery*, Vol. 82, No. 4 (October 1955), pp. 295–9.

Buzzard, Anthony W., 'Massive Retaliation and Graduated Deterrence', *World Politics*, Vol. 8, No. 2 (January 1956), pp. 228–37.

Buzzard, Anthony W., 'Graduated Deterrence: The Next Step', *The Spectator*, Vol. 196, No. 6663 (March 1956), pp. 305–6.

Buzzard, Anthony W. et al., 'The H-Bomb: Massive Retaliation or Graduated Deterrence?', *International Affairs*, Vol. 32, No. 2 (April 1956), pp. 148–65.

Buzzard, Anthony W. et al., 'On Limiting Atomic War', *Bulletin of the Atomic Scientists*, Vol. 13, No. 6 (June 1957), pp. 216–22.

Cameron, Neil, 'Defence in the 1990s', *Journal of the Royal Society of Arts*, Vol. 128, No. 5289 (August 1980), pp. 603–17.

Carter, J. E. L., 'Engineering in Extremis', *Royal Engineers Journal*, Vol. 69, No. 1 (March 1955), pp. 35–50.

Carver, R. M. P., 'Tanks and Infantry: The Need for Speed', *The RUSI Journal*, Vol. 96, No. 3 (June 1953), pp. 452–6.

Centaur, 'Some Thoughts on Nuclear War', *Royal Engineers Journal*, Vol. 69, No. 1 (March 1955), pp. 83–7.

Clarke, D. S., 'The Bertrand Stewart Prize Essay, 1953', *Army Quarterly*, Vol. 67, No. 2 (January 1954), pp. 161–74.

Cleeve, S. M., 'Super-Heavy Artillery: The Problem in 1945', *Journal of the Royal Artillery*, Vol. 73, No. 2 (April 1946), pp. 133–40.

Crean, G. P., 'Death of a Dinosaur', *Army Quarterly*, Vol. 73, No. 1 (October 1956), pp. 102–10.

Crosthwait, M. L., 'Speed and Surprise in an Atomic War', *Royal Engineers Journal*, Vol. 68, No. 2 (June 1954), pp. 124–9.

Crystal-Gazer, 'Looking Ahead', *Royal Engineers Journal*, Vol. 65, No. 4 (December 1951), pp. 363–7.

Curtis, J. H. P., 'The Principle Weapon', *Journal of the Royal Artillery*, Vol. 83, No. 4 (October 1956), pp. 244–50.

Curtis, J. H. P., 'The Army of the Future', *Military Review*, Vol. 37, No. 9 (December 1957), pp. 38–47.

Cygnus, 'Is My Regiment Really Necessary?', *Journal of the Royal Artillery*, Vol. 82, No. 3 (July 1955), pp. 219–24.

Dennis, M. E., 'To-Day and To-Morrow', *Journal of the Royal Artillery*, Vol. 74, No. 1 (January 1947), pp. 12–14.

DeReus, Clarence, 'Through the Atomic Looking Glass', *Military Review*, Vol. 35, No. 3 (June 1955), pp. 4–11.

Dick, Charles J., 'The Goodwood Concept: Situating the Appreciation', *The RUSI Journal*, Vol. 127, No. 1 (1982), pp. 22–8.

Dixon, R. L. C., 'The Bertrand Stewart Prize Essay, 1956', *Army Quarterly*, Vol. 73, No. 2 (January 1957), pp. 162–82.

Duckworth, G. L. D., 'Tank Crews in Atomic Warfare', *Royal Armoured Corps Journal*, Vol. 9, No. 2 (April 1955), pp. 73–5.

Dunbar, C. W., 'Airportability', *British Army Review*, No. 1 (September 1955), pp. 71–8.

Editorial, 'Nuclear Fission', *Royal Armoured Corps Journal*, Vol. 1, No. 1 (July 1946), p. 8.

Editorial, 'c', *Royal Armoured Corps Journal*, Vol. 1, No. 3 (January 1947), pp. 169–70.

Editorial, 'Atomic Broadcasts', *Royal Armoured Corps Journal*, Vol. 1, No. 4 (April 1947), pp. 235–6.

Editorial, 'The British Atomic Explosion and the New Warfare', *Army Quarterly*, Vol. 65, No. 2 (January 1953), pp. 130–1.

Editorial, 'Atomic Warfare', *British Army Annual*, No. 1 (July 1954), p. 6.

Editorial, 'Editorial Notes', *Royal Armoured Corps Journal*, Vol. 8, No. 3 (July 1954), p. 113.

Editorial, 'Editorial Notes', *Royal Armoured Corps Journal*, Vol. 9, No. 4 (October 1955), p. 169.

Editorial, *British Army Review*, No. 3 (September 1956), p. 2.

Farndale, Martin, 'Counter Stroke: Future Requirements', *The RUSI Journal*, Vol. 130, No. 4 (1985), pp. 6–9.

Fitzgerald, D. J. O., 'The Bertrand Stewart Prize Essay, 1950', *Army Quarterly*, Vol. 62, No. 1 (April 1951), pp. 33–54.

Ford, E. N., 'The Platoon Commander Training for War', *Army Quarterly*, Vol. 63, No. 1 (October 1951), pp. 106–12.

France, R. L., 'Armoured Engineers', *Royal Engineers Journal*, Vol. 71, No. 3 (September 1957), pp. 239–45.

Fuller, J. F. C., 'The Tank in Future Warfare', *Royal Armoured Corps Journal*, Vol. 7, No. 1 (January 1953), pp. 31–41.

Gale, R. N., 'Infantry in Modern Battle: Its Organization and Training', *British Army Annual*, No. 1 (July 1954), pp. 8–14.

Gavin, James M., 'The Tactical Use of the Atomic Bomb', *Bulletin of the Atomic Scientists*, Vol. 7, No. 2 (February 1951), pp. 46–7.

Gavin, James M., *Military Review*, Vol. 35, No. 12 (March 1956), p. 107.

Gibson, T. A., 'A Plea for the BAT', *British Army Review*, No. 1 (September 1955), pp. 30–4.

Goodship, J. D., 'Divisional Engineers in the Atomic Era', *Royal Engineers Journal*, Vol. 71, No. 2 (June 1957), pp. 125–30.

Graham, D. S., 'The Great Misconception', *Royal Armoured Corps Journal*, Vol. 10, No. 4 (October 1956), pp. 140–2.

Graham, D. S., 'The Future of the Regiment', *Journal of the Royal Artillery*, Vol. 84, No. 2 (April 1957), pp. 108–13.

Hackett, J. W., 'Panzer Battles', *British Army Review*, No. 3 (September 1956), pp. 30–5.

Hearn, J. N. W., 'Nuclear Weapon Effects and Target Response', *British Army Review*, No. 5 (September 1957), pp. 14–22.

Howell-Everson, D. N., 'Are We Training for the Right War?', *Journal of the Royal Artillery*, Vol. 81, No. 4 (October 1954), pp. 287–8.

Hulbert, R. C., 'Silver Medal Essay 1946/47', *Journal of the Royal Artillery*, Vol. 74, No. 4 (October 1947), pp. 367–78.

Jackson, A. F. J. G., 'Fighting Formations of the Future', *The RUSI Journal*, Vol. 100, No. 598 (1955), pp. 229–35.

Jolly, A., 'Armour and the Next War', *Royal Armoured Corps Journal*, Vol. 1, No. 1 (July 1946), pp. 52–9.

Landon, L. H., 'What Sort of Army?', *Journal of the Royal Artillery*, Vol. 82, No. 3 (July 1955), pp. 213–18.

Landon, L. H., 'What Type of Army?', *Military Review*, Vol. 36, No. 12 (March 1957), pp. 100–4.

Lawrie, W. G. A., 'The Years Between', *Royal Engineers Journal*, Vol. 69, No. 3 (September 1955), pp. 209–28.

Liddell Hart, B. H., 'How to Quicken Manoeuvre and Gain Flexibility in Land Warfare', *Army Quarterly*, Vol. 60, No. 2 (July 1950), pp. 181–95.

Lloyd, T. I., 'Nuclear Arms and the Service Man', *Royal Engineers Journal*, Vol. 68, No. 4 (December 1954), pp. 353–7.

Lyne, L. O., 'The Future of the Tank, Part II', *Army Quarterly*, Vol. 67, No. 2 (January 1954), pp. 175–83.

Macksey, K. J., 'The George Knight Clowes Memorial Prize Essay, 1956', *Army Quarterly*, Vol. 72, No. 2 (July 1956), pp. 161–72.

Majumdar, B. N., 'Logistical Concept for an Atomic War', *Army Quarterly*, Vol. 75, No. 1 (October 1957), pp. 107–12.

Martel, Giffard, 'The Future of the Tank: Part III', *Army Quarterly*, Vol. 68, No. 1 (April 1954), pp. 75–82.

McCloy, A. C., 'Wham!', *British Army Review*, No. 5 (September 1957), pp. 23–9.

McLeod, R. W., 'Some Elements of Mobility', *Army Quarterly*, Vol. 75, No. 1 (October 1957), pp. 50–7.

Mears, K. J., 'David or Goliath', *British Army Review*, No. 3 (September 1956), pp. 60–4.

Montgomery, B. L., 'A Look Through a Window at World War III', *The RUSI Journal*, Vol. 99, No. 596 (November 1954), pp. 507–23.

Montgomery, B. L., 'Organization for War in Modern Times', *The RUSI Journal*, Vol. 100, No. 600 (1955), pp. 509–31.

Moore, P. N. M., 'Goose Eggs', *Army Quarterly*, Vol. 69, No. 2 (January 1955), pp. 229–38.

Mountbatten, Louis, 'A Military Commander Surveys the Nuclear Arms Race', *International Security*, Vol. 4, No. 3 (Winter 1979–80), pp. 3–5.

Musketeer, 'The Tactical Employment of Atomic Weapons', *Royal Armoured Corps Journal*, Vol. 7, No. 2 (April 1953), pp. 60–5.

Naib, V. P., 'Mobile Defence', *The RUSI Journal India*, Vol. 86, No. 364 (July 1956), pp. 223–8.

Navarino, 'Is It Happening Again?' *The RUSI Journal*, Vol. 92, No. 568 (1947), pp. 593–6.

Nickerson, Hoffman, 'Atomic Military Theory: Some Reflections on Pre- and Post-Atomic Military Theory', *Journal of the Royal Artillery*, Vol. 73, No. 3 (July 1946), pp. 218–24.

O'Balance, E., 'Thoughts of an Infantryman Under Nuclear Pressure', *British Army Review*, No. 2 (March 1956), pp. 50–3.

Ogorkiewicz, R. M., 'Armoured Formations: Past and Future', *Royal Armoured Corps Journal*, Vol. 10, No. 3 (July 1956), pp. 98–102.

Ogorkiewicz, R. M., 'The Organisation and Role of Armoured Formations', *Royal Armoured Corps Journal*, Vol. 11, No. 4 (October 1957), pp. 170–6.

Phillips, Thomas R., 'The Atomic Revolution in Warfare', *Bulletin of the Atomic Scientists*, Vol. 10, No. 8 (October 1954), pp. 315–17.

Pickett, George B., 'Squeeze 'Em an' Blast 'Em', *Military Review*, Vol. 35, No. 6 (September 1955), pp. 56–60.

Pyman, H. E., 'Armour in the Land Battle', *Royal Armoured Corps Journal*, Vol. 8, No. 3 (July 1954), pp. 119–31.

Pyman, H. E., 'Armour in the Land Battle', *The RUSI Journal*, Vol. 99, No. 594 (1954), pp. 219–29.

Ratnam, O. D. P., 'Atomic Warfare and Conventional Forces', *The RUSI Journal India*, Vol. 85, No. 361 (October 1955), pp. 334–7.

Reynolds, R. C., 'The Future of Anti-Aircraft', *Journal of the Royal Artillery*, Vol. 73, No. 2 (April 1946), pp. 97–102.

Roberts, M. R., 'The Importance of Patrols in Nuclear Warfare', *The RUSI Journal*, Vol. 100, No. 60 (1955), pp. 575–8.

Romulus, 'Future Employment of Airborne Forces', *The RUSI Journal*, Vol. 100, No. 598 (1955), pp. 236–40.

Rowny, Edward L., 'Ground Tactics in an Atomic War', *The Army Combat Forces Journal* (August 1954), pp. 18–22.

Scotter, W. N. R., 'Streamlining the Infantry Division', *The RUSI Journal*, Vol. 98, No. 592 (1953), pp. 597–602.

Scotter, W. N. R., 'A Role for Non-Mechanised Infantry', *The RUSI Journal*, Vol. 125, No. 4 (1980), pp. 59–62.

Slessor, John, 'The Great Deterrent and Its Limitations', *Bulletin of the Atomic Scientists*, Vol. 12, No. 5 (May 1956), pp. 140–6.

Slessor, John, 'British Defence Policy', *Foreign Affairs*, Vol. 35 (July 1957), pp. 551–63.

Smithson, N. B. M., 'To Be or Not to Be? Is That the Question?', *Journal of the Royal Artillery*, Vol. 83, No. 4 (October 1956), pp. 285–9.

Smithson, N. B. M., 'How Clear Is My Crystal?', *Journal of the Royal Artillery*, Vol. 84, No. 3 (July 1957), pp. 214–25.

Solomon, M. A., 'Dispersion Is Not the Answer', *Military Review*, Vol. 31, No. 3 (June 1951), pp. 41–8.

Sutherland, R. J., 'The Future of the Armoured Division', *Army Quarterly*, Vol. 53, No. 1 (October 1946), pp. 86–92.

Tobin, P. A., 'Trench Gascoigne Prize Essay, 1952', *The RUSI Journal*, Vol. 97 (1952), pp. 364–77.

Train, William F., 'The Atomic Challenge', *Military Review*, Vol. 36, No. 8 (November 1956), pp. 3–14.

Tuck, G. N., 'The Engineer Task in Future Wars', *Royal Engineers Journal*, Vol. 68, No. 2 (June 1954), pp. 108–23.

Tugwell, M. A. J., 'Future of Airborne Forces', *Army Quarterly*, Vol. 70, No. 2 (July 1955), pp. 155–8.

Tuker, F. S., 'Nuclear Energy and War', *The RUSI Journal India*, Vol. 76, No. 322 (January 1946), pp. 68–74.

Turner, P. S., 'Duncan Gold Medal Essay 1955', *Journal of the Royal Artillery*, Vol. 83, No. 2 (April 1956), pp. 81–96.

Waddy, J. L. L., 'Helicopters for the Army', *Army Quarterly*, Vol. 69, No. 2 (January 1955), pp. 194–200.

Ward, D., 'Divisional Organization', *British Army Review*, No. 3 (September 1956), pp. 4–7.

Wharry, D. F., 'Nuclear Fission and the Principles of War', *Journal of the Royal Artillery*, Vol. 83, No. 1 (January 1956), pp. 45–64.

Whitting, F. Le. G., 'Duncan Silver Medal Essay, 1954/55', *Journal of the Royal Artillery*, Vol. 82, No. 2 (April 1955), pp. 81–94.

Wilkinson, P. J., 'Tactical Atomic Support of Ground Forces', *Journal of the Royal Artillery*, Vol. 81, No. 2 (April 1954), pp. 123–31.

Williams, G. G. R., 'Atomic Weapons and Army Training', *The RUSI Journal*, Vol. 99, No. 596 (1954), pp. 570–3.

Wilson, A. J., 'The Future of Armour as the Arm of Mobility', *The RUSI Journal*, Vol. 91, No. 563 (1946), pp. 396–400.

Wright, M. J. W., 'The Cooper's Hill War Memorial Prize Essay 1956', *Royal Engineers Journal*, Vol. 70, No. 3 (September 1956), pp. 215–37.

Wright, R., 'Docking the Tail', *British Army Annual*, No. 2 (March 1955), pp. 98–100.

Wynne, G. C., 'Pattern for Limited (Nuclear) War: The Riddle of the Schlieffen Plan—I', *The RUSI Journal*, Vol. 102, No. 608 (1957), pp. 488–99.

Young, D., 'New Look Artillery', *Journal of the Royal Artillery*, Vol. 81, No. 4 (October 1954), pp. 289–98.

# 3. Secondary Sources

## Books

Alger, John I., *The Quest for Victory: The History of the Principles of War* (London and Westport, CT: Greenwood Press, 1982).

Allport, Alan, *Demobbed: Coming Home after the Second World War* (London and New Haven, CT: Yale University Press, 2009).

Bacevich, A. J., *The Pentomic Era: The U.S. Army Between Korea and Vietnam* (Washington, DC: National Defense University Press, 1986).

Bagnall, Nigel, *The Punic Wars: Rome, Carthage, and the Struggle for the Mediterranean* (New York, NY: Thomas Dunne Books, 2005).

Bagnall, Nigel, *The Peloponnesian War: Athens, Sparta, and the Struggle for Greece* (New York, NY: Thomas Dunne Books, 2006).

Barnett, Correlli, *Britain and Her Army, 1509–1970: A Military, Political, and Social Survey* (London: Penguin, 2000).

Baylis, John, *Ambiguity and Deterrence: British Nuclear Strategy, 1945–1964* (Oxford: Clarendon Press, 1995).

Baylis, John and John Garnett (eds.), *Makers of Nuclear Strategy* (London: Pinter, 1991).

Baylis, John and Kristan Stoddart, *The British Nuclear Experience: The Role of Beliefs, Culture, and Identity* (Oxford: Oxford University Press, 2015).

Baynes, J. C. M., *The Soldier in Modern Society* (London: Eyre Methuen, 1972).

Bennet, Huw, *Fighting the Mau Mau: The British Army and Counter-Insurgency in the Kenya Emergency* (Cambridge: Cambridge University Press, 2012).

Biddle, Stephen, *Military Power: Explaining Victory and Defeat in Modern Battle* (Oxford and Princeton, NJ: Princeton University Press, 2006).

Blackett, P. M. S., *Military and Political Consequences of Atomic Energy* (London: Turnstile Press, 1948).

Blaxland, Gregory, *The Regiments Depart: A History of the British Army, 1945–1970* (London: William Kimber, 1971).

Bloch, I. S., *Is War Now Impossible?* (London: Grant Richards, 1899).

Bond, Brian, *The Victorian Army and the Staff College, 1854–1914* (London: Eyre Methuen, 1972).

Brodie, Bernard, *Strategy in the Missile Age* (Santa Monica, CA: The Rand Corporation, 1959).

Brodie, Bernard, *Escalation and the Nuclear Option* (Princeton, NJ: Princeton University Press, 1966).

Cairncross, Alec, *Years of Recovery: British Economic Policy 1945–51* (London: Methuen, 1985).

Campbell, Isabel, *Unlikely Diplomats: The Canadian Brigade in Germany, 1951–64* (Vancouver: University of British Columbia Press, 2013).

Carver, R. M. P., *The Apostles of Mobility: The Theory and Practice of Armoured Warfare* (London: Weidenfeld and Nicolson, 1979).

Clark, Ian and Nicholas J. Wheeler, *The British Origins of Nuclear Strategy, 1945–1955* (Oxford: Clarendon, 1989).

Clausewitz, Carl von, *On War*, trans. Michael Howard and Peter Paret (London, Toronto, and New York, NY: Everyman's Library, 1993).

Comfort, Kenneth J., *National Security Policy and the Development of Tactical Nuclear Weapons, 1948–1958* (Cohoes, NY: Public Administration Institute of New York State, 2005).

Cornish, Paul, *British Military Planning for the Defence of Germany, 1945–50* (London: Macmillan, 1996).

Cropley, David H. (ed.), *The Dark Side of Creativity* (Cambridge: Cambridge University Press, 2010).

Daalder, Ivo H., *The Nature and Practice of Flexible Response: NATO Strategy and Theatre Nuclear Forces since 1967* (New York, NY: Columbia University Press, 1991).

Delaney, Douglas E., *Corps Commanders: Five British and Canadian Generals at War, 1939–1945* (Vancouver: University of British Columbia Press, 2011).

Dewar, Michael, *Brush Fire Wars: Minor Campaigns of the British Army since 1945* (London: Robert Hale, 1984).

Dixon, Norman F., *On the Psychology of Military Incompetence* (London: Pimlico, 1994).

Dockrill, Saki, *Britain's Policy for West German Rearmament 1950–1955* (Cambridge: Cambridge University Press, 1991).

Douhet, Giulio, *The Command of the Air*, trans. D. Ferrari (Washington, DC: Air Force History and Museums Programme, 1998).

Duffield, John S., *Power Rules: The Evolution of NATO's Conventional Force Posture* (Stanford, CA: Stanford University Press, 1995).

Edmonds, Martin (ed.), *The Defence Equation: British Military Systems Policy, Planning and Performance* (London: Brassey's, 1986).

Farrell, Theo and Terry Terriff (eds.), *The Sources of Military Change: Culture, Politics, Technology* (London: Lynne Rienner, 2002).

Fox, Aimée, *Learning to Fight: Military Innovation and Change in the British Army, 1914–1918* (Cambridge: Cambridge University Press, 2017).

Freedman, Lawrence, *The Evolution of Nuclear Strategy*, 3rd ed. (London: Palgrave Macmillan, 2003).

French, David, *Raising Churchill's Army: The British Army and the War Against Germany 1919–1945* (Oxford: Oxford University Press, 2001).

French, David, *Military Identities: The Regimental System, The British Army, & the British People c. 1870–2000* (Oxford: Oxford University Press, 2005).

French, David, *The British Way in Counter-Insurgency, 1945–1967* (Oxford: Oxford University Press, 2011).

French, David, *Army, Empire, and Cold War: The British Army and Military Policy, 1945–1971* (Oxford: Oxford University Press, 2012).

Fuller, J. F. C., *The Foundations of the Science of War* (London: Hutchinson & Co., 1926).

Fuller, J. F. C., *The Dragon's Teeth* (London: Constable & Co. Ltd, 1932).

Gat, Azar, *British Armor Theory and the Rise of the Panzer Arm: Revising the Revisionists* (Basingstoke: Macmillan, 2000).

Godefroy, Andrew B., *In Peace Prepared: Innovation and Adaptation in Canada's Cold War Army* (Vancouver: University of British Columbia Press, 2014).

Grant, Matthew, *After the Bomb: Civil Defence and Nuclear War in Britain, 1945–1968* (Basingstoke: Palgrave Macmillan, 2010).

Grant, Matthew and Benjamin Ziemann (eds.), *Understanding the Imaginary War: Culture, Thought and Nuclear Conflict, 1945–90* (Manchester: Manchester University Press, 2016).

Groom, A. J. R., *British Thinking about Nuclear Weapons* (London: Frances Pinter, 1974).

Grove, Eric J., *Vanguard to Trident: British Naval Policy since World War II* (London: The Bodley Head, 1987).

Hackett, John, *The Third World War: August 1985* (London: Sidgwick & Jackson, 1978).

Heilbrunn, Otto, *Conventional Warfare in the Nuclear Age* (London: George Allen & Unwin Ltd, 1965).

Heuser, Beatrice, NATO, *Britain, France and the FRG: Nuclear Strategies and Forces for Europe, 1949–2000* (Basingstoke: Macmillan, 1997).

Heuser, Beatrice, *Nuclear Mentalities? Strategies and Beliefs in Britain, France and the FRG* (Basingstoke: Macmillan, 1998).

Heuser, Beatrice, *The Bomb: Nuclear Weapons in Their Historical, Strategic and Ethical Context* (London and New York, NY: Longman, 2000).

Heuser, Beatrice, *The Evolution of Strategy: Thinking War from Antiquity to the Present* (Cambridge: Cambridge University Press, 2010).

Hoffenaar, Jan and Dieter Krüger (eds.), *Blueprints for Battle: Planning for War in Central Europe, 1948–1968* (Lexington, KY: University Press of Kentucky, 2012).

Hogg, Jonathan, *British Nuclear Culture: Official and Unofficial Narratives in the Long 20th Century* (London: Bloomsbury, 2016).

Holden Reid, Brian (ed.), *Military Power: Land Warfare in Theory and Practice* (London: Routledge, 1997).

Holden Reid, Brian, *Studies in British Military Thought: Debates with Fuller and Liddell Hart* (Lincoln, NE: University of Nebraska Press, 1998).

Holden Reid, Brian and Michael Dewar (eds.), *Military Strategy in a Changing Europe* (London: Brassey's, 1991).

Hooker, Richard D. (ed.), *Manoeuvre Warfare: An Anthology* (Novato, CA: Presido Press, 1993).

Howard, Michael (ed.) *The Theory and Practice of War* (London and Bloomington, IN: Indiana University Press, 1975).

Irwin, Christopher, *The Security of Western Europe: Towards a Common Defence Policy* (London: Charles Knight, 1972).

Jackson, William and Edwin Bramall, *The Chiefs: The Story of the United Kingdom Chiefs of Staff* (Washington, DC, New York, NY, and London: Brassey's, 1992).

Johnson, Franklyn A., *Defence by Ministry: The British Ministry of Defence, 1944–1974* (London: Duckworth, 1980).

Jomini, Antoine-Henri, *Summery of the Art of War*, trans. G. H. Mendell and W. P. Craighill (Philadelphia, PA: J. B. Lippincott & Co., 1862).

Kahn, Herman, *Thinking about the Unthinkable* (London: Weidenfeld and Nicolson, 1962).

Kahn, Herman, *On Escalation: Metaphors and Scenarios* (Washington, DC: Hudson Institute, 1965).

Kaldor, Mary, *The Imaginary War: Understanding the East-West Conflict* (Oxford: Basil Blackwell, 1990).

Kaufmann, William W. (ed.), *Military Policy and National Security* (Princeton, NJ: Princeton University Press, 1956).

Kier, Elizabeth, *Imagining War: French and British Military Doctrine Between the Wars* (Princeton, NJ: Princeton University Press, 1997).

King-Hall, Stephen, *Defence in the Nuclear Age* (London: Victor Gollancz Ltd, 1958).

Kingston-McCloughry, E. J., *Global Strategy* (London: Jonathan Cape, 1957).

Kissinger, Henry, *Nuclear Weapons and Foreign Policy* (New York, NY: Harper, 1957).

Kissinger, Henry, *The Necessity for Choice: Prospects of American Foreign Policy* (London: Chatto & Windus, 1960).

Liddell Hart, Basil, *Deterrent or Defence: A Fresh Look at the West's Military Position* (London: Stevens & Sons, 1960).

Lider, Julian, *British Military Thought after World War II* (Aldershot: Gower, 1985).

Mackenzie, J. J. G. and Brian Holden Reid (eds.), *The British Army and the Operational Level of War* (Camberley: Tri-Service Press, 1989).

Mallinson, Allan, *The Making of the British Army* (London: Bantam Press, 2009).

Mastny, Vojtech et al. (eds.), *War Plans and Alliances in the Cold War: Threat Perceptions in the East and West* (London: Routledge, 2006).

Mataxis, Theodore and Seymour Goldberg, *Nuclear Tactics, Weapons and Firepower in the Pentomic Division, Battle Group and Company* (Harrisburg, PA: The Military Service Publishing Company, 1958).

McInnes, Colin, *Hot War, Cold War: The British Army's Way in Warfare, 1945–95* (London and Washington, DC: Brassey's, 1996).

Merrill, Dennis and Thomas G. Paterson (eds.), *Major Problems in American Foreign Relations, Volume II: Since 1914*, 7th ed. (Stamford, CT: Cengage Learning, 2010).

Miksche, F. O., *Atomic Weapons and Armies* (London: Faber and Faber Ltd, 1955).

Miller, David, *The Cold War: A Military History* (London: John Murray, 1998).

Mitchell, William, *Winged Defense: The Development and Possibilities of Modern Air Power—Economic and Military* (Tuscaloosa, AL: University of Alabama Press, 2009).

Mockaitis, Thomas R., *British Counterinsurgency, 1919–60* (London: Macmillan, 1990).

Mockaitis, Thomas R., *British Counter Insurgency in the Post-Imperial Era* (London: Macmillan, 1995).

Murray, Williamson and Allan R. Millett (eds.), *Military Innovation in the Interwar Period* (Cambridge: Cambridge University Press, 1996).

Myers, Kenneth A. (ed.), *NATO: The Next Thirty Years* (Boulder, CO: Westview Press, 1980).

Nagl, John A., *Learning to Eat Soup with a Knife: Counterinsurgency Lessons from Malaya and Vietnam* (Chicago, IL: University of Chicago Press, 2005).

Nichols, Tom, Douglas Stuart, and Jeffery D. McCausland (eds.), *Tactical Nuclear Weapons and NATO* (Carlisle, PA: Strategic Studies Institute, 2012).

Paret, Peter (ed.), *Makers of Modern Strategy: From Machiavelli to the Nuclear Age* (Oxford: Clarendon Press, 1986).

Peden, G. C., *Arms, Economics and British Strategy* (Cambridge: Cambridge University Press, 2007).

Pierre, Andrew J., *Nuclear Politics: The British Experience with an Independent Nuclear Force, 1939–1970* (London: Oxford University Press, 1972).

Posen, Barry R., *The Sources of Military Doctrine: France, Britain, and Germany Between the World Wars* (London and Ithaca, NY: Cornell University Press, 1984).

Quinlan, Michael, *Thinking about Nuclear Weapons: Principles, Problems, Prospects* (Oxford: Oxford University Press, 2009).

Rogers, Mike, *VTOL Military Research Aircraft* (New York, NY: Orion, 1989).

Rosecrance, R. N., *Defense of the Realm: British Strategy in the Nuclear Epoch* (London: Columbia University Press, 1968).

Sanders, David, *Losing an Empire, Finding a Role: British Foreign Policy since 1945* (Basingstoke: Macmillan, 1990).

Schmidt, Gustav (ed.), *A History of NATO: The First Fifty Years, Vol. I* (Basingstoke: Palgrave, 2001).

Schroeer, Dietrich, *Science, Technology and the Nuclear Arms Race* (New York, NY: John Wiley & Sons, 1984).

Seldon, Anthony, *Churchill's Indian Summer: The Conservative Government, 1951–1955* (London: Hodder and Stoughton, 1981).

Self, Robert, *British Foreign and Defence Policy Since 1945: Challenges and Dilemmas in a Changing World* (Basingstoke: Macmillan, 2010).

Shamir, Eitan, *Transforming Command: The Pursuit of Mission Command in the U.S., British, and Israeli Armies* (Stanford, CA: Stanford University Press, 2011).

Slessor, John, *Strategy for the West* (London: Cassell & Co., 1954).

Stanhope, Henry, *The Soldiers: An Anatomy of the British Army* (London: Hamish Hamilton, 1979).

Stoddart, Kristan, *Losing an Empire and Finding a Role: Britain, the USA, NATO and Nuclear Weapons, 1964–1970* (Basingstoke: Palgrave, 2012).

Stoddart, Kristan, *Facing Down the Soviet Union: Britain, the USA, NATO and Nuclear Weapons, 1976–1983* (Basingstoke: Palgrave, 2014).

Stoddart, Kristan, *The Sword and the Shield: Britain, America, NATO and Nuclear Weapons, 1970–1976* (Basingstoke: Palgrave, 2014).

Strachan, Hew (ed.), *Big Wars and Small Wars: The British Army and the Lessons of War in the 20th Century* (Oxford: Oxford University Press, 2006).

Tiratsoo, Nick (ed.), *The Attlee Years* (London: Pinter, 1991).

Tuker, Francis S., *The Pattern of War* (London: Butler and Tanner, 1948).

Van Cleave, William and S. T. Cohen, *Tactical Nuclear Weapons: An Examination of the Issues* (New York, NY: Macdonald and Jane's, 1978).

Young, F. W., *The Story of the Staff College, 1858–1958* (Aldershot: Gale & Polden, 1958).

Zisk, Kimberley M., *Engaging the Enemy: Organization Theory and Soviet Military Innovation, 1955–1991* (Princeton, NJ: Princeton University Press, 1993).

Zuckerman, Solly, *Nuclear Illusion and Reality* (London: Collins, 1982).

## Journal Articles

Alderson, Alexander, 'The Army Brain: A Historical Perspective on Doctrine, Development and the Challenges of Future Conflict', *The RUSI Journal*, Vol. 155, No. 3 (2010), pp. 10–15.

Alderson, Alexander, 'Influence, the Indirect Approach and Manoeuvre', *The RUSI Journal*, Vol. 157, No. 1 (2012), pp. 36–43.

Baylis, John, 'Britain, the Brussels Pact and the Continental Commitment', *International Affairs*, Vol. 60, No. 4 (1984), pp. 615–29.

Baylis, John and Alan Macmillan, 'The British Global Strategy Paper of 1952', *Journal of Strategic Studies*, Vol. 16, No. 2 (1993), pp. 200–26.

Bernstein, Barton J., 'Eclipsed by Hiroshima and Nagasaki: Early Thinking about Tactical Nuclear Weapons', *International Security*, Vol. 15, No. 4 (1991), pp. 149–73.

Bluth, Christoph, 'Offensive Defence in the Warsaw Pact: Reinterpreting Military Doctrine', *Journal of Strategic Studies*, Vol. 18, No. 4 (1995), pp. 55–7.

Bundy, McGeorge et al., 'Nuclear Weapons and the Atlantic Alliance', *Foreign Affairs*, Vol. 60, No. 4 (1982), pp. 753–68.

Caddick-Adams, Peter, 'Footprints in the Mud: The British Army's Approach to the Battlefield Tour Experience', *Defence Studies*, Vol. 5, No. 1 (2005), pp. 15–26.

Cohen, S. T. and W. C. Lyons, 'A Comparison of US-Allied and Soviet Tactical Nuclear Force Capabilities and Policies', *Orbis*, Vol. 19 (1975), pp. 72–92.

Cohn, Carol, 'Sex and Death in the Rational World of Defense Intellectuals', *Signs*, Vol. 12, No. 4 (1987), pp. 687–718.

Creveld, Martin van, 'Thoughts on Military History', *Journal of Contemporary History*, Vol. 18, No. 4 (1983), pp. 549–66.

Douthwaite, Jessica, '...“what in the hell's this?” Rehearsing Nuclear War in Britain's Civil Defence Corps', *Contemporary British History*, advance online publication (2018), pp. 1–21.

Dyer, Philip W., 'Will Tactical Nuclear Weapons Ever Be Used?', *Political Science Quarterly*, Vol. 88, No. 2 (June 1973), pp. 214–29.

Elliot, David C., 'Project Vista and Nuclear Weapons in Europe', *International Security*, Vol. 11, No. 1 (Summer 1986), pp. 163–83.

Enthoven, Alain C., 'U.S. Forces in Europe: How Many? Doing What?', *Foreign Affairs*, Vol. 53, No. 3 (1975), pp. 513–32.

Festinger, Leon, 'Cognitive Dissonance', *Scientific American*, Vol. 207 (1962), pp. 93–106.

Foley, Robert T., Stuart Griffin, and Helen McCartney, 'Transformation in Contact: Learning the Lessons of Modern War', *International Affairs*, Vol. 87, No. 2 (2011), pp. 253–70.

Gadsby, G. Neville, 'The Army Operational Research Establishment', *The Operational Research Society*, Vol. 16, No. 1 (March 1965), pp. 5–18.

Ghamari-Tabrizi, Sharon, 'Simulating the Unthinkable: Gaming Future War in the 1950s and 1960s', *Social Studies of Science*, Vol. 30, No. 2 (2000), pp. 163–223.

Grissom, Adam, 'The Future of Military Innovation Studies', *Journal of Strategic Studies*, Vol. 29, No. 5 (2006), pp. 905–34.

Hall, David, 'The Modern Model of the Battlefield Tour and Staff Ride: Post-1815 Prussian and German Traditions', *Defence Studies*, Vol. 5, No. 1 (2005), pp. 37–47.

Heuser, Beatrice, 'Warsaw Pact Military Doctrines in the 1970s and 1980s: Findings in the East German Archives', *Comparative Strategy*, Vol. 12, No. 4 (1993), pp. 437–57.

Heuser, Beatrice, 'Victory in a Nuclear War? A Comparison of NATO and WTO War Aims and Strategies', *Contemporary European History*, Vol. 7, No. 3 (November 1998), pp. 311–28.

Heuser, Beatrice and Kristan Stoddart, 'Difficult Europeans: NATO and Tactical/Non-Strategic Nuclear Weapons in the Cold War', *Diplomacy & Statecraft*, Vol. 28, No. 3 (2017), pp. 454–76.

Howard, Michael, 'The Use and Abuse of Military History', *The RUSI Journal*, Vol. 107, No. 625 (1962), pp. 4–10.

Huntington, Samuel P., 'Conventional Deterrence and Conventional Retaliation in Europe', *International Security*, Vol. 8, No. 3 (Winter 1983–4), pp. 32–56.

Ikle, Fred Charles, 'NATO's "First Nuclear Use": A Deepening Trap?', *Strategic Review*, Vol. 8, No. 1 (Winter 1980), pp. 18–38.

Kasurak, Peter, 'Canadian Army Tactical Nuclear Warfare Doctrine in the 1950s: Force Development in the Pre-Professional Era', *Canadian Military Journal*, Vol. 11, No. 1 (2010), pp. 38–44.

Kier, Elizabeth, 'Culture and Military Doctrine: France between the Wars', *International Security*, Vol. 19, No. 4 (1995), pp. 65–93.

Kikuyama, Kaoru, 'Britain and the Procurement of Short-Range Nuclear Weapons', *Journal of Strategic Studies*, Vol. 16, No. 4 (1993), pp. 539–60.

Kirby, Maurice and Matthew Godwin, 'Operational Research as Counterfactual History: A Retrospective Analysis of the Use of Battlefield Nuclear Weapons in the German Invasion of France and Flanders, May–June 1940', *The Journal of Strategic Studies*, Vol. 31, No. 4 (August 2008), pp. 633–60.

Macmillan, Alan, 'Strategic Culture and National Ways in Warfare: The British Case', *The RUSI Journal*, Vol. 140, No. 5 (1995), pp. 33–8.

Mahnken, Thomas G., 'Uncovering Foreign Military Innovation', *Journal of Strategic Studies*, Vol. 22, No. 4 (1999), pp. 26–54.

Martin, Laurence W., 'The Market for Strategic Ideas in Britain: The Sandys Era', *The American Political Science Review*, Vol. 56, No. 1 (March 1962), pp. 23–41.

Mawby, Spencer W., 'Détente Deferred: The Attlee Government, German Rearmament and Anglo-Soviet Rapprochement 1950–51', *Contemporary British History*, Vol. 12, No. 2 (Summer 1998), pp. 1–21.

McInnes, Colin, 'The British Army's New Way in Warfare: A Doctrinal Misstep?', *Defence and Security Analysis*, Vol. 23, No. 2 (2007), pp. 127–41.

Mearsheimer, John J., 'Nuclear Weapons and Deterrence in Europe', *International Security*, Vol. 9, No. 3 (Winter 1984–5), pp. 19–46.

Meilinger, Phillip S., 'Trenchard and "Morale Bombing": The Evolution of Royal Air Force Doctrine before World War II', *The Journal of Military History*, Vol. 60, No. 2 (April 1996), pp. 243–70.

Michaels, Jeffery H., 'Revisiting General Sir John Hackett's *The Third World War*', *British Journal for Military History*, Vol. 3, No. 1 (2016), pp. 88–104.

Moody, Simon J., 'Was There a "Monty Method" after the Second World War? Field Marshal Bernard L. Montgomery and the Changing Character of Land Warfare, 1945–1958', *War in History*, Vol. 23, No. 2 (2016), pp. 210–29.

Moody, Simon J., 'Enhancing Political Cohesion in NATO during the 1950s or: How It Learned to Stop Worrying and Love the (Tactical) Bomb', *Journal of Strategic Studies*, Vol. 40, No. 6 (2017), pp. 817–38.

Park, Jihang, 'Wasted Opportunities? The 1950s Rearmament Programme and the Failure of British Economic Policy', *Journal of Contemporary History*, Vol. 32, No. 3 (July 1997), pp. 357–79.

Rivera, Joseph De, 'Facing Nuclear Weapons', *American Behavioural Scientist*, Vol. 27, No. 6 (1984), pp. 739–56.

Ruiz Palmer, Diego A., 'The NATO-Warsaw Pact Competition in the 1970s and 1980s: A Revolution in Military Affairs in the Making or the End of a Strategic Age?', *Cold War History*, Vol. 14, No. 4 (2014), pp. 533–7.

Schwenger, Peter, 'Writing the Unthinkable', *Critical Enquiry*, Vol. 13, No. 1 (1986), pp. 33–48.

Shephard, R. W., 'War Gaming as a Technique in the Study of Operational Research Problems', *Operational Research Quarterly*, Vol. 14, No. 2 (June 1963), pp. 119–30.

Smalley, Edward, 'Qualified, But Unprepared: Training for War at the Staff College in the 1930s', *British Journal for Military History*, Vol. 2, No. 1 (2015), pp. 55–72.

Soutor, Kevin, 'To Stem the Red Tide: The German Report Series and Its Effects on American Defense Doctrine, 1948–1954', *Journal of Military History*, Vol. 57 (1993), pp. 653–89.

Strachan, Hew, 'Conventional Defence in Europe', *International Affairs*, Vol. 61, No. 1 (Winter 1984–5), pp. 27–43.

Tannenwald, Nina, 'The Nuclear Taboo: The United States and the Normative Basis of Nuclear Non-Use', *International Organization*, Vol. 53, No. 3 (1999), pp. 433–68.

Toye, Richard, 'Churchill and Britain's "Financial Dunkirk"', *Twentieth Century British History*, Vol. 15, No. 4 (2004), pp. 329–60.

Turco, R. P. et al., 'Nuclear Winter: Global Consequences of Multiple Nuclear Explosions', *Science*, Vol. 222, No. 4630 (1983), pp. 1283–92.

Walker, J. Samuel, 'Recent Literature on Truman's Atomic Bomb Decision: A Search for Middle Ground', *Diplomatic History*, Vol. 29, No. 2 (2005), pp. 311–34.

Wingen, John van and Herbert K. Tillema, 'British Military Intervention after World War II: Militance in a Second-Rank Power', *Journal of Peace Research*, Vol. 17, No. 4. (1980), pp. 291–303.

Wood, James A., 'Captivated Historians, Captivated Audiences: The German Military History Program, 1945–1961', *Journal of Military History*, Vol. 69 (2005), pp. 123–48.

## Theses and Occasional Papers

Bitzinger, Richard A., *Assessing the Conventional Balance in Europe, 1945–1975* (Santa Monica, CA: RAND, 1989).

Caddick-Adams, Peter, 'Footsteps Across Time: The Evolution, Use and Relevance of Battlefield Visits to the British Armed Forces' (PhD thesis, Cranfield University, 2007).

DePuy, William, *Generals Balck and von Mellenthin on Tactics: Implications for NATO Military Doctrine* (McLean, VA: The BDM Corporation, 1980).

Doughty, Robert A., *The Evolution of U.S. Army Tactical Doctrine, 1946–76* (Kansas, MO: Combat Studies Institute, 1979).

Grant, Charles, 'The Use of History in the Development of Contemporary Doctrine' in John Gooch (ed.), *The Origins of Contemporary Doctrine*, The Occasional No. 30 (Swindon: Strategic and Combat Studies Institute, 1997).

Hoffenaar, Jan and Christopher Findlay (eds.), *Military Planning for European Theatre Conflict During the Cold War: An Oral History Roundtable, Stockholm 24–25 April 2006* (Zurich: The Centre for Security Studies, 2007).

Howard, Michael, 'IISS: The First Thirty Years—A General Overview', *The Adelphi Papers*, Vol. 29, No. 235 (1989), pp. 10–19.

Latawski, Paul, *The Inherent Tensions in Military Doctrine*, Sandhurst Occasional Papers No. 5 (Camberley: Royal Military Academy Sandhurst, 2011).

Lee, Sangho, 'Deterrence and the Defence of Central Europe: The British Role from the Early 1980s to the End of the Gulf War' (PhD thesis, King's College London, 1994).

Macmillan, Alan and John Baylis, *A Reassessment of the British Global Strategy Paper of 1952*, International Politics Research Papers 13 (Dept. of International Politics, University of Wales, Aberystwyth, 1993).

Ney, Virgil, *Evolution of the U.S. Army Division, 1939–1968* (Fort Belvoir, VA: Technical Operations Inc., 1969).

Roberts, John E. and George Bell (eds.), *Nuclear War and Peace: The Facts and the Challenge, Peace Aims Pamphlet No. 60* (National Peace Council: London, 1955).

Stockfisch, J. A., *The 1962 Howze Board and Army Combat Developments* (Santa Monica, CA: RAND, 1994).

*The Army in the Nuclear Age: Report by the Army League Sub-Committee* (London: St. Clements Press Ltd, 1955).

Trauschweizer, Ingo, *Nuclear Weapons and Limited War: The U.S. Army in the 1950s* (Florence: European University Institute, 2009).

# Index

For the benefit of digital users, indexed terms that span two pages (e.g., 52–53) may, on occasion, appear on only one of those pages.

www.ingramcontent.com/pod-product-compliance
Ingram Content Group UK Ltd.
Pitfield, Milton Keynes, MK11 3LW, UK
UKHW021456220125
4237UKWH00007B/70

9 780198 846994